The Watcher on the Quay

OLMA MIGNACCA

NEW HOLLAND

For Alan Barringham, the skipper,
with love and thanks.

Published in Australia in 1998 by
New Holland Publishers Pty Ltd
3/2 Aquatic Drive
Frenchs Forest
NSW 2086 Australia

Project Co-ordinator: Anna Sanders
Cover and design concepts: Patricia McCallum
Editor: Susan Lawrence
Typesetter: Midland Typesetters
Printer: McPhersons Printing Group

National Library of Australia Cataloguing-in-Publication Data:

Mignacca, Olma.
The watcher on the quay: one Australian woman's story of circumnavigating the world.

ISBN 1 86436 322 3.

1. Mignacca, Olma - Journeys. 2. Voyages around the world.
I. Title.

910.41

Cover photograph: Copyright © 1998 Olma Mignacca

Windigo's voyage across the oceans

Pacific Ocean

Atlantic Ocean

Indian Ocean

CONTENTS

CHAPTER 1

beware of tranquillity • learning about boats
wedding bells • Cyclone Joy
a brewer's nightmare • over the top

A decade ago I took no interest in boats and sailing, my experience being limited to trips on the Manly ferry. The sea, however, becomes a subliminal element for those who live beside it as I have done for a large part of my life.

Standing beside Pittwater with my partner one sunny afternoon in December 1985 I said, 'Alan, let's buy a boat and sail around the world.' Alan remained motionless, as if he had not heard. I was so shocked by what I had just said that I dared not repeat it.

Time passed. We stood in silence. Finally Alan looked at me and spoke.

'I'm probably dreaming but I could have sworn you just said that you wanted to buy a boat and sail around the world.'

That is how it all began.

It was to be an adventure; an informal and heuristic journey that would carry us forward with the relentless momentum of a great wave, a tsunami, for the next ten years. But we were unlikely participants in such an adventure; unskilled, lacking in knowledge and experience, tied to the land. Furthermore, we were happy and contented with our lives.

As the principal of a large government primary school, I felt both successful and challenged, while Alan enjoyed teaching at the local school near our home on Pittwater. He had been my partner for many years and we still walked hand in hand. My daughter, Velia, who was studying Arts/Law at the University of Sydney, lived at home and our relationship was close and loving. The three of us lived comfortably, travelling overseas each year, enjoying camping in wilderness areas, sharing interests in literature and the arts and enjoying being together. Our friends were generous and loyal. All in all, life was as close to perfect as one could desire.

Why then did I suddenly wish to cast aside everything that was so comfortable, so safe? Perhaps W.R. Hearst understood when he wrote, 'Beware of tranquillity. It proclaims the toppling-over stage. It is the sleep that precedes dissolution.'

But I had not read his words then. My explanation to family and friends was along the lines that we pass this way but once so it behoves us to make the most of our time on earth. Their curt reply was, 'You must be mad.'

In Ulysses, that great adventurer of another era, there seems to be an irreconcilable contradiction between the man who wants to remain on Ithaca with his loving wife, Penelope, in security and stability, and the man who cannot resist adventure. Perhaps women as well as men have both desires within them, and one may predominate at any time. Usually we choose the secure and stable way, but sometimes we choose adventure. And even after the adventure has satisfied our desire, it seems that a restless conflict remains within us, driving us, unsettling us, continually threatening to upset the tranquillity again.

Having chosen adventure, I worried. Could Alan and I immerse ourselves in something overwhelming, something grand and terrifying, bigger than self? Had I the courage to leave education, to start again at the beginning? How could I bear to leave Velia? Was I being fair to Alan? Could I learn new skills that were at the moment beyond my comprehension?

Alan had had some experience of weekend sailing with friends on Sydney Harbour before we met, but to me a bar was a place for drinking and basic terms like 'bow' and 'stern', 'port' and 'starboard', 'sloop', 'cutter' and 'yawl' threw my mind into confusion. So, early in 1986 we enrolled as evening students at Brookvale TAFE. Alan breezed through the Coastal Navigation course while I struggled with the strange concepts and cursed a lifetime of muddled thinking about speed, time and distance, slide rules and the compass rose. We also studied Meteorology and passed practical courses in Survival at Sea, Fire Fighting, Seamanship, First Aid, Radar and Marine Radio.

For me, learning to sail was humiliating. It was not until we had paid for the series of lessons and were out in the middle of Pittwater that our instructor changed from a seemingly benign man into a pig.

'I might as well tell you now that women and boats are bad news. The two just don't go together,' he announced. 'Why not take up gardening if you want something to do.'

'I want to sail around the world,' I stubbornly informed him.

'Everyone says that,' he replied.

He was relentlessly chauvinistic about women and I cried with frustration after each lesson. Soon Alan declared that we would be happier teaching ourselves to sail.

It was time to buy a boat. Since the day of the momentous decision to circumnavigate, we had spent every spare minute reading books and magazines about sailing, cruising and yachts. We felt daunted by the choices: a hull of fibreglass, aluminium, timber, concrete, or steel; a cutter, sloop, schooner or ketch; a centre or an aft cockpit. There were questions about the ideal length of a cruising boat, the best type of marine engine, the sail wardrobe.

In the end it was a question of philosophy that governed our decision. The respected yacht designer, Joe Adams, had been building yachts on Pittwater for decades. We read what he had to say and felt at ease with his views. A streamlined shape with low freeboard appealed. We chose steel for safety, particularly in reef areas, and a centre cockpit for the convenience of having a private aft cabin. A length of 40 feet or 12 metres seemed a manageable size for two people to sail. We never seriously considered building our own yacht although many cruising sailors do so. It would have taken some years to complete the building project and we were impatient for the adventure to begin.

Early in 1987 at Port Stephens we found *Windigo*, a 40-foot Adams-designed steel cutter with a centre cockpit and a shallow draft. We fell hopelessly in love with her. To finance the purchase, we sold an investment unit we had owned for some years.

Windigo's interior was lined with teak and there were enough white surfaces to give her a feeling of lightness and space below decks. She comfortably slept seven people; two in the forepeak, two in the saloon, one in the pilot berth in the linkway between the fore and aft parts of the boat, and two in the aft cabin. Her galley was compact and intelligently designed. And she had an aura, a personality. She seemed to say, 'I've been waiting for you to come along.'

Because the hull and mast were painted mid-blue, people thought her name was clever — a W in front of *indigo*. But we knew her name stood for *Wind, I Go*. We toyed with the idea of choosing our own name, but we felt a loyalty to the man who built her. Gerard Nymeyer had a sincere and engaging personality and we quickly became friends. He had built *Windigo* to sail back to his native Holland with his wife, Harmke, but, after an illness, Gerard felt that the voyage would be too strenuous.

We sailed *Windigo* at the weekends and during the school holidays throughout 1987. Left to our own devices we learnt quickly, responding to the lift of the wind in the sails and the sound of the hull cutting cleanly through the water. We were in the grip of an obsession which alarmed our families and friends. But we felt elated and joyous and we walked on air.

More than two years passed after Alan and I made the decision to go to sea. In that time we successfully completed the necessary courses. We read widely, found *Windigo*, fitted her out with new safety gear, some new sails, navigational aids, a new stove, a refrigerator and a freezer. And we taught ourselves to sail.

In May 1988, we resigned from our respective schools and

Windigo became our new home. Tenants moved into our house. Our furniture and belongings were stored in a shed on my family's sheep property and our lovely Velia moved into lodgings. Until we left she would spend the weekends with us on the boat. When I am asked what was the most difficult part of the circumnavigation, I always answer that it was leaving Velia to fend for herself. She clung to me like a limpet and wept.

'Please don't go. I can't bear it.'

I buried my face in her hair.

'I must. I must.'

Despite the mounting sadness, aboard *Windigo* I felt like a child with a new cubby. Everything seemed so small, so compact. There were lockers in all the nooks and crannies; mysterious little storage spaces that one stumbled across over a period of some days. I packed, and then unpacked, moving our belongings about until a logic developed and we began to feel as comfortable on the boat as we once had felt in the house.

Until we moved aboard I had been insistent that Alan and I would be equal partners. The galley chores, the washing, the cleaning, the watches, the route planning, the navigation would all be equally shared. Alan had agreed — it seemed just and fair.

Not long after we became 'live aboards' Alan commented, 'You've never climbed the mast, Olma.' I held my breath, hoping he had not said it at all, but he continued. 'It's important that you learn everything. You may have to climb up there at sea if something bad happens to me.'

Pittwater was calm. Why then did I feel a rising panic? Unconcerned, Alan strapped me into the bosun's chair and proceeded to winch me up.

'I'm not really enjoying this,' I yelled down as my feet rested on the first spreaders.

'You're doing fine,' Alan replied.

At the second spreaders, Alan looked like a dwarf below me on the deck, and the mast was swaying alarmingly. I clung to it for dear life.

'I don't think I should go to the top,' I called down.

'It's only a few more feet. You're almost there. It's important that you see how things work up there.'

'Bloody hell,' I thought.

When my feet touched the deck again I crumbled into a jellied heap, entangled in the bosun's chair. Perhaps it was time to re-think the whole equality issue.

The Yanmar diesel engine provided further food for thought on the topic. I tried to understand its idiosyncrasies but the affection that Alan obviously felt for it eluded me. He would happily tinker with it for hours, learning its ways and mastering its foibles. At a pinch I may be able to replace an impeller, manage an oil change, bleed air from the fuel lines, but it was Alan who assumed responsibility for the shining grey machinery, and I was relieved and grateful.

So, as time passed, our roles were defined quite naturally. We each ended up doing what we did best. Alan had been a brilliant student of navigation while I had struggled to pass the examinations, so it was safer for him to navigate. And because there can only ever be one captain on a ship, I happily agreed that Alan be the skipper. I knew him to be a fair and loving man who never shouted, so it was not a problem for me.

But, despite what may appear to be clearly defined gender roles, the reality of life aboard *Windigo* was one of sharing. Alan helped me with the washing and cooking and other boat chores, while I helped him with the general maintenance, and we discussed route planning and navigation problems until we were satisfied that the best decision had been made.

There are few dangers within the protected waters of Pitt-water and we realised that before we took on the oceans of the world, we would need a wider range of experiences. In 1988, and again in 1989, Alan and I sailed from Sydney to Cairns and back to Sydney in order to practise. On both occasions we left in June and returned in December before the cyclone season began. During the summer months we lived aboard *Windigo* on Pittwater. Alan did some casual work while

I kept up the maintenance and made flags, stowage bags, new awnings and covers. Nothing lasts for long in the marine environment.

Some changes and repairs were necessary at the end of the first trip. As a result of faulty workmanship, the new stove had burst into flames near Brisbane, so the manufacturers replaced it. The freezer would not freeze properly until an extra plate was installed and the autopilot required a bigger junction box to increase its power.

The memory of our first night at sea in 1988 is still vivid. The weather bureau had forecast gentle conditions from the south so we decided to sail through the night to Coffs Harbour on our first overnight passage.

We were excited. Perhaps that was why we were not unduly concerned when the wind increased and we had to reduce sail. By dark the wind was strong, the south setting current was making the waves stand up and a radio message warned that the lighthouse at Seal Rocks, north of Newcastle, was on reduced power. It would be difficult to see the warning light in the worsening conditions and at that stage we had no radar. At 2 a.m. the lights of Port Stephens beckoned like the sirens' song, luring us towards the land but we considered it too dangerous to approach in the prevailing conditions. We headed out to sea.

At dawn there was no land to be seen, only featureless ocean.

'Don't worry,' soothed Alan. 'Australia is so big that if we steer west we'll find it.'

He rested on the saloon floor after steering most of the night. I took the helm. The seas had increased during the night and when I turned *Windigo* towards Australia, water and spray swept into the cockpit, belting me in the chest and forcing water under my wet weather gear.

We had installed an autopilot the previous week but had had no time to learn how to use it. In hindsight, though, it would have been overpowered by the conditions. Sometimes the force of the waves almost wrenched my hands from the helm and my body strained against the safety harness clipped to the cockpit floor. When I caught glimpses of Alan's face between the waves, he looked thoughtful.

'Aren't you frightened?' he finally yelled from below.

'No. I'm wet and cold and tired, but not frightened,' I answered. 'Should I be? Isn't this what it's like at sea?'

'No! This is terrible,' he shouted through the companionway hatch. 'Are you telling me that you wanted to sail around the world thinking the oceans would be like this?'

It was hard to explain exactly what I had thought. I did not know why I was not frightened. Perhaps it was because at that time the world was new, inchoate, and I was newly born. It was too soon for fear. I was accepting, and as yet unsure of exactly what to fear.

'You're an unusual woman,' I heard Alan yell above the noise of the waves. 'But I love you,' he added.

I longed for Velia each time we left. When we reached the Queensland border on the second passage, Alan and I agreed that it would be better if Velia joined us on the circumnavigation. She could finish her law degree at some time in the future. But her response was puzzling when I rang her from Tin Can Bay. I had expected a joyous acceptance of my proposal, but Velia was coy and mysterious.

'I would prefer to finish Law,' she said. She sounded happy.

It was not until we arrived back in Sydney that we understood. Velia had fallen in love. She and Graeme, a colleague, planned to marry in the following October.

At the time of the wedding, Alan and I were back in Cairns and *Windigo* was installed at the Cairns Cruising Yacht Club in Trinity Inlet. We flew to Sydney for the wedding. Velia was a beautiful bride and I sobbed as she walked down the aisle, radiant, happy and free.

After three trips to Cairns from Sydney, Alan and I felt we had practised enough. I now knew that bars were not merely places for drinking, but perils at the mouths of coastal rivers that sensible sailors approached with trepidation. I had learnt to respect the power of the ocean. We both learnt patience when the wind blew from the wrong direction, resilience when we were forced to remain at sea.

All along the coast we had favourite places to which we kept returning — the lovely river at Ballina, Hinchinbrook Island and spectacular Zoe Bay, Fraser Island with its crystal lakes and pristine beaches, Lady Musgrave lagoon and Fitzroy Reef, and the anchorages in the Whitsundays where the charter yachts never go.

The wedding provided the opportunity for Alan and me to drive our car to Cairns. We would need it in the months we would be living there. Alan found a job as a cleaner because the flexible hours gave him time to work on the boat during the day. And all the time we prayed there would not be a cyclone. Somewhere I had read that if the energy contained in an average cyclone could be transformed into electricity, it would supply the world's electricity needs for five years.

Cyclone Joy hit Cairns two days before Christmas after hovering offshore for almost a week. A collective groan rose from the beleaguered people of Cairns when an announcer at the local radio station signed off saying, 'I wish you all joy for Christmas.'

Alan and I had had no experience of cyclones but we had read widely on the subject and studied the phenomenon in Meteorology. When the Port Authority ordered all vessels to take shelter in cyclone holes in the mangroves, we found a narrow channel deep in their protective arms and tied *Windigo* to their muddy roots with a maze of long lines.

Until then we had had no time to feel frightened. But as the wind quickly built to a whistling screech and stripped the mangroves of their foliage we felt vulnerable and we cowered below, fearful that the lines would break and worried that we had not found the time to move our car to a protected place.

Velia and Graeme were expected for Christmas but the airport was closed and Cairns was without power and water. In circumstances such as these it is best to believe in miracles so while Joy raged around us I baked the Christmas cake and Alan hung the decorations.

Christmas morning dawned clear and still. Extricating *Windigo* from the maze of lines formed by the sheltering vessels seemed to take hours. The car was still where we had left it and as we hurried across the airport lounge, we saw Velia and Graeme step onto the tarmac. To us it was a miracle.

Our neighbours at the Cairns Cruising Yacht Squadron were two orthodontists, Don and Robyn Gilchrist. Their yacht, *Stylopora*, is named after an obscure sea creature and that is what Don, with a height of six foot four, reminds me of — something gangling and spidery like a stiff-legged octopus. Alan and I quickly grew accustomed to his blustering antics, and from the first meeting we respected Robyn's gentle earnestness.

Like us, the Gilchrists were preparing to circumnavigate, so, at the end of the cyclone season in May 1991, *Windigo* and *Stylopora* sailed out of Cairns together, bound for Gove in the Northern Territory where we planned to join the inaugural Over The Top Fun Race from Gove to Darwin.

As the two boats left Trinity Inlet and turned north from Cairns, my mind was still whirling from the intensity of the final preparations. I had flown to Sydney for a few days to say farewell to Velia and Graeme; we had had to leave our car with friends in Cairns to sell, because we had needed it until the final day; and I had brewed 60 bottles of beer.

I have no experience of brewing. But many yachties are beer makers of repute so I reasoned that the task could be within my capabilities. I had learnt many new skills in the last four years, so why not add brewing to the list? Alan disapproved of the experiment and would take no interest in the bubbling drum and the bottles that cluttered the cockpit and became a hazard on the pontoon approaches.

Like many aspects of life on a marina, my brewing became a public affair. It seemed that everyone who passed knew how to brew beer. But they always directed their remarks at Alan.

'You should use proper beer bottles, mate. Stubbies aren't strong enough,' a knowledgeable Queenslander advised.

'Give the caps three rhythmic whacks,' another said. 'The rhythm's important.'

'When's the party, mate?' they all wanted to know.

The bottles filled three lockers in the saloon. The skipper was tight-lipped as I packed them in.

'This is ridiculous,' he said.

The first explosion occurred at Lizard Island at 7 p.m. Alan was blasted into the cockpit in unseemly haste and I leapt from my bunk in naked terror. The first explosion was quickly followed by several more ear-splitting booms and ominous crackles, and then there was silence.

'It's your bloody beer,' Alan groaned. 'It's lethal. We need a bomb disposal expert.'

The saloon was a shambles. Beer dripped from the ceiling, the upholstery was quietly absorbing puddles of it, cushions were scattered, broken glass littered the horizontal surfaces and thin slivers and shards had been driven into the teak bulkhead by the force of the blasts.

Alan and I sat in the cockpit in shocked silence. I felt too anguished to speak and Alan looked as if he would never speak again, at least not to me. Finally, though, we had to face cleaning up the mess below.

With great care and concentration, Alan covered each bottle in folded towels, carried it to the cockpit and lowered it into the dinghy tied alongside. The task took most of the day. We were miserable with tension because we expected each bottle to explode in Alan's face. When it was over we laughed with relief and I promised Alan that I would never brew beer again.

However, the problem was only half solved. Several times through that night we were jolted awake by fresh bursts of artillery fire from the dinghy, where constant rocking further agitated the brew. The next morning Alan tipped the contents of the remaining bottles into the sea and we stowed the empties in plastic bags to be put in a bin at the next town.

In the Great Barrier Reef Reserve near Lizard Island lies the famous Cod Hole, where a family group of enormous potato cod lives in a 12-metre-deep pool. Some fish weigh 90 kilograms and are more than a metre in length. We sailed *Windigo* from our anchorage at the island and picked up a mooring directly above the Cod Hole.

Potato cod are mysterious fish in that, when hooked, they can change their appearance to that of a common grouper. Consequently, many fishermen do not realise they have killed a protected species. Well, that is their story.

The name 'potato cod' refers to the potato-sized black splotches that cover the fishes' white body. Alan and I thought the fish beautiful as we lay on the surface of the Cod Hole watching the dappled denizens swimming slowly below us in water with the clarity of gin. Several times they came close to the surface, peering at us with enigmatic round eyes, before circling in slow motion to the cold depths.

'I'll feed them now,' Alan said eventually and he reached into *Windigo*'s scuppers for the fish pieces we had already prepared. In the water Alan is like a fish — graceful, strong, and at ease with his environment. I enjoyed watching him from the surface, the sun warm on my back as he swam down to meet the fish.

The attack was unexpected. One minute the fish were lazily swimming; a second later they pulsated with an awful energy, thrashing their mighty tails and darting at Alan like crazed killers. The water flashed with silver and spots of red and Alan struggled to fight off his attackers as he battled towards the surface. One fish worried his elbow, another bit at his hand, others ripped at his wetsuit.

Then he was beside me panting for breath, his eyes sad behind the goggles. When I saw that he was safe, I forgot all the rules for swimming in reef areas, thrashed back to *Windigo* at full speed, and clambered aboard. Alan followed at a sensible pace. I cleaned and bandaged his wounds while he tried to come to terms with the fact that the sea creatures he loves and always treats as treasures could treat him so unkindly. The wetsuit was beyond repair.

Sailing along with the Great Barrier Reef to starboard and the wild and lovely Cape York Peninsula to port is like gliding through a wonderland. Princess Charlotte Bay lies about halfway along, a grand expanse of water bordered by a river-washed wilderness and dotted with untouched anchorages. The area teems with barramundi, mud crabs, prawns, crayfish and crocodiles. There are acres of saucer-sized oysters.

'I think we should hurry around the world so that we can get back here before someone stuffs it,' Alan commented.

We set out our crabpots in the mangroves and in the morning we found a large and aggressive mudcrab in one. The crab snapped and fought in the bottom of the dinghy, making it impossible to tie its legs, but by forcing it into a large bucket we managed to get it aboard *Windigo*.

'I'll cook it, if you kill it,' I told the skipper.

We discussed different methods. Filling the bucket with fresh water to drown the crab seemed the most humane way. But in the morning there was no sign of the angry crustacean. We searched the boat just in case.

Portland Roads, a hamlet of six houses, is the only coastal settlement between Cooktown and Cape York. The tiny outpost dates from the Second World War when the Americans built an airfield nearby as the main base from which to fight the Battle of the Coral Sea. The handful of colourful inhabitants helps to give the attractive backwater an unusual atmosphere.

'Watch out for the big crocodile that wanders along the track beside the beach,' they warned. 'He's already eaten most of our dogs.'

On a meticulously painted sign at the entrance to one of the houses is a cryptic message:

> To be happy for a day, get married,
> To be happy for a month, kill a pig,
> To be happy for ever, plant a garden.

The line about the pig puzzled us. It was not until we reached Shelburne Bay, 40 miles farther north, that we understood.

Behind the dazzling white of the silica sand dunes there are lakes, so we set out to find them. Alan armed himself with a machete although we were unsure how he would use it. When we were some distance inland we smelt the pigs. The grass was shoulder high and we had passed the last tree some distance back. Pig tracks criss-crossed the grass, turning it into a maze of tunnels, and all around the grunting and scurrying of the invisible creatures mingled with their foul smell in the heat of mid-morning. Alan and I were unnerved.

'I won't even have time to swing the machete if one suddenly charges out of the grass,' Alan said.

I mumbled something about discretion and valour as I led the hurried retreat to the safety of Shelburne Bay.

The last anchorage before 'the Tip' at Cape York Peninsula is at Escape River, which is the natural boundary between two Aboriginal tribes, the once-warlike Jadhaigana to the south and the more docile Djadaraga to the north. It was near the anchorage here that the unlucky explorer, Edmund Kennedy, was speared and killed by the Jadhaigana as he was on the verge of being rescued by the Djadaraga. Jackie-Jackie, Kennedy's faithful friend and guide, escaped to the ship that was waiting in the Albany Channel just a few kilometres away.

To have reached the northernmost tip of Australia seemed to us to be quite an achievement until we saw the crowd of tourists gathered there on rocks covered with graffiti which Alan Lucas, the guru of Australian cruising yachties, rightly describes as 'the gaudy reminders of the passing of fools'. Still, there is a magic about the barren point pushing into Torres Strait, with the Arafura Sea to the west. It was this sea that we were now about to cross and it was to be our first passage of any length — five days, we anticipated. Gove lay on the other side, on the eastern tip of Arnhem Land.

On 14 June 1991, almost a month after leaving Cairns and in company with *Stylopora*, we set sail from Possession Island where a monument to Captain Cook commemorates his taking possession of the east coast of Australia.

Before leaving Sydney, Alan and I had intended studying celestial navigation at TAFE but for various reasons we had been unable to do so. In Cairns we enrolled and paid our fees but the course was cancelled because of a lack of students and our fees were refunded. We regard as foolhardy those who go to sea unable to use the sextant to find their way by the heavenly bodies, so we taught ourselves celestial navigation by the sun from books, and we practised on the passage north from Cairns.

An unusual increase in sunspot activity upset *Windigo*'s satellite navigation system on our first day in the Arafura Sea. It was impossible to obtain a fix so we could not plot our position. For a few seconds we felt vulnerable. Then we remembered the sextant and the worksheets we had photocopied in Cairns.

Four days later, Alan smiled with satisfaction as we made a perfect landfall in Gove. He had enjoyed using the traditional method of finding position from the sun and, in his enthusiasm, he vowed to continue studying until he could use the moon and the stars as well.

Gove harbour was full with some 50 yachts; an unexpected sight in this far-flung outpost. Twenty were there for the race from Gove to Darwin, while many of the others were the homes of sailors from the south who had come to work in the flourishing bauxite industry.

Situated beside the beach, Gove Yacht Club is welcoming and comfortable. It is the social focus of an area where the red bauxite dust settles over everything in a suffocating film and gives rise to an impressive thirst.

'If it weren't for the red dust, mate, we wouldn't drink half as much,' the locals told us. 'Couldn't exist up here without beer, y'know.'

The passage from Gove to Darwin has always been a difficult one for yachts. The route is poorly surveyed and there are scores of scattered islands, reefs, rocky outcrops, shoals and tidal rips.

The coastline borders an area that has been officially recognised as Aboriginal tribal land for most of this century, and entry has always been controlled. As the Aboriginal ownership of land becomes more controversial and the Aborigines grow more determined to protect their lifestyle from the ravages of drink and other destructive influences of white society, the problems associated with visiting the area become more acute.

Perhaps it was these factors that spawned the idea of a yacht race from Gove to Darwin. There would be greater safety in sailing with others, and the obtaining of entry permits to the Arnhem Land Aboriginal Reserve would be facilitated.

Tony Jacques, the race organiser and the fleet's bosun, was an ex-Sydney man who with his wife, Effie, had been working in Gove for a couple of years. Tony was confident and charming with obvious leadership qualities. He began the first briefing at the Yacht Club by worrying people like Don and Robyn who were experienced competition racers, and delighting those who, like me and Alan, knew nothing about racing.

'This is to be a fun race,' Tony began. 'Any serious racing will be dealt with severely. The event is referred to as a race only in order to attract sponsorship.' Tony glared at the group. 'But there's to be no racing. Only fun! So drink up and get to know each other.'

From the elegant *Fine Romance* came Ion who possessed a clear tenor voice. He would lead the sing-songs around the campfires on remote moonlit beaches. Will Townsend, the skipper of *Blueflyer* had sailed from Canada. He was a retired naval commander and a member of Alcoholics Anonymous. It was probably because of the latter that he was chosen to judge the winners of the various events organised by the bosun for the evenings ashore.

There were to be champagne barbecues under the stars, games, dances, dress-ups and theatre sports. In that windswept and wild isolation, the group members quickly forgot who they were. We grew gregarious and convivial, playing like children, carefree and spontaneous. Alan and I had seldom felt happier; we had never had so much fun.

The first obstacle in the Over The Top Fun Race, as the event was called, was the Gugari Rip, known as The-Hole-In-The-Wall. It is a narrow passage between two islands in the Wessel group, a few hours' sail from Gove. Currents race through the passage at nine knots so yachts must wait for slack water at the change of tide before entering. The fleet tacked up and down at the entrance, the skippers afraid to be the first to test the waters. Finally, a yacht aptly named *Gunadoo* led the charge.

The small fleet sailed south-west to Elcho Island, then west to Goulburn Island. The overnight leg between the two was sponsored by a Darwin chandlery and the leg was called The Crocodile Classic because the course curved to the north of the Crocodile Islands. Thirty metres of braided rope was the prize for winning. And all sailors love braided rope.

'Let's try racing,' Alan said.

Sailors have an instinct to race. Whenever there are two boats on a stretch of water, it is inevitable that they will do so, although the skippers may pretend to be simply admiring the scenery. The serious racing skipper buys a boat that is specifically designed for the purpose. Speed is paramount. On land it would be irresponsible to drive your Ferrari at top speed but the owner of a fast yacht has no such limitation; hence the fascination.

There were no racing yachts in the Over The Top fleet, only

racing skippers. With her handicap, *Windigo* had the same chance as the other boats.

'Yes, let's try racing,' I replied.

Yachts respond in different ways to the conditions and on this occasion both the strength and the direction of the wind were perfect for *Windigo* to hold a broad reach, her best point of sailing. She quickly found her groove and set off like a rocket with Alan hand-steering and shouting for glee all through the night. His effort was rewarded the next day when he received 30 metres of braided rope.

'Sneaky bugger,' the other skippers yelled good-naturedly.

I cannot describe the coast of Arnhem Land as beautiful in the conventional sense, for it lacks intimacy. Coming from Pittwater, our idea of a bay is of a small and protected place. Up north, a bay is a stretch of water so wide that you cannot see from one end to the other. The distances are formidable, the scale immense. We felt like insignificant specks in incalculable space.

And we were hot. The trade winds were light that year and the sun beat down relentlessly. The water was clean but murky, and we could not swim because of the crocodiles.

The fleet stayed for three days at the pretty inlet at Port Essington. It was ironic that some years previously, Alan and I had spent hours unsuccessfully stalking the illusive *benteng*, the native cattle of Indonesia, in an area near Pangandaran in Java when all the time there was a herd right there in Port Essington. Timorese ponies and tame deer wandered through the grounds of the exclusive Seven Seas Resort, and farther on at Popham Bay there were rookeries of flying foxes in the mangroves that lined the bay.

Cape Don, on the tip of the Cobourg Peninsula, is a dangerous point with swirling rough water, reefs, and fierce currents. It is marked by one of the few lighthouses in northern Australia. We rounded it safely and on the 11th day after leaving Gove, the fleet sailed past Melville Island and through the complex hydrostatic patterns of Van Diemen Gulf, to Darwin. The lights of the city lit the waters of Fannie Bay as we anchored.

CHAPTER 2

blessed by a 'sadhu' • going like the clappers
'selamat jalan' and 'selamat tingal' • Bali

nchored in Fannie Bay off the Darwin Sailing Club were more than 100 yachts, at least 60 of which had gathered there for the annual Darwin to Ambon Yacht Race. Alan and I were sitting in the cockpit enjoying breakfast on the morning after our arrival when an American from a nearby luxury yacht powered across in his inflatable.

'Hi there! My name's Clifford. The wife and I are organising a little get-together at the yacht club tonight to celebrate American Independence Day and we'd sure like you to join us.'

Of course! The Fourth of July. We accepted. We were in Darwin to take part in the 1991 race to Ambon and the celebration would be a pleasant way to meet some of the other contestants.

Darwin Sailing Club is an attractive open-plan building overlooking the bay. Spacious lawns sweep to the water's edge and, as we crossed the brown beach, wide at low tide, we could see the rows of tables festooned with American flags, coloured balloons and candles, set out on the grassy sward beneath the casuarinas. The 'Battle Hymn of the Republic' rang across the bay and a large group had already gathered.

It was easy to spot Clifford in the crowd — indeed, in any crowd. He made an imposing figure and his style was flamboyant.

'Ah, there you are,' he boomed. 'Come on over here and meet the American contingent, but first have a drink.'

He poured two large cognacs from a bottle at his elbow and thrust them at us.

'I come from Texas and down there we consume a lot of this stuff. You probably prefer beer, but tonight — this is America!' And he swung his arm in an arc that appeared to encompass the whole of northern Australia.

In my childhood in rural New South Wales I had taken piano lessons at the local convent where Sister Regina had felt it incumbent upon herself to broaden my black stump horizons with renditions from *National Anthems of the World*. That night, when we all stood to sing 'The Star-Spangled Banner' at the beginning of the meal, I was able to recall every word and I sang with the gusto of a born-again. The Americans looked impressed and I felt virtuous.

From San Francisco, on the sleek yacht *Northern Lights*, came Andre, an architect turned developer, and his boat-proud wife, Barbara. And from New Orleans, the irascible JB Dewar, with his patient partner, Rosa, had sailed the aptly-named large black cutter, *Anaconda*, across the Pacific to Darwin. JB Dewar was an ex-military man, ex-motorbike rider, ex-mountain climber. *Anaconda*'s flag, like her skipper, was aggressive — an intimidating rectangle depicting a writhing serpent with exaggerated fangs. My intuition told me that JB and I would view the world differently, but I had no way of knowing that our differences would resound around many quiet bays from Darwin to the Mediterranean, causing those anchored within earshot to shake their heads and say, 'Oh no, they're at it again.'

The Hastwells on sweet *Maisie Dotes* hailed from West Virginia. Woody, a lean limping farmer, came quickly to the point.

'You know Olma, I'm one of the good guys. Worked hard all my life. Made my money from tobacco. And I always treat my niggers well.'

I glanced at Ellen, his wife, expecting her to reproach her husband for his racist remark, but she met my eyes with candour and added, 'Yes, he does treat them well, and his niggers love him.'

Most of the guests were Australian. Colin Henderson, a rosy-cheeked accountant who was invariably called upon to play Santa

Claus, had sailed *New Address* from Adelaide, while the trim and tiny couple on *Interlude*, Bret and Debbie, had approached from New Guinea. Aboard *Big Drum*, a cumbersome condominium of a boat ablaze with lights every night, lived farmer George and earth-mother Vi who lavished a cloying friendship upon the only Japanese sailors we were ever to meet, Kuni and his wife, Nobby. Too polite to reject the company of the plodding farmers, the Japanese sailors displayed an infectious sense of fun whenever they were free of their mentors. Their boat was named *April Fourth II* or 442, the date of their wedding.

Of the New Zealand skippers we met that night, Desmond Benson on *Panache* had the greatest swagger and, like JB Dewar, he was ex several things — journalist, boxer, pub owner, fishing charterer. Tall and slim, his Chinese and Maori ancestors reflected in his handsome face, he gave the impression of being able to respond to most experiences with aplomb as did Laurie, his wife, who was friendly and optimistic.

And as the evening wore on we met others, but most were racing sailors and they did not share the preoccupations of those whose aim it is to sail around the world.

Darwin in the Dry is a city where almost everything takes place in the open, the weather being so reliable that people plan functions and book open-air facilities years in advance. Nevertheless, we felt the cold when the temperature dropped to 27 degrees, and at night we used a blanket for the first time in months.

Many years after Cyclone Tracy the city still has a newborn appearance; a little awkward and raw around the edges, but it is burgeoning with promise and growth. There are over 40 nationalities living in Darwin, so a remarkable range of cuisines is offered in the Singapore-style markets and outdoor eating places. On Thursday evenings it is the custom for families and groups to bring their own picnic tables and chairs, to position themselves strategically on the lawns surrounding the food stalls at

Mindil Beach, and to spend the evening eating and drinking.

On our first visit we were unsure of the etiquette. No-one had explained about the tables and chairs so we purchased our first course, a fiery laksa, and chose the best looking unoccupied outdoor furniture we could see and sat back to enjoy the evening. We paid scant attention to the members of a small family group which arrived soon afterwards, laden with food and drinks. They sat in silence on the grass nearby and I remember thinking they seemed surly. Eventually Alan stood, asking if I would like barbecued squid on a skewer. The head of the family on the grass also stood.

'Sorry mate,' he said, 'But we want to go home now, if you don't mind.' We stared at him.

'You're sitting on my furniture.'

On the morning of the race there was to be a champagne breakfast at the club at 6 a.m. We would leave at 11 a.m. The last few days were busy with final preparations and provisioning, and *Windigo* gradually sank on her marks as we loaded her with stores, some of which had to last us well beyond Bali, five weeks away. The freezer was packed solid with meat and I had prepared three casseroles in case it was too rough to cook during the race. Duty-free drink filled the starboard lockers in the saloon where the explosive brew was once stored, and the port side ones bulged with dried and tinned goods.

We attended the Darwin–Ambon Race briefing at the club and took part in the mass vaccination against tetanus and rabies. The race officials came aboard for the safety check. Alan's preparation was meticulous so I was not apprehensive, although he paced about like an expectant father. 'Top marks,' they said.

The race rules state that each yacht must carry at least three people so we had to find a crew member. Ted Baker was around 70 years of age, fit and tough, and with a lifetime of experience with yachts and sailing. We valued his expertise and welcomed his advice. His party trick was to stand on his head for extended periods and, although we had yet to witness the feat, those who had done so were impressed. Ted's favourite topics of conversation, after the sea and boats, appeared to be his war adventures and his wife, Beryl, but, because we had to hand steer to comply with the race regulations, we would be too exhausted to indulge in prolonged discussion of these topics or, indeed, of any other topic.

Crews arrived each day from the south so there was soon a confusion of new faces. *Stylopora* had four crew who, according to Don, were his best mates, grand chaps and gung-ho racers.

'With men of the calibre of my friends aboard *Stylopora*, we'll piss it in!' joked our Don. Robyn, who is possibly a more skilful and intuitive sailor than any of them, had been relegated to the galley for the race. At least she would not have to stand watches.

We asked a *sadhu* to join us for lunch one day. It seemed a good idea at the time. John, for that was his name, introduced himself when we were having lunch at an Asian food stall near the bay. With his patrician features and aura of mystique, we were titillated, as I suspect he knew we would be. On his forehead he carried a caste mark, across his right shoulder hung the holy thread of Brahma, and his white dhoti gleamed in the penumbra of the large fig tree that protected us from Darwin's fierce heat of noon. In a cultured voice, he explained why he was a devotee of the fat and grinning guru, Sai Baba.

'I felt a growing alienation from Sydney's North Shore where I once lived, and from the values of the business world where I worked, so I went to India to ask Sai Baba what to do.'

'Was it Sai Baba who caused you to change your lifestyle?' I asked.

'Oh, yes. He told me to renounce my past and to become a *sadhu*.'

'Is it true that Sai Baba levitates?' I wanted to know.

'Just to be in his presence is to be uplifted,' he replied.

'I was not referring to you, but to Sai Baba. Does he actually float?'

'He too is uplifted by his own purity and power,' he said.

It seemed impolite to persist, so we talked of other things, of music and literature and the problems of living in the far north. At the end of the meal as we rose to leave, John said, 'You too, are *sanyassin*: searchers after the truth. That's why you've chosen to sail around the world — to find the truth.' We had never thought of it quite like that, but he continued.

'As a *sadhu*, I must bless your boat before you leave. Then Sai Baba will be aware of your quest and will watch over you and keep you safe.'

It seemed risky to reject him. We had yet to find out what it was like to sail around the world but we knew enough to realise that any bit of help must surely be a bonus.

The next day John arrived in the dinghy with Alan who had gone ashore to pick up our guest. The holy man's flowing dhoti gave him the appearance of a large white moth. He carried an old leather suitcase, which caused some trepidation on my part — perhaps he intended coming with us. But when he opened the suitcase on the saloon sole I saw that it contained only his tools of trade.

Twigs, incense sticks and exotic things like frankincense and myrrh burned in a small metal bowl while John sat cross-legged before it, singing mantras and meditating for the hour before lunch. He ate the vegetarian fare with relish, enjoyed the wine, and soon afterwards asked Alan to take him ashore, announcing as he disappeared that he would bless the fleet as it left in the morning. We have no way of knowing what spiritual preparations other yachties make to ensure a safe return to their homeland, but we felt that we had made the most of the opportunity offered.

The day of departure dawned clear and still and as the sun rose over the low hills of Parap, the suburb behind Fannie Bay, a gentle breeze ruffled the water. It would build by 11 a.m. and the racing division would be ecstatic.

Having raced only once before, I was apprehensive about the start. One does not relish denting another yacht or sustaining damage to one's own in the jockeying for position that is part and parcel of such events. Although we were up before dawn, there were so many last minute chores that we ate breakfast aboard *Windigo, sans* champagne, and at 10.30 a.m. Alan pulled up the anchor whilst I pondered that it would be years before it once again sank into Oz mud. But there was little time to wax sentimental, with dozens of spectator craft and more than 60 yachts under sail, milling around at the start line.

At the crack of the starter's pistol, sails filled with a whoosh and we were away on our first ocean passage; the start of the adventure. Our awareness of each other and of the dangers ahead added a piquancy, accentuated by the knowledge that for the first time in our lives we would be totally in charge of our own destiny. It was an exhilarating thought. As we turned in the cockpit to gaze at our homeland for the last time, puffs of smoke rose from the headland at Dudley Point. We exclaimed in unison, 'Holy Smoke!', and laughed as we shared a vision of a handsome *sadhu* alone on a headland blessing the white sails that flickered on the horizon of the Arafura Sea.

According to the experts, the wind was supposed to blow from the south-east at that time of the year, but for the first two days and nights it blew from the north-east, forcing us to beat into the conditions instead of running before with the wind 'up our bum', a pleasant sensation on a boat. *Windigo* leaned at an alarming angle, green water raced along the side decks and waves broke over the bow. The wind appeared to increase during my watch on the second night, just before Ted surprised me by appearing in the cockpit early, already wide-awake.

'Have I told you about my old mate Jack, who was stationed in Bougainville during the war,' he began. 'He was ...'

'Ted, I'm sorry to interrupt, but we need to reduce sail,' I told him. He cast an experienced eye over the sails and the sea and the sky and quickly made his decision.

'She's going like the clappers, my girl. Going like the clappers. Now, I was telling you about Jack.'

'Yes, I agree that we're doing well but *Windigo* is a cruising boat, not a racer,' I persisted. 'We could break something, and it's mighty uncomfortable. I think we're over-canvassed.'

'At this rate, and with our handicap, we could get a place,' Ted pointed out. 'I've sailed in the Sydney to Hobart race and this isn't uncomfortable. This is great sailing.'

He was right of course. I could have enjoyed it on a sunny afternoon in the relative safety of a harbour, but halfway between Australia and Indonesia I felt tired and tense.

'Now when Jack was in Bougainville ...'

'Please Ted, I must get some sleep.'

'Jolly good. I'll tell you that story tomorrow,' he replied. And as I scrambled below, I heard him shout with glee as he slapped the back of the cockpit.

'You little beauty! You're going like the clappers!'

Ah, the treachery of weather. For the following two days there was no wind. 'As idle as a painted ship', we wallowed in a flat and oily sea, until finally the three of us agreed to turn on the engine and announce our withdrawal from the race on the next radio sked, little knowing that most of the cruising division were making the same decision.

Pulau Sematong in the Muluku group, provided the first sight of Indonesia. Too far away to show any details, it rose as a dark smudge on the horizon just as a lovely painted *prahu* with turquoise sails and a man playing a guitar on the foredeck slid across our bow. In the gentle kaleidoscope of aquamarine that had become our world, Alan and Ted gossiped about boats and sailing while I read *The Mayor of Casterbridge*, part of my 'Hardy Revisited' phase with *The Return of the Native* next on the list.

And later in the balmy moonlight, we sipped our sundowners in the cockpit and decided that it did not matter that we would miss the Welcome to Ambon dinner, nor that the race was a fizzer, nor even that *Anaconda* had motored all the way from Darwin and was already sitting in the prime anchoring spot in Ambon harbour.

Sixteen miles out, the island of Ambon still hid mysteriously in the clouds but we were conscious of its presence and we could smell its fecundity. Suddenly, four miles off, it theatrically appeared as if accompanied by a drum roll, a lush land pendent beneath the monsoon clouds clinging to its invisible peaks in a strange varietal phenomenon. We had arrived.

When the Customs launch pulled up beside *Windigo*, ten heavily perfumed officers piled into the saloon. The people of Ambon love boats and the Ambonese sailors are famous for their prowess on the sea, so any opportunity to inspect a foreign boat is not to be missed. Who cares that 20 polished black boots will leave ugly scuff marks all over the boat. The officers' eyes darted everywhere and when they met mine they sparkled with good-will and Indonesian mischief, and the air in the saloon grew dense with the smoke from the *kretek rokok*, their clove cigarettes. Alan and I had travelled extensively through Indonesia and we loved the land and its people. Arriving in Ambon felt like coming home.

We celebrated our arrival by joining the rest of the fleet at the nearby Tirta Kercana Hotel. It was time to let our hair down, to swap sailors' tales, to drink and be merry, and to dance with anyone who remained vertical, until the wee small hours.

The next morning, more or less recovered, we boarded the fleet of five buses that the Ambonese had provided to take us on a tour of the island.

'You'll see the plantations of cloves, the sago palms, nutmeg, cinnamon and mace. You're in the Spice Islands, you know,' explained Siti, our guide, an attractive young woman dressed in the traditional sarong and *kebaya*.

Her English was fluent but her pronunciation was unusual, as if she had learnt it from someone whose native tongue had not been English.

'We'll give you a traditional Ambonese luncheon in the mountains, and then we'll show you the holy heels,' she continued.

During the morning I heard a couple of people ask Siti about the holy heels but she merely laughed in a confused way and did not answer. I too was puzzled. Where were the hills? I could see only mountains.

Lunch was set in a large open pavilion with a backdrop of mist and jungle. It was cool in the clove-scented air and the food was spicy and aromatic. Mounds of *nasi putih* in flat woven baskets towered above a collection of *sajur* dishes (curried vegetables); pork, chicken and beef satays; fiery *sambalan* and fried *tahu*. Years before, Alan and I had learnt to taste first by taking a small amount of each Indonesian dish, because to the uninitiated or careless eater a mouthful of *sambal* is like swallowing molten lava. There was cold Bintang beer, fresh coconut milk and saucers of sweet black rice.

'Now it's only a short walk to the holy heels,' announced Siti. 'The track is too narrow for the buses. Please follow me.'

So we did. Well, not everyone — those who were still convalescing after their over-indulgence of the previous night preferred to stretch out on the soft grass for a quiet snooze.

A narrow path wound upwards from the valley until we could look down upon the buses resting like toys beside the thatched pavilion. The heady aroma of spices wafted on the still air and beside us a stream had formed clear pools as it tumbled down the mountains. Comprehension slowly dawned as Siti explained.

'The heels are in the pools and the heel man will now feed them with raw eggs.' As if by magic, a man stepped out of the jungle and dribbled egg into the water. From the dark recesses under the banks glided grey saurian shapes, writhing and twisting in a frenzy. Huge eels. Holy eels! No-one seemed to know why they were holy; they simply were.

Back in the warm humidity of Amahusu, the village closest to the anchorage, we had barely left the bus when a young man sidled up to Alan.

'I'd like to introduce myself,' he began. 'My name's Nick and I live near your boat.' He held out a soft, damp hand.

'How do you know which is our boat?'

'I've been watching you. Your boat is *Windigo*. I am right, no?' He grinned at us, displaying a large mouth overcrowded with teeth and eyes bright with cunning.

'I'll be your guide while you're in Ambon,' he said. 'I'll show you special things.'

'Thanks Nick, but we don't need a guide,' Alan told him.

'I'll do it for nothing — just for you.'

'Sorry, but we prefer to be alone.'

Then, *sotto voce* to Alan, whom he had pulled aside, Nick said, 'I can get you a girl. Very cheap. Very clean. Pretty too.'

'No thanks, Nick.' Alan glanced at me mischievously, 'Not tonight.'

'Australian men like Indonesian girls when they come to Ambon. I know many girls who love Australian men,' Nick continued. He was irrepressible, chatting on about girls as if about the weather until we reached the beach where he helped us launch the dinghy before giving a cheery wave of farewell.

'See you tomorrow,' he called. '*Selamat sore.*'

Most Ambonese live in small villages called *negeri* which comprise several patrilineal groups attached to something sacred like a pool, a spring, a rock, even an eel, I suppose. Amahusu was originally an animist village but when the missionaries decided that animism was not the way to salvation, the people were converted to Christianity and received Christian names, hence Nicholas.

Nick had a younger brother and three nubile sisters who giggled and flirted, causing their brother to scowl disapprovingly and to hover protectively around them, seemingly unaware of the hypocrisy of his role in the procurement of other Ambonese women for the enjoyment of the visitors.

Because of the strategic proximity of their house, Nick's family and friends regarded *Windigo* as their special boat, paddling out with gifts of cloves, nutmeg, coconuts, evil tasting sago cakes, and *pisang goreng* made from plantain, too dry and starchy for our tastes. I grew to dread their visits and particularly the monotonous conversations that ensued as they scrambled into the cockpit.

'What your name?' they ask.

'My name's Olma.'

'Where you from?'

'I come from Australia.'

'Oooo, so far. How old are you?'

'It's a secret.'

'What is secret? How old are you?'

'I never tell anyone my age.'

'Why not?'

'I don't want to.'

Then in case they think I am being perverse, I try to explain.

'In Australia some people don't like to tell their age.'

My punishment for this eccentricity is invariably swift and to the point. They glance towards Alan and giggle.

'We think you his mother,' they say.

'Well, you can think what you bloody well like,' I say to myself, squirming under Alan's amused grin.

Sometimes I lie, in an attempt to escape the interminable interrogation.

'Sorry, but I am feeling *sakit* today.'

'Oooo, Olma *sakit*. No good Olma *sakit*. We bring medicine for Olma. No more *sakit*.'

On the first Sunday in Ambon the visiting yachts were expected to take the Ambonese for a sail up the harbour to repay them for their hospitality. The adults preferred to step aside in favour of the children and *Windigo*'s group began to assemble on the shore two hours before departure. Through the binoculars I could count 20 children. Ted and I were worried by visions of Alan being drowned under tons of impatient youngsters if they upturned the dinghy in their enthusiasm to scramble aboard.

I had bought biscuits and sweets and soft drinks for the multitudes, but had I bought enough? How many would there be? Could we control them and keep them safe? All my worst school principal nightmares resurfaced and left me sweating. And Clifford, as he swept by in his inflatable, made a remark that worried me.

'I'd kill myself before I'd take 30 American or Oz kids on board,' he shouted. 'But they tell me that Indonesian kids are different.'

The group of 20 grew to 32, three of whom were adults, mothers of some of the children. Ted and I were correct in assuming that Alan could be drowned because each time he went ashore the dinghy was almost swamped by a rush of excited youngsters who took flying leaps onto Alan as he struggled to maintain control of his inadequate craft.

Once they were aboard *Windigo*, we only imposed one rule: 'Thou shalt not go below.' The children quickly found their own spaces around the deck and settled down. They were the children of fishermen and were at home on the water, one lad of 11 steering the boat competently for the entire trip. They politely ate everything I had prepared and they were so restrained and obedient that we relented and allowed them below in groups to inspect the interior.

Some yachts, no doubt fearful of having children aboard, refused to join in the sail past, whilst others like *Maisie Dotes* with 57 children aboard their beautiful yacht, were gracious in their support.

Ted left the next morning, catching a small plane to Ujang Pandang from the airport on the opposite shore. We luxuriated in being alone again as most people do when the guests depart. We never did see him stand on his head.

The fleet dispersed in several directions. Many yachts, including our friends on *Stylopora*, headed back to Darwin. Some set sail for Ujang Pandang to take part in a regatta, while others, singly and in small groups, took the island-hopping route towards Singapore. At last there were only five yachts left in the anchorage at Ambon as the village reverted to its normal somnolence.

Alan and I left at dawn the next day with *New Address* and *Panache*, crossing the Banda Sea with its great depths of eight kilometres, to Sulawesi, and from there to the Tiger Islands to spend some time diving and snorkelling over their reefs.

Our friend, Col, on *New Address*, had fallen in love with one of his crew, a beautician who could not swim. Cosmetica's long red nails and glossy lips flashed in the sunlight as she flirted her way into Col's heart. Her commitment to accompanying him on an extended circumnavigation was unclear at that time, so Col was a man caught between two dreams — a life of wedded bliss in Adelaide or a life of adventure on the high seas.

During the passage from the Tiger Islands to Flores we were hit by a mortifying flash of memory. In order to pass the safety check for the Darwin to Ambon race we had borrowed some flares from *Stylopora* to supplement our own supply, intending to return them in Ambon. But they were still aboard *Windigo*, and *Stylopora* was heading in the opposite direction. Our embarrassment was acute; our guilt profound. Luckily we knew of one crew member who was returning to Darwin from Bali. Perhaps she could return the flares for us.

Despite its tropical beauty, that part of Indonesia was shabby and depressed. We avoided islands where stealing from yachts was reported on the radio by those ahead, and we often felt insecure in isolated anchorages, particularly when surrounded by a dozen canoes filled with villagers who wanted to come aboard. They were poor but we had little to give because yachts, with their constraints of space and weight, seldom carry anything superfluous. Sometimes we bartered for squid and the occasional lobster but the canoes were generally empty and the reefs barren. We watched helplessly one day as villagers dynamited their reef, scooping up the dead fish when they floated on the surface.

There were days of shimmering heat on cool turquoise seas followed by luminous sunsets in gentle anchorages. From the cockpit we watched monkeys play on the beaches and swing from vines high overhead, and we fell asleep to jungle sounds floating across the water.

Labuanbajo, on the island of Flores, is a miserable place, stinking of excrement and rotting fish. We anchored there to fill up with water, having given away a considerable amount of the precious liquid to fishermen on the reefs in the Tiger Islands. On going ashore to make inquiries, we met the harbourmaster who insisted on being taken to the boat. He grinned at me in a conspiratorial manner which was both puzzling and annoying. Because the visit was unexpected, we had not taken the usual precaution of hiding the liquor, and the harbour master's eye immediately fell upon the bottle of Johnny Walker we had opened the previous night.

'You give me that, I give you water,' he bargained.

As I handed it to him, his hand closed over mine, and he applied a suggestive pressure. 'Tonight I sleep on your boat.'

'*Tidak!* No!' countered Alan.

'Yah, I sleep here,' he persisted.

'We don't want you here. Please get in the dinghy.' Alan took him firmly by the elbow and propelled him through the companionway hatch.

As we finished tying *Windigo* to the rotting wharf, an insolent looking young man slouched from the harbour master's office.

'No water. Tap turned off,' he said.

Our Indonesian visas had almost expired and we had two days to reach Bali where we could renew them. There was no alternative but to sail non-stop on a difficult passage which was made more so because of our fear of arriving late.

Benoa harbour was crowded with yachts, many of which we recognised. There was also an assortment of other craft: decorated *prahus*, brightly painted Taiwanese fishing trawlers that resembled Chinese junks and leaned perilously when manoeuvering; inter-island ferries of obscure vintage; modern charter yachts and catamarans for the tourists. Weaving the whole into a tapestry of shapes and colours were the Balinese canoes paddled by sinewy brown fishermen under broad-brimmed conical hats.

A few metres from the harbour wall was the immigration office, a plain building softened by tropical growth. In the front office sat the chief immigration officer behind a desk devoid of the usual paraphernalia, apart from a neat stack of paper on which rested a biro. He did not look Balinese.

We introduced ourselves to Dr Kadir, handed over our passports and Security Clearance and explained that the visas expired that day.

'At what time does the immigration office in Denpasar close?' asked Alan.

'At two o'clock.'

'Good. It's now ten,' Alan commented. 'We should have plenty of time.'

Dr Kadir glanced thoughtfully at us, his eyes cold and his smile enigmatic.

'I'm from Lombok,' he began. 'My son is attending Cairo University where he is enrolled in the faculty of Islamic Studies. It's very expensive for me. To assist in his studies, the yacht captains give me presents. You can give me one too.' We stared at him.

'I'm sorry but we don't wish to give a present,' Alan told him.

'Perhaps you may have difficulty in getting to Denpasar by two', Dr Kadir answered.

The officials at the other offices: harbourmaster, navy, health, Customs, were friendly and easygoing and therefore slow, but finally we returned to Dr Kadir with everything complete. Like a *dalang* playing with puppets, he tediously inspected each page before turning to us.

'You will need three copies of everything for me to sign,' he pointed out. 'You have only one.'

Alan looked puzzled. 'Why didn't you give us three copies in the beginning ?' he asked.

'Ah, you see, Indonesia's a poor country,' said Dr Kadir. 'So I can't give you any more forms. Just one copy of everything.'

We gathered the papers, caught a taxi to the outskirts of Denpasar ten kilometres away, found a small office that did photocopying, scrambled back into the taxi and once more presented our now considerably thicker bundle to the wily Dr Kadir. He laboriously inspected both sides of each sheet before slowly picking up the biro. Then, with the studied pace of one who is learning to write, he began to sign. Finally he pushed the bundle at a snail's pace across the desk towards us.

In silence Alan picked it up and we walked, with what we hoped was poise, until we were out of sight. There the scene changed to resemble a silent movie as we raced to find another taxi to Denpasar. As the main doors of the Immigration Office were closing, we squeezed through and collapsed on the cool leather sofa to recover before approaching the counter. The pretty Balinese woman who accepted our papers was smiling and serene.

'Welcome to Bali,' she said. 'You seem to find the heat not to your liking.'

Whenever things went wrong on *Stylopora*, Don would say, 'Now we're in deep shit,' an apt description of the predicament Alan was in when he took *Stylopora*'s flares to the airport. As he walked through the entrance, he was seized by Security Police who believed the flares were incendiary devices for blowing up the airport. Expecting him back halfway through the morning, I worried when he had not returned by early afternoon, and grew alarmed when a police launch headed across the harbour towards *Windigo*.

'You come with us to ring this number,' an officer ordered as he leaned across to hand me a sheet from a notepad.

On the phone, Alan's voice was tight with torment.

'They've arrested me because they think I'm a terrorist. You'd better come.' And then he added, 'Don't wear shorts. Get dressed up. Try to look respectable.'

'Well, thanks,' I thought.

When I got to the police station, Alan was sitting in a small, bare room, looking white-faced and worried. He had been questioned for most of the morning but was always treated kindly by the six men on duty, who provided him with glasses of Balinese coffee and a free lunch.

Shortly after my arrival, a high-ranking officer from Headquarters in Denpasar took Alan away for further questioning. Both men looked serious when they returned.

'Your husband has committed a serious offence. We're still deciding what to do about it,' the officer said, looking at me severely before continuing. 'He may now return to the boat to sleep, but he must remain on board until he returns to this office at 7 a.m. I'm holding his passport.'

We walked out quickly into the dusk. A reprieve. Ignorance of the law does not mean that one is innocent, but perhaps the police would reason that we seemed unlikely terrorists and that it might be more convenient to forget the whole silly episode.

All through the next long day we sat together in the bare room, re-reading an ancient *Time* magazine and staring at the patterns of mould and verdigris, the ordered shadows of the barred window creeping across the far wall as the sun moved to the west, and the silent gecko clinging to the wall in a dark corner above the door.

Finally the officer reappeared, his eyes inscrutable.

'As I said yesterday, you have broken Indonesian law. This is serious. You're a very lucky man, Mr Alan, because if you'd committed the offence today instead of yesterday, you'd probably now be dead.' We stood ashen-faced while he continued. 'Today we have two very important visitors to our airport, the heads of the Indonesian and the Singaporean military forces. Security is tight.'

We pictured the tension of the heavily armed guards and knew that what he said was true. The officer's face softened.

'We've considered all aspects of this unfortunate incident, Mr Alan, and we've decided that you're not a terrorist, but simply a silly man. Here's your passport. You're now free to go.' Then he laughed and placed an arm around Alan's shoulder.

'Without the flares, of course,' he added.

There had been enormous changes since our first visit to Bali 20 years before when the capital, Denpasar, was hardly more than a large village. Acres of rice fields had disappeared forever under streets and buildings, large supermarkets now sold non-essentials like chandeliers and potted plants, and many teenagers arrive at school on motorbikes or driving cars. At Ubud, in the mountains, there was no electricity, just one simple restaurant run by the inimitable Okawati, and few places to stay.

My old friend, Atjin, was born in the village of Padangtegal near Ubud, the son of Bapak, the man who once cooked for the Dutch artist, Walter Spies, in his bungalow on the Tjampuan River. Atjin had grown into a fine man, handsome, intelligent and respected. His wide mouth flashed easily into a friendly grin and his dark eyes sparkled with energy and fun. When he was not engrossed in his work as the principal of the local secondary school, he was busy painting in his studio in a corner of the family compound, or taking part in the affairs of the *banjar*.

Swasti, Atjin's wife, came from a village on the island of Lombok. She was taller than many Balinese, clean-limbed, svelte and willowy, with the soft eyes of a deer. She moved around the compound with a lissom grace, seldom speaking, serene and gentle. She and Atjin had not long been married when I first met them.

Twenty years before, Bapak had spent much of his day grooming his splendid cocks at the back of the compound, or tending his pet pig, a massive sway-backed sow whose bloated belly dragged on the ground — making it impossible for her to escape from her low-walled enclosure.

Ibu, Atjin's mother, ran the compound with an iron will when she returned each morning from her stall at the Ubud market where she sold rice and dried legumes. Ibu was a fierce old woman with shrewd and watchful eyes and she enjoyed a formidable alliance with Johnny, the family dog, who was strangely similar to her in temperament.

The times I spent with them in those early years were rich in both tender and terrifying experiences. There were nights of blackness when, suddenly woken by a cold stream of rat's urine falling on my face from the rafters beneath the thatch roof, I would imagine I could hear the spirits moving — Rangda, the queen of the undead or perhaps the evil *leyaks* that gnaw at the entrails of unborn children.

I remember Swasti's first taste of ice-cream, her shock at the unexpected and unfamiliar coldness of it, and then her lovely face softening with a delighted grin as the magic of the new sensation took hold, and she wanted more.

Swasti is now an elegant and sophisticated woman. She speaks fluent English, competently manages the two pleasant homestays that she and Atjin have built in the Monkey Forest area, and runs her own jewellery shop in the main street. Two of their three children attend the University in Denpasar and the youngest will no doubt join them later.

Atjin is proud of his wife's Pygmalion transformation. He sat relaxed and contented beside the quiet pool where we had gathered to chat and his face was animated as he talked of the future.

He would soon retire from teaching to paint, and to play a more active role in the affairs of the *banjar*. Bapak busied himself between the compound, the *banjar*, and the two homestays, while Ibu, at a loose end since her grandchildren had become independent, had returned to the Ubud markets to sell rice and dried legumes.

Colin Harrison was the first to greet us when we returned to Benoa harbour a week later.

'Cosmetica has gone! Flew back to Adelaide yesterday.'

We looked sheepish.

'I know that's what you call her,' he said. Then he grinned and added, 'Actually, it was a good name for her.'

We were not sure how to react, but he continued.

'It just wouldn't have worked out. We wanted different things.'

Alan and I relaxed a little.

'But it's tough sailing single-handed, Col. Are you sure you will be able to manage?' Alan asked.

'Oh, I won't be single-handing,' replied Col. 'Marcelle, a very nice French lady, has agreed to sail with me on *New Address*.'

Mount Gunung Agung, with its cone in the clouds, was our last sight of Bali. As it faded, hundreds of fluttering moths, the sailing *prahus* boats of Bali, returned home. They criss-crossed each other's path, searching for the particular ribbon of orange light that stretched like a warm umbilical cord far out to sea from the homing fire that is lit above each village at sunset.

The tiny islands of the Java Sea should have been untouched, splendid in their isolation, but many were raped and denuded. As we sailed north, the air became progressively smokier until, at Serutu Island, off the western coast of Borneo, breathing became difficult and visibility was severely reduced. Islands and reefs hid in the gloom, making navigation tricky and dangerous. We felt weak and nauseated.

Approaching Borneo at night we narrowly missed a freighter and, half an hour later, two trawlers without lights. And then there were the drift nets, evil wire tendrils that stretched for miles, forcing sailors to make great detours to avoid becoming ensnared.

Sailors of small vessels pray that they will be able to pass through the area around the equator without encountering a *sumatra*, but few escape the dreaded line squalls. The balls of turbulence appear suddenly, and explode with vicious power.

Most of the time we were in the area we anchored with other yachts for safety, but on one occasion we pulled in behind a speck of an island and we were alone. We should have heeded the sudden quiescence, the eerie light and the strange tension, but we sat in the saloon enjoying the evening meal, oblivious to what was approaching.

Suddenly our world erupted. Ice-cold rain fell as a solid mass, soaking and bending us as we rushed into the cockpit. There was a roar, a shrieking savagery all around as the wind picked up *Windigo* and swung her in crazy arcs. Balls of electrical energy exploded like cannon fire around our heads as the continual lightning plunged into the sea, turning the blackness into a blinding white nightmare. *Windigo* was blown aground, and we cursed our independence and desire to be alone as we cowered on the floor of the cockpit, hugging each other in terror and wondering if one died a painless death from a direct lightning strike.

A *sumatra* is quickly over; spent, drained, burnt out, after a brief and brilliant crescendo. One moment we were in an inferno, then it passed, and there was silence. We existed in a blessed state. Even as we pondered how to float *Windigo* again, we felt her move slightly, then more, until we were floating free in the current.

In the lovely Lingga Islands just south of Singapore, a rowdy King Neptune, looking incongruously like Santa Claus, scrambled aboard *Panache* to preside over the 'Crossing the Equator' ceremony. Those aboard the yachts gathered there agreed that a day to recover was necessary before pushing on to Singapore.

CHAPTER 3

*Singapore and Changi • bacon or Baygon
cats and cruisers • more is more in Phuket*

A year had passed since Velia and Graeme had married, and it was now October 1991. Many times each day I glanced at Velia's wedding photograph on the bulkhead in the saloon and often I cried with longing for her, especially during the lonely watches. People who came below would ask, 'Who is that beautiful girl?', and I would puff out my feathers and proudly reply, 'That's my daughter, Velia.' I love her because she is honourable, as well as beautiful. Parting was not 'sweet sorrow'. It was a wrenching, tearing sense of loss.

We had reached Singapore. Its skyscrapers rose like misty spires from the smoke haze and long before the image gained definition the outlines of the first of the anchored ships appeared on the horizon. Singapore, strategically placed, is the world's fourth busiest port, with hundreds of vessels anchored in the approaches to Singapore harbour as they awaited their turn at the wharves.

The silent monoliths of steel, even at rest, appeared threatening, and we felt insignificant and exposed as we wove warily between them. Even the ungainly ketch, *Big Drum*, approaching from our stern, looked lightweight and delicate in their midst as it followed us to the anchorage at Changi.

There is an unpleasant association in many people's minds with this outlying suburb of Singapore but in reality it is leafy, affluent and beautiful. The millions of visitors who pass through Changi International Airport seldom explore its surroundings and so they remain ignorant of its charms. However, people remember the infamous Changi prison, where the Japanese incarcerated Allied prisoners after the fall of Singapore.

None of this is visible from the anchorage, however. We looked across to a wooded shore sprinkled with gracious bungalows and exclusive clubs set amidst golden *angsana*, red flame trees and evergreen oaks. Changi Yacht Club is ritzy with the usual facilities, the best from the yachties' point of view being the hot showers. We ate at Changi Village Food Centre a short stroll from the club, where dozens of stalls offer a bewildering array of cuisines at little cost, and where the *matabak* maker entertains by flinging his lumps of dough in the air in ever-increasing circles to create paper-thin pancakes.

Lugubrious George and his heavy wife paddled across from *Big Drum* soon after we arrived. They had taken on three crew members in Darwin; young backpackers in search of adventure. There was Sven and Ondine, a Swedish couple, and Bevan, a lad from New Zealand working his way to Europe. We had met them briefly in Darwin.

'Never take on backpackers,' George began. 'We've just had to order ours off the boat.'

And so began a protracted tale of woe. Their backpackers had eaten all the food, drunk all the liquor, told foul jokes, stolen Vi's jewellery, and were generally 'not shippy'. It was a depressing tale that took the edge off our excitement at arriving safely in Singapore and we made a mental note to avoid the gloomy pair in the future.

If Changi has a drawback it is its distance from the centre of Singapore, but with the new Mass Rapid Transport, this is not a major inconvenience, especially when this underground rail system is such a modern wonder. Spotless, airconditioned, perfumed, swift and efficient, it is without partitions, just one continuous serpent in which it would be impossible to rape or pillage unless one were prepared to do so within sight of the entire train. Mind-teaser games on large television screens alleviate the tedium of waiting, and some station entrances, rich with marble and chandeliers, resemble the foyers of plush hotels.

Hong Kong apparently has a similar solution to the mass movement of people and we wished that Sydney were similarly endowed.

Lean times were ahead for us as we drank the last of our Australian wine. We feared we would be unable to afford wine again until we reached the Mediterranean. In Singapore a cask of Australian wine was selling for $36.

Hospital care was also beyond our means. Not long after arriving, I felt too ill to leave the boat and a lump the size of a golf ball developed in my groin. At Changi Hospital the young Chinese doctor insisted that I undergo tests that would necessitate a night in hospital, but when I discovered that the accommodation alone would cost $2000, I began to feel better, and I hastened the recovery with a course of antibiotics from the ship's medical kit. The lump slowly diminished in size and I gradually felt well again.

On previous trips to Singapore we had visited the famous places and had little desire to do so again, although we kept telling ourselves that when we had fully prepared *Windigo* for the next leg, we would revisit Jurong Bird Park, one of the most sensitively designed and attractive wildlife parks we had ever seen. But there was provisioning to be done, borrowed charts and cruising guides to photocopy, a fault in the radar to investigate, the engine to overhaul, and a string of boat chores to finish. So we never returned to Jurong, but we did return to the zoo.

Years before, Alan had fallen in love with a gibbon at the Singapore Zoo. It had reached out and embraced him affectionately. It had stroked his hair and kissed his forehead and whispered gibbon secrets in his ear. He had never forgotten it. One day when we were in that area, we went to see if the gibbon was still there — but it was hard to tell.

The owners of *Beata Maria*, a Swedish yacht with two young children on board, bought a small monkey in Bali. It swung on its chain on the bow, baring its teeth and snarling at everyone who came close. I thought it an unpleasant animal and often wondered how the five occupants of *Beata Maria* managed at sea when the monkey, of necessity, would have to remain below.

One day after the family had gone ashore, the monkey broke its chain and swam after them. A new arrival in the anchorage saw it swimming past his boat and fearing its demise, felt duty-bound to rescue it. He set off in his dinghy in hot pursuit and on catching the small creature, leaned over to lift it to safety. The ungrateful beast leapt at his face, sank its teeth into his neck and dived back into the water to continue swimming towards the shore. The well-intentioned sailor also continued towards the shore, where he raced in panic across the sand and through the cantonment to Changi Hospital for a rabies shot.

After a month in Singapore we yearned for a less earnest environment, for a rowdier, naughtier place, free from the tedium of uniformity set in train years ago by the island's adroit elder statesman, Lee Kuan Yew.

The Strait of Malacca was once notorious for pirates, but Alan said (and I wanted to believe him) that their activities were at that stage concentrated in the South China Sea and the Phillip Channel just south of Singapore. Nevertheless, while we were in the Strait a freighter was boarded by pirates and the captain and crew held at knife point while the pirates raided the safe and the crew's quarters.

It was during our second night in the Strait, still and leaden with the threat of thunderstorm, that we most feared pirates. We motored parallel to the main channel to avoid the big ships, picking our way through the fishing boats and straining to see the floats and traps in time to avoid them. Without warning, the engine stopped and *Windigo* glided to a halt. She became immediately at risk, vulnerable to boarding pirates.

While Alan worked below on the engine, I kept watch in the cockpit, willing him to hurry as a boat without lights slowly approached from our stern.

'If they're coming to help, why approach unlit?' I asked myself, yelling at Alan to hurry as I made out the shapes of four men paddling softly and now only metres from our stern. Suddenly *Windigo*'s engine roared into life and we slowly gathered speed. From the cockpit we watched with relief as the men stopped rowing and faded into the gloom.

By morning we were in the northern part of the Malacca Strait and approaching Port Klang, the seaport that serves the city of Kuala Lumpur. We had come there to take part in the annual Raja Muda Regatta, a race from Port Klang to Lankawi Island on the border between Malaysia and Thailand. Our interest was more to do with safety than competition — safety in numbers, and protection from the gunboat which would accompany the fleet.

The two mature women who organised the regatta and managed the yacht club were upper North Shore in accent, clothes, jewellery, make-up and hairstyles.

'We sailed here on separate yachts a couple of years ago and have been here ever since,' Virginia said, as if that explained everything.

'You're obviously busy with the extra work of the Regatta,' Alan commented, indicating the piles of entry forms, pennants and flags that covered most surfaces.

'Yes, this is the largest fleet we've ever organised,' Vanessa agreed.

'Perhaps a reflection on the success of previous regattas?' I ventured.

'I think not,' replied Vanessa. 'The 40 yachts of the Europa fleet are arriving today and they have all entered the regatta. That's why we're busier than usual.'

Our spirits dropped. Jimmy Cornell, the author of *World Cruising Routes*, the bible of cruising yachtspeople, had organised the first of the 'Around the World' cruising races, later to become regular events. Stories of the fleet of large and expensive yachts, with big crews and seemingly unlimited spending power, had already reached us and the general feeling was that we should avoid them either by keeping ahead or staying well behind so that officials and providers of services had time to recover from the inflated expectations fanned by the big spenders.

But they had crept up on us. As the days passed, the handful of yachts that had sailed together from Darwin felt increasingly like Cinderellas and we huddled together for support, ignored by the Europa fleet which had long ago formed a tight-knit group. We had a preview of what to expect in the Mediterranean as the marine radio bands were monopolised by Italian, German and French speakers. At least it forced me to start brushing up my Italian.

Unlike Singapore where demolition and construction have developed a callous momentum, Kuala Lumpur has retained most of its historic structures like the old Masjid Jame on the river, marking the site of the city's beginnings; the law courts; the Royal Selangor Club (in front of which a game of cricket was in progress on the green); and that strange blend of Moorish architecture and British whimsy, the railway station. Kuala Lumpur, a relatively small city, appears grand in scale, spread as it is around gardens, parks and stands of rain forest.

A *ringgit* goes a long way in Malaysia so we were shocked when the Chinese meal we enjoyed one evening cost a small fortune. Perhaps we were caught off guard, our concentration broken by the arrival of Bevan towards the end of the meal. The Kiwi crew member from *Big Drum* seemed pleased to see us, and he sat at our table and ordered a beer, having already eaten somewhere else.

'How did you get to Kuala Lumpur?' we asked.

'By bus,' he replied. 'I left *Big Drum* in Singapore, together with the Swedish pair.'

We remained silent, but he must have noticed the flicker of interest in our faces, for he continued.

'That George was a mad bugger. Dangerous. They were both off the rails. Paranoid, both of them.'

'Perhaps they were finding life at sea more than they'd bargained for,' I suggested. 'They were farmers, you know.'

'Bloody hell I know!' Bevan declared. 'They never stopped talking about cows. They imagined things too. Vi even accused me of stealing her jewellery. And Sven of telling dirty jokes. Perhaps he did in Swedish, but his English was too rudimentary even for clean jokes.'

We laughed, and he continued.

'They tried to starve us, you know. We had to sneak things to eat. Finally, one night just south of Singapore, George got pissed out of his brain and attacked the three of us with a broken boathook. Like a crazy man.' Bevan took several long gulps from his glass of Tiger beer, watching our faces over the rim.

'Any chance of crewing on *Windigo*?' he asked.

We attended a poolside banquet graced by the Sultan on our last night in Port Klang. Of the 13 Malaysian states, nine have sultans; rich, British-educated, powerful. Those who support them argue that they keep alive the culture and traditions of Malaysia.

The skippers were told to shake hands with the Sultan, but few did. Rather than appear churlish, Alan was about to comply when he spilt curry down the front of his white pants and did not wish to appear in front of royalty in a soiled state. When people started to fall in the pool, the Sultan withdrew to his palace, the Darwin group returned to their boats, and the evening was left to the Europeans.

A *shaman*, hired by the regatta organizers to ensure there would be wind for the beginning of the race, was obviously inept. There was no wind. Most yachts, after drifting around for a couple of hours, withdrew and motored ahead. Opportunistic, we reasoned that because there was virtually no-one left in the race, with our handicap we might win if we persevered. But finally we were forced to turn on the engine and follow the fleet.

The bridge to Butterworth spans the southern approach to

Pulau Penang. A mile farther on, beneath the battlements of Fort Cornwallis, was the anchorage, with the splendid old Empire and Orient Hotel a little farther to the right.

The building guards the ghosts of those members of the East India Company and their families and friends who stayed on when the Straits Settlements of Malacca, Penang and Singapore became a crown colony under British rule. The dust of crinolines, faint whiffs of oil of macassar and old roses still float in its grand ballroom, and its long corridors echo with the sounds of distant laughter and a tinkling piano. The Empire and Orient was to be our base while we were in Penang, and we relished its cool dark spaces in the heat of the day.

Peter on *Scimitar* had sailed single-handed from Bali to Penang, preferring the freedom of being alone to sharing his 36 feet with comparative strangers. One night, after joining in the revelries at the Empire and Orient, he paddled back to *Scimitar* and was soon sleeping soundly in the forepeak. Around midnight he was awakened by the sound of the engine and realized that his boat was underway.

'The anchor must have dragged and one of my mates has come to the rescue,' he reasoned as he scrambled to the companion-way. But the man at the wheel was Asian, a stranger, and from the surprise on the intruder's face it was clear that he had not expected anyone to be on board.

On reaching the cockpit, Peter saw that the lights of Penang were fading as *Scimitar* headed out to sea.

'Who are you? What are you doing with my boat?' he yelled. But the stranger at the helm stared straight ahead in silence, his hands in a vice-like grip on the wheel.

Peter is a slight man, not given to physical violence and he feared close contact with someone who may have been carrying a knife. In desperation he screamed.

'I'll shoot you, you bastard. I'll get the gun and I'll shoot you.'

He dived below in search of something that in the gloom might resemble a firearm. A winch handle would have to do. When he turned, pointing it into the cockpit, there was no-one there.

'Am I drunk or dreaming?' Peter wondered as he hurried to take the wheel. Turning *Scimitar* in an arc towards the lights of Penang he saw reflected in their glow, the rhythmic splashing of a swimmer heading in the same direction.

'I hope he makes it,' thought Peter. 'But I'm not going to pick him up.'

At Penang we withdrew from the Raja Muda Regatta and proceeded at our own pace to Langkawi, a tropical archipelago of 104 islands, only a half dozen of which are inhabited. Once the hiding place of pirates, the islands lie in the far north of the Malacca Strait, close to the Andaman Sea.

The Langkawi archipelago was the most beautiful area we had seen since leaving the Queensland coast. Arcane and alluring, its waterways often form slender straits between high-sided limestone islands that appear to be toppling inwards under the weight of their crowns of foliage. So slimly serpentine are some of the channels that I feared *Windigo* would not squeeze through, or that her mast and spreaders would catch in the jungle vines.

We had heard of a freshwater lake high on one of the islands where childless couples came to drink. It was called the Lake of the Pregnant Maiden and we tried to find it. The climb was steep and we were hot, relishing the thought of a swim in a cool mountain lake.

Rounding a bend in the path, we suddenly saw it shimmering above the heads of scores of Japanese tourists crowded along its edge. They giggled and jostled, shattering the tranquillity, causing us to turn and walk away. If we could not tolerate sharing this remote place with tourists, we wondered how we would manage in the famous places of Europe where their numbers would be tenfold. No longer did we consider ourselves tourists, but travellers.

Having withdrawn from the misadventures of the Raja Muda Regatta before leaving Penang, we nevertheless attended the final banquet at the luxurious Pelangi Beach Resort on the main island. A free meal and drinks in surroundings such as those were too tempting to ignore.

It was to be the end of high living for us, the swansong to free meals and yacht clubs and rajas and regattas. From here on, we would be on our own, admittedly part of a moving caravan of yachts heading towards the Mediterranean, but without an organisation or regular skeds or route plans, or indeed, any help at all.

We had entered the north-east trades and were now able to sail most of the time. The stability of the south-east trades had lulled us into a false sense of security. The weather once again became an obsession. The nights were cooler, we slept under a sheet and were comforted by the thought of the blanket folded at the foot of the bunk.

Kuah, the only town in the Langkawi group, is a free port. A bustling place with a Wild West shantytown appearance, it hugs a pleasant bay with wide, black mud flats at low tide. These make it impossible to approach by dinghy unless one uses the tides.

There are more liquor stores in Kuah than I have seen in any other town of its size. The prices are cheap and *Windigo*'s lockers were once again packed tightly. We even managed to buy some Australian cask wine and a few bottles of champagne for special occasions.

We had not eaten bacon for some time and were craving it. The only supermarket was no more than a large shop with a sign outside saying 'Supe market'. The owner was a tough Chinese woman who snapped at the three employees and fiercely regarded the customers. Nevertheless, she seemed the best one to approach. I smiled and said good morning in Malay. She scowled.

'Bacon?' I asked. 'You have bacon?'

'Aha, Baygon,' she replied, with a flash of understanding.

'No, no. Bacon. I want bay-con. Bay-con. Not Bay-gon,' I persisted.

'Bay-gon. Bay-gon. Ya, ya.' She nodded vigorously and pointed towards the shelves where I could see a couple of cans of the lethal stuff. She grabbed one and slammed it down in front of me in triumph.

'Bay-gon!' she crowed.

I fought back panic. In desperation I searched in my bag for a pencil and paper whilst my Chinese torturer waited impassively. Carefully I drew a fat pig with a curly tail, then an arrow from the pig to a rasher of bacon and another arrow from the bacon to a frying pan. My mother would have been proud. She had always maintained that I had artistic talent. When I turned the paper towards the woman, her face lit with comprehension.

'Ahhhhh,' she exhaled.

Then she dropped from sight and began rummaging around under the counter. Her search seemed interminable and as I waited I thought that possibly the bacon would be more appetising if it were kept under refrigeration in that climate. I was beginning to have second thoughts about buying it. At last she rose in front of me and her face fairly glowed with victory. Triumphantly she placed an antiquated rat trap before me.

'Ahhhhh,' she said once more, this time with a smile of satisfaction.

You recognise defeat when it stares you in the face. I paid for the rat trap and hurried from the shop. That afternoon we left Kuah and crossed into Thailand. Just on dusk, a victory yell from Alan made me think that we had finally caught a fish and I hurried to the cockpit from where I had been reading on the foredeck. But the trolling line was slack.

'I've worked it out!' Alan exclaimed. 'That Chinese woman couldn't clear her mind of Baygon and its association with vermin. She thought your pig was a fat rat, the rasher of bacon was a flattened rat and the frying pan was the weapon of destruction. Her solution of the rat trap was a lot less messy.'

By the time we reached Thailand the small group that had sailed together from Darwin knew each other well. We knew about each other's families and their problems, and we were confident and convivial with each other.

'How's your mother since her operation?'

'Heard from the kids lately?'

'Come over for sundowners.'

We were mindful of idiosyncrasies and had learned when to withdraw gracefully. Generally though, political and social affairs were discussed with considerable passion and without any lasting rancour. Cruising sailors are at heart nonconformist, some of us verging on anarchic in our annoyance at the constraints of rules and regulations. The irony was that we were now placing ourselves at the mercy of foreign laws that appeared far more draconian than those we had left behind. JB, though, was unrelenting in his criticism of Australia.

'Socialism has ruined your country. Australians are a race of dole bludgers. You expect the government to look after you, wipe your arses for you.'

'But JB, the good old USA also looks after its poor and needy, perhaps not so successfully as Australia does, but its problems are greater,' I pointed out. 'You also have welfare programs. That's what it means to be civilised.'

'We're not discussing my country. I'm telling you what is wrong with yours.'

The conflict in Laurie's heart was now known to all of us; her longing to be with her two daughters in New Zealand, the younger of whom was pregnant with her first child, her excitement at the thought of seeing her son Tod who worked in the charter industry in Greece, and her desire to sail the world on

Panache with Des. Her husband said little about his feelings on those issues but contributed with passionate and ribald language to all other controversies.

Bret and Debbie on the streamlined and racy *Interlude* had been given a kitten by the cook at the Singapore Yacht Club. He had rescued it, along with three siblings, from a bag floating past the dining room. The kitten's eyes were still closed when *Interlude* left Singapore so keeping it alive had been demanding and time consuming for the young dentist and his wife.

'How's the little mite today?'

'Slowly getting her sea legs.'

The little mite was a pretty ball of fluff patterned in tan, yellow and white, and she was called Miffy. However, as the weeks passed she began to display signs of aberrant behaviour, clinging to people with embarrassing intensity and sucking desperately on any exposed skin. Was the first letter of her name disguising a certain transience, we wondered.

Anaconda's cat, too, was developing annoying habits that the choleric JB tried to overlook. His wife, after all, was a past president of 'Cat Lovers of America'. Paris, an enormous feral cat taken on board in Darwin as a kitten, had grown increasingly obdurate and arrogant. He would sulk in a dark corner beneath the saloon table while watching hapless visitors with a malevolent eye, treacherous and cunning. Slowly the hairs along his broad back would rise and his body curve like a tiger before he sprang in a pulsating parabola at the bare ankles of his victim, drawing blood and causing screams of outrage and terror.

The elegant interior of *Anaconda* was beginning to show wear and tear from Paris's time on board and a piece of carpet that JB had tied to the leg of the saloon table for the cat to claw was now in tattered shreds. You could sense a mounting tension.

Alan and I had already visited Thailand and so did not share our friends' enthusiasm for trips to the famous places, of which there are many, from the opium-growing hill tribes of the north to exotic and suffocating Bangkok and the stilt villages and mosques of the south. It is a fascinating land of enigmatic people and golden Buddhas. This time, however, we preferred to spend our time exploring places that could be visited only by boat.

Unlike Malays, who do not approach a yacht on their own initiative, the Thais have no such reticence and in this regard are like the Indonesians. Once again we locked the boat and removed all the deck gear before leaving *Windigo* or going to bed. By placing the dinghy upside down over the aft cabin we could open the hatch above our bunk for air, at the same time making it impossible for even a small Thai to squeeze through.

Most of our visitors were charming, but curious about us and the boat. We gave them cool drinks, chocolate and cigarettes and they reciprocated with squid and coconuts. Others, however, made us feel vulnerable in the isolated anchorages. The three members of one group who tied up alongside *Windigo* were dirty and dishevelled, spitting, burping and cleaning their nostrils in the cockpit. One, a smutty lad of around 13 years, was obviously saying lewd and vulgar things about me to his two older companions, men in their 40s, I imagine. All three guffawed loudly, flicking their pink tongues and showering spittle.

The main anchorage and clearing port on Phuket is at Ao Chalong, a wide bay on the southern side of the island which is joined by a causeway to the mainland. The bay is ringed with seafood restaurants, bars and simple hotels, but compared to Patong Bay, on the other side of the island, it is undeveloped and unpretentious.

In the centre of Phuket town, 15 minutes by *tuk-tuk* from Ao Chalong, is a simple restaurant where we had eaten years before. It had not changed in any noticeable way. Our servings of mussels still came in two metal pots, battered and dented, but with lids firmly clamped.

Clouds of aromatic vapour rose from the perfectly cooked shellfish which had been steamed open in the layers of green leaves and fresh herbs lining the pots' interiors. A pungent dipping sauce accompanied the mussels. The fried bananas which followed were coated with an airy cake batter and they oozed like rich cream when cut. They were served with a sweet clear sauce flavoured with vinegar and cloves.

At Patong Beach there was another restaurant where we had eaten when Patong was a small village instead of the crass duplication of German suburbia, brothels included, that it is today. We searched along the beachfront for the old circular restaurant with its thatch roof, not really expecting to find it amidst the glitz but finally we did. Inside another restaurant, big and loud and sleazy, the circular gem of our memories was now the bar.

On Phuket island there is madness. The domestic and street architecture of the *nouveau riche* and the *nouveau arrive* is plagued by blatant featurism. Often, three or four styles of tiles, porticos and arches are used in the same building, together with 1960s abstract murals in cyclamen, green and yellow. 'More is more' is the maxim.

This applies also to sex. There is rampant exploitation of women and children, and the 'adult bar' is a freak show where women and girls perform amazing feats with their vaginas, like blowing smoke rings, firing darts, and popping out ping-pong balls in rapid succession.

In Phuket town, not far from our favourite restaurant, there was once a brothel. It is a now a heap of charred ruins in an allotment that will always remain vacant in memory of the 27 girls who were chained in their rooms when the brothel caught fire and burned to the ground over a decade ago.

Away from Phuket in Phang Nga Bay there is beauty of the kind that bewitches. Phang Nga is timeless. Thirty-five kilometres long, the sheltered waterway contains countless islands ranging from a few large inhabited ones to the tiny spindle-shanked limestone columns that rise like bulbous needles from the sea. There are cathedral-like caves, and hidden lagoons that can only be reached by dinghying by torchlight through twisting black tunnels. There are stalactites dripping from ceilings covered in bats, each suspended in its private wing-wrapped cocoon. There are fish and herons and swallows, and the tranquil, floating feeling of having reached the Happy Isles.

Our first Christmas away from Velia was spent on a pearly, powder-sand beach with *Northern Lights*, *Maisie Dotes* and *Interlude* and several other yachts from Darwin. Alan and I felt sad and lost without her, and we were happy when the day was over. It was almost time to move on. The trade winds had firmed and we set about preparing *Windigo* for sea.

CHAPTER 4

a stopover in Sri Lanka
'The Sultan's Turret in a Noose of Light'
a gold watch and a twisted nipple in Oman
a Chinese banquet in Yemen

S ri Lanka has been known by many names. The Greeks and the Romans called it Taprobane, Sinbad's Arab sailors knew it as Serendib, the Portuguese as Ceilao, the Dutch as Ceylan and the British as Ceylon. The name, Sri Lanka, dates from the mists of the Ramayana.

Six and a half days after leaving Thailand in mid-January 1992, the lighthouse on Dondra Head blinked on the horizon and we were almost there. At sunrise we were passing Weligama where we had caught dengue fever several years before, and a few hours later we were tied up in Galle harbour after a smooth and uneventful passage during which civil war had erupted in Sri Lanka and the Tamil Tigers were once again active in the north of the island.

Galle harbour, our home for the next couple of weeks, is protected from the wind and, we hoped, from the fighting. It is an intimate harbour with a backdrop of colonial buildings covered in a tropical patina. Brightly decorated fishing canoes weave among the yachts in the late afternoons.

It is when you step ashore to be greeted by groups of bedraggled men begging for the garbage you are carrying to the bin that you wonder if your serendipity will still be intact at the end of your visit to this troubled island.

The Europa Around the World fleet had sailed a few days previously, and the people of Magalle, of which Galle is an outlying suburb, were rapacious and persistent as they followed us through the streets demanding that we pay the inflated prices paid by those who had preceded us.

'You want to buy gems, Memsahib? I take you to the best gem shop in Sri Lanka. Very close. Very cheap,' they say.

'No thank you,' I reply.

'I am a human being,' they yell.

The town is a squalid place of decaying buildings, pot-holed streets and opportunistic inhabitants who make it impossible to conduct business with any degree of success. We would have to use a shipping agent to provision for the next leg to Oman.

His name was Marty and his stomach hung in folds over his low belt as he moved ponderously around the dusty office at the front of his house, his pudgy hands making damp marks. He sweated profusely in the humid heat and beads of moisture seeped through his thick, black moustache. He licked at the salt as he spoke.

'Do you have any cheese, Marty?'

'Oh, so very difficult to obtain, Memsahib.'

'Why is that, I wonder.'

'I do not know, Memsahib.'

'Surely we're not the first vessel to require cheese. You must keep it in stock,' I insist.

'Oh, no, no, no. Not in stock.'

'Can you get me a large block of cheese then?'

'Yes Memsahib. It may cost more, Memsahib.'

'How much more? More than what?'

'Very difficult to explain. I give you good price.'

'We are leaving soon. When will it be here?'

'Oh, you can have it now, Memsahib.'

Even the simplest of excursions somehow became complicated and exasperating. We set out to find a laundry, armed with an address that had been given to us by another yachtie, but the street names had either fallen off or had faded in the tropical conditions. We stopped a passer-by to ask directions.

'Can you show us where this house is, please?'

'Yes, I can arrange that for you.'

'We don't want you to arrange anything,' we tell him.

'Commission is very small for this service,' he persists.

Our friends on *Anaconda* and *Interlude* hired a car to explore the island, leaving their boats and their cats in our care. Miffy and Paris were a constant source of anxiety, Miffy because she cried day and night and Paris because his owners insisted that he be brushed each day.

'It tames him, and he likes it,' explained JB.

For the first few minutes it appeared that JB was correct. Paris would lie on his back like a dog, perfectly still, and despite his lack of purr he appeared to be grinning contentedly. Without warning, however, he would coil his body around the brush and sink his claws into the back of one's hand before disappearing into one of his private places, refusing to show himself again. After his second display of ingratitude, we left him unbrushed.

THE PASSAGE TO OMAN — 6 February 1992 (based on extracts from the ship's log)

DAY 1. The new moon shone only briefly and the night is now pitch black. One consolation is that during the two weeks it will take us to reach Oman, each evening will be brighter than the last. So far there has been no wind.

We left Sri Lanka with few regrets, happy to be at sea again. We both feel a frisson of excitement at the thought of reaching Oman, a land we know little about — probably because foreigners are not encouraged. Yachts, however, are welcome because the Sultan and his people have had an affinity with the sea since the time of Sinbad. Oman will be the first country we have not previously visited so we approach it with a sense of wonder that has been missing from our reactions to the places we have sailed through. To our north lies the teeming Indian subcontinent and ahead of us the Arabian Sea.

DAY 2. Away from the land we found strong wind and just after dark we spent at least three hours picking our way through an enormous fishing fleet. The sea ahead looks empty, a wall of black with no visible horizon. *Interlude* is 45 miles ahead of us and *Anaconda* a day behind us. *New Address* and *Northern Lights* will leave tomorrow with three other yachts, leaving *Maisie Dotes* to wait until Woody's leg, infected for weeks, has improved. For looking after Miffy and the boat, *Interlude* gave us a large bag of avocados.

DAY 3. No wind, not even a zephyr, ruffles the surface of the sea, which at sunset became a billowing sheet of crimson satin. There appears to be no movement, but a strong south-setting current is pushing us at least 20 degrees off course. Most of the other yachts bought GPS in Singapore but we are still using our satellite navigation. We greatly admire the navigators of old, who had no electronic gadgets to guide them.

Alan has injured his knee on a winch. I have bandaged it but it is still very painful and he cannot bend his leg.

DAY 4. Near midnight, Bret radioed for help. *Interlude* was entangled in a driftnet. Donning scuba gear, and with Debbie shining a powerful torch through the water, he had managed to cut the net away from the hull. But it had wound itself around the propeller, and damaged the gearbox.

There was no wind and Bret was worried that *Interlude* would drift back onto the net and that the owners would return at dawn and be unhappy when they saw the holes he had cut in it. We were worried about approaching an unlit net as we did not want the same fate to befall *Windigo*, and we doubted our ability to be of much assistance with enraged fishermen.

We changed course, however, and five hours later we spotted *Interlude*'s light through the binoculars. A breeze had come up with the dawn and she was some distance from her original position and sailing well. The four of us were relieved to leave the area before the return of the trawler with its vengeful fishermen, and as we sailed, Bret told his story over the radio.

'I was scared, Alan. For a while, I was too frightened to function. I just sat in the cockpit like a lump of jelly, unable to come to terms with jumping into the heaving blackness. I guess it's the way parachutists feel the first time they jump from a plane except they want to do it and I had no choice.

'It was a terrible experience. My main concern was avoiding entanglement in the net. It kept moving with the waves, threatening to hold me down. At one stage, I became paralysed with panic. I could feel something slimy brushing against my legs and all I could think of was sharks. After what seemed a lifetime, in the beam from Debbie's torch I saw that it was a large black plastic bag which had become caught in the net.

'Then, because of the movement of the boat, I kept banging my head on the hull and I worried that I would be knocked unconcious.'

'Are you feeling all right now, Bret?' Alan asked.

'I've had a brandy. I think I'm OK, Debbie had one too.'

DAY 5. In four days we have covered 300 miles. There are still 1500 to go. Again we are without wind. *Anaconda* has caught up and is towing *Interlude*. I feel relieved because we have never towed anyone and I am not entirely sure of what to do. I have read of the difficulties encountered when the yacht being towed sails faster than the one that is towing and I worry about our lack of experience. But Alan says that we will never be experienced if we do not do these things. He is right, of course.

We are due north of the Maldives and passing close to an Indian island called Minicoy, taking care that the current does not set us sideways onto reefs.

When we are not sleeping, we read. I am halfway through Paul Theroux's *Riding the Iron Rooster* and no longer have any wish to visit China. I love the book, though.

DAY 6. Through the binoculars we saw a gunboat approaching. At times it was clearly visible as it rode high on the waves, but then we would lose it in the troughs. However, it always returned like some sinister configuration, and through the bin-oculars we recognised it as an Indian coast patrol. In another couple of hours we would have reached the relative safety of international waters but here we were still in Indian territory. As it came closer we saw the armed soldiers standing at the ready along the side decks and the machine gun mounted on the bow.

'I'm not going to stop,' Alan declared as he hurried below to the radio. The vessel was keeping pace with *Windigo* on our port side and I wondered how this would end as I listened to Alan giving the details of our vessel.

'Indian coast patrol. This is the Australian yacht *Windigo*. Two people on board. We are sailing from Galle to Oman. Do you copy?'

'Lower your sails and stop the boat. We are coming aboard,' was the curt reply.

'In these seas a boarding operation would be dangerous,' Alan pointed out. 'We have legitimate right of passage through these waters. I will not stop.'

Silence. The armed men still held their rifles at the ready as they braced themselves against the rolling of the ship. I could see four men talking earnestly in the wheelhouse. Our refusal to stop had thrown them into a dilemma. They were left with two alternatives: to board us against our wishes or to open fire, both uncivilised acts. The radio crackled.

'Why are you here? Where have you been? What are you carry-ing? Why has it taken you so long to get from Galle to here? Where have you stopped?'

Alan patiently explained that we had not stopped since leaving Galle, that the currents had been against us, that there had been little wind, that we carried no drugs or firearms and that we were very sorry that we had not had time to visit their beautiful country but next time we were in the area, we would call in. He also pointed out that a radio check with Galle would verify most of what he had said.

Again there was silence. Then 'Thankyou, Sir. You may

proceed. Do you need assistance with anything? Enough water? Fuel? Safe passage, Sir.'

When they disappeared over the horizon we felt lonely.

DAY 7. This morning we worked out that we had used half our fuel and we had only covered one third of the distance. We can no longer use the engine to push the boat along, but must instead conserve fuel for running the fridge and freezer and powering the batteries.

The days seem short and the nights tediously long. I take the first watch until midnight, and my second from 4 a.m. until around 7 a.m. After that I can sleep for as long as I like but to my annoyance I invariably wake around nine. By the time I do the usual morning things — breakfast, wash up, clean and tidy the boat — the morning has gone. After lunch we read, listen to music, and enjoy being together. Alan keeps radio skeds with other yachts every six hours and these are often fun if there is a 'Recipe Swap' or a 'Trivial Pursuit' or some other light-hearted attempt to brighten the day. Their greatest value, though, is in the passing on of information about conditions ahead: sea state, wind strength, weather, traps and nets, other shipping, floating objects, schools of fish.

DAY 8. We move through a world of air and water. There must surely be fish and birds, dolphins and whales but so far we have seen none. We prayed for wind (not literally) but whoever is in charge of these things lacks a sense of proportion and we now have too much. It is uncomfortable and it was frightening until we managed to reduce sail, a tricky process as it is so long since we have had to reef the main that we are out of practice. We could not remember the last time we wore a safety harness.

Although we steer higher than our course to compensate for the current, we are still heading south towards Africa. One of the yachts ahead of us has been unable to reach Oman for this reason and is now sailing for Aden. It is not a major problem, but we will be disappointed if we cannot make the northing to reach Oman.

Anaconda's mainsail has blown out and *Northern Lights* has had to turn into Cochin for more fuel. It is too rough to shower or to cook.

DAY 9. We are halfway there, 800 miles to go. Conditions are unpleasant. *Windigo* rushes and plunges and rolls. The seas have increased, the wind howls and our muscles ache from the constant bracing and hanging on. I am feeling grotty, my hair is stiff with salt and it is too rough to think of washing it. This must surely be one of the most unglamorous things a woman can choose to do. I think of Velia and Graeme soundly sleeping on solid earth and I wished this passage would end.

DAY 10. It is almost midnight and conditions are once again fierce after a reasonable day during which we managed to shower and wash our hair. I even shaved my legs and put clean sheets on the bed. Our morale has improved but we wish that the wind would ease. I am not sure why I made up our bed because we cannot sleep in it for fear of being thrown out, so we take it in turns to sleep in the pilot berth where we are held in by the lee-cloth.

DAY 11. Tonight conditions are perfect. A huge silver moon follows us in a sky swept clear and clean and I know that if there were anything to see, its outline would be crisp and sharp. The seas have calmed and a gentle breeze pushes us effortlessly along with 500 miles to go. Four more days, we think. Each day is noticeably cooler and at night we use a blanket and we wear tracksuits in the cockpit.

Today we had our own encounter with a driftnet but we were lucky. I was so engrossed in studying an orange object in the distance that I did not see the long row of similar objects that we were approaching at full speed. By then it was too late to do anything except listen to the sound of the net rubbing along the hull as the boat passed over it. If we had been using the engine the net would no doubt have fouled on the propeller. *Anaconda*, too, came across a net today and had to sail ten miles off course to pass around it.

Today, an outsider (not one of the Darwin group) came up on the sked. The voice was American and remarkably high-pitched.

We listened with interest as Rosa spoke to the newcomer.

'Hi there. We read you loud and clear. Where are you from?'

'I'm from Kansas and there's just me and my cat on board. I stumbled across your sked a couple of days ago. You all sound like mighty fine people to me. It's sure nice to talk to someone. Hope you don't mind me butting in.'

'Not at all. You're most welcome,' Rosa replied. 'It's unusual to find a single-hander who is a woman. I know of only two others. By the way, my name's Rosa. What's yours?'

'I'm James.'

Rosa fumbled her way out of the faux pas and we discovered that James's position was halfway between *Anaconda* and *Interlude*, about 100 miles ahead. No doubt we shall meet him in Oman. In the meantime, Alan and I try to picture him and we think he will be young, with a slim build and sun-bleached blond hair.

DAY 12. Conditions are perfect for ambling along but we do not want to amble. We want to get there. If we had more fuel we would motor-sail. Tonight we are almost becalmed. Pleasant but frustrating. Today I baked two large loaves of bread and the smell of them cooking was a lift to the spirit.

DAY 13. It is so still that if a butterfly were to land on the surface of the sea, it would cause ripples. Despite the fact that we are short of fuel, we are motoring in the hope of finding wind. If we do not, we shall be 150 miles short of our goal and we are not sure what will happen then. James, who is 20 miles ahead, has said that we may use his spare fuel and if conditions do not improve we may have to accept his generous offer.

We now know that James has lived on his boat for 15 years and has sailed 100 000 miles so we have had to revise our impression of him. I suspect that we will find him an old salt with many a tale to tell.

Usually, yachts arrive at the end of a passage in a bit of a mess, *Windigo* included, but this time is going to be different because we have spent the day cleaning her from bow to stern. Last night, a seabird about the size of a gull, with a forked tail like a frigate bird, sat above the companionway hatch for hours. We missed it when it flew away, just as we had missed the Indian patrol boat some days earlier.

DAY 14. Today the sea was like a mirror. Suspended in an upside-down world with the sky and its puffy fair-weather clouds above and below us, *Windigo* purred along drinking precious diesel. Fish jumped around us for most of the day, but none was tempted by the sparkling gold and silver lure. Snub-nosed dolphins played beside the boat, rolling on their sides to look at us with one mischievous eye before leaping and diving in our bow wave while we clapped and cheered their ballet.

Late this afternoon a breeze came up and tonight we are sailing slowly. James, and any extra fuel we may have taken on board, are now 30 miles behind us. He is having engine trouble. We offered to go back but he prefers to sail slowly and accept assistance from *Maisie Dotes*, 300 miles behind him, if he should need it.

Anaconda and *Interlude* have just arrived in Oman but they are waiting until dawn to enter the harbour.

DAY 15. I could tell from Alan's voice, when he woke me in the pre-dawn, that as I stepped into the cockpit I would see lights. And there they were, the lights of Oman twinkling on the horizon. The wind was howling at near gale force, the seas were steep and nasty, but for once I did not mind as I clung to the steering pedestal and watched the shore lights dim as the eastern sky lightened.

The Arabian Nights skyline slowly emerged from the desert haze. Domed slender pavilions, white and pale pink, appeared ethereal along the shoreline, and in my mind the phantasm of Scheherazade wafted like a gossamer waif through their slim, silver columns. We were to learn later that the lovely pavilions were the seaside facades of Omani beach resorts.

Nestling into a curve in the desert, the small harbour of Mina Raysut and the military compound surrounding it could have been part of a *Lawrence of Arabia* film set. Turreted white buildings formed an apron at one end, behind a wide promenade along the harbour wall. Handsome men in flowing white garments strolled along the promenade, the sun glinting on their ornate turbans and glittering scimitars. There was not a woman to be seen.

In the opposite wing the mysterious desert stretched away in rolling dunes and, silhouetted against the ochre sky, a row of camels trudged in file with their ageless plodding gait.

Journey's end is sweet, arrival sublime; a goal reached, a haven found. We sat in the cockpit with cold drinks and studied our new environment. Those who had arrived before paddled across to welcome us. Each brought a small offering — a couple of pieces of fresh fruit, a cold beer, a loaf of freshly baked bread, a lettuce — thoughtful gestures of friendship and celebration.

Oman is a maritime country with a long tradition in the building of Arab dhows. No nails or screws are used in the construction of these ancient carvel-planked vessels. Instead, everything is held together with oiled coir rope of varying thicknesses. The dhows are gaily painted craft, each with a large eye on either side of the bow to ward off the evil spirits.

It was to Muscat, the capital of Oman, that the intrepid adventurer and historian, Tim Severin, came for the building of his dhow, the craft he used to replicate the voyages of the Arab sailors of ancient times. The sailors used the north-east and south-west monsoons to establish trade routes across the Indian Ocean to places like Mozambique, Zanzibar and Mombasa, and as far away as China.

The small well-constructed harbour bustled with oil tankers and trading vessels, and rusting Indian freighters packed with live sheep and fish. When the hot wind blew from the desert across the stinking cargoes, the harbour filled with a noisome stench and the sounds of pitiful bleating.

On the morning after our arrival we were boarded by the Customs officer and several of his henchmen. Moustafa Abid was a self-opinionated, plump little man who stared at my legs, only visible below the knee. His mellifluous voice did not disguise the vulpine nature of the petty official and I found his presence in the close confines of the saloon disturbing.

'Where do you keep your liquor?' he asked me as Alan filled in forms. I pointed to the starboard lockers.

'I must seal them. You cannot have liquor.'

'But surely we can have some to drink while we're in port?' I asked.

'Last year we had big problems here, Madam,' he replied. 'The western sailors held parties. Wild parties. Drunken and noisy parties. This is not the way to behave.' His face grew blacker. 'This year we are sealing up all the liquor supplies. So, no more parties.'

I cleared the cushions from the lockers, forcing most of the officials to retreat to the cockpit to make room, then removed two bottles of whisky.

'One will be enough,' Moustafa Abid said, as he sealed the lockers with strips of adhesive tape. 'Now I must see where you sleep.'

I pointed towards the aft cabin and sat back to wait, relishing his disappointment at not being able to find what he was looking for. We had heard from other yachties that Muslim officials believe that westerners are avid readers of pornographic literature.

Alan was still filling out forms when Moustafa returned, his eyes cold when they met mine. He reached in front of Alan and picked up our passports.

'These I will keep until you leave. You are not permitted to go out of the harbour compound on Thursdays or Fridays and when you leave on the other days, you must obtain a pass at the gate and be back in the compound before the 6 o'clock curfew.'

We had already been made aware of the rules by our friends, so we were not dismayed.

'We won't find that a problem,' Alan said.

'For your sake, I hope not,' Moustafa replied. 'When you leave the compound, you must be fully clothed,' he continued. 'Men and women must be covered. No bare skin may be shown.' This time, he glanced at Alan's bare legs.

We were prepared for this too, knowing that to flout the dress code in a Muslim country is to invite censure and unpleasantness. Besides, we were excited at the prospect of seeing something of Oman and we were prepared to sweat in the heat to do so.

The closest town to the port was Salalah, 20 kilometres away. There are two Salalahs in Oman, the other near Muscat, but I was never sure at which one the Queen of Sheba found her alluring frankincense.There is no public transport in this part of Oman because everyone owns a car and no-one would dream of driving past someone on foot in the desert without stopping to offer a lift.

The first vehicle to come along was a police lorry and we sped through the desert on a modern highway. Probably by the time we reached the end of the Red Sea we would have had enough of deserts, but we gazed across that one with a sense of wonder at its shimmering honeyed mirage, the low lavender hills in the distance, the desiccation, the searing heat. And everywhere there were camels. There are one million Omanis and two million camels. The anachronistic beasts wander freely, no longer used since the oil-rich Omanis started driving cars.

I longed to ask questions of the dour and silent man at the wheel but he seemed uneasy in my presence and made no attempt to return any overtures of friendship. Soon the white town of Salalah sparkled in the dunes and we were in an exotic place.

Many of the buildings were sumptuous, most were new. They glinted in the clear light, their turrets casting patterned shadows across green lawns. Even the phone boxes were turreted minia-tures of grander structures.

There were shops full of western goods. There were olives; good cheeses; plump dried fruits; sheets of tough apricot jelly, translucent and sticky; a variety of breads; figs; fresh dates; fruits and vegetables.

One section of the spotlessly clean town was devoted entirely to jewellery shops, a fantasy world of sparkle and illusion where all surfaces, including ceilings, were covered with mirror mosaics, and gold was piled on the counter tops and reflected all around.

It was a daytime world of perfumed and bejewelled men swanning around in flowing white robes. Across their shoulders they wore brightly patterned scarves and their twisted turbans made them appear tall. They paid little attention to me, walking past as if I did not exist. I tried to interpret the look in their eyes. I think it was disdain. But it could have been pity.

Before leaving the harbour I asked one of the yachties what the women were like.

'Well, there are none,' he replied.

During our time in Oman we saw only four. Each wore a full, brightly patterned skirt that fell in a train and dragged through the dust as she walked. Over everything went the black *burka* with the small peephole covered in black lace so that not even eye contact was possible. From what we could gather, women were allowed out after dark. But this was when yachties had to remain within the port compound.

As we stocked up with fresh fruit and vegetables, I tried to chat with the stallholder, telling him that we were enjoying his town.

'The people are so courteous,' I said. 'They pull up and flash their lights whenever one wants to cross the street. So different from Sydney, where I come from.'

'We do that for camels too,' he replied.

We took *Windigo* to the wharf to fill up with fuel and water, an operation that normally takes an hour but because of the bureaucracy in Oman, we had to spend the day there. Bret and Debbie kept us company and at one stage we were joined by a young soldier who lost no time in telling us that his father was a general.

The soldier wore a long skirt and a wonderful T-shirt, black with the national emblem of crossed scimitars and chain emblazoned in gold across the front. Debbie and I both wanted one.

'Where can I buy one of those T-shirts?' Debbie asked.

'No need to buy,' the soldier replied. He stood in the cockpit, peeled off the T-shirt and presented it to Debbie with a low bow, before stepping ashore to his Range Rover and returning dressed in a similar shirt, this time in mauve with the emblem in black.

'Perhaps you should give him a T-shirt in return,' I suggested to Debbie. I was feeling slightly miffed.

'I'd have to go back to *Interlude*,' Debbie complained. 'Besides, our T-shirts wouldn't fit him. Look at the way he is built.'

So, taking one of Alan's new T-shirts from the aft cabin I handed it to our visitor, little thinking that I would start a chain reaction.

The soldier immediately removed the elegant gold watch from his wrist and placed it in my hand.

'For you,' he smiled.

Nothing I could say would make him change his mind so in the end I had to accept the gold watch, at the same time wondering if there was an Omani custom in giving of which we were ignorant. I feared the soldier would drive away saying to himself, 'That bloody woman forced me to relinquish my beautiful gold watch for this cruddy T-shirt.'

His Majesty, Sultan Said bin Taimur, who ruled Oman with an iron fist after he came to power in 1932, was one of a line of isolationists. Oman remained as it had been in medieval times. In 1970, his son, Sultan Qaboos bin Said, took over from his father and immediately began to change the country into an Arab dreamworld. The discovery of oil brought fabulous riches to the people of Oman.

We met a couple of expatriates working in the Omani oil

industry as they strolled by to chat to the yachties.

'Have you ever seen Sultan Qaboos bin Said?' I asked John, the younger of the two men.

'Yes, often,' he replied. 'On special days, he throws money to the people in the streets. They love him. He has modern ideas and the will to carry them through. He's brought prosperity to the people.'

His friend Bill added, 'He's quite a guy, the Sultan. He's British educated, cultured and urbane.'

'His father was of the old school,' John chipped in. 'You know, chop off their hands, stone the adultresses to death. They packed him off to England for medical treatment and somehow had him certified insane. Then his son took control. Jolly good thing too, if you ask me.'

'Sultan Qaboos bin Said sounds young,' Alan commented.

'Yes, he is rather,' Bill replied.

'He doesn't appear to have altered the status of women in this society,' I complained.

'No. Well, he's not the slightest bit interested in women, I'm told,' Bill replied.

Of the 60-odd yachts that left together from Darwin, only seven remained. The majority returned to Australia or stopped off along the way. Two of our most colourful companions, Des and Laurie on *Panache*, were the last to drop out. They decided to work for a year in the Maldives where they would be in charge of a game-fishing boat attached to a Japanese resort. Perhaps we would meet again in the Mediterranean.

Col, on *New Address*, parted company with Marcelle in Thailand and now had Sue aboard. Sue was a pretty Thai girl from Phuket, confident, vivacious, and a good cook, which possibly compensated for her lack of sailing experience and her vanity. She refused to wear glasses and so often failed to notice ships at sea, particularly at night.

We met James at a gathering aboard *Interlude*. He had just been towed into port by *Maisie Dotes* and as he scrambled aboard from his battered dinghy, it was obvious that he did not fit anyone's preconceived ideas. Here was a very large man of well over six feet, in his late 40s. A Vietnam veteran with a thick mane of shoulder-length black hair under a cowboy hat, he was hearty, exuberant and extroverted: a powerful personality. In the days that followed, though, he showed a mellower side, with the result that we all grew to like having him as part of the group. One of the sailors later named her firstborn James, after him.

Clearing out procedures were always tedious, but when police, Customs, port authority and immigration are scattered through the dunes of a burning desert, one requires stamina as well as patience. Alan's knee had not mended and when we were ready to leave Oman he could not walk more than a few metres. I would have to deal with the officials, a prospect I dreaded.

The men of Oman have had no experience in dealing with women professionally, and they consider western women no better than prostitutes. I covered up as best I could, short of wearing a *burka*, and set off into the desert.

At the port authority and again at immigration, the transactions were carried out in a dismissive silence, the officials ignoring my greeting and regarding me with contempt. At the police station I approached the duty officer at his desk, but he lowered his eyes and refused to deal with me. I waited. Men came and went, each one promptly and cordially attended to.

I placed my papers in front of him. He pushed them aside. Had I the determination to outwait him? What would Alan think when I did not return in a reasonable time? What would happen if I told the little shit what I thought of him and his brothers?

Hours seemed to pass, but it was probably more like 20 minutes before another policeman entered. I recognised him as one of the officials who had been aboard *Windigo* when we checked into the country, and I quickly stepped in front of him, blocking his path.

'We want to leave now. Please give me clearance.'

In silence, and without meeting my eyes, he accepted the papers, signed them and handed them back. There was one more hurdle, the customs officer.

Moustafa Abid was not a man to treat lightly and I expected difficulties. He surprised me, however, when he welcomed me into his large office with exaggerated politeness, and closed the door firmly behind me.

'You now wish to leave Oman?' he asked with oily charm.

'Yes, I need a customs clearance.'

I sat on a chair in a corner while he completed the forms at his desk. Finally he rose and walked towards me. The smile on his face and his outstretched hand caught me off guard. Automatically I extended my hand, and then gasped with pain. Moustafa Abid had reached past my hand, grabbed my breast and twisted the nipple.

I stared at his smug expression, sick with fury and loathing. I felt an almost overwhelming urge to spit in his face. But that would have been unwise, so I snatched up the forms and hurried from the building, feeling impotent and violated.

An hour later, we were heading out to sea on our way to Yemen.

'Aden looks like my idea of hell,' JB informed us on the radio as we approached the harbour at dawn. 'Do not contact the harbour officials before you enter,' he continued. 'They'll send out an escort and charge you $60.'

In the 1950s I had passed through Aden in a passenger ship on my first visit to Europe, but my memories of the city did not prepare me for the Aden of the 1990s, a civil war and several coups later. For once I found myself agreeing with JB. It was closer to hell than any place I had seen.

Mountains of barren black rock rise from the narrow strip of flat land bordering the sea. It is a stark and desolate place where nothing grows. The city, fragmented on the small pockets of flat land, resembles a battlefield, which is what it has been for much of the 30 years since the British left.

Partly destroyed buildings crumble in the pervasive air of neglect that hangs over the city and those buildings still in use are riddled with bullet holes and scarred by shrapnel. Signs, shot to shreds, flap noisily in the wind and piles of debris from the latest skirmish still clutter the streets. Through it all creep hundreds of cats, emaciated, misshapen creatures with an aggression born of starvation and terror. I felt that if one were weak and defenceless, they would attack like a pack of wild dogs.

The doors of Aden, though, are picturesque and reminiscent of happier times. Faded now, their once strong colours are muted and delicate, a romantic contrast to the grim, grey landscape. There is beauty, too, in the people of Aden who are generous of spirit, fun-loving and colourful. For Ramadan, many of the men had dyed their hair a bright shade of orange, probably because Mohammed was supposed to have had red hair and a red beard. Some women wore long black robes but, for Ramadan, their fingernails were bright red and many had designs painted on their hands and feet.

There was a fervour that we had not experienced in the Muslim countries of South-East Asia during the month of Ramadan. In Yemen, women are forbidden to look at the most devout Muslim men, those dressed in white. One of the women on a yacht from Gibraltar was ignorant of the rule so when she was joined in a lift at a hotel in the northern capital, Sana, by one of the devout, she smiled and said 'Good Morning'. This enraged the man in white, who felt that he had been insulted and violated, so he whipped out a knife and threatened to slice her open.

'I suppose you'll be using Abdullah as your adviser,' the skipper of a nearby yacht called out. The advisers or agents of the Red

Sea are infamous for their gall and perfidy and long before arriving in Aden, we had determined to have nothing to do with them.

'No, we prefer to sort things out for ourselves,' Alan told him.

'Why did you recommend Abdullah, then?' our neighbour asked.

'I've never heard of Abdullah,' Alan replied.

'But I agreed to use him because he had a letter of recommendation from *Windigo*.'

Alan explained that he had not written a recommendation for anyone and that as soon as we went ashore, he would find Abdullah and destroy the letter.

'Well, I'm pleased you explained because I couldn't understand why you would recommend someone like Abdullah. Wait till you see him.'

But of course, we never did. We searched the port area but everyone was vague.

'Oh, Abdullah. Haven't seen him around lately.'

'Oh, Abdullah. He had to go to Sana. His wife is ill.'

'Oh, Abdullah. He's gone to Port Sudan on a big ship.'

Apart from the Hotel Aden, the only other place that offered food in reasonably hygienic conditions was a Chinese restaurant in the suburb of Crater, so named because it is in the crater of the extinct volcano that forms the backdrop to the city. Faded blue paint flaked from the walls and a large glass fish tank of the type that is used to hold live lobsters, was now a rubbish receptacle. There was not an Asian in sight and the group of friends we were with became restive and there were mumblings of discontent.

'A Chinese banquet in this dump! You are mad,' JB finally informed us.

Seconds later, two large platters piled high with steaming crab were placed at either end of the table, followed soon after by bowls of surprisingly tasty shark-fin soup. There were dishes of shrimp, platters of king prawns, succulent squid, juicy grilled lobster tails, a whole fish in a tangy sauce, crisp and delicate small spring rolls. And there was a dish of sliced beef for which no-one had any appetite after the splendid seafood.

Had it not been for Ramadan we would have explored more of Yemen, especially the capital, Sana, where many of the people live in a type of mud-brick medieval high-rise. But the Muslim religious festival makes day-to-day living difficult for westerners, who do not understand how to plan around it.

So it was time to begin our passage up the Red Sea, that cigar-shaped stretch of water that links the Indian Ocean with the Mediterranean Sea. Sailors have always feared its fierce headwinds, which are created by the funnel effect of the landmasses.

As the first rays of sunlight struck the black cliffs of Aden, we motored towards the harbour exit through the strange assortment of craft that cluttered it: the stripped hulks of Russian naval vessels, leaning freighters packed with refugees from Mogadishu, dhows of all sizes, and half-submerged wrecks with the low sun making pinpoints of light through the bullet holes.

As we looked back at the sad city behind us, we thought of the cruising yacht which had been sunk in the harbour during the last skirmish. It was an Australian yacht named *Innocent Bystander*.

CHAPTER 5

a caravan of 47 camels • 'marsas'
Luxor and Aswan
fat-tailed sheep and Molly Meldrum in Cairo

*E*arly on the morning of 17 March 1992, we entered the Red
Sea through the Straits of Bab el Mandeb, a narrow opening
through which howl the winds, often at gale force. Yachts proceeding north, of necessity favour the western side because
Saudi Arabia possesses almost the entire eastern shore. However,
both Ethiopia and Eritrea on the western side are also unfriendly
to yachts. One of the 'Around the World' fleet skippers ignored
the warnings and anchored one night off the coast of Ethiopia.
Those on board were arrested and the yacht confiscated. It was
only through the intervention of Jimmy Cornell, who paid the
US$4000 ransom demanded by the Ethiopians, that the sailors
were released.

Strong headwinds forced us to tack up the middle of the Red
Sea past Eritrea for five days until we reached the first safe
anchorage at Khor Narawat in southern Sudan. This was a lovely
wilderness area of clear water, coral reefs, white beaches, fish
and prolific birdlife, and it was here that we saw our first
flamingoes.

The elegant pale pink birds allowed us to approach within a
couple of metres before moving slowly into a line and delicately
stepping backwards. Then, as if in response to a baton, they all
opened their wings. There was a burst of crimson as they lifted into
the air and circled above our heads like a line of beautiful dancers.

Towards evening, as we sat in the cockpit listening to the
sounds of the desert creatures, a caravan of 47 camels plodded
in a slowly moving frieze against the blood-red sunset.

The desert nomads we met there and at the next anchorage at Trinkitat were tall and graceful with high cheekbones and calm eyes. Their hair stood high in stiff tangled masses and their clothing was little better than rags, but they were proud, confident and friendly.

Near Port Sudan the anchorages change to *marsas* which can best be described as natural channels through the reefs to the protected water inside, which often takes the form of large lagoons. *Marsas* are a peculiarity of the Red Sea and their entrances are often difficult to find until you are on top of them. The colours are striking — deep navy fading to emerald green before the white lace of the reefs, and then to pale turquoise where the water laps the yellow dunes, beyond which mauve foothills merge into purple mountains in the distance.

At most anchorages we fished, swam, snorkelled and walked in the desert. Often there were five or six yachts together in an anchorage for a few days while we sat out blows from the north, so we socialised and made new friends.

At Princess Charlotte Bay on the Queensland coast, we had met Max and Gloria on *Anhinga*, a gleaming yellow ketch. They were also on their way around the world. We had parted with the usual 'See you at the next anchorage', but our paths were not to cross again until they sailed into Marsa Sheik Ibrahim.

Gloria was a mature woman of whom people said, 'She must have been a beauty in her youth.' To me she was beautiful in her maturity, with a glamorous face and perfect legs that were smooth, glossy and free from blemish. Bret, who professed to be knowledgeable in such matters, maintained that Gloria's legs were naturally hairless, but I believed that she shaved them like the rest of us. We wagered a loaf of fresh bread but when we knew Gloria well enough to ask about her legs, it was I who lost the wager. Her husband, Max, was a retiring man who probably regretted the tattoos of his youth that decorated his biceps.

We met John and Jenny from Sydney on the yacht *Burramys*, Fiona and Mike from New Zealand on *Syrah*, and Harry and Olive from Darwin on *Sunbird*. All three yachts had left Darwin at around the same time as *Windigo* but had followed different routes and travelled independently. John, with red hair and red beard like the Prophet, was treated with a certain reverence during Ramadan, and he hoped the effect would continue to gain him kudos in Muslim countries. He holds degrees in engineering and geology and explained that a *burramys parvus* is an Australian mountain pygmy possum. Jenny, quiet and retiring, seldom left the boat without her sketchbook and paints.

The accountant, Mike, would talk for hours about boats if his effervescent wife did not pull him into line.

'Please pause for breath now, dear. Then someone else can say something.'

The pair on *Sunbird* had survived Cyclone Tracy. Harry had been a lecturer in a northern Australian college of advanced education, and he delivered his stories in the manner of one grown accustomed to a silent and submissive audience while Olive gazed at him in adoration. It appeared that 30 years of marriage had done nothing to change her starry-eyed view of the tall, lean man who bore such a striking resemblance to his favourite poet, Henry Lawson.

Most of the yachts had sustained damage on the long bash to windward from Bab el Mandeb. There was no possibility of finding help ashore so those with skills gave a helping hand to anyone in need, and gradually the repairs got done. Those yachts with weather faxes passed on information to the rest, but reception was intermittent and the only available weather forecast came from Jiddah, delivered by a man whose English was indecipherable.

We based our decisions to leave an anchorage on our own observations. There appeared to be a pattern of three or four calm days followed by five or six of gale force winds, so we moved north in the calms and sat out the blows. *Northern Lights* received the news that their daughter, Arden, had decided to marry, so Andre and Barbara were under pressure to reach the Mediterranean where they could leave the boat in safety to fly home. They pushed ahead in calms and blows.

'I must get there in time to stop the bridesmaids wearing red,' Barbara explained.

Twenty miles south of Port Sudan lies an ancient settlement called Suakin on an island in the reefs. It was to this old slave-trading town that the early Arab sailors came in their dhows across the Indian Ocean, having discovered that at certain times of the year it was possible to sail as far north as Suakin before being stopped by headwinds. So the settlement became a thriving commercial and pilgrimage centre with camel-train routes across the desert to the interior, and a dhow route across the Red Sea to Jiddah, the port for Mecca. Over the centuries the reef had grown and the entrance to the now tiny harbour was through a narrow, winding *marsa* that gave little room for error.

As we rounded a bend in the *marsa*, the splendid ruined town of Suakin unfolded, luminous in the heatwaves of the desert and the reflections from the water lapping at the foundations. It had a grace and faded splendour that was breathtaking. Towers, minarets, domes, crumbling walls and some intact structures were grouped as if by an inspired hand to form a surreal arrangement of shapes like a de Chirico painting.

We anchored beneath the camel-coloured city and watched a small crowd of curious desert people gather to stare. Young women and girls, dressed in sari-like garments in glowing colours of orange, yellow, purple and magenta, giggled and chased each other through the ruins like brilliant butterflies. I thought of the seven virgins of Suakin.

The name derives from *'Sava Ginn'*, ('The Spirit did it') and refers to a time when the King of Abyssinia presented seven virgins to the King of Egypt. So that nothing would happen to the precious maidens, they were accompanied on their journey by a reliable eunuch. However, when they arrived in Cairo not one of the virgins was still as she should have been.

The only explanation that the eunuch could give was that

when they had stopped to rest at the island in the lagoon, the island spirit had taken conjugal possession of the girls while they slept. The King thereupon sent the girls back to the island. They and the children born of the union with the spirit became the ancestors of the colourful crowd laughing on the shore, and that night, as the moon bathed the ruins in a ghostly white light and hundreds of bats circled overhead, I imagined I saw seven filmy white figures with enigmatic smiles, floating through the silvery ruins.

Port Sudan was the first place after Aden where it was possible to buy provisions and after three weeks in the Red Sea most yachts were out of fresh food. It was a dusty, windswept town where the pace of life was exceedingly slow. There was a little less squalor than in Aden and fewer women with covered faces but the people lacked the sparkle of the Yemenis.

In Port Sudan the people appeared lethargic: lolling about, leaning, sitting in the dust, lying in the shade, shuffling slowly with feet protruding from heel-less sandals that appeared to be leaving the wearer behind. Many of the men were very tall, some with faces like ebony. Many wore colourful caftans and gold jewellery. Everywhere there were beggars. Camels, donkeys and goats were often used as beasts of burden but some wandered about the town untended.

Provisioning there was challenging. There were only three or four shops, each with a few fly-spotted containers on the dusty shelves. The meat market made us wish that we were vegetarian, as, indeed, we thought seriously of becoming until we reached Egypt. Whole carcasses, bits and pieces, severed heads and feet of goats, entrails and skins hung under curtains of black flies in the desert heat.

With the River Nile flowing through Sudan, we expected the fruit and vegetable market to provide for our needs, but here, too, we were sickened by the smell of rotting produce and annoyed by the crowds of urchins, each with a couple of plastic bags, rushing at us and yelling 'Kiss. Kiss.' It was some time before we realised that they were probably using the local Arabic word for bag.

There were brilliant red tomatoes, unformed and white in the middle, luscious looking purple aubergines which began to drip through the grub holes within hours of purchase, huge orange mangoes that inside were like balls of string with the taste of kerosene. There were no green vegetables, not even a cabbage. But there were spectacular grapefruit, heavy with juice, with a bright salmon-coloured sweet flesh. Everywhere there were tarpaulins covered with dates drying in the heat and dust.

At the post office the young woman behind the counter made it obvious that my request for Poste Restante was a nuisance. Finally, though, she found a battered shoebox brown with age and pushed it across the counter towards me.

'Is this all there is?' I asked.

She assured me that it was. There were about 20 sad-looking letters for people who had long since gone.

Tom and Mary Mathews, Yacht *Sundowner*. Port Sudan.

Achmed Aziz, Poste Restante, Port Sudan.

Timothy Baird. Crew member. Urgent. Any yacht who knows him.

Bill and Susan Roberts, Yacht *Far Away*. Port Sudan. Please forward to Suez after two weeks.

There was nothing for *Windigo*.

'Ring her,' Alan said, when he saw me fighting back tears.

Of the six phone booths, only one was functional. A crowd of people waited in the bare, dusty room for their turn. There were no seats, so they sat on the floor and lounged against the walls. Some slept, their heads resting in their arms as they lay full-length. I carefully picked my way to the counter and waited until one of the four idle women behind it gave in to the urge to look my way.

'How long is the wait to use the phone?' I asked her.

'Could be two days,' she replied.

'I was hoping to ring Australia.'

'Impossible from Port Sudan,' she said. 'You must go to Khartoum.'

The capital, Khartoum, was 640 kilometres away, two days by train. Next we tried sending a fax to Graeme's office. I waited an interminable time for my turn, only to be told that there were no fax facilities, only telex. In desperation we approached Bret on *Interlude*. His father was a ham to whom Bret spoke regularly and he promised to ring Velia from Townsville where he lived.

The next day the port officials sealed all our radios with tape so that they could not be used in port. There was no logical explanation for this apart from some mumbled nonsense about security.

There are two grand old colonial hotels in Port Sudan — the Red Sea Hotel on the outskirts, past the hovels of the poor and the wealthier merchants' houses farther on, and the Palace Hotel, closer to the port. The former is a substantial stone building with wide verandahs and the air of dignified repose that old British tropical clubs seem to acquire with the help of cane furniture and slowly oscillating ceiling fans.

The Red Sea Hotel is run as a training school for waiters, but where will they work when they have finished their training? We struggled through an appalling meal which left us wondering what the poor ate, if the rich were expected to enjoy such bad fare. The staple in that part of Sudan appeared to be dates and *foul*, not as in feathered but as in broad beans, dried and ground into a flour, then reconstituted and mixed with mysterious ingredients. The *foul* is sold from large, flat pans unprotected from the dust which rises in clouds from the unsealed streets.

As we prepared to leave, the ludicrous Sudanese bureaucracy threatened to smother us. We had been warned by Customs to avoid using the black market, but when each of the six banks in the town found some excuse to refuse Alan service, we had no alternative.

When Alan asked the harbourmaster for permission to fill up with water, the rotund, jolly man replied, 'But of course you may have water. In desert areas, if someone refuses to give you water, you must kill him. That's our law.'

The hose, with a diameter of about six inches, and operated by a diesel pump, would have blown *Windigo* out of the water.

'The hose is far too big,' Alan complained.

'Oh, I'm so sorry, Sir,' the roly-poly one replied. 'But if you have a carton of cigarettes for me, I can find a smaller hose for you.'

'We also need to fill up with diesel while we are tied to the wharf,' Alan pointed out.

'That's only for the big ships,' the wily harbourmaster explained. 'Yachts must obtain their diesel through an agent who will bring it to you in 44-gallon drums. Then you must transfer it in your fuel containers to your boat.'

'That's the most ridiculous procedure I've ever heard of,' exclaimed Alan.

'Nevertheless, that's the way it must be done. Now my brother, Mahmud, is the best agent. You go and see him.' He scribbled an address on a greasy scrap of paper.

Yachties ahead of us had warned that Port Sudan was 'a bugger of a place', but it is strategically placed halfway along a sparsely populated stretch of water. There was nowhere else to go, but we disliked being there. As it faded from sight, we consoled ourselves by saying, 'Well, that's over. Now let's look forward to Egypt.'

The Taila Islets, 40 miles north of Port Sudan, is a lovely complex of islands with marvellous coral and fish, and strange birds and turtles, but we could not linger because of the exposed nature of the anchorages. The wind was once again raging, forcing us to find a safer place. JB and Rosa had decided to push on, but were hit by 55-knot winds which tore their headsail to shreds and destroyed the roller-furling system.

Through Marsa Khor Shinab, Marsa Wasi, Marsa Gwilaib to Marsa Umbeila, we towed *Interlude* in the calms and light airs. The repairs to their gearbox in Oman had not lasted. We discovered that towing another yacht is not for the faint-hearted, especially in reef areas where the smallest error of judgement can have dire consequences. There were times when we missed reefs by the smallest of margins, times when all four of us dreaded having to do it, and times when, towing under sail in light airs, *Interlude*, the faster boat, kept creeping up on *Windigo*.

At Marsa Gwilaib we saw a tree, the only one for hundreds of kilometres. Where had it come from and how did it survive? Here, too, in less than two hours, we caught a mackerel, a large schnapper, a trevally, and several reef fish. I was able to use my 2000-year-old Venetian recipe for *zuppa di pesce*, which required at least six varieties of fish.

Farther on at Marsa Terifa the wind was so strong and the sandstorm so biting that we were forced to remain below for three days. For all of the first day, a lone woman in a long puce garment and a black shawl over her head waved urgently from the shore, sometimes sitting in the sand to rest before once more waving her arms and beckoning. Disturbed, we watched from a porthole and wished she were not there, because the wind was too strong for us to launch the dinghy to go to her assistance. The next morning she was gone.

At the end of 20 kilometres of coast defaced with resorts, we sailed into the tourist town of Hurghada simmering in the heat. A Sheraton hotel in the prime position in the middle of the beach was flanked by a plethora of smaller establishments.

It was to the Sheraton that Bret and Debbie took us for our first Egyptian meal or, more accurately, for our first meal in Egypt, since the food was bland international. However, there were few western tourists. Most were wealthy Egyptians who sat around the pool after dinner, sucking on their gurgling hubbly-bubblies and watching the plump belly dancers.

With *Interlude*, we hired a car to visit the pharaonic sites around Luxor and Aswan in the Nile Valley, several hundred kilometres to the south-west. Masouf, a strong young man with the neck of a wrestler, was to prove a competent driver but he insisted on bringing along his younger brother, Mohammed.

'But we don't wish to pay for two people,' we told him.

'Mohammed is free. I need him to drive when I'm sleepy.'

But Masouf was never sleepy. He was a fractious, irascible young man, ignorant and violent and it gradually became obvious that the gentler Mohammed was there for Masouf to bully and taunt until the younger man snapped. Then the car became their alter ego and we sped through desert towns like cowboys, with horn blaring and our two tormentors shouting and spitting at each other and at those who were slow to get out of the way. They scattered goats and Bedouins and missed outraged camels by inches. Squashed in the back seat, Bret was the first to crumble.

'This is a crazy way to drive, Masouf,' Bret complained. 'Slow down before we have an accident.'

Masouf caught Bret's eye in the rear-vision mirror and burped.

I tried. 'Masouf, the speed's making us ill. We're not used to speed. We can't enjoy the scenery.'

'For you, dear lady, I'll slow down,' came his unctuous reply. And he did so, until the next incident triggered a fresh speeding frenzy.

At a small village, we stopped to buy bottled water.

'You stay here,' ordered Masouf. 'We'll buy the water. These people are thieves, but we know what to do.'

Within seconds a full scale brawl was in progress with loud shouting and recriminations, clenched fists and waving arms. We had hoped to stretch our legs but it seemed safer to get back into the car. The brothers ran to join us and with a shower of gravel and screeching tyres, we were gone. Behind us, the small group of Bedouins at the roadside stall was throwing rocks in our general direction.

The narrow strip of fertile land on either side of the Nile ends abruptly in desert. The river flows like a thin thread of bright green cotton stretched across a length of canvas, and from pharaonic times the *fellahin* have tended the precious river soil in ways that have not changed.

The Ptolemys, if they could see it now, would be undismayed. As we drove beside the great river, ancient Egypt was all around us. The water, the fields, the date palms, the dun mud villages, the *shadoofs* and the wooden ploughs were of our time and theirs. It is an ever-flowing landscape in which the occasional tractor or electric pump only emphasise the ancient rhythms and the conservative lifestyle of the *fellahin*.

On the site of ancient Thebes, the lovely temple of Luxor sits beside the water, romantic and leafy in cool lawns. By moonlight there is magic in its silver columns and mysterious shadows. In contrast, the powerful Dandera temple with its massive stone roof still intact, sits on the edge of the desert and reflects its stark and brooding solitude.

During the height of Theban prosperity and power, the Temple of Karnak was the most important in all of Egypt. The complex is mammoth. We stood in the great hypostyle hall feeling overwhelmed, then regained our sense of proportion in the avenues of sphinxes and the colonnaded courts and groves.

Death and the dead intruded upon the business of living in the Valley of the Nile and nowhere more so than in the Valley of the Kings, an aristocratic *wadi* in which were buried the pre-served and mummified bodies of the great and powerful to await resurrection in the afterlife. We followed the funerary passages deep into the earth, relishing the cool darkness after the searing desert heat.

Aswan is a well-planned city with wide boulevards along the river which is busy with floating hotels, tourist boats and swallow-sailed *feluccas.* The city is within easy distance of the Aswan High Dam, the famous temples of Kalabsha, Philae and Idfu and the tomb of the Aga Khan. Our hotel rooms were on the fifth floor so we enjoyed an uninterrupted view of the river from our balconies.

Not so at Luxor, though, where the hotel was a couple of blocks back from the river in a narrow, noisy market street. There we were on the fourth floor and we looked across to the flat roof of the building opposite. On its fourth floor lived five sheep with long fat tails and in the early mornings their bleating mingled with the crowing of the roosters and we were away to an early start.

The two hotels we stayed at were both clean with ensuite bath-rooms and hot and cold running water, but they both had an intriguing and entirely unsatisfactory solution to the bidet. Inside the toilet bowl was a metal J-shaped tube, up which spouted water when a small tap was turned on. Unfortunately, the only way to avoid contact with the metal tube in the normal course of events, was to climb on the toilet seat and squat, an athletic and dangerous procedure but all we could think of at the time.

Masouf and Mohammed were slightly more subdued on the return journey. We had no idea how they had spent their nights and did not ask. On one occasion, we noticed a group of Bed-ouins, dressed in black and red clothing, shepherding a flock of goats along the road ahead. Masouf brought the car to a screech-ing halt and both brothers leapt out and began to scream at the Bedouins in a loud and abusive tirade, following them off the road and as far as the nearest dune before returning panting to the car. As so many of their antics over the last few days had left us doubting their sanity, we simply remained silent and longed

The Watcher on the Quay

to be back on our yachts swinging sweetly at anchor.

'Don't you want to know why we had to yell at the nomads?' Masouf finally asked in a hurt voice.

'Not really,' Alan replied.

'Well, Mr Alan, I'm going to tell you,' bully-boy insisted. 'You see, the government builds good brick houses for them. Makes a town for them. Free schools, free hospitals, water, everything. But they will not live in the houses.'

We had seen the small villages in a couple of places in the desert as we sped along. They were attractive, modern, gleaming white, and utterly deserted.

'We have to live with our parents,' Masouf complained. 'We can't get married because there's no room. Why can't we have those houses instead of those stupid nomads? Animals. Ignorant animals.'

The pace of evolution is slow. It would be a mammoth leap for the desert nomads to change a lifestyle so ingrained as to be almost biological. A square white block beside a highway is not to their liking. We have a similar situation with some Aborigines in Australia and the solution eludes us too.

We all shook hands at the quay in Hurghada.

'You promise to tell your friends about us,' Masouf insisted.

'We promise. We promise.'

North of the Gulf of Aqaba, the Red Sea narrows and the winds funnel down with increased force, laden with dust from the Sinai. The air is exceedingly dry and most of the time I felt like a prune. It was a relief to sniff steam whenever an opportunity arose and we looked at our fast diminishing stock of Sorbolene with alarm, not knowing when we would be able to buy more.

Interlude proceeded under its own power due to some lateral thinking on Bret's part. He discovered that by turning the gearbox back-to-front, the reverse gear, not damaged in the fish net, would drive the boat forward.

If someone had asked me to describe our worst experience at that stage of the circumnavigation, I would have told them of the terror of almost being crushed to death by a supertanker. A group of five yachts left the anchorage at Marsa Zeitiya just after dark when the wind eased. We hugged the edge of the busy main shipping channel to avoid a collision with the supertankers and the mass of smaller vessels bunched together in the narrow waterway. Alan was in bed while I concentrated on steering the boat through the maze of oil rigs and lights.

I saw three yachts turn back and wondered why they had done so but I could not leave the cockpit to use the radio. Later they explained that they were too confused by the traffic to continue. Suddenly *Interlude*, a couple of hundred metres ahead, turned sharply to port at a right angle to the course. I banged on the aft cabin to wake Alan. Something was wrong.

I turned too, thinking that Bret must have had a good reason to change course so dramatically. Then it was upon us. A towering black hulk of steel like a 15-storey apartment block rose from the darkness and bore down upon *Windigo* as Alan staggered into the cockpit.

'Fuck!' he said.

That was all. We could feel the monster's heat and we pulsed with its vibrations. A lifetime passed with it as we watched helplessly, its great bulk sliding by a few feet from our stern. Why a supertanker was out of the main channel we shall never know, and such was our terror that we could not remember any of the vessel's particulars.

Two miles out of Suez, three launches raced towards us, their drivers waving and shouting as they circled the boat.

'Hello, Mister. I'm Abdul, the honest agent. I've come to look after you.'

'Hello, Mr Windigo. I'm Ibrahim, the best agent in Suez. You come with me'

'Good morning, Sir. Oh, and Madam too. I'm 'The Prince of the Red Sea'. Everyone uses me. I'm famous.'

We knew that it was impossible to function in Suez without an agent and that 'The Prince of the Red Sea' was famous, but for some reason we chose Ibrahim. They all charged $140 so it did not seem to matter a great deal.

To celebrate our safe arrival in Suez, we searched the town that night for a restaurant but there appeared to be only one within walking distance of the port. Ritzy French would best describe its appearance, but it was 9 p.m. and we were the only customers.

'When do Egyptians eat?' I asked the waiter.

'Three times a day,' he replied haughtily.

Our hotel in Cairo again overlooked the Nile and from our eighth floor window we once again looked across at sheep, this time on the roof of the seven-storey building opposite. Egyptian sheep have obscene tails, swollen like melons, all fat. Because there is no grass, the sheep are fed on beans and this causes a build-up of fat in their tails. At least that is what I was told by the young man who insisted on showing us the sights of downtown Cairo as soon as we set foot outside the hotel.

From our elevated room, we could see a seething dun-coloured city beneath a grime of age and desert dust, a city where the impact of the 20th century has been without grace. Gleaming skyscrapers tower over tenements; *feluccas* glide by on the river while cars and buses roar over its bridges; laden camels wait at traffic lights, patiently chewing their cuds. A glance in one direction takes in skyscrapers and concrete blocks and, in another, the minarets and domes of an ancient city. This confusing, dirty, noisy place is also a treasure-trove of many of the world's most revered monuments and works of art.

So engrossed were we in the wonders of the Cairo Museum, that it was not until after 4 p.m. that we realised we had not eaten since breakfast. By chance we stumbled upon the extraordinary Felafel Gardens restaurant with ceilings of stained glass, tables of solid timber 20 centimetres thick, a collection of old sewing machines and gramophones, cages of live birds, exotic fish in tanks, an arbor hung with bunches of plastic grapes, and other assorted bric-a-brac. We could not resist the ambience, and the packed tables suggested that this was the time when Egyptians ate.

We ordered humus and pita bread for starters, followed by a plate of piping hot stuffed vine leaves on a bed of fried onions and crisped chicken skin. Then came an ornate silver platter of mixed kebabs with grilled whole tomatoes, tiny eggplant and capsicum on a salad base of onion rings and shredded carrot in a tangy dressing. With icy Stella beer, it was a feast for a Pharaoh.

Multifarious are the antics of the Cairo tourist touts in eliciting custom. As we strolled through the streets and *souks*, we resisted them all until one young man caught us off guard.

'Oh, so you're from Australia. Then you must know my good friend, Molly Meldrum,' he said.

In the perfume shop owned by the young man's family, a large poster of Molly held pride of place amongst the rows of tiny bottles. I bought a phial of Chanel No. 5 oil made from 'a secret family recipe'. It subsequently leaked all over our clothes in the luggage compartment of the bus returning to Suez.

After our experiences with the crazy brothers on the trip to Luxor, we decided to study drivers' faces before choosing a taxi driver. We avoided those with thick necks and those who tried to bully us into hiring them. There was a line of cabs outside our hotel.

'I take you to Pyramids. I good driver. Cheap, very cheap.'

'Where you want to go? I take you anywhere.'

'You want to change money? See beautiful belly dancer?'

At the wheel of one cab was a plump man with a smooth round face and button features, who said nothing. His brown eyes were calm and his name was Joseph. When we commented on his name, he explained that he was a Coptic Christian.

Before the arrival of Islam in the 7th century, Christianity had been the predominant religion of Egypt. St Mark began preaching there in AD 35, but it was not until the 4th century that Christianity became the official religion. Copt is derived from the Greek word for Egyptian.

'We are different from other Christians,' Joseph explained. 'We believe that Christ is divine, not both human and divine.'

We wanted to know if life was difficult for a Coptic Christian living in an Islamic country. His answer had a familiar ring.

'Life for Coptic Christians is very difficult in Cairo,' Joseph replied. 'Our people are intelligent. We understand banking and how to organise things but when we're successful, the Muslims become jealous and attack us.'

If Joseph felt bitterness it did not affect his love for Cairo, nor his readiness to explain the history of the places we visited.

We began with a dawn drive to the ancient temple city of Sakkara, 32 kilometres from Cairo, a fascinating collection of tombs and tunnels, many with walls of carved alabaster, the translucent white surfaces delicately etched with scenes of life in the times of the Pharaohs.

Back in the city, at each museum or mosque Joseph would say, 'I'm saving the best until last.' We smiled indulgently, wondering if there could possibly be some place to surpass what we had seen so far.

'I'll bet he's going to take us to the Coptic Museum,' Alan said. Of course. Joseph glowed with pride as he led us up the steps. The displays were not of interest to us, being mainly the mysterious accoutrements of the religion, but the building was wonderful with a harmony of lovely spaces, courtyards and fountains. It had an air of tranquillity that was a haven from the heat and noise of the city. Intricately carved panels in varnished wood covered the walls and ceilings and the interior of the domes. Joseph beamed when he saw our delight.

'I told you this was the best,' he crowed, his face crinkling with a proud smile.

Most people choose to ride camels or donkeys to the Pyramids but we had grown tired of the surly camel and the donkey seemed too small a beast to accommodate Alan's height so we settled for horses. When I told the turbaned attendant that I could ride, he returned from the stable with a prancing chestnut gelding. The horse was spirited and sure-footed and I enjoyed the ride alone through the desert, laughing each time I looked over my shoulder to where Alan, far in the distance on a flea-bitten old grey, was being led through the dunes by a small child.

The Pyramids and the Sphinx at Giza epitomise ancient Egypt in the minds of most people but when I first saw them from the top of the closest dune they appeared small and insignificant, and I felt a momentary disappointment. Quickly though, a sense of scale developed: the enormity of the great orb of the sky, the camels at the base mere specks, and the people barely visible at all. It was then that the power and grandeur of the indestructible monoliths became manifest.

The thrill of the Sphinx was in being there, touching it. Dwarfed beside the pyramids, it is a poor battered old thing, defaced by Napoleon and other marauders. Its nose is in London, along with the Elgin Marbles and other treasures pilfered in a less-enlightened era. But still never returned.

For sailors, one of the thrills at Giza is the Sun Ship, a beautifully preserved and sensitively restored barque which was used to carry the Pharaoh across the Nile to his tomb. Until the 1950s it had lain beneath the hot dry sand before the Great Pyramid for millennia. We loved its slim romantic lines and its graceful, clean curves.

It is probably wise to avoid being in Cairo at the time of the Haj. Towards the end of our stay, the city became packed with pilgrims on their way to Mecca — armed guards patrolled the streets and stood at each corner, and riot police were poised for action. There were serious traffic jams as thousands of cars filled with pilgrims passed through on their way to Suez and thence across the canal to Mecca. Crowds lined the streets to wave banners and to cheer the pilgrims on their way. There was a disturbing electricity in the air and people's eyes were wild.

We said farewell to Joseph and returned to Suez to find our friends in the anchorage saddened by the news that Woody and Ellen on *Maisie Dotes* had flown to the US to attend the funeral of their daughter. She had been burned to death on board her own yacht when a gas water heater exploded while she was taking a shower. *Maisie Dotes* sat alone at a mooring in a far corner of the harbour.

On the morning we were to begin our transit of the Suez Canal, the pilot for the first half of the passage to Ismailia arrived promptly at 8 a.m. as promised by the agent, Ibrahim, who had paid him in advance. Abdul Aziz was a fat, simian-featured man with one eye and a hollow charm.

The infamy of the Suez Canal pilots is well known among yachties. Alan and I had formed an idea of how much baksheesh to pay by listening to other yachties on the radio skeds. Sailors who paid more than the going rate created problems for those who followed.

Nearing Ismailia, Abdul Aziz looked at me with his calculating brown eye.

'Where is my baksheesh, Missus?'

I tried to ignore his effrontery and told him it was below.

'How much baksheesh are you giving me?' he asked.

'Thirty pounds and two packets of cigarettes,' I replied.

'That's not enough,' Abdul Aziz said. 'You must give me 80 pounds.'

'Thirty is the top rate this year,' I told him. 'That's all you are getting.'

'I want it now, please, Missus,' Abdul Aziz said.

'No, Abdul Aziz. When we get to Ismailia you can have it. Not now,' I told him. His face pouting and pleading, he turned to Alan.

'Captain Alan, please give me my baksheesh now,' he wheedled.

'You know that baksheesh is given when the job's finished,' Alan replied. 'You can have your baksheesh when we arrive, not before.'

Abdul Aziz threw his hands in the air, let out a long scream of anguish and sank into a corner of the cockpit where he began a pathetic wailing, at the same time banging the heel of his hand against his head in a frenzy of frustration.

'Please stop that, Abdul Aziz!' I pleaded.

His wailing increased. I grew impatient.

'You're behaving like a child, Abdul Aziz,' I told him. 'This is ridiculous. Please behave like a man. You're 60 years of age, for heaven's sake. Stop it!'

But he would not. Then Alan remonstrated with me.

'I don't think you should speak to him like that,' he said.

I replied that it would be best if he concentrated on steering the boat and left the pilot to me.

Abdul Aziz continued to wail and bang his head. It was a trick that always worked in the end. I handed over the baksheesh. He stuffed the money into his trouser pocket and the cigarettes into his socks.

'Why are you putting the cigarettes in your socks?' Alan asked.

'If the others see that I have cigarettes, they'll take them from me,' Abdul Aziz replied.

When we dropped anchor in the harbour at Ismailia a small launch drew alongside to take Abdul Aziz ashore. As he stepped aboard, the three men in the launch shouted to us. 'Cigarettes. You give us cigarettes. Please, Mister, cigarettes.'

'I already have,' Alan replied. 'Abdul Aziz has them. They're in his socks.'

Early the next morning, fortified by experience, we awaited the arrival of the second pilot for the run to Port Said. Achmed, who carried his top teeth in his shirt pocket, was soon chatting in a relaxed manner to Alan in the cockpit. I sat and watched the desert slide by on either side of the canal and thought of Ferdinand de Lessops and the thousands of men who had died there during the construction of this massive feat of engineering. I could picture the 3000 camels carrying fresh water from the Nile in an endless train, and the fanfare and celebrations, the fireworks and the feasts that Pasha Ismail had planned for the inauguration ceremony.

Up to 80 ships a day pass through the canal and as I looked at a convoy ahead at a slight bend in the canal, they appeared to be sailing on sand. Then I remembered standing on the stern of a ship in the 1950s, probably in this same place. I remembered having heard, above the muted roar of the engines, someone calling my name. 'Olma, Olma.' There on the bow of the following ship was a girl I had not seen since schooldays. We shouted our promises to meet in Naples, the next port, but I never saw her again.

Through the fog of memories, I realised that Achmed was asking me something.

'Can I have a whisky, please, Madame?'

'But it's only nine in the morning, Achmed. It's too early for whisky.'

'In Egypt it can be taken at any time. I want some whisky now, Madame.'

A drunk canal pilot is probably not that much worse than a sober one, I reasoned. Achmed sipped contentedly for the rest of the day, remaining alert and not once referring to his baksheesh until we were nearing Port Said.

'Where is my baksheesh?' he asked.

'*Et tu*, Achmed,' I moaned.

Then Alan stood in front of Achmed.

'Look Achmed, we have baksheesh for you,' Alan told him. 'We'll give you 30 pounds and some cigarettes. You've already drunk nearly a bottle of Scotch. That's all we'll give you. Not a penny more. When you're standing on the wharf, we'll pass your baksheesh across to you. Don't mention it again. Do you understand?'

'Yes, Captain Alan. Thank you, Captain Alan.'

We dropped Achmed and his baksheesh on the main wharf and continued through Port Said and into the Mediterranean Sea. I stood in the cockpit and sang bits of 'Joy to the World' at the top of my voice. We had spent almost three months in the Red Sea and as we hugged and danced in the cockpit we felt a heady sense of freedom and exhilaration. A few miles offshore, we turned *Windigo* east, towards Israel.

CHAPTER 6

Jaffa, Jerusalem and Akko
brides in a runabout
octopuses in a washing machine

*I*srael is the Holy Land to Jew, Christian and Muslim alike, haunting the imagination of the three religions. It haunts, too, the Jordanians, the Lebanese, the Palestinians, the Syrians, the Egyptians and other groups that live near the borders of this single Jewish state in a sea of Islam.

Few places have had such a long and luminous history, a story of human savagery on one hand, and the most profound of spiritual perceptions on the other; from the conquerors like Solomon, Nebuchadnezzar, Herod and Suleiman, to the great spiritual leaders, Elijah, Christ, Peter the fisherman, and Mohammed the Prophet. So Alan and I approached the land of the Bible in awe, not because of any religious belief, but because the land sang with the voices of the past as no other land could.

Jaffa, where we spent a month, is *Yafo* in Hebrew, which is derived from either *yafe*, meaning 'beautiful' or from the name of Noah's son, Japheth, who established the town after the flood. It is also the place of Jonah's experiences with God and the whale, and it is the world's oldest seaport. And, yes, the name also conjures up visions of bright citrus and little orange chocolate balls. Once a separate town five kilometres along the coast from Tel Aviv, it is now more like an outer suburb of that sprawling, modern city.

Jaffa's harbour is small and crowded with a tight entrance between the fabled Andromeda Rock and the end of the breakwater that holds back the Mediterranean Sea. It is lined with seafood restaurants, behind which Old Jaffa rises in steps of gardens and medieval buildings that form the nucleus of an artists' colony. It is a bohemian enclave, rich with the colour and friendly eccentricity of our neighbours.

Off our bow was a large black yacht that was used as a houseboat by a flamboyant New York Jew who greeted our arrival with humorous disdain.

'Welcome to Jaffa, my dears,' he called. 'You look straight. Such a pity! *Peccato!* I was hoping for someone more my type, a little bent. Absolutely bent would have been perfect.'

'Sorry about that,' Alan laughed. '*C'est la vie*, I suppose. Are you alone on your boat?'

'At the moment, yes,' our new friend replied. 'I've been alone since Rudy left. Lovely boy, Rudy. But he found greener pastures, the little fairy.'

He looked longingly past us, his eyes soft.

'Now there's a lad I could love, but he won't speak to me.'

We followed his gaze to a French cruising boat behind us. A boy of around 16 was turning away, the back of his neck pink with embarrassment.

Also behind us was Jacques, a vigorous man of perhaps 70 with long white hair under a 1930s gangster-style felt hat. His other item of clothing was a wide G-string. This did not appear to bother anyone, possibly because Jacques was lean, tanned and fit. His wife, Simone, was in her early 30s. A ballet dancer, she part-owned a ballet school in Sydney and taught dance in Tel Aviv.

The yacht on our port side appeared to serve a couple of functions. Sometimes sailing types took it out for a spin, but most of the time there was a succession of pretty young things and their partners who stayed overnight and were not seen again.

Vera, mother of five, lived aboard a houseboat with the children, several dogs, some cats, two birds, a collection of hanging plants and possibly a husband, but we never saw a man around.

Jean-Pierre was the shy 16-year-old who lived aboard the family cruising yacht so that he could attend school in Tel Aviv. His parents and a younger brother lived in France. Often Jean-Pierre called in to chat, beginning the conversation with, 'I won't stay long. Too much homework.' But two hours later he was often still there, earnestly discussing a range of serious topics and showing great interest in our opinions. The gay guy from New York bothered him.

'He's always asking me to his boat,' Jean-Pierre complained. 'I don't want to go. What should I do? I'm embarrassed about it.'

Our neighbours on the starboard side were Lew, a retired pilot who had flown in the Entebbe raid and appeared to have lived a life of adventure and danger, and his wife, Sima, an attractive woman who shared her husband's relaxed urbanity and sense of fun.

'The moment I saw her I loved her, and I still do,' Lew told us. 'She was 18. She walked towards me looking amazingly sexy in her army uniform, swinging her semiautomatic and grinning at the world as if she owned it. I just had to stop her. I had to have her.'

'I saw him before he saw me,' Sima retorted. 'If he hadn't stopped me, I would have stopped him. I had to have him too.'

They both laughed and threw their arms around each other.

Lew and Sima appeared to spend most nights of the spring and summer on the yacht where it was cooler to sleep than in their apartment overlooking the harbour. They often kept us entertained into the early hours and we invariably cursed them the next morning as we staggered to the Jerusalem bus stop.

We always enjoyed the 40-minute ride to Jerusalem. In the late spring, the countryside was a blaze of colour. Orchards, orange groves, fields of sunflowers, rows of red, pink and white oleander, flowering desert shrubs and golden mimosa lined the highway. There were reminders, too, of ambushes, skirmishes and battles past, where flowers reverently placed on bullet-riddled trucks and jeeps made shrines to those gunned down there.

On the first bus trip, we sat in the front seat for a clearer view, but were politely told to move because that seat was reserved for the armed guard. On the one occasion when an armed soldier did not accompany the bus, we felt uneasy.

Most people in Israel are armed and we soon grew accustomed

to girls and boys in military uniform nonchalantly swinging their Uzis, teachers armed with submachine guns escorting crocodiles of children on excursions, and the bomb-laden convoys of helicopters that flew along the coast towards Lebanon, from where the Hezbollah terrorists launch their attacks upon Israel. At the time of our visit there was no *intifada* so we were seeing people at their most relaxed.

We grew accustomed, too, to people laughing unaffectedly and showing affection in public, to spontaneity and warmth, to lovers kissing and people hugging. We noticed a relaxed acceptance of our presence and a caring response to any request for assistance.

Jerusalem is one of the world's most fascinating cities. We approached it after we had spent considerable time at the Diaspora Museum in Tel Aviv in an attempt to gain an understanding of Jewish history and, although the time spent was inadequate, it helped us appreciate the richness and historical significance of Israel's treasures.

The Via Dolorosa runs from the Muslim to the Christian quarter and it is supposed to be the route along which Jesus carried his Cross, but the way has changed many times over the centuries and the route is now more symbolic than accurate. Wishing to be independent of guides, touts and 'friends', we set off alone to find the 13 stations of the Cross, became lost and managed to find only five before we were standing at the doors of the Church of the Holy Sepulchre, the sacred site of Jesus' crucifixion, burial and resurrection.

Had we been devout Christians we may have been saddened by the carnival atmosphere of this, the holiest church in the Christian world. As it was, we were just a little sad, and mostly amused.

We approached the Holocaust Museum with dread, doubting our ability to withstand such a rape of the senses. The impressive and haunting memorial to the six million Jews who had been tortured and murdered during the Second World War stands on a pine-covered slope overlooking the Holy City. The building rests gently in a forest of young trees. There are 8000 trees, one for every person who risked his or her life to save a Jew from the Holocaust. Each tree has a plaque with the person's name and country inscribed upon it. Inside, the main exhibits are restrained. There was nothing morbid or sensational, just the brutal facts, sickening, chilling, incomprehensible.

An exhibition of wall hangings based on the Holocaust hung in one section. It is strange how something abstract can hit you in the gut harder than a photograph. We had to sit under the trees to sob.

A little way through the pines was the Memorial to the Children, also totally abstract. You enter from a strong, even brutal environment of concrete ramps and threatening forms into a soft, warm void deep in the earth where for a few seconds you are blind. But you feel safe and comforted, as if in a womb.

Gradually you become aware of lighted candles floating in a mirrored blackness — 1.5 million tiny flames, one for every murdered child — above, below and all around. The feeling is like floating in the Milky Way, in infinity. We felt disembodied, spiritual, and finally heartbroken as somewhere in the distance a voice softly called the name and age of each murdered child. We will always remember the beauty and the pain of that place.

One day, suffering from an *embarras de richesses*, we decided to stay on board to consolidate, to sort out our impressions and to plan for the rest of our stay. *Anhinga* had been at Jaffa when we arrived, but Max and Gloria had been strangely aloof, and we had been too excited by Israel to pay much attention. Now, here was Max on the pontoon, looking desolate.

'Mind if I come aboard?' he asked.

I made some coffee and the story was told.

Interlude, now in Cyprus after having bypassed Israel, had grown tired of their cat's strange behaviour and at Port Said, Bret had decided to drown her. Gloria, much against her husband's advice, adopted Miffy and, despite the cat's odd ways, quickly became devoted to her.

On heat for the first time in Tel Aviv marina, Miffy caused havoc. One night her screams were so terrible that Max put her in the dinghy. She woke the other yachties who yelled abuse at gentle Max. The occupants of the high-rise apartments that hug the marina became incensed and threw things down upon the yachts. There was confusion and mayhem. And the cats of Tel Aviv that were within earshot all converged on the marina and joined in the fray, along with a few dogs that were upset by the noise. So desperate was Max that he disposed of Miffy there and then. We did not ask how, but Gloria had not spoken to him since.

'What can I do?' asked Max.

'I'll talk to her. It'll be OK,' I rashly promised.

'Bloody cats!' Max continued. 'You may not have heard that *Anaconda*'s cat jumped ship in Tel Aviv marina before JB and Rosa left for Cyprus.'

'Really jumped ship?' Alan asked. 'On his own initiative?'

'Well, that's what JB said on the radio,' Max replied. 'I saw Paris a couple of days ago stealing food from the garbage bins near the marina. I'm sure it was him. Much thinner of course, but when I called out "Paris", he stiffened and turned to look at me. Wouldn't let me near him, though. Gone feral again, I suppose.'

A couple of days later we were listening to the early morning sked when we heard an Australian yacht calling *Anaconda*.

'*Anaconda, Anaconda*. This is the yacht *Peace and Plenty*. We're in Tel Aviv and I have good news. I've found your cat.'

'Oh.'

'Yes, I'm certain it's Paris,' continued *Peace and Plenty*. 'Same markings. Answers to his name. I'll catch him and bring him across to Cyprus for you.'

'That's not really necessary,' JB tried to assure him.

'No trouble, mate,' *Peace and Plenty* persisted. 'Be there in a couple of days.'

'We're leaving,' JB said. 'Please don't bother.'

'Well, if you're not there, we'll meet you somewhere in Turkey with the cat. You must be missing him terribly.' The voice trailed off into what sounded suspiciously like a suppressed giggle.

'Listen here, *Peace and Plenty*,' JB, said. 'That bloody cat jumped ship and I do not want him on board again. He's an Australian feral animal. It's impossible to tame them, and I never want to see him again. We may not go to Turkey. We could go anywhere. You'd be wasting your time. *Anaconda* clear.'

Bethlehem on the West Bank is a large Arab town, quite unlike the 'little town of Bethlehem' of the Christmas carol. The Church of the Nativity overlooks Manger Square, a bustling space filled with souvenir shops, restaurants and tourist traffic. Heavily armed Israeli guards are positioned in vantage points along the roofs surrounding the square, their guns trained at the people below. In a sunny corner of the square, Alan squirmed as he chatted to an Israeli soldier whose finger hovered over the trigger of his submachine gun which was pointed at Alan's legs.

Inside the church, we wormed our way through tight passages to where the Star of Bethlehem hangs over the place where Christ was born or, at least, the place that is generally accepted as the site of his birth. In the confined space Alan crashed into a precious wooden panel and almost succeeded in wrecking Christ's supposed birthplace and decapitating himself at the same time. The black-hooded Armenian priests abruptly stopped chanting and glared at him through the slits in their hoods, and I quickly walked away and pretended that I was part of a group of pious-looking people who were sitting in silent prayer in a nearby crypt.

The road to Masada, that symbol of Jewish courage and freedom, winds through the valley of the Dead Sea along the Jordan rift, the deepest valley in the world. King Herod built a fortified palace on the top of the great mountain spur, but at the time of the famous siege the palace was occupied by a group of 1000 Jewish zealots. Rather than become enslaved or killed by the invading Romans, the people decided to die by their own hands. Today, new army recruits are sworn in at the mountain fortress of Masada.

Herod's many-tiered holiday villa was decorated with painted plaster and marbled walls. There were wide balconies and porticos, rotundas and vine-cooled terraces, and a view across the desert, dotted with *wadis*, to Jordan on the other side of the shimmering Dead Sea. On the day of our visit the heat was intense, and the silvery water looked inviting in the distance.

But at the En-Gedde oasis on the shores of the Dead Sea, Alan recoiled when he saw that the water was pink. He refused to swim in it.

'It won't hurt you,' I told him, but without great conviction. 'Look at all the other people swimming in it.'

'That doesn't mean they'll survive the experience,' he replied.

But no germ could have lived in the dense salinity. The water tasted bitter and, yes, I was able to sit in it and read a book because of the buoyancy caused by the build-up of minerals and salt as the water evaporates. Despite its resemblance to normal water, swimming felt like floundering in thick gel.

In the 40-degree heat, the thought of cool waterfalls motivated us to hike through the nearby national park, but the waterfalls were elusive. However, we saw deer and hyraxes, little hare-like animals that scurried into holes in the rocks when we approached. Signs warning of what to do if one encountered a leopard prompted a quick return to the safety of the shores of the Dead Sea.

Returning one day from the domed museum that houses the Dead Sea Scrolls, we found our way blocked by a moving mass of black that swallowed several streets like some huge amorphous slug. Thousands of Orthodox Jews had gathered to protest about their perceived lack of adequate representation in the affairs of Israel. The protest of the Hasidim was silent and, possibly for this reason, ominous. Jewish fundamentalism is a threat to the inner stability of a country in which unity is essential for survival. Lack of unity has always weakened the Arabs, who have been unable to vanquish the determined and united Israelis; but if the Israelis cannot work as one, the risks of attack increase and their survival will be threatened.

The next day a fire started in a workshop on the outskirts of Jerusalem where a Jew and his son employed a group of Arab workmen. Students at a neighbouring Hasidim school concluded that the Arabs were burning the Jews, and rushed to attack. This was despite the protests and pleadings of the two Jewish employers who fought to protect the innocent Arabs and were seriously injured as a result.

Over dinner with Lew and Sima on our last evening in Jaffa, we once more discussed the problems of Israel. Alan and I had just returned from a visit to Ben Gurion's house in Tel Aviv, and Lew reminisced about the Tel Aviv of his childhood.

'It was built in a hurry, so one cannot describe it as beautiful,' he said. 'But it's a vibrant and exciting city despite the haste of its birth.'

'In some ways Tel Aviv reminds us of home,' we told them. 'We hope to see you some time in Sydney.'

'I don't think so,' Lew replied. 'We sail to different parts of Europe each summer but we always get homesick for Israel and often cut short our trips so that we can return home. Australia is too far. We couldn't bear to be away for so long.'

'Lew always feels that unless he's here to push his opinions down other people's throats, the country will go to the pack,' Sima teased.

We had heard Lew's opinions several times already and he now offered his latest thoughts on the subject.

'It is possible for Jews and Arabs to live in peace,' he began. 'The Arabs have been our brothers for thousands of years. Here in Jaffa, an Arab town, we live side by side without many arguments. It's no different from towns all over the world. You'll see the same peaceful coexistence in Akko when you get there.'

He took a long sip of wine before continuing. 'Now, I get angry about places like the Gaza Strip where things have happened to divide the people. Take Rafah, for example, where we have friends. When the Sinai was returned to Egypt in 1979, part of the town of Rafah went with it. This resulted in our local Berlin Wall, a fenced-off strip of land separating families and friends who now must shout to each other across it.'

'I'm not so easygoing about our situation as Lew,' Sima said. 'It's the refugee problem which divides us. The Arabs are forever blaming us for their refugee status and I can understand their angst. But they conveniently forget the 700 000 Jewish refugees who have been forced to flee from their homes in the Arab countries because of outbreaks of anti-Jewish violence.'

'I'm not easygoing, Sima,' Lew told her. 'I want to live in peace. I've grown tired of fighting. I want our children and our grandchildren to be safe and I want us to spend the days of our retirement together.'

He stopped. When he spoke again, his voice had softened. 'I don't want to ever leave you again, Sima. I doubt if I could bear it.'

I blinked back tears as his eyes held Sima's and she reached out her hand to him.

'Nevertheless,' he resumed, standing tall in the cockpit. 'If my country needs my poor old skills at any time in the future, I will not refuse.'

A little farther north along the coast, past Haifa, is the ancient town of Akko to which we sailed after a month in Jaffa. We imagined we would never again find a harbour so special. But Akko also had its share of charms. Standing on a small promontory on the Bay of Haifa, it was once the principal port of the Holy Land. Built by the Phoenicians long before biblical times, it was called Ptolemais in the New Testament and Acre by the Crusaders after St Jean d'Acre.

The old city is a fascinating mixture of styles, predominantly Christian and Turkish, with the splendid green-domed El Jazzar mosque dominating the highest point in the centre. There are at least six smaller mosques dotted around the harbour, so when the *muezzins* called the faithful to prayer there was a cacophony such as we had never heard before.

Most evenings at sunset we watched a parade of Arab brides and grooms from our vantage point in the cockpit. They waited in their finery to be whisked around the harbour three times in a small, flower-bedecked runabout with barely room to stand. The significance of the ritual eluded us, but we presumed it had something to do with life's voyage as a married couple.

Many men wore dinner suits and those who did not showed a preference for tan suits. Regardless of colour and style, though, all the men rolled up the sleeves of their jackets to the elbow, thus destroying any claim to sartorial elegance. We wondered about the significance of this too.

Some brides, unaccustomed to the movements of boats, appeared terrified by the rocking runabout and had difficulty balancing in their high heels whilst at the same time holding their veils and headdresses with one hand and the unsteady grooms with the other. The bridal trains were a further encumbrance, sometimes filling suddenly with air and threatening to lift the bride skywards like Mary Poppins.

To add to the tension, some brides wore large collars similar to those worn by children dressed as flowers at school concerts. There was one who caused the small boat to tilt dangerously when she and the groom battled to control an elaborate shoulder construction of wire, satin and lace that resembled an exaggerated Elizabethan collar, or a Winged Victory.

Not all the brides wore white, some preferring green, the colour of Islam. But the style was invariably western. One young woman wore a black velvet gown with a tan lace veil and we wondered about this, and one groom handed his jacket and his shirt to a friend to hold as he escorted his bride in his white singlet.

Our favourite bride was an elaborately gowned beauty in a huge hooped skirt and a voluminous veil. Seed pearls, spangles, beads and sequins caught the last rays of the setting sun and she sparkled and flashed as she climbed aboard and waved exuberantly to the crowd. The driver, obviously enchanted, threw the small boat into gear and gripped by elation, flew around the harbour in three great bursts of speed that left spray in a shining fan behind the boat and created waves that rocked the yachts in the harbour and splashed the feet of the waiting couples on the shore.

The bride blew like a paper doll in the wind, her veil horizontal, the hoops of her crinoline pressed hard against her body in front and bulged in a great satin bubble behind. At the end of the run, she stepped triumphantly from the tiny boat and the yachties in their cockpits spontaneously stood and cheered.

I commented to one of the waiting grooms that the brides generally looked unhappy.

'It's because they're not yet married,' he replied. 'We do this first, you see. Then we have the wedding ceremony and the feast. After that, they're happy'.

The bus from Haifa to Tiberius passes through what is probably the most productive agricultural region in Israel, with green valleys, forests and farmlands. The area is known as the Land of the Bible because it was here that Jesus did most of his teaching and recruited several of the disciples.

The beautiful Sea of Galilee is a serene lake beneath the Golan Heights which runs along its eastern banks. A few kilometres to the north is Capernaum and to the east, Nazareth. The River Jordan flows into the Sea of Galilee in the north and out in the south. I found the hymns, psalms and prayers of my childhood flooding back in that evocative place and I sang to myself as we explored. 'Oh, little Sea of Galilee . . . '

Around the leafy shores were spas, hot springs, landscaped bathing places and restaurants in a cool setting of lawns and fountains and shade trees. The water was fresh, cool and clear.

We had read about Saint Peter's fish and knew that this would be our only opportunity to eat one because they exist nowhere else in the world. Their correct name is *musht* and they are a flattish fish with a large dorsal fin and a taste rather like trout, but with a coarser flesh. In the intense midday heat, we relaxed with the waters of the Sea of Galilee lapping at our feet and the breeze rustling the leaves of the large shade trees that formed a dappled ceiling above the lakeside restaurant. Crisp chips and salad, with cold beer and Saint Peter's fish, seemed to us the perfect lunch for our last day in Israel.

Our first Mediterranean summer had already begun. It was mid-July 1992. We were sad to leave Israel but could not dally longer if we were to see something of Cyprus before crossing to eastern Turkey to escape the tourist hordes of August. A Homeric hymn offers homage to Cyprus with the words:

> I will sing of Aphrodite,
> the stately one, the fair one, the golden-crowned one:
> sea-girt Cyprus and its walled cities are her sole domain.

Cyprus lay hidden in the summer haze until we were approaching the marina at Larnaca on its southern shore. Then we were too close to catch more than glimpses of the low, flat land to one side of the town and a long, grey beach running into the distance in the opposite direction.

Here was a new country, a new culture, about which we knew

little. Years ago I had read Lawrence Durrell's *The Alexandria Quartet* and now wished we had it on board. *Bitter Lemons* was one of the many books we argued about taking with us when we left our house and we subsequently regretted many of the decisions made in the name of 'keeping the boat light'.

We had picked up a little information from cruising guides. We knew that Cyprus was the third largest island in the Mediterranean after Sicily and Sardinia, and that, like Israel, it was a troubled land. When the British left in 1960, the Cypriots appeared at last to be free to follow their own destiny. But in 1974 the Turkish army invaded and partitioned the island. Some 200 000 Greek Cypriots living in the north of the island were forced to abandon their property and possessions and flee to southern Cyprus, while 45 000 Turkish Cypriots fled to the north. International recognition of Turkish Cyprus has never been given and the only country which recognises its existence is Turkey itself.

In this complicated stalemate, there were regulations that affected us:

> A yacht may cross from Turkey to Turkish Cyprus (or from Turkey to Greek Cyprus) and from Turkish Cyprus to Turkey but may not cross from Turkish Cyprus to Greek Cyprus. A passage from Greek Cyprus to Turkish Cyprus is not forbidden but should be undertaken with caution.

Larnaca marina is large, impersonal and packed with cruising yachts, mainly British. The English regard Larnaca as their special place and treat the Australians and New Zealanders as interlopers, ignoring our presence and only grudgingly returning greetings.

On our first Sunday at the marina I noticed the English yachties attending a 'Book Swap' in the common room.

'Do you mind if I swap some books too?' I asked the organiser, a tall gentleman of military appearance and manner.

'But you're not a "permanent",' he informed me in a refined voice.

'Does that matter?' I asked.

'Well, I suppose not,' he grudgingly replied. 'But I must warn you that we only swap good literature. No Westerns, or Mills and Boon or anything like that.'

'What about Barbara Cartland?' I asked.

'Yes, she's suitable. Some of the ladies are rather fond of her.'

The water in the marina is crystal clear and every effort is made to keep it pristine. A marina official wanders around every morning, peering between the yachts to check that there is no floating excrement. Yachties who pump their toilets are fined. Whilst approving of the environmental zeal, I personally found the mornings tedious and stressful as a result.

You see, the toilets are half a kilometre away, so when the urge comes, one is faced with several alternatives. You can walk the distance as sedately as possible and hope that the desire will still be strong on arrival; you can set off without an urge and hope that everything will work out by the time you arrive at the ablutions block; you can run along the pontoons if you get caught with a sudden urge but this causes them to bounce so alarmingly that boat-bound dogs rush out and bark at you; or if you own a bike, you can run to the bike racks, unlock your transport and pedal along the narrow, heaving pontoons, hoping that you will not emulate the woman who ended up in the water astride her bike a couple of days after we arrived.

I still preferred the bike. But despite its relative speed, I often arrived *sans* urge and had to return to *Windigo* for another cup of coffee before setting out on the second sprint. Alan's system appeared less temperamental and his calm assurance so early in the morning further added to my woe.

The beach next to the marina is a dead shade of grey and it is lined with brassy restaurants with photographs of their best dishes on hoardings outside. The fare is English, and most dishes are smothered in chips. Some restaurants have replaced photographs of food with lurid snaps of nauseating stunts. Our favourite was of an expressionless waiter cutting off his arm with a blood-spurting butcher's knife.

The promenade along the beach is a Pommie enclave with a few Germans who strut with an impressive proprietary, considering that they are severely outnumbered. There are strong odours of abused cooking oil and sickly suntan lotion, and the air is loud with Pommie soccer accents as the tourists jostle between the line of restaurants on the beachfront and the tourist shops and stalls on the other side of the promenade.

The unfit bodies of the new arrivals resembled suet and those who had been there for a few days were pink and peeling and moist in the folds. Some men wore shirts open down the front. The shirts blew back in the breeze to reveal abdomens bulging over the waistbands of shorts worn with black socks and sandals. Some men wore singlets, others promenaded bare to the waist. All appeared to be hot and their skins oozed beer.

The women, too, exposed as much bare skin as they considered decent and they favoured short, tasselled skirts, crocheted tops, white cowboy hats and high-heeled sandals. After one walk along the beachfront, we decided to cut straight to the centre of the town from the marina to avoid the depressing view of humanity at leisure.

Away from the beach, the life of Larnaca bubbled along with a momentum and charm that seemed completely divorced from the squalid hedonism of the seafront. The winding streets with their metre-wide footpaths were crammed with banks and shops selling shoes, fabrics, clothing and island crafts. They radiated from a central market, a large pavilion with stalls crammed with fruit and vegetables, meat, fine white Cypriot lace and cotton goods. Other stalls sold bread, wine, nuts, dried figs and apricots and Cypriot delicacies.

Turkish delight is called Cypriot delight, but there is also the delicious *soudzoukou* which are thick necklaces of almonds strung together with thread and then dipped like candlewicks into vats of grape syrup and rose water until a chewy, semi-transparent covering is formed around the almonds. And there are long bars of *pastellaki* made from sesame seeds, peanuts and grape syrup. We tried to limit our consumption of either to ten centimetres per day — five each.

A few days after our arrival in Larnaca we joined a group of cruising friends for an evening at a taverna in one of the seedier parts of the city not normally frequented by tourists — an area which, according to George, the gatekeeper at the marina, was 'pure Greek Cypriot'. In a corner of the large room at the top of the black staircase, a man sang traditional songs accompanied by a spirited *bouzouki* player, a *sandouri* (a type of dulcimer) player, a violinist, a flautist, and a castanets player.

Characteristic of the Greek Cypriot cuisine are the *mezedhe*, which can be eaten as appetisers or as a complete meal, when anything from 16 to 32 different items may be served before the cook calls, 'That's all, my friends!' or the diners call, '*Voithia!*' (Help!). Most distinctly I remember the *haloumi*, a salty goats' milk cheese which is sliced and then fried, the mint-flavoured *dolmadhe*, the *keftedhe* (cumin flavoured meatballs), the tiny grilled lamb cutlets, and the *sheftalia* (spicy grilled sausages). These were interspersed with small servings of fish and vegetables, dips and pita bread and wine.

As the meal progressed, the taverna filled with Cypriots, the noise level rose, the singing and playing grew ever more passionate, people began to dance, Greek style, and the mustachioed castanets player dashed across the room and pulled me onto the dance floor as if to say, 'Enough of eating and drinking. It's time to dance.'

So relax Olma! Feel the wine, respond to the beat, think of Zorba, enjoy, click the fingers, move the hips, flirt with the crazy castanets player. "Dance, Dance, wherever you may be, I am the Lord of the Dance, said he". Whirling, twirling, clicking, dreaming. A sea of faces floating below. Dancing on the tables. Someone sounding far away is saying, 'It's 3 a.m.! Time to go.'

'If you have a tree you also have shade,' says a Cypriot proverb. I thought of this as we drove in a rented car through the coastal plain to the foothills of the Troodhos Mountains. It was an area largely denuded of trees, kilometres of sun-bleached rocky land with goats and donkeys, and pockets of soil where black-clad women toiled in unshaded labour.

Later, in the High Troodhos, I thought that the Cypriot proverb, like all other proverbs, had a ring of truth. In the well-managed forests of the peaks and lush foothills grew Aleppo pines, cypresses, oaks and cedars, olive trees, eucalypts, fruit and nut trees. For two days we followed the narrow mountain roads in search of the nine Byzantine, barn-roofed churches in the UNESCO list of heritage sites. The churches, many with rare frescoes and mosaics, cling to the mountain peaks or nestle in cool, green valleys beside streams where icy water flows softly over pebbled beds.

At the pretty mountain village of Kakopetria we stayed the night at 'Olga's'. Our eponymous hostess was a large, friendly woman in a businesslike blue and white checked apron which seemed to auger well for dinner that night. She ran a clean, homely establishment of four or five rooms which opened onto a sunny, vine-covered deck above a gurgling stream.

The crisp mountain air made us hungry and I imagined Olga, her arms covered in flour to the elbows, busy in the rustic kitchen preparing the evening meal of hearty Cypriot lamb, or maybe a *moussaka*, or even some freshly caught mountain trout. But Olga's apron was only an illusion, for she served some of the worst food I have ever eaten. A thrice-fried chicken thigh was string tough, saturated with rancid oil and served with fried half potatoes, and potato chips. Alan chewed his way through something he thought was goat, but at least it was hot.

Interlude sat forlornly on land at Larnaca marina with a gaping hole in her hull through which the gearbox had been removed. Bret carefully packed it and sent it to England for repairs, but an employee of the company which manufactures it, dropped the parcel and the gearbox was smashed. The company accused Bret of sloppy packing and then refused to proceed with the repairs. The only solution was the installation of a new engine. Bret and Debbie left to work in England for a few years, before continuing their circumnavigation.

Of our American friends, *Anaconda* was the only one left. Andre and Barbara on *Northern Lights* were heading towards Crete on their way back to America. It appeared that their motivation was to circumnavigate rather than explore the world. *Maisie Dotes* still sat in Port Said. JB and I avoided all mention of Israel, and cats. I felt frustrated and so did he, but our silence on those issues suited everyone else. JB sidled up to me one day in Cyprus and sheepishly offered a book, *The Arabs* by Thomas Kiernan.

'You must read this, Olma,' he said. 'Then we can find a quiet spot away from all the wimps to have a discussion. By the way, it's written by a Jew,' he ended triumphantly.

'Thank you, JB,' I replied. 'Have you read *The Haj*? No? Well, while I'm reading *The Arabs* you might like to read what Leon Uris has to say.'

Later in the day Alan mentioned that he had seen JB walking through the marina with a copy of *The Haj*.

'That's a good sign,' he commented. 'It means he's prepared to look at another point of view.'

When I did not answer, he looked at me quizzically. 'Oh, no! You gave it to him, didn't you? You said you wouldn't incite him.'

'Look what he's given me to read,' I said.

Alan threw his hands into the air like a frustrated Italian. 'You're both as bad as each other,' he replied.

As we gathered each evening in someone's cockpit for drinks, it became obvious that the tight-knit little band of travellers who had left Darwin together would soon be part of our own diaspora. From Cyprus, each yacht would explore the Mediterranean according to personal whim and interest. So we swapped addresses, wrote sentimental poems in each other's Yacht Books, and promised to keep in touch via the skeds for as long as possible. Of them all, I would miss JB the most.

Next to *Windigo* was a small red yacht owned by Michael Topakas, a whimsical Greek Cypriot who, with his wife Marea, had been forced to flee from Famagusta to a refugee suburb of Larnaca when the Turkish army invaded. Michael had bought the bright red yacht at auction after it had been confiscated from two Arabs who had stolen it in Israel and sailed it to Cyprus. He had little knowledge of or interest in sailing, his passion being octopuses. Two or three times each week, Michael would motor out to his secret octopus hunting ground and return with several writhing specimens.

'You'll be very tired after bashing those against the rocks one hundred times each,' Alan commented one afternoon.

'Oh, I never do that any more,' Michael replied. 'Years ago I bought an old washing machine specifically for tenderising the octopuses. Now, all I do is throw them in and turn on the machine. Takes about half an hour, sometimes more. Depends.'

'That's a marvellous idea, Michael,' Alan told him.

'Yes, most of my friends now have old washing machines under their houses. Come to dinner tomorrow night and Marea will cook a traditional Cypriot meal with octopus.'

The Topakas home was comfortable, even lavish in some respects. In an outlying suburb, leafy with fruit trees and grape vines, the house sat on a large block in the back of which Michael had planted pear, orange, lemon, apricot, pomegranate, persimmon and fig trees, and sweet-smelling jasmine. He felt a need to be involved with the sea and the soil. There was a cage of canaries, and another of rabbits as large as wombats and just as fierce, but they showed no fear of Michael. In a corner was a large cage of pigeons so grotesquely inbred that they resembled small vultures with their naked pink necks and twisted beaks.

'They still make a good pigeon pie,' Michael explained in their defence, whilst I prayed that pigeon pie was not part of the traditional Cypriot meal we had been promised.

Linda, Michael's hunting dog, for which he had paid $2000 as a pup, cowered shyly in a corner of her kennel.

'Linda's not a very good hunting dog,' said Michael fondly.

'Perhaps it's her name,' I suggested. 'Boadicea or even Joan may have made her more bellicose.'

'Linda's my favourite name. I don't mind that she doesn't like hunting. We enjoy walking together.' He smiled kindly at her before ushering us inside.

Family photographs of Larnaca and faded ones of Famagusta lined the mantelpiece and vied for space with religious icons on the lid of the white with gold trim baby-grand piano. There was an old photo of the Larnaca marina under construction.

'My father designed it,' Michael explained.

We asked about their life in Famagusta before the invasion.

'We can never go back,' Marea said, 'but we still miss it. We miss our friends, our old neighbours. They were Turks, but they were like family.'

'They cried when we had to flee. We all cried,' Michael added. 'Like my father, I was an engineer. We owned land and two houses but we had to leave everything behind. We barely escaped with our lives.'

'Now we are separated by the Green Line, the buffer zone controlled by UN forces,' his wife pointed out. 'It runs just south of Famagusta and cuts Nicosia in half, like the Berlin Wall. It's crazy!' Marea threw her hands into the air in a gesture of frustration.

'We were amongst the lucky ones,' she continued. 'There were 1600 of us who were not able to escape in time and those people are still unaccounted for.' Her eyes were moist as she turned away.

'Come now, Marea,' Michael said. 'Our guests come from a free and happy land. These old stories will make us all sad. By the way, we very nearly migrated to your country along with thousands of other Cypriots after the invasion. We have friends in Melbourne who return each year to visit family. They say they're now Aussies and that it's a great place to live.'

We gave them our address.

'Perhaps some day you will come to Sydney,' we said.

Michael and Marea had two sons, both out for the evening, but their good-looking faces smiled from the piano. Thoroughly modern Katarina, their 16-year-old daughter, joined us for dinner. She chatted gaily about her friends and the secondary school she attended, and afterwards she played some Chopin that sent the family cat stalking out fastidiously. We left laden with fruit and Marea's homemade delicacies, and we felt sad that we would probably never see them again.

I had recently read Oriana Falacci's inspiring book, *A Man*, and now I thought of it again. No doubt the political instability in Greece at the time of the Colonels had contributed in no small way to instability in Cyprus. There are those who would argue that the Turks invaded to protect their own people. On the other hand, Cyprus is a very convenient meeting place for three continents, Europe, Asia and Africa, so it is conceivable that the Turks opportunistically used the period of instability to acquire a foothold on this strategically placed island.

Soon we would be in Turkey. We would possibly spend the winter there. It was time to clear our minds of preconceived ideas and to allow the dynamism of discovery to sweep us along paths as yet unfamiliar.

CHAPTER 7

the southern coast of Turkey • Greek interludes
the Nightingale sings • snow on the decks
Ismail, the teacher • Pamukkale and Ephesus

What amazed us on the crossing to Turkey in 1992 was the stillness of the sea and the intensity of the sun's rays. It was August, the month in which the countries along the Mediterranean come to a standstill, gripped in a wave of high summer swelter that forces the people from the stifling cities and towns to those with a sea breeze and a place to swim. August then is the month of Mediterranean madness, tourist hordes and crazy prices, which were some of the reasons we were heading for a part of Turkey where foreign tourists seldom go.

As the Anatolian landmass rose from the sea we wondered what to expect, feeling that we understood something of Frenchness, Englishness, Greekness, Italianness, and the quintessence of some other nationalities, but not Turkishness. What were the implications of being an Islamic country which functioned as a republic with a clear separation of church and politics? Had the mighty Kemal Atatürk, who defeated the Anzacs, the British and the French at Gallipoli, created 'a state of society entirely modern and completely civilised in spirit and form' as he set out to do in 1923 when he created the republic from the shambles of the old Ottoman Empire?

The tiny commercial harbour at Taşucu in eastern Turkey is a port of entry and it was here that we made our landfall. *Windigo* had to be tied stern-to, a common practice in the crowded anchorages of the Mediterranean but one to which we were unaccustomed. The procedure involves dropping the anchor well out from the quay and then backing into the space, but

Windigo has a mind of her own in reverse and we seldom ended up where we wanted to go. There were helping hands ashore, however, and we were soon sitting in the cockpit making plans for the next few days.

Suddenly there was a commotion. Ferries from Cyprus had been jostling for position when a young man, dressed in only a pair of jeans, dived overboard amongst the milling boats and swam desperately for the shore. He scrambled up the rocks, raced full-pelt along the promenade and disappeared along the main road. Everyone watched transfixed as sirens wailed and police poured from cars that seemed to materialise out of thin air. Roadblocks were quickly in place and men in jeans without shirts were hauled from cars and taken away. We felt uneasy.

A group of black-robed women prayed in the nondescript main street of Taşucu. Many young people wore western clothes but most older men and women were dressed in the traditional *salvar*, long baggy bloomers with crutches at knee level, and as we strolled through the town the small wiry men avoided looking at me, but the plump peasant women in their headscarves were smiling and curious. Two older men wore the fez. That surprised us because the old form of headgear had been banned by Atatürk, who had regarded it as a symbol of Islamic and Ottoman orthodoxy.

In that boondocks part of Turkey the people were inquisitive. 'Why are you here?' 'How did you know about us — about this village?' 'How did you come here?' 'How did you find your way without getting lost?' 'Where are your children?'

At nearby Silifke we found a bustling market town with good food and cheap fabrics. We bought new upholstery material for *Windigo*, a Rousseau-inspired floral design on thick cotton in greens, pinks, browns, mauves and gold.

In the centre of the town square stood Atatürk's statue with the inscription: *'Ne mutlu Turkum diyene!'* ('Happy is the man who calls himself a Turk!'). The young woman at the adjoining tourist office explained.

'Kemal Atatürk was our father. You'll see his statue in every city and town in Turkey. Even the smallest hamlet will probably have his statue, or at least a plaque with one of his sayings.'

'You speak of him with reverence,' I remarked. 'But you're so young and he died so long ago, certainly before you were born.'

'His memory lives,' she replied. 'At military passing-out ceremonies his serial number is still called ... 1238, and then the soldiers say in unison, "He is among us." My brother is a soldier,' she added with a smile.

Her name was Guldan. She was an attractive young woman in smart western dress. Her English was fluent and she quickly covered our map of the area with crosses, squiggles, asterisks, arrows and circles so that we became confused and wished she would stop. As she tapped her coloured biros at each of the historic sites, she said, 'It's a long way to walk in the heat and it's really just a ruin. Little more than a pile of rocks. Perhaps a wall or two. Still, if you really want to walk about in this heat ...'

Perhaps it was only for mad dogs and Englishmen after all, because any enthusiasm we had felt for exploring the ancient sites of Silifke evaporated as Guldan spoke. But she had recommended that we visit Atatürk's house near the centre of the town.

It was a pleasant timber bungalow that was lovingly cared for, as if he were expected at any moment. The beds were made, his belongings laid out, photographs brightened the walls, his desk was in readiness, an open book lay beside his easychair.

Atatürk's stay in Silifke had been brief, but we would not have been unduly dismayed had he walked through the door saying, *'Hosgeldiniz!'* ('Welcome to Turkey').

The southern coast of Turkey falls roughly into four sections, each one named after the ancient civilisations whose people settled along its shores: the Carian Coast, the Lycian Coast, the Pamphylian Coast and the Cilician Coast. It is a wondrous coastline, wild and rugged where the towering Taurus Mountains rise sheer from the sea. The valleys are rich in cotton fields, orchards and orange groves.

Everywhere there are ruins — castles, forts, tombs, walls — all weathered by time and bleached in the fierce heat of the summers. We often discovered that the perfumed walks through pine and jasmine and wild herbs with views across the sparkling sea were more alluring than the ruins.

At Alanya stands a magnificent castle on a fine headland high above the sea, so high that we caught a bus to the top. There was something unusual about the small bus, like a riddle with an illusive solution that one should know. As we sat waiting for the bus to fill, we suddenly realised that it was upholstered in the fabric we had bought in Silifke. It looked feminine and joyful; not the fabric one expects to find on a bus. But we were thoughtful as we wound up the narrow road to the summit. Was the person who chose the fabric for the Alanya buses a particularly sensitive and imaginative official; or did we have public transport tastes.

The Lycian coast between Marmaris and Antalya presents a hostile front to the sailor, but it is majestic, almost primeval. The mountains, split by deep ravines, plummet into the sea, and caves and caverns where pirates once hid gaped with black menace as we glided by. But at lovely Phaselis, where the ruins of the city that had been founded in 690 BC nestle around three small bays that were loud with the screeching of locusts, we felt protected and safe.

Most of the Lycian area, though, is now awash with affluence. It is the Mediterranean's latest tourist mecca. There are miles of condominiums, Club Meds, discos, casinos and the holiday homes of Europe's wealthy.

One of the pleasures of cruising is that the yacht is your floating home: self-contained, comfortable, able to supply all your needs for long periods. Yachties always have the best view, so in places where the tourists and the touts made us feel trapped and annoyed, we retreated to *Windigo*. From our vantage point in a bay, the world looked entirely different — clean, quiet, picturesque. At night the floodlit castles and forts, the illuminated streets and restaurants, were reflected in the black waters of the bays and we lived in a fairyland.

Kekova Roads is a resplendent roadstead protected from the sea by the slim island of Kekova Adassi. Here, ruins drip from every outcrop. Acropoli and necropoli cascade down the slopes into the turquoise sea, and burial chambers honeycomb the hot rock walls. There are camels and goats, olives and herbs, and few people. We snorkelled above a sunken Lycian city, swimming into rooms and along streets lined with fallen columns and broken amphora in water of splendid clarity.

Saint Nicholas is apparently not only the patron saint of children but also of sailors, so we thought it appropriate, even wise, to pay our respects at the church of Baba Noel at nearby Kale and to visit the restored amphitheatre at Myra where he was the bishop. His remains, however, are not here, having been taken to Bari in Italy by a band of Italian merchants in the 11th century.

Kastellorizon, clearly visible from the Turkish mainland, is a small Greek island which was once a busy port for Levantine trading vessels. Alan and I had read of its beauty so we decided to make the short detour. Today the harbour is deserted except for the few visiting yachts in the summer months. The lovely old town that hugs the harbour and nestles into the mountainside is home for a scant 200 people where once had lived 20 000. Most sought their fortunes in Australia and the majority of those now living in Kastellorizon are Greek Australians with strong Australian accents.

There is an electric quality in the sparkling whitewashed walls and steps, draped with purple bougainvillea and red geraniums, against the sharp turquoise of the harbour and the deep blue of the sea. Two men strolled by in animated conversation and we eavesdropped as they passed *Windigo*, tied to the quay.

'There's a poet out there called Banjo. Banjo Paterson,' we

heard one say. Then, in a resonant voice, he began to recite:

> In far away Queensland,
> On the outer Barcoo,
> My dad owns a fruitshop,
> And a bloody good one too.

We missed the rest of the doggerel as they moved away.

Ashore, the little town felt forsaken, palpable with the longings of those who had gone to the other side of the world. One felt a forlorn nonpresence in which the homes of those who had remained or returned glowed like flames in the crumbling ruin.

Still, we were happy there. It was pleasant to be among Greeks again. We felt an empathy that so far had eluded us with the Turks, despite our wish to understand and the Turks' civilised manner towards us.

Back on the Turkish coast we shared a quiet anchorage with *Burramys, Anhinga* and swarms of huge brown wasps which made life almost intolerable. John was bitten and swelled alarmingly, possibly because his red hair and beard excited the wasps, and Alan's red swimmers caused such activity around his privates that it was dangerous to wear them. Sadly, this was to be our last secluded anchorage for some time.

The area around Bodrum and Marmaris is one of the Mediterranean's most popular cruising grounds, and there were thousands of *gulets* and charter yachts jostling for space in the harbours and anchorages. I liked the appearance of the *gulets*, though. The traditional Turkish sailing boats are built of timber, and they are glossy with layers of varnish and crisp with white canvas awnings and cushions. Their Turkish skippers, almost without exception, are considerate sailors.

Not so the charter-boat skippers, nor those on most of the European private yachts. After several attempts at friendship, we learned to ignore other yachts as they did us. The ways of the Mediterranean were not our ways, but there we were and there seemed little we could do about the customs.

The Germans were the most arrogant, turning their backs when addressed, refusing to give thanks when helped to tie up, ramming their boats into others and refusing to apologise or even to acknowledge that they had caused a problem. The few friendly ones who accepted an invitation to drinks in the cockpit never returned the hospitality.

One evening just on sunset a yacht with five large fat German men on board arrived in the small harbour where we had spent the day with *Burramys*. As the yacht slid into the space beside us, one of the two men at the bow turned his back to us, pulled down his shorts and loudly farted five times. They all laughed.

Rhodes, the largest of the Dodecanese Islands, had been occupied in 1912 by the Italians, who intended to create another Capri, and it certainly is a place of great beauty, like a garden. It is probably Greece's main tourist island but luckily only a few stragglers remained when we sailed across from Turkey in late October. The days were still hot, but the nights were cool. We knew that we would soon have to anchor down somewhere for the winter.

The Colossus of Rhodes, the 37-metre statue of the sun-god Helios which once straddled the narrow entrance to the harbour, was destroyed by an earthquake in 227 BC. As *Windigo* passed between the two entrance columns, each topped by a bronze deer, we entered a theatre, the curtains already raised on a medieval set of grand proportions with castles, battlements, gardens, windmills and cannons.

At any moment Caesar, Brutus, Antony, Cicero and Tiberius would enter stage left and stroll along the waterfront, deep in discussion of their studies in maritime law and military strategy for which Rhodes was the centre. The Knights of Saint John would take their places centre stage, exchanging gossip of the

Crusades and worrying about the rapid advances of the Ottoman Empire. The past was all around us.

In Rhodes we were woken by church bells. Crowds were gathering along the promenade and there was an air of excitement and purpose.

'What's happening?' we asked a group of well-dressed people gathered around a collection of furled flags.

'It's *Okhi* Day!' they exclaimed.

'There'll be a big parade,' said one man.

'It's a national holiday,' said another.

'Find a good spot to watch it,' advised a woman.

'But *okhi* means 'no', doesn't it?' I asked.

'*Ne*,' they replied, nodding and laughing.

So this was to be a 'No Day' celebration. In 1942, Mussolini had asked the Greeks for permission to land Italian troops on Greek soil. The Greek President replied with one word, '*Okhi*', and ever since then, the Greeks have celebrated the day in much the same way as Australians celebrate Anzac Day.

There were flags, banners and bands, groups in national dress, marching girls, old soldiers, young soldiers, the Fire Brigade, Sea Scouts, Boy Scouts, plus every child on Rhodes, so it seemed to us. The children marched with their teachers in school groups, confidently and with pride.

The Greeks, with centuries of glorious battles from which to choose one to celebrate as a national day had chosen *Okhi* Day. It seemed to say something about the Greek character, the fierce pride, and the audacity.

There are three distinct parts to the city of Rhodes: the Italianate section around the harbour, the tatty concrete hotels and suburbs of the holiday town, and the lovely ambience of the old town with its paved streets, exquisite stonework and dozens of small shops selling pottery, furs, unusual umbrellas, gold jewellery, costume jewellery, postcards, and rude things.

Heavy stone balls are scattered everywhere in the medieval part of Rhodes. They have lain in the city for more than 2000 years. Polioketes, a determined invader, built a fantastic machine called the Helepolis. It was estimated to be nine stories high and was rolled to the city walls on enormous oaken wheels. From it sprouted huge catapults, drawbridges which could be dropped down to release troops, and a shielded nest on top for the archers.

The stone balls were the missiles. They did great damage but the stubborn Rhodians refused to surrender. Polioketes finally ordered that the siege machine be dismantled and sold and the money used to build the Colossus of Rhodes, one of the Seven Wonders of the ancient world.

In Rhodes we discovered a supermarket with an Asian section and we rejoiced because we had finished our stocks of noodles, curry pastes and spices. And on the outskirts of the old town we discovered a large weekly market where farmers from the surrounding valleys sold their produce from makeshift stalls and the trays of their trucks. The local fishermen were grouped together at one end. It was a noisy and good-humoured gathering, but bargaining with the tough traders was a battle that we mostly lost. We filled the freezer with pork and bacon before our return to Turkey.

At the castle built by the Knights of Saint John, I asked to see the bedrooms.

'They're not open to the public,' the guide, a Greek woman from Melbourne, informed me.

'Is that because they're not yet restored?' I asked.

'They're beautifully restored, but they're kept locked,' she replied.

'Why is that?' I persisted.

'Well, the manager became angry about something that recently happened in one of the bedrooms. You know,' she coyly explained.

Some people specialise in having sex in unlikely places like the Eiffel Tower, aeroplanes and confessionals or the tip of Saint Peters but I wished they could have ignored this particular medieval castle.

Maybe a time would come when we would grow tired of whitewashed alleys ablaze with sunlight, hibiscus and bougainvillea but at that moment, possibly as a contrast to the greyness of Turkey, we delighted in them. Lovely Lindos a few miles along the coast from the city of Rhodes, was such a place. But it was here that the temperature plummeted, the leaves of the deciduous trees covered the ground in a crackling carpet, and the first of the winter gales blew. It was time to hide.

We chose to spend our first Mediterranean winter in Fethiye (ancient Telmessus) on the Lycian coast of Turkey, mainly because of the protection offered by the enclosed bay along which the town is built. The setting is attractive, the town squeezed onto the narrow strip of land between the sea and the sheer rock walls that mark the wide base of the Taurus Mountains. Parks and gardens line the waterfront and disguise the ordinariness of the town, at least from the water, for Fethiye was flattened by an earthquake in 1957 and hurriedly rebuilt as rows of reinforced concrete boxes.

When we passed through in the summer on our way to the Dodecanese it was a bright and breezy tourist town, taking advantage of its location in the popular and beautiful area. There were outdoor restaurants, colourful gift shops crammed with the local crafts, water sellers and ice-cream vendors in traditional costumes, and balloon sellers and wandering minstrels in the parks.

By December most of the restaurants had shut and those that remained open had moved indoors. The tourist shops, too, had either closed or changed their stock to items that the local people needed. So the trinket seller now sold quilts and the T-shirt vendor sold raincoats and rubber boots and many of the tourists shops lined their walls with balls of angora, mohair and wool for the knitters of the town.

There were shops selling farm equipment that we had not noticed in the summer, and there were several with displays of gardening tools, heaters and bellows, paints and varnishes, horseshoes and saddlery. The ubiquitous *cayhanesi*, the tea shops, still functioned as before as clubs for the dour men of the town and surrounding farms who sat for hours sipping flavoured teas in the dark bars that the women never entered. From the teashops, young men in aprons dashed about the town bearing glasses of tea in silver holders on silver trays.

The people also seemed to have changed. Gone were the rather hip young things who appeared to be running the town in the summer. Gone, too, were the signs in German and we were no longer addressed in that language. Few people spoke English, however, so we had to battle along with sign language and the rudiments of Turkish. When Turkish is combined with a most confusing body language it is a difficult tongue to decipher.

A Turk saying 'yes' (*evet*), nods the head forward and down, and saying 'no' (*hayir*), nods it up and back. To us the differences between 'yes' and 'no' were barely noticeable and it took some time before we realised that raising the eyebrows in silence also meant 'no' and was not an indication of rudeness.

There were ten cruising yachts at anchor in the bay in front of the town and all were busy with maintenance that had been neglected during the summer. There was painting and varnishing to be done, engine repairs, sail repairs, the replacement of worn sheets and ropes, the control of rust or osmosis or rot, depending on the material of the hull. Our major concern was with condensation and the mould that grew when we were forced to keep the boat closed against the cold.

Cruising folk have three options in the European winters, the choice partly dictated by finances and partly by inclination. Some put their yachts 'on the hard', a suggestive expression which simply means 'on the land', others move to a marina, and some swing at anchor.

Apart from *Burramys* and *Syrah* who were with us in Fethiye, our friends were scattered. *Anaconda* was in Larnaca marina while JB and Rosa had flown home to New Orleans for the winter, *New Address* was also there, Col having returned to Adelaide. Woody and Ellen, no longer happy cruising since the death of their daughter, returned to Port Said to collect *Maisie Dotes* and then hurried through the Mediterranean and were already in the Caribbean.

Anhinga and *Sunbird* were at anchor in Preveza harbour in Greece. Don and Robyn on *Stylopora*, who returned to Cairns after Ambon, were now in Thailand, and Des and Laurie on *Panache* were preparing to leave the Maldives to sail to Oman and then up the Red Sea.

Halfway through December the tops of the mountains behind the town were covered in snow and in the early mornings their peaks glowed rosy-pink above curtains of mist. On the calm days we sat as if on a lake of glass, the snowy peaks perfect mirror images around us.

Often there were gales and along the three-kilometre fetch to the east the waves built if the wind blew from that direction. The yachts pitched and plunged so wildly that it became too dangerous to leave them. A particularly strong gale hit on Christmas Eve and plans to share the celebrations with *Burramys* and *Syrah* had to be postponed.

Normally we would have been sad spending our second Christmas without Velia but two days before we had received a letter from her with the glorious news that she and Graeme would be joining us somewhere in Greece at Easter. So we felt buoyant and joyous and immediately started making plans to arrive in Athens a week before them.

Most of the yachts wintering in Fethiye were English and they tended to stick together. The first to visit us was Catherine, who paddled across soon after our arrival.

'I've been told you're teachers,' she began. 'I've done some teaching myself but I didn't much like it. I'm really an intellectual. I came across to meet you because I hoped you would be intellectuals too. Are you?'

Catherine described her husband as a musician and composer, but we seldom saw him and only recognised him in the street as a phantom-like figure in a long fawn overcoat and woolly cap which almost completely hid his face. Without the coat and hat, he would have been a stranger to us.

The friction between John and Judith on *Dover* was sparked by any mention of John's once-beautiful, hand-knitted Aran pullover of exquisitely complicated design. The first time the couple came on board, I made the mistake of asking who had knitted it.

'Well, certainly not Judith,' John replied with a bitter edge to his voice. 'She can't knit.'

'Your mother knits for you, so why should I bother,' Judith snapped.

'At least you could mend it and wash it,' he answered, poking his fingers into a few of the larger holes.

'How can I do that when you sleep in the bloody thing,' his wife replied.

Turning to me she said, 'It's his security blanket. It's his bloody mother hugging him. That's why he can't take it off. That's why it's falling to bits.'

None of us saw much of Hans and Inge, a pleasant Swedish couple who were always busy on their boat, Inge as an artist, mainly in watercolours, and Hans as a freelance writer. They worked hard throughout the winters, returning to Sweden each summer to exhibit and to negotiate with publishers.

There was Pieter, a German single-hander, who moved into a hotel every time we had a gale. I envied him, but doubted that his behaviour was entirely shippy. And there were Tom and Lisa who tied their boat to the quay whenever it was calm in order to feed the three stray dogs that yachties before them had dumped.

The dogs loved yachties but they hated Turks. Some of the local fishermen, with their mates from a nearby construction site, spent their lunch breaks baiting the dogs, then belting them off with sticks. If they saw a yachtie approaching, they would saunter away whistling, pretending innocence.

If I was alone, the men would stop the baiting and stare at me with silent insolence. In this essentially male society, Turkish men believe that they must protect their women. It is something to do with honour and virility, so when they see a woman who walks alone with a confident step, they feel threatened. They also believe that western women have no sexual inhibitions. They are like prostitutes — trash. With Alan, tall and well-built beside me, there was seldom a problem, and if there was I would keep quiet because it was safer that way.

As the winter progressed, we grew fond of Wilson and Ayse on *Gladiator*. Like the Ancient Mariner, Wilson felt driven to tell of his brush with death and disaster in the Red Sea a decade before. Just north of Port Sudan, Wilson had made a navigational error and *Gladiator* sailed onto a reef.

The constant pounding on the rocks had holed the hull and the boat began to fill with water. Wilson had been a sheep farmer in Victoria and he was well prepared. He mixed mutton fat and cement and plugged the holes. With the bilges pumped dry, Wilson and his wife were able to kedge the yacht free and the couple sailed her to Cyprus for repairs.

Wilson's first wife had died in her 20s. Heartbroken, he had fled from London to Australia where he remained, taking out Australian citizenship and eventually buying the sheep station and marrying again. The experiences in the Red Sea had caused a permanent rift in the relationship, and Wilson and his second wife divorced. Now he was married to Ayse, a slim, attractive Turkish girl from Istanbul.

Ayse's large dark eyes shone with an intriguing intensity and she reminded me of the Young Turks, those idealists of the 1920s, who, fired by Atatürk's dream, had striven to bring about change in their orthodox and backward country. Ayse had a PhD (Economics) from the University of Istanbul. She was politically aware and critical of many aspects of Turkish life, especially after being arrested for accusing some of the top employees of the local PTT (postal department) of corruption. Her case had been called without any warning so that she had been unable to contact her brother, a barrister in Istanbul, to act in her defence, and hence had had to fight her own case.

Ayse was hesitant to talk about her experiences but they had clearly sobered her. Instead, she bombarded me with questions about the status of women in Australia and the rights of people who found themselves at loggerheads with authority. There were other questions as well. What was it like to cross an ocean? Was I ever afraid? Would she be able to work in Australia? Did I feel free there? Were there many Muslims there? Which law did they obey — Australian or Islamic?

Ayse was endearing: restless, intelligent, intense, and in love with Wilson.

'Ayse needs a challenge,' Wilson said hugging her. 'Possibly a baby would have been the answer but I had a vasectomy years ago — long before I met Ayse.'

'I knew that when I married you,' Ayse reminded him. 'I don't want a baby, Willy.'

'She's always talking about sailing to Australia,' Wilson continued, as if Ayse had left the cabin. 'But I'm 60 and she's only 30. She knows nothing of sailing, how tough it can be. I've grown tired of it. I just want to paddle about in the Mediterranean like all the other armchair sailors. I've crossed my oceans. I feel that I can't do it again.'

'Surely for me, you could do it, Wilson,' Ayse cajoled.

'You have no idea of the power of an angry ocean,' Wilson told her. 'We'd have to cross the Atlantic and the Pacific to reach Australia. It's on the other side of the world, my lovely Ayse.'

We discussed the options. Perhaps one could sail back along the same route as we had come. But no decisions were ever made.

Ayse liked to cook and, aboard *Gladiator* during the winter, we often ate hearty Turkish meals washed down with the rough Turkish wine and rounded off with fiery *raki*, which the Turks call 'Lion's Milk'. Often there were Turkish guests, like Ayse's girlfriend, Demet, a dentist in the town and the only dentist I have ever met who had a black gap where a tooth was missing in the front. There was also Hasan, a young friend of Ayse's brother.

'Have you been to Gallipoli?' he asked one night. We explained that we would stop there on our way to Istanbul in the spring.

'You must go there,' he stressed. 'The memorials are striking. It was after that famous battle that our leader became Atatürk, The Father of the Turks. Before that he was known as Mustafa Kemal.'

'And before that, simply as Mustafa!' Ayse chimed in.

'Yes,' Hasan replied. 'Every second man in Turkey is called Mustafa. When Atatürk was a student of mathematics in Salonika where he was born, his maths master was also called Mustafa along with several others, teachers and students. One day the teacher called our future leader to him and said, 'It's too confusing for both of us to be called Mustafa. You are more brilliant than I, so you will be called Mustafa Kemal — Mustafa of Perfection. I will remain plain Mustafa.' When he became our leader, though, he decreed that all men were to have two names to avoid confusion between the millions of Mustafas, Ahmets and Mehmets.'

'And Hasans,' Ayse joked.

'You're the first Australians I've met, apart from Wilson,' Hasan said. 'Your losses at Gallipoli were horrible. Why did you come here? It seems such a stupid thing to do — to come from the other side of the world to fight us, a people you did not know, and who never threatened you. Why did you come?'

Once a week, Fethiye bustled with a large market, most of it in the open air despite the cold and the muddy ground. On that day, the town filled with families from the surrounding valleys. They were solid peasant folk with their bloomers tucked into rubber boots because the roads were unsealed away from the centre of town. For warmth they wore layers of hand-knitted pullovers and shawls. The women covered their heads with scarves and knitted caps and the men wore hunters' caps or felt hats.

As the winter wore on, the villagers became less grave and serious towards us. They would laugh and joke and press extra produce into our bags while giving us a friendly pat on the shoulder. Wondrous were the stalls selling various types of Turkish delight and plump dried figs, huge walnuts and fruits preserved in syrups. Turkish bread is without variation all over Turkey. It is brilliant when fresh with a shiny, crackling crust but when it has been left for a few hours it becomes tough and rubbery and the Turks then soak it in milk.

On the way through the park we sometimes saw a man on a swing. He was about 50 years of age, trim and immaculate in a suit and tie. Like most Turkish men, he wore a neatly trimmed moustache. A serious man, he would stride purposefully from the business part of the town, place his briefcase carefully beside the swing support, settle himself on the seat, and swing — higher and higher and higher until it seemed that he must turn full circle. Then he would allow the swing to lose momentum until all movement ceased, when he would stand, straighten his clothes, retrieve the briefcase and walk briskly back the way he had come.

One day the winter calm of Fethiye was shattered by a cavalcade of cars with horns blaring as they processed slowly through the centre of town. I thought of funerals, but this was too noisy and the people were waving and cheering. At the head of the procession was an open car and in it stood a boy of about ten. He was dressed as a king, resplendent in crimson satin with an elaborate velvet cloak and a sparkling gold crown. The boy grinned and waved to the people who clapped and cheered him. I then thought of birthdays, and imagined it was Turkish custom for boys to be King for a Day.

'How sweet,' I said to Alan. 'I hope that the girls get to be Queen for a Day. That would only be fair.'

'Fairness has nothing to do with it,' Alan replied. 'The boy is on his way to be circumcised.'

The *sunnet* or circumcision is an important event in Turkey and seems to take place at any age, although most of the boys we saw were around seven or eight. A party is held after the ceremony but it seemed to me that the one in whose honour the party is given is hardly in a fit state to enjoy it.

On another occasion, we noticed preparations being made for an event in the park.

'What's happening?' we asked.

'A concert,' they replied. 'You must come tonight. The Nightingale will sing.'

When we arrived, the park was packed with people of all ages. Everyone stood because there were no seats, apart from a few packing cases that those with foresight had brought. On the makeshift stage an ancient 'living treasure' was playing a traditional wind instrument. He played and played, so fragile and determined. The people stood in rapt silence, their collective soul attuned to the old man and his music, and when he was gently assisted from the stage by two young men, the people clapped thoughtfully for a long time.

The Nightingale was a surprise. We expected a woman in traditional costume, but here was an elegant and beautiful blonde dressed in a skin-tight, shimmering black sheath and stiletto heels. Her voice was strong and clear and she sang through a lengthy repertoire of Turkish songs with excellent crowd control. This was just as well, because the men in the audience did amazing things while she sang.

Some danced in a trance-like state, their eyes upon The Nightingale, while others ran onto the stage to kiss her hand and present her with flowers. She sang on regardless. Men, young and old, clapped and shuffled to the beat. Some lit sparklers and waved them as they danced. The stage attendants set off crackers and spun catherine wheels with rocket-like fireworks that sprayed sparks over sections of the audience. People slapped at their hair and clothing. One man fell to the ground and when two policemen failed to make him stand, they left him there and continued to gyrate to the beat. And leathery old guys, their desires rekindled, clicked their fingers and stomped beside their plump and silent wives.

On the opposite side of the large bay on which Fethiye stands is an exceptionally lovely place called Skopea Liman, known to the yachties as Fethiye lagoon. It is like an inland lake surrounded by steep slopes and fed by numerous mountain streams. There are dozens of small secluded anchorages with evocative names like Tomb Bay, Ruin Bay, Wall Bay, Tersane Creek and Yassica Adalari.

The area is a wilderness inhabited by a couple of sheep farmers and their families. There are three basic waterside restaurants established by some enterprising peasants to cater for the yachts that gather there in the summer months. Deep in the far end of the lagoon is the tiny ramshackle village of Gocek, its minaret like a beacon clearly visible as one approaches by boat.

Towards the third week in January the weather was perfect with clear skies, hot sunny days and a blissful calm. The lagoon became irresistible so we up-anchored and sailed across to some of the places we had enjoyed in the summer. *Windigo* was the only yacht there, and the serenity and charm of the lagoon was bewitching.

Several times each day we tuned into a Greek weather forecast given in English, but we shrugged off the warnings of 'cold conditions with leet and no'. The balmy weather continued and newborn lambs gambolled along the beach, tossing their heads in dismay when they tasted the salt water. Then quite suddenly the barometer plummeted and we headed for the village of Gocek where we knew we could sit out a blow in safety.

Snow began to fall the next day. Soft flakes like thistledown soon covered *Windigo* and built up on the spreaders before falling with soft thuds to the deck whenever the boat rocked. All was silent and still, as though the village slept.

The next morning Gocek was a huddle of soft white mounds in a soft white world. Only the minaret stood clearly defined. Snow drifts had built up in the cockpit and on the aft deck and the buckets of fresh water we had collected for washing were frozen over. Ashore, adults and children were excitedly building snowmen and pelting each other.

'Thirty-seven years!' one old man shouted at us, almost losing his front teeth in his excitement. 'Thirty-seven years, no snow.' He counted off three tens and a seven with his gnarled hands.

Ismail, the teacher

Kayaköy is a ruined Greek village on the other side of the mountain range behind Fethiye. In the 1920s, 25 000 Greeks lived there, but they were driven out by the Turks. Such is the hatred of the Turks for the Greeks that, despite the poverty of the area, the Turks have always refused to live in the village. However, a couple of tourist restaurants have recently opened on the outskirts, and the Turks charge the tourists an entrance fee to the village in the summer months.

We took a taxi to the top of the mountain range before hiking down the other side. In the foothills we came upon a small school — a one-roomed building set in a large yard in the corner of which was a rockery ablaze with flowers. Beside it, a teacher sat reading to a group of eight children of varying ages. He looked up as we approached, smiled and waved, and called out in perfect English, 'Please come in and meet the children. It's good for them to meet strangers.' His name was Ismail. He was handsome in an Omar Sharif fashion and seemingly just as urbane. We sat on the grass beside him as he introduced each of his small charges.

'This is Yusuf. He's ten and just learning to read.'

'Here's Hussein. He's also ten but he's just started school.'

'This is Ali.' He ruffled a small boy's hair. 'You're a good lad, Ali,' he said, smiling at the boy. He turned to us. 'Well, he isn't really. But he tries hard.'

'Now meet Rifki, who is 12. This is a good day because he is here. He'll be here for another week, then he'll go. Rifki comes from a family of nomads so he seldom gets a chance to attend, although he sometimes goes to schools in other places.'

'Is there just the one girl?' I asked.

'Yes,' Ismail replied. 'This is my favourite, Handan.' He gave her a hug and they all laughed. And so it went on until all had been introduced.

We drank apple tea in the sun and while the boys played and Handan sat quietly with us, Ismail told us something of his life. He, too, had grown up with a black nomad tent as his home, but early in life he had discovered that he must escape from the nomadic lifestyle if he were to prosper. He was aware of the tourists and the opportunities they provided to make money, so he taught himself four languages, English, French, Italian and German, all of which he now spoke fluently. In the summer he worked in the tourist industry, often travelling outside Turkey for his employer, and in the winter he taught in the little school.

'I love the teaching best,' he said. 'I look forward to the winters in this pretty valley.'

'Aren't all children supposed to go to school?' I asked. 'I read that universal education was one of Atatürk's reforms.'

'That's true,' Ismail replied. 'But sometimes the Turkish people have other ideas, and in this area the children are kept at home to work on the tobacco farms. Rifki, of course, is a nomad but the other seven are from wealthier families. There are 20 children enrolled, but not all attend each day.'

'It's sad that there is only one girl,' I commented.

'Little Handan is my niece. That's why she's here. If I hadn't talked my brother into letting her attend, there would be no girls.'

At Kayaköy the flaking whitewashed alleys and crumbling walls of the once splendid Greek village were picturesque, but depressing in their neglect and emptiness. We sat beside the well in the silent main square and imagined the once lively tavernas, the cries and the laughter and the clip-clop of the donkeys as they struggled under baskets of supplies up the steep alleyways. But the only sound in the still air was made by a Turkish workman banging nails into the corrugated iron roof of one of the restaurants.

Halfway through February we spent a week exploring inland, leaving the key to *Windigo* with Burramys John, as he was now known to most of us, and rigging up a second anchor on the bow in case we dragged in a gale. The bus followed a tortuous route above the snowline of the mighty mountains and down the other side to the ugly industrial town of Denizli.

The man opposite, who had also joined the bus in Fethiye, waved his arm to encompass the broad sweep of the range and said, 'Poor people. All poor people.' We nodded. Not only were they poor but they were tiny, their backs bent under huge loads of firewood, brambles and hay, like beasts of burden.

Life was tough in the winter in the damp stone hovels that sat in muddy yards. There were donkeys and a few camels but these too appeared stunted and lethargic. In the pockets of soil carved from the rocky mountainside a few men struggled with single-furrow, horse-drawn ploughs in the freezing air. Atatürk had said, 'The peasant is the master of the country', but these struggling people may not have agreed.

At Denizli the bus driver walked along the aisle with a large bottle of strongly scented lemon essence, carefully pouring a measured amount of the refreshant into each passenger's cupped hands like a priest giving Holy Communion. We were unsure of how to use it so we watched the other passengers. The technique seemed to entail splashing it quickly onto the face and rubbing the remainder on hands and wrists. Alan and I would have preferred eau de cologne but lemon essence was used on every bus we caught.

So strange and ethereal and foreign is Pamukkale, 64 kilometres farther on, that it could be on another planet. Shimmering white cascades of petrified waterfalls form castles of crystal that rise from the middle of a flat brown plain. They sparkle and glisten as the mist rises from the stepped pools, the hot water from the thermal springs laden with calcium oxide. It is as if the rice terraces around Sian in Bali were turned to crystal and powdered with snow and piled up one on top of the other in a glittering heap.

We did not swim despite the tempting hot water because we feared undressing in the freezing air, and none of the pools was deep enough to cover the body completely. Within walking distance of 'The Cotton Castles', as they are called, are the splendid ruins of Hierapolis, an ancient Greek city.

The goddess Aphrodite was the symbol of sensual love and all things exquisitely feminine. People came from afar to worship her at the beautiful marble city of Aphrodisias, which had been built in her honour. The fine stadium alone could hold 30 000 people and we marvelled at the magnitude of the ruins and the grace of the city's design.

Farther on at Selçuk we hoped to see the camel wrestling for which the town is famous but Turks tend to tell you what they think you want to hear and when we arrived there, the camel wrestling was not on. 'Maybe tomorrow,' they said.

The museum was worth visiting, however. We found the tiny clay Priapus with his outsize penis that we had seen on postcards all along the coast of Turkey, and the larger marble one where he balances a tray of fruit on his mighty organ. There were two impressive statues of Artemis, the goddess of fertility with her three rows of breasts, or maybe they are eggs for they lack nipples. And a few kilometres down the road was our main reason for making the trip in the first place, the marble city of Ephesus.

Turkey has more Greek sites than Greece, and more Roman sites than Italy. Only a small percentage have been excavated and Ephesus is still being discovered. But what there is to see is magnificent. Even the baths and brothels are imposing, but nothing more so than the Roman Library of Celcus, a white marble creation so grandiose that it towers over the city like a sentinel. Saint John brought the Virgin Mary to Ephesus and Saint Paul preached his gospels here, but the people preferred Artemis and shouted him down.

There were few tourists so we were able to fill the empty streets and squares with nubile maidens strolling beside their toga-clad companions while gladiators gossiped in the sun outside the baths. We imagined chariots bouncing noisily along the marble-paved Acadiana and it seemed that we could hear Caesar calling to Cleopatra from Zilve, near Ankara, *'Vini, Vidi, Vici!'* Two condoms, swinging in the breeze outside the main entrance to a brothel, brought us back to the present.

On the walk back to Selçuk, we were offered a lift by a man who we thought was merely showing kindness.

'I'll take you to my carpet shop,' he said when we were underway.

'No, thank you,' said Alan. 'We're not interested in buying a carpet.'

Sitting in his shop a few minutes later we puzzled over how we came to be there, having successfully eluded carpet sellers all along the Turkish coast.

'We're not buying a carpet,' Alan said through clenched teeth. 'We can't carry any more luggage.'

'Of course not,' I replied.

Aslan was the man's name. He proudly told us that it meant 'lion' as he proceeded to spread carpets before us, explaining the differences in dyes and designs. There were Bergama rugs based on ancient geometric patterns, expensive pure silk carpets with intricate and delicate designs, rugs woven by the nomads of the Taurus Mountains. They were all beautiful.

When we showed our purchase to the family with whom we were staying (they also owned a carpet shop) they laughed.

'Aslan said that his mother wove it,' I told them defensively.

'Aslan's mother died years ago, and she never made carpets,' they replied.

Alan seldom mentions the carpet but when he does, he refers to it as the yellow carpet.

'But it's not yellow. It's basically brown,' I protested the first time he said it.

'It's our "egg on face" carpet,' he replied.

At the end of our stay in Turkey we still felt that we did not understand the Turks. They remained enigmatic and mysterious. Atatürk saw them as conservative, fatalistic, stubborn and dour, but that was more than 70 years ago when his plans for change were agonisingly slow. To us they were mostly friendly and kind, but always restrained.

Intuitively I felt that things were not as Atatürk would have liked. How democratic was this democracy? How secular was this state? Most nights on Turkish television we saw rows of handcuffed prisoners, their backs to the cameras, their heads bowed. They were passive and subdued. As the camera panned over neatly arranged piles of guns and ammunition, we were told they were terrorists. The neat lines of weapons were always the same. Only the prisoners changed.

Also on television we watched Turkey's elegant, blonde, westernised Prime Minister, Ms Tansu Çiller, talking to her people and I wondered how she was received in the homes of the Muslim fundamentalists. At official functions, she was often flanked by the wily Süleyman Demeril and the plump and pompous Turgut Özal. Who really holds the power?

May 27 is a Turkish national holiday known as Revolutionary Day to commemorate the bloodless coup that removed Prime Minister Menderes from power in 1960. One of his many repressive measures had been censorship, and editors and reporters who published articles critical of the government had been arrested. Yet while we were in Fethiye, the outspoken editor of one of Turkey's most influential newspapers was shot in Ankara, the capital. The people mourned his death and in the town hall in Fethiye a large blank book was placed on a table beneath the dead man's black-draped photograph. Each day, lines of brave Turks wrote their feelings in the book, usually just a few lines, sometimes more, sometimes a poem. Then they signed it with their name and address.

So it was with mixed feelings that we sailed away from Turkey in the early spring of 1993. Maybe we would find some of the answers when we returned to Turkey to visit Gallipoli and Istanbul in the summer.

CHAPTER 8

through the Dodecanese and the Cyclades
reunion in Piraeus • where is Windigo?
monasteries at Meteora • Pelion Mountains

S ailors disregard the ancient Coptic calendar at their peril.
On the day we planned to leave Turkey to cross the Aegean,
the Coptics forecast eight days of bad weather. On the sixth day,
however, it cleared. We crossed to Rhodes and the next morning
proceeded west through the Dodecanese to the island of Simi
where the monks live beside the bay in a monastery that resembles a grand hotel on the shores of an Italian lake.

The island of Astapalaia, a day's sail farther on, is barren
except for isolated clumps of grass that provide fodder for the
long-tailed sheep. Not for these ruminants the leisurely graze of
sheep in pastures — they have to run from one sparse clump to
the next to survive. The young lambs are segregated from the
ewes during the day because they are unable to maintain the
frantic pace of their mothers, whose eyes have the hungry look
of predators.

Islands dotted our route to the Cyclades. The weather was still
cold, and snow covered the highest peak of many, usually called
Mount Olympus. Scattered over the sparkling Aegean, the islands
were alluring, but we had no time to linger as we hurried to
Athens before Easter to meet Velia and Graeme. Some islands
were winter brown, others already green. Tiny villages, white
and cubist, clung to precipitous slopes and hugged the shores of
protected bays in which we were the only yacht.

The island of Serifos floated beneath misty clouds that inter-
mittently hid from view the white *chora* clinging to the highest
peak. When the sun broke through the mist, a rainbow played over

the valley that swept down to Livardi on the bay. We had made good time and could afford to rest for a couple of days before continuing to Piraeus. There were no tourists, and we walked alone through gentle valleys where newborn lambs bunted their mothers' bellies and gambolled in daisy-strewn meadows.

Piraeus is the port for Athens, ten kilometres inland. The port city covers a promontory in the Saronic Gulf and is protected from the wider Aegean by the island of Salamis. A guidebook states that 'the only reason to go to Piraeus is to catch a boat and to eat fish', but I do not agree. For those interested in boats and the sea, Piraeus is an intriguing mixture of the romance and enterprise associated with shipping. The harbour is awash with ferries and liners from Crete, the Dodecanese, the Cyclades, the Aegean, Italy and other parts of the Mediterranean, and the surrounding streets are crammed with travellers from dozens of countries. There are fish restaurants and shops selling a range of the useful and the exotic.

Still commonly known by its Turkish name of Paşalimani, Zea lies on the other side of the promontory. Zea marina, built around the suburb's circular bay, is packed with the cruisers and yachts of the wealthy. One yacht, called *The Other Woman*, carried a four-wheel-drive vehicle, a motorbike, and two runabouts labelled *The Mistress* and *Lady in Waiting*.

It was into that jetset world of brass buttons and blazers that we sailed to pick up Velia and Graeme who were to arrive from Venice by overnight ferry. Despite our comparatively humble vessel, we were treated with respect and we found the cost reasonable for a short stay.

Velia and Graeme were expected to arrive late in the afternoon, but instead turned up halfway through the morning, having been given a lift by the crew of the overnight ferry. We were caught unprepared but it did not matter. We were ecstatic. But Velia looked pale and drawn and when I asked if she were feeling unwell, Graeme replied in an ominous voice, 'Velia has something to tell you.'

'My God!' I thought. 'She has some incurable disease, they're getting a divorce, she's lost her job, she wants to return home immediately.'

'I forgot to bring your radio part,' she sobbed. 'I had it ready to pack but I simply walked out of the door and left it there. I'm so sorry.'

Alan and I were speechless. Our HF radio had developed a fault six months previously which meant that we could pick up only those channels that ended in even numbers. We had rung the firm in Sydney and arranged for a new panel to be sent to Velia. We had been counting on it, but there was nothing else to do but hug her and kiss away her tears.

The following morning the four of us set sail for Epidavros in warm spring sunshine. It was too early for the annual festival, but the open-air theatre 30 kilometres inland is a fine piece of classical architecture that stands alone. Its acoustics are so perfect that a faint whisper on stage can be heard in the back rows.

The island of Hydra is barren of all trees. I find it difficult to believe that it has always been so, fearing that the Greeks probably chopped them down to build ships. We walked on carpets of wild flowers where the film *Boy on a Dolphin* was made. Hydra is the home of artists and some of the rich and famous. While close to the coast of the Peloponnese we also visited lovely Poros with its tranquil anchorages in Vidhi Bay, where the fragrance from the scented lemon groves along the shore at Galatas wafted on the air.

When we returned to the island of Serifos, Alan and I relaxed on board for a couple of days while Velia and Graeme hiked to the *chora* and explored the green valleys. On Mikonos, that most popular of all Greek islands, the town is a dazzling white cluster of cubist shapes, narrow alleyways, and touches of brilliant blue. There are enormous tame pelicans with multicoloured beaks, pink and yellow and blue. The ponderous birds wander into the tavernas scrounging for food. Perhaps we would hate Mikonos in the summer, but in the early spring it was a delightful place to be.

The island of Delos, a few miles off the coast of Mikonos, was the holy island of the ancient Greeks and the birthplace of the divine twins, Artemis and Apollo. The harbour is unsafe for yachts in windy weather so we caught the small tourist ferry from the harbour at Mikonos. The skipper and the mate were men of advanced years, dishevelled, rough and tough, with an easy swagger and bold laughter, and they resembled pirates. They inspired confidence in Alan and me, but Velia and Graeme viewed them with concern.

A strong *meltemi* had blown for days. The seas were short and steep and the little ferry plunged and heaved as she fought her way through the waves. Drums of oil slid wildly across the cabin floor, forcing the frightened passengers to dodge about the cabin like demented soccer players or to lift their legs onto the seats for protection. The skipper and his mate ploughed on regardless, ignoring the yells of pain, the bruised shins and the flying missives that were thrown loose from shelves and lockers.

Waves broke over the boat with shuddering thuds, and every few seconds we appeared to sink into green water. Several passengers turned grey in the face and some began to vomit, while those who had been caught outside at the start, now stood dripping miserably over the floor.

'I'm frightened,' Velia whispered. 'Does it ever get as bad as this on *Windigo*?'

An Englishman in a new Panama hat loudly proclaimed that the whole adventure was suicidal and that the authorities should have cancelled the ferry. He obviously did not know that ferries are never cancelled in Greece if there are tourists about.

Conditions on the way back were only marginally better. Although everyone arrived safely, albeit bruised and shaken, Alan and I were the only passengers to thank the two wild seamen for the safe passage. One reciprocated with such a hearty slap on the back that Alan was sent reeling down the gangplank.

Siros will long remain in our memories as the island where *Windigo* floated away. With Velia and Graeme, we had spent the day sightseeing at the town of Ermoupolis, 30 kilometres from the anchorage. Late in the afternoon, the bus rounded the last bend above the bay of Finikas and we saw with horror that *Windigo* was not where we had left her at anchor.

In a state of shock, we scanned the harbour. Then we saw her — tied to a mooring close to the wharf. As we approached we noticed that seaweed littered her foredeck and that the anchor chain was draped in an untidy bundle on the bow.

A tall young man with sun-bleached blond hair and peeling nose greeted us.

'Looking for a yacht?' he asked, laughing at our startled faces. 'I'm Lucas Hofman.' We introduced ourselves and he explained what had happened.

'Your boat was blown across the bay in the 30-knot winds that blew here today. She was close to those rocks over there. I couldn't rescue her alone so I asked the owner of that red motor cruiser at the wharf to help me. We managed to haul your anchor on board, and then we towed *Windigo* across and tied her to Peter's mooring. Peter's the owner of the red motor cruiser. Michael, that young man on the white yacht, also helped.'

We had heard horror stories of outrageous salvage claims for yachts rescued in the Mediterranean, so we were particularly nervous about the owner of the shiny red cruiser, which had the name *Dirty Diana* flamboyantly emblazoned across its stern. Lucas was embarrassed when we offered him money and he assured us that Michael would not consider accepting any payment either.

'All I know about Peter is that he seems rich,' Lucas told us. 'So he doesn't need the money. That may help. Oh, and his wife's father owns an airline.'

The problem had to be faced, though. The alternative was to simply sail away in the night and hope that nothing happened.

It was tempting, but I doubted that the two lawyers aboard would agree to anything risky.

Peter was a good-looking, confident young Greek who spoke perfect English. He laughed gaily when we asked how we could repay him for his kindness. Throwing an arm around Alan's shoulders, he said, 'Take me and my wife out to dinner! You can tell us of your adventures. We'd like that. By the way, my wife's name is Diana.'

'Can't wait to meet her,' Alan said to me as we walked across to the line of waterside tavernas bordering the bay. We chose the most elegant and ordered a Greek banquet for eight people for the following evening.

Diana was stunning. A New York Greek, she was poised, vivacious and pretty, with mischievous black eyes. When the waiter arrived she sprang from her chair and warmly embraced him, ruffling his hair and talking excitedly in Greek.

'We played together as children,' she explained. 'This is my father's island. He still owns a lot of it. He used to bring us here from New York when we were children. Now I come because I love it here.'

As a young man Peter had joined the Greek merchant navy. On two occasions he had been shipwrecked and he spoke with feeling of the risks others had taken to rescue him. When we asked him if he were still in the navy, he replied that he now ran a business in London and another smaller one on the island.

Lucas Hofman was a Dutch computer programmer on leave for the summer. He had sailed his Australian-designed catamaran single-handed from Bari in southern Italy and was heading for Istanbul. Because we would follow a similar route, it was likely we would meet again. Michael, from a wealthy Scandinavian family, was working on a charter yacht to gain experience before buying a small boat of his own.

The taverna filled, the music grew wilder, the people danced and sang, the *retsina* flowed, the courses kept coming and we all grew merry.

'This is a great taverna,' I shouted to Peter above the din.

'Yes, you and Alan chose well. It's the best on the island.' Then he added with a grin, 'I own it.'

After stops at the islands of Kithnos and Kea, we watched the Temple of Poseidon on Cape Sounion guide us to the anchorage at its base. This is one of the most imposing sites (and sights) in Greece. On the highest point, the remaining 16 massive columns of the Temple of Poseidon, built in the 5th century, guard the entrance to the Saronic Gulf and sailors for centuries have said a prayer as they passed beneath — even the sceptics on *Windigo*.

After wandering at will through the Greek islands for a month, we returned to Piraeus so that Velia and Graeme could catch their flight to Sydney. It was a sad farewell in the dark and cold pre-dawn at Athens airport and we wondered when we would see them again. Later that morning Alan and I sailed around Cape Sounion once more and then continued north to Porto Rafti, a pretty bay about 16 miles from the cape. The weather remained cold, overcast and windy, and we were sad, so we stayed on board for a couple of days feeling sorry for ourselves. Then we provisioned and sailed north along the Evvoia Channel.

In mythology, Poseidon raised his trident and, with a mighty blow, severed the long island of Evvoia from the mainland of Greece. Evvoia became his favourite island and he lived there in a fantastic palace with his wife, Amphitrite.

The winding channel thus created narrows to bridge-width halfway along at Khalkis before taking a dogleg turn into the Gulf of Volos. It was down the Evvoia Channel that invading armies from the north travelled to attack Athens and southern Greece, and many were the bloody battles fought along its shores, particularly at the Pass of Thermopylae and the Field of Marathon where the burial mounds are clearly visible from the sea.

A disturbing aspect of the channel for sailors is the contrariness of the currents. On some days they can change as many as 14 times, so it was with some trepidation that we approached the bridge at Khalkis and anchored a short distance off. Alan contacted the controller by radio.

'*Kalimera*. This is the yacht *Windigo*. When do you think you will open the bridge?'

'Don't know,' the controller replied. 'Could be soon, could be later. Maybe tomorrow.'

'Is that because *Windigo* is the only boat waiting to go through?' Alan asked.

'No. It's because we can't anticipate the currents. You must stand by your radio until we call you.'

The rest of the day passed in radio silence. We read and waited. I stood radio watch until midnight when Alan took over. Dozing off, I heard the crackle.

'*Windigo. Windigo*. Be ready to proceed at 0100 hours.'

The closer we came to the narrow neck the more pronounced were the currents. We felt *Windigo* being thrown off course, and Alan, at the helm, battled to control her. Then, above us, we saw a couple of hundred people lining the shore on both sides, a surprising sight at that hour of the morning. We presumed that boats passing through the bottleneck often provided an exciting spectacle if the helmsman lost control.

'Reminds me of Ballina,' Alan shouted.

Years before, crossing the bar at Ballina on Australia's east coast, we had had a similar experience. Unknown to us, the coastguard had closed the bar because of the dangerous seas. Somehow, word had spread through the town that a yacht was attempting to enter and the townspeople had lined the breakwater and watched in silence as *Windigo* surfed down waves and battled the maelstrom at the entrance.

Volos is the town from which Jason and the Argonauts set sail in the *Argo*, and, in the square beside the harbour, a bronze model of their ship commemorates the event. Achilles also set sail from this bay on his journey to Troy. It is an attractive place with a palm-fringed promenade along the waterfront and thickly forested mountains behind. We left *Windigo* tied to the quay while we explored inland.

On the edge of the Plain of Thessaly, in the foothills of the Pindos Mountains, are the curious rock formations of Meteora. The rock pencils soar high into the air, singly and in clusters, and the monks have built monasteries on the tips of the highest and most inaccessible.

We stayed in the picturesque village of Kastraki which nestles at the foot of the vertiginous pinnacles in a sylvan valley soft with butterflies. Storks had built their nests on lampposts and isolated outcrops, and from the balcony of our room in a small family hotel we could watch the parents feeding their young in a feverish regurgitating ritual.

Not long after our arrival the landlady asked, 'Have you brought a skirt with you?'

'No,' I replied, wondering why she had asked.

'That's OK,' she said. 'There are several hanging beside the front door. You may borrow one. Women can't enter the monasteries in jeans.'

'Are men permitted to enter in jeans?' I asked.

'Of course,' she laughed.

Early the next morning, we followed the winding track to the summit. There were signs saying, 'Please do not shout. Preserve the unequalled character of this area.' But I would have liked to shout — for spring, for joy, for simply being in that spectacular place, for Alan's hand in mine, as well as for the echo that would have bounced from the rock walls and rung around the valley.

There are six monasteries open to the public. All except one are occupied by secretive monks. The Rousanou Monastery, which is for nuns, is described on a sign at its base as 'a nannery'. The arcane places date from the 14th century, but even before that time solitary anchorites had lived in the caves there.

To make the monasteries impregnable, access had originally been by wooden scaffolding and a series of ladders wedged precariously between the rocks. Later, the monks and any visitors courageous enough to make the ascent were winched aloft in nets at the end of long ropes. The nets and windlasses are now used for hauling supplies as steps have been cut into the rocks for easier access for visitors.

Some of the monasteries are cantilevered from the rockface, so it was easy to imagine the terror of swinging at the end of a hemp rope over a yawning gorge hundreds of metres deep while the rope slipped and groaned on the wooden winch.

Outside the first monastery I pulled the skirt over my jeans as Alan watched in amused silence and I squirmed as a serious man commented, 'It's gratifying to see women respecting the Greek Orthodox faith. Thank you.'

The monastery courtyards were leafy retreats, often with orange or lemon groves. The churches, however, were invariably gruesome with Byzantine murals and frescoes depicting the unseemly things done to martyrs, like impaling, boiling alive, cutting in half, or turning on stretch wheels while the faces of the victims and the torturers remained equally impassive.

We saw a kitchen and a charnel house and, in the distance, the monks' prison, although one wonders what crime a monk can commit while perched on a perilous pinnacle. There were collections of icons and saintly relics, vestments and crucifixes, and a minute testament produced by a monk with a magnifying glass and the patient piety of the zealot.

I have often fantasised about being in a restaurant when the waiter approaches bearing a bottle of fine wine on a silver tray and says, 'With the compliments of the management.' The closest I have come to realising the dream was on the way down to Kastraki from Meteora. Almost at the bottom, we stopped to eat at the first taverna we saw. The meal in the late afternoon under spreading plane trees was excellent, and we were on our second bottle of beer when the waiter approached bearing a silver tray on which was a third bottle.

'With the compliments of Costos,' he said.

How could we drink yet another bottle of beer? Who was Costos? Then we remembered.

Costos was the Zorba-like character we had met the previous day in a glade on the outskirts of Kastraki where he had been collecting water from a mountain spring.

'Where are you from?' he had asked.

'From Australia,' we replied.

'That's far away! That's 30 hours flying time away!'

'We didn't fly. We sailed,' we told him.

'How long did it take?' Costos asked.

'We left our home port of Sydney in May 1990, three years ago.'

'*Ela!* What a hobby!' he shouted.

So we asked Costos if he had a hobby.

'Oh yes,' he replied. 'I own a taverna.'

It was purely by chance that we chose Costos's taverna for our late afternoon meal.

Behind and to the east of Volos is a mountain area called Pelion which is lush with orchards, walnut and chestnut trees, and forests of oak and beech. Icy streams trickle over rocky beds and tracks cobbled in river stones link the tiny villages. Many of these were established in the 13th century when they had formed a semi-autonomous district at the time of the Turkish invasion. The Turks probably found it too bothersome to destroy the isolated mountain settlements, so the inhabitants had been left in relative peace to become a centre of Greek culture that was to provide an impetus to the revival of folk art and traditional architecture.

It was mainly for the latter that we made the journey into the remote hills, because up there the people live in traditional timber houses with roofs of grey-green slate. The Pelion area above Volos is protected by a World Heritage listing and at the villages of Makrinitsa and Portaria there are splendid examples of carved and painted decoration and stained-glass inserts. Curving chimneys, heavy iron and opaque white glass chandeliers and intricately beamed and buttressed ceilings are typical features.

When it was time to return to the warmth of Volos at sea level we asked an elderly woman when the next bus was due.

'*Dhen ksero!*' ('I don't know!') she said with a friendly shrug and a rocking of her outstretched hands. Nearby, in a warm patch of sunlight grew a cherry tree laden with ripe black fruit and we gorged until a passing motorist driving a small red car yelled out, 'Volos?'.

It seemed not to occur to our driver that we could not understand more than a few words of Greek, for the elderly man chatted without pausing for breath all the way down the mountain side. He laughed gaily and waved his arms in a disturbingly cavalier fashion as he negotiated the hairpin bends at a terrifying speed. He bore out what we had always said — never trust those who drive red cars because they are invariably daredevils.

The Sporades Islands lie in a curving chain, except for Skyros and Skyropoula, halfway down the coast of Evvoia. They are unlike the other Aegean islands, being pine-covered and soft in profile. Skiathos, the first island on the Greek side, had too many tourists so we sailed past to Skopelos where thick pines soughed in the breeze and we had our first swim of the season in the sudden 33-degree heat. For us, the islands of the Sporades, although beautiful, lacked the zing, the clarity and the deft touch of the other Aegean islands.

Sixty miles farther on, the large island of Limnos is halfway between Greece and Turkey and almost at the mouth of the Dardanelles. From a distance its low hills, burnt-ochre and brown in the heat of early summer, reminded us of inland Australia. Perhaps the island had been green a fortnight before, but summer had arrived suddenly and the days were once again hot and still.

In days of yore Limnos had fallen into disrepute as a result of the so-called 'Limnion Deeds'. The women of Limnos had become angry with Aphrodite and they had refused to worship her because she was making her husband miserable with her numerous affairs. Aphrodite, not a goddess to be trifled with, was resentful and inflicted the women with a terrible smell, so pungent that their menfolk refused to have anything to do with them, preferring the captive women from Thrace.

The women of Limnos were so enraged that they drugged the island wine and slit the sleeping men's throats. When Jason and the Argonauts arrived at Limnos, they found an island of frustrated women, and so had a merry old time repopulating Limnos. One presumes that the smell had disappeared by that stage, or that Aphrodite took pity on her sisters.

The evening before we were to leave Limnos for the Dardanelles, a German skipper dropped his anchor on ours.

'We're leaving at 5 a.m.,' Alan called out to him.

'So?'

'You've dropped your anchor over ours.'

'I have not!' the German replied. 'Do you think I don't know where I dropped it?'

In the grey of the following dawn, we laughed when we looked over the stern and saw the German in his underpants stagger on deck to reset his anchor.

CHAPTER 9

we remember at Gallipoli
trouble in the Sea of Marmara
at Bebek in the Bosphorus • Istanbul

The Dardanelles is a narrow, winding strait that links the Aegean Sea with the Sea of Marmara. It was known to the ancients as the Hellespont, while the Turks today call it Canak-kale Bogazi. The entrance to the strait, which has featured prominently in the affairs of humankind since ancient times, is both impressive and sobering.

On the tip of the Gallipoli Peninsula stands the colossal Turkish war memorial, a silent sentinel of four towering granite columns joined across the top by a massive granite slab. It is stark, lonely and grand. A little farther inland stands the British memorial, a soaring single column of white marble, and in the distance you can see the blurred shapes of other memorials rising from the scrubby, pine-dotted hills.

The ancient city of Troy once stood on the Asiatic side and from *Windigo* we could see the two sepulchral mounds that Homer wrote about in the *Iliad* and referred to in the *Odyssey*. There are several tumuli ashore but only the two largest are visible from the water. They are supposed to contain the bones of Achilles and his friend, Patroclus.

To us it was wondrous that these 'great and glorious mounds' were still there, despite the battles that have raged over them, and the zeal of modern-day archaeologists to uncover their secrets.

Fierce currents, headwinds and heavy shipping make the Dardanelles a challenging stretch of water for those in small vessels. We were passing through a giant crack in the earth between two continents and I thought of the earthquakes that had moved the seabed and flattened towns and cities. Despite these, though, no less than 46 strata of civilisation have been identified by the archaeologists in and around Troy.

It was at Çanakkale that the Persian king, Xerxes, built a bridge of boats across the Dardanelles to land his troops in Thrace. Today you look across at the giant figure of a soldier painted on the hillside at Gallipoli. Under him in large white letters is written: 'This earth you thus tread unawares is where an age sank. Bow and listen. This quiet mound is where the heart of a nation throbs.'

On the Çanakkale side, on another hill, is painted '18th March 1915' which is the day on which Turks celebrate the Battle of Gallipoli. It is indeed a sombre place, a reminder of death and mourning, of muffled drums and last posts, requiems and remembrances.

Because we arrived in Çanakkale on 26 May 1993, Revolutionary Day, everything was shut. Çanakkale is the clearing-in port of the Dardanelles so we flew the yellow pratique flag and waited for something to happen. Within a few minutes a young man arrived in a dinghy. His moustache was untrimmed, giving his face a tough appearance.

'I'm your agent. You can call me Sammy,' he said as he climbed on board.

'We don't want an agent,' Alan told him.

'Then you must sit on your yacht for the next two days,' Sammy replied, looking pleased with himself. 'The port officials are all on holiday.'

He and Alan settled on a price of $30 and we handed over our documents to be stamped. Sammy returned within the hour with everything completed.

'Oh, Mr Alan. So sorry. Now you must pay me $80.' Sammy whined.

He told a story about having to pay this one, that one and the other one.

'You must have known all this when you quoted $30,' Alan

pointed out. 'Besides, I don't believe you. We agreed on a price. We shook hands.'

Sammy looked stubborn. 'If you don't pay me I'll keep your passports,' he said.

What nonsense! I sprang across the cockpit and snatched our documents from his hands. Then I sat on them.

'Well, that seems to be that,' Alan said. 'Here's your $30.'

Sammy sulkily left the cockpit and roared off.

The entire Gallipoli Peninsula has been designated a national park by the Turks. It is large, so without a car the only way to see it is to join an organised tour. Our guide was an intelligent and compassionate man, a history teacher in the winter and a Gallipoli guide in the summer. His passion was the battle and his knowledge remarkable, as was his grasp of Australian politics and culture. The other pilgrims in the small bus were Australians and New Zealanders in their 20s and late teens.

Although many of the memorials are beautiful, all are stark reminders of death and all are surrounded by the graves of thousands of young men. Shrapnel Gully, Murphy's Ridge, The Nek, Lone Pine will now haunt us for ever. Before, they were simply names. So, too, will the trenches and Anzac Cove where we walked along the beach barefooted and paddled in a sea that had once turned red with the blood of slaughtered youth. Simpson's grave is above the beach, not far from a marble slab on which the following words are inscribed:

> There is no difference between the Johnnies and the Mehmets to us,
> Where they lie side by side here in this country of ours,
> You, the mothers who sent their sons from far away countries, wipe away your tears;
> Your sons are now lying in our bosom and are in

peace after having lost their lives on this land,
They have become our sons as well.

Atatürk

The lone pine burnt down 40 years ago but another was planted
in its place. We sat in its shade before the Lone Pine Memorial
with its thousands of names of the unburied dead and we wept
for what had happened there: the stupidity, the callous loss of
life, the savagery, the courage and the pride.

Just north of Çanakkale is a sharp bend in the Dardanelles where
the strait narrows again and it was here at Sestos that the tragedy
of Leander and Hero occurred. Hero was a priestess in the temple
of Aphrodite but she fell in love with Leander, who regularly
swam across the Hellespont at night to meet her. Hero would put
out a lantern to guide her lover, but one windy night the flame
blew out and Leander drowned, confused by the darkness and
the strong currents. Heartbroken, Hero drowned herself. In an
act of homage to the romance of Hero and Leander, Byron swam
across the Hellespont at Sestos.

It seemed to us that the people of the Dardanelles and the Sea
of Marmara were different from those along the southern shores
of Turkey: less welcoming, secretive. The younger women wore
the traditional 'raincoat', a form of Muslim dress that is particularly unflattering. Perhaps that is the purpose of it. Lacking the
mystery of the *chardar*, it combines the head scarf with an ankle-
length gaberdine fawn-coloured raincoat, thick stockings and
clumpy shoes. The older men favoured brown suits, the coats cut
short and the trousers cuffed, and while there were many young
men in the international uniform of jeans, T-shirt and sneakers,
the few young women who followed fashion dressed in the style
of the 1950s.

In the Sea of Marmara we had an experience that unsettled us for several days. Anchored in a bay close to an ugly and stinking village, we were tired after sailing since dawn. Around 10 p.m. we were preparing for bed when we heard loud thumping on the hull and male voices calling *Windigo*. We rushed into the cockpit.

Hanging onto *Windigo* from a boat pulled alongside were three young Turkish men who were taking it in turns to suck long gulps from a bottle of *raki*. Their faces, lit by the lights of the village, were flushed and their mouths slack and wet. From the way they leered at me, it was apparent that they were not there for any slight transgression but for something degenerate and vicious. I could smell their lust in the soft air as the one in the stern flicked his pink tongue and rubbed his hand up and down the hard bulge against his belly. I remembered noticing them staring as we dropped the anchor at sunset while they motored by.

'Get below! Get out of sight,' Alan ordered. 'Put on more clothes.'

Beside a jungle track in Indonesia, I had found a heavy walking stick cut from a green branch. Alan had thought I was crazy to keep it. I dragged it from under the pilot berth and stood poised at the foot of the companionway. I could not see what was happening but I could hear Alan shouting.

'You lying bastard! That's old blood. I did not squash your leg between the boats. Now leave us alone. Fuck off! Fuck off, the lot of you.'

Several times the men tried to climb aboard *Windigo*, but Alan had been able to push them off. Then one had let out a cry of pain and pulled up the leg of his trousers to display an ugly and recent scar. He had shouted and screamed at Alan, accusing him of causing the wound and insisting that his wound be treated aboard *Windigo*.

In the shaft of light from the saloon I saw Alan pick up an oar and raise it above his head ready to strike. There were more shouts. Then I heard their motor kick over — they were going. But they left angrily, shaking their fists, threatening and unrepentant.

'We can't stay here,' Alan said. Then he saw my face. 'I know it's been frightening, but we must leave now. I'm afraid they'll return from the village with their mates. Turn off all the lights.'

In the blackness we slid from the bay using the radar and depth sounder to guide us. For the next couple of hours we stared aft, searching the blackness for lights that could indicate that someone was following us. They would not have the assistance of radar and depth sounder but they would know the area like the back of their hands. Alan's voice broke through my thoughts.

'Olma, I just said that we don't have a chart of this area and you didn't respond.'

Then I remembered. My God! No chart. We had charts of every inch of our route from Darwin to the Caribbean — except for this one chart. Alan had asked many yachts for it but, because it was off the main route to Istanbul, no-one had a copy. Not in our wildest dreams had we imagined navigating that reef-strewn stretch of water in the dark, but there we were.

The moon rose from our stern, bright and full, and it was only then that we saw the white line of breakers ahead. A reef! In the darkness we may have heard the breaking waves in time to avoid hitting it, but I doubt it. We abruptly changed course until an hour later we were forced to sail closer in again to feel our way around the next headland because the anchorage we were heading for was only a few kilometres farther on. As we rounded it we noticed a light flashing out to sea and another answering it close in shore.

Sailing nearer, we saw, silhouetted against the shore, the black shape of a ship in total darkness. *Windigo* had to pass between two vessels that were obviously engaged in an illegal activity. We felt exposed and sick with the fear of being boarded or fired upon, but it was too late to turn back.

'Surely if we hold our course they'll realise that we want to ignore them,' Alan reasoned.

Just after 3 a.m., almost drained of adrenalin, we dropped

anchor at a town called Karabiğa. We poured two large whiskies and talked until dawn.

There is no other city in the world like Istanbul, for part of it stands in Europe and the other part in Asia. It is a city that sparkles in water: the Sea of Marmara, the Golden Horn and the Bosphorus. And it is by water that one should approach it, for then it beckons and tantalises and slowly reveals its splendour. Palaces, towers, domes and minarets reflect in the sunlight and the city floats like a mirage from Arabian Nights. The buildings we had only seen in books rose from the sea and we thrilled with the recognition and the wonder of it all.

'There's Topkapi Palace on Seraglio Point.'

'That must be the Blue Mosque, but it isn't blue.'

'There's Hagia Sofia.'

'I've counted 20 minarets.'

'Look! Sinan's Suleiman Mosque is to port.'

As we passed the Golden Horn and proceeded up the Bosphorus, the grandiose Dölmabahce Palace gleamed white on the shore and the Bosphorus Bridge was clearly visible ahead.

Yes, it was a superb site for a city — strategic, romantic, splendid. Byzas, the legendary founder of Byzantium, had consulted the Delphic oracle about where to build his city and she had answered, 'Opposite the blind'. For years Byzas had wandered around wondering what she meant, until he reached the place where the Golden Horn meets the Bosphorus and the Sea of Marmara and, looking across to the opposite shore, he saw a settlement.

'If those people can't see that this is by far a superior place for a settlement, then they must be blind,' Byzas is reputed to have said.

His city, Byzantium, flourished for 1000 years until it surrendered to Constantine and became known as Constantinople. Atatürk preferred its present name of Istanbul ('The City'). Like

Rome, it is built on seven softly undulating hills and many of the spacious parks and gardens where the rich Ottomans had spent the summers in luxurious kiosks still exist.

Just south of the Bosphorus bridge, in a leafy area on the eastern shore, we saw a vacant mooring buoy, which we picked up. We were not certain what to do. In Istanbul, yachting is for the rich and marina charges are among the highest in Europe. This was obviously an affluent area, the shores on both sides lined with palaces, palatial wooden mansions called *kali* and exclusive waterside restaurants. As we looked at our splendid surroundings a tanned, bald man with a walrus moustache and bulging shoulders, rowed towards us.

'Permission to come aboard, Sir,' he called to Alan. He shook hands firmly with both of us.

'My name's Oldun. Welcome to Bebek. That's my yacht over there.'

He pointed to a beautifully maintained, attractive old-style timber yacht nearby. A boy sat in the cockpit, polishing the brass.

'You'll be happy here, my friends,' Oldun said. 'I'll look after you. My friend lives in that house just there and if you have any problems, you must go to him. He's the head of the CIA in Istanbul and he can get things fixed quickly and without any fuss. Just say, "Oldun sent me". ' We thanked him, and I offered coffee.

'I'd prefer beer,' our guest said. 'Do you have any?'

I asked if the boy polishing the brass were his son.

'Oh no, he's my boat boy,' Oldun laughed. 'You don't have boat boys in Australia? In Turkey, if you have a yacht, you have a boy. Any age, it doesn't matter. Some are old, but we still call them boys.'

'I suppose someone owns this mooring,' Alan said.

'Don't worry about it,' Oldun replied. 'The owner's a friend of mine. He's gone for a short cruise to the Princes Islands. You would have passed them on your way in. When he comes back you can move. Will a week be long enough?'

We assured him it would, feeling intuitively that to stay longer would be putting a strain on someone's hospitality, even though we were not sure whose. So here we were in the lovely suburb of Bebek, five kilometres from the centre of Istanbul and it wasn't going to cost us a Turkish lira.

'There's a tap in the back of that little mosque that you can use when you're short of water.' Oldun indicated the building at the water's edge. 'Bebek shopping centre is just there and the bus into town runs every few minutes and stops at the mosque.' Perfect!

Oldun chatted on. He explained his bulging biceps by telling us that he had swum the English Channel, the Loire, the Danube, and from Capri to Naples.

'And many times across the Bosphorus, my friends,' he continued. 'The currents here are fierce. Don't be tempted to try it.' We looked across to the lines of tankers, cargo vessels, liners and *gulets* passing north and south and felt no urge to swim across.

The Bosphorus is a strait 30 kilometres long. At Bebek it is narrow, a mere 700 metres across. but where it enters the Black Sea it is three kilometres wide. So the water funnels past Bebek at three to five knots and, because of the sinuous nature of its path, strong eddies and currents swirl around the anchorage making it essential to be securely tied to a mooring. According to Oldun there are two currents, a surface one from the north and a lower one from the south.

'How do you know that ?' Alan asked him.

'Speak to the fishermen,' Oldun replied. 'They'll tell you that at certain times of the year, if they lower their nets into the lower current, they'll be pulled north against the south setting surface current.'

'I read in the *Pilot* that the winds can make conditions chaotic at times,' Alan commented.

'Yes, even large ships sometimes have problems,' Oldun told us. 'They've been known to crash into the shore, destroying the fronts of buildings.'

'Does it ever ice over in winter?' I wanted to know.

'No,' replied Oldun. 'But sometimes icebergs float past.'

Finally Oldun stood to leave, promising to return to tell us more about his beloved city.

'Now I go to teach Tansu Çiller's two small sons to swim,' Oldun declared as he lowered himself into his dinghy.

'Nothing but the best for the Prime Minister's sons,' I joked, not being quite sure whether he was serious.

'I've known her since she was a child. She grew up around here. I love her,' he cried.

Crossing the park in front of the glittering Dölmabahce Palace, we passed four men, each leading a large brown bear on a chain. I waved to one of the bears and it waved back. Outside the palace, guards dressed in chain mail stood on either side of the elaborate gates and an Ottoman band played military music on ancient instruments. We were in a time warp.

Inside, the tourists were placed in language groups — German, French, Turkish, Arabic and English, and we were back in the present. No-one in our group spoke English to each other and when they heard us talking their faces remained blank. Four spoke Italian, but the origins of the rest were a mystery.

For sheer unbridled extravagance and poor taste, Dölmabahce Palace must surely be of world prominence. Perhaps the giant chandeliers, or the crystal staircase, or the alabaster bathrooms could have achieved a certain elegance by themselves, but surrounded by acres of kitsch, they simply added to the confusion. Feeling saturated by the vulgarity, we sat beneath the trees on the Bosphorus to recover. The inhabitants of Istanbul bustled before us on the water in a melee of ferries, fishing boats and rowing skiffs and the scene had a refreshing candour and validity after two hours of the Dölmabahce.

Built 1000 years before St Peters in Rome, Hagia Sofia, deep pink in colour, is an architectural masterpiece with a massive dome that appears to float above it. Once, the interior had been covered with gold and mosaics but these had been plastered over by the followers of Islam. High in an apse, however, is a lovely mosaic of "mother and child" in blues and gold, and several others still exist in out-of-the-way corners. In 1935 Atatürk declared that he did not wish to see Christians and Muslims fighting over Hagia Sofia, one of the world's greatest treasures, so he turned it into a museum to be shared by everyone.

In my ignorance I expected the Blue Mosque to be blue, but so lovely is this multi-domed memorial to Sultan Ahmet, with its six needle-like minarets, that its exterior greyness mattered little. Its name derives from the exquisite Iznik tiles on the interior walls and the painted arabesques inside the domes.

As I replaced my shoes in the dark entrance at the end of our visit, the attendant slid his hand beneath my breast.

'Piss off.'

'So sorry. So sorry,' he simpered.

Each morning we were up before sunrise, excited by the city whose most famous treasure is probably Topkapi Palace. It is breathtaking, and it seemed that it would take several days to explore it, so vast and intricate are its spaces and so sumptuous its treasures. The harem section alone has 400 rooms and it once held 300 of the Sultan's wives, children and odalisques, plus the Black Eunuchs who guarded them.

Topkapi was the nerve centre of the far-flung Ottoman Empire and each new sultan added to it as he thought fit. Generally, though, there are three main sections: the outer palace, the inner palace and the harem. The Palace stands on the spot where Byzas once stood when he looked across to the blind ones and it was once a city within itself with thousands of people living and working within its walls. The guards and gardeners, the bakers and butchers and all the artisans and providers of services were then dressed in colour-coded uniforms. There are gardens and pools, fountains and baths, and mosques and mazes. Once there was a hospital, a tulip garden, a circumcision pavilion, and even a zoo.

The Topkapi Diamond in the treasury has been an inspiration

for poets and writers. It glows with a brilliance that makes one gasp, as do those in the handle of the famous Topkapi Dagger, the subject of a Hollywood film. But so overwhelming are the riches of the treasury that after an hour or two they lose their glitter and appear to be no more precious than pieces of coloured glass.

Certainly for us the harem was the most evocative section. Lavish with tiles, mosaics and painted decoration, the rooms run in a labyrinth around ornate fireplaces, marble fountains and decorated hallways. But of the hundreds of rooms, only a small number are open to the public, perhaps 20. I asked an attendant what the other rooms were used for.

'They're not used at all,' he replied. 'They're kept locked.'

'Have you ever been into them?' I asked.

'Certainly not, Madam,' the man replied. 'No-one has entered them since the last woman left the harem in 1909.'

'Are they still full of furniture and belongings?' I wanted to know.

'I believe so, Madam. As I said, they haven't been entered since that time. Nothing has been touched.'

I had read Eric Newby's account of wandering through some of those rooms, but he did point out that it was practically impossible to get permission to view them. Nevertheless, I longed to see into them. I could imagine the dust and the cobwebs, the fading mirrors and the musty smell of women. I could see the yellowing frills lit momentarily by shafts of dusty sunlight through chinks in the thick curtains, and I could hear the whispered secrets.

Atatürk, of course, put a stop to all the nonsense of sultans, concubines, harems and numerous wives, believing that men and women were equal partners in marriage as in everything else. So he passed a family law that introduced a form of secular marriage which gave women monogamous rights.

'Is it possible that, while one half of the community stays chained to the ground, the other half can rise to the skies?' he had asked.

The Istanbul Archaeological Museum, one of the great museums of Europe, had received a special UNESCO award for excellence. Its pride exhibit is the magnificent Alexander sarcophagus from Sedan in Lebanon, a massive white marble tomb. Horses and warriors rear from its walls and lid through a marble forest, and little of the decoration is broken or even cracked.

Then there is the Museum of Turkish Ceramics where the building itself is a museum: a Taj Mahal-style 15th century glory with stark white interiors decorated with Iznik tiles.

The interior of the enormous old barracks at the Military Museum on the Bosphorus was surprising, possibly because one has certain expectations of what the interior of an army barracks will be like — rather drab and masculine with fading photographs of brave colonels on the walls and displays of swords and ancient firearms and torn and bloody flags. But the massive old doors opened onto a starkly modern entrance, bright and strong. You could feel the power of a mighty army but there were no artefacts to suggest its physical presence.

Every so often in our wanderings I saw something which made me think, 'That's to die for.' The Ottoman campaign tents displayed in the Military Museum had that effect. About a dozen were fully pitched in a huge space and they were so beautiful that for a moment I believed they were painted there, part of a mural, not real.

Made of fine cotton and silk, every inch was decorated with a form of hand-stitching: appliqué, braiding, drawn thread work, beading, fancy stitching, fine rope work for the windows, tassels and frills and flaps and flounces. There were patterns in gold and silver thread against pinks and creams and turquoises which extended under the flies and onto the exterior.

The tents ranged in size from a huge, elaborate banquet tent to those the size of an average room. The interiors, soft with diffused light, were intimate, romantic spaces and I became unreasonably possessive if someone entered a tent while I was there. The groundsheets were also decorated, and the tent poles carved with designs of flowers, ivy and humming birds — painted, then detailed in gold leaf. The tents had been hand-stitched and decorated by the soldiers of the Ottoman armies while they waited for the next battle to begin.

The Mehter, the oldest military band in the world, was an Ottoman Janissary group that had first played in 1035. Alan and I sat on plush red velvet seats in the starkly modern theatre and we looked down upon a brick-paved, oval stage. Precisely at 3 p.m. the entire back wall of the theatre silently slid away to reveal a fountain spurting columns of water high into the air against the backdrop of a formal garden flanked by fine trees.

In the distance we caught the glitter of uniforms and brass and heard the roll of drums as the modern Mehter, dressed in copies of the 11th century uniforms, marched along a gravel path towards us. They played as they advanced and circled the stage, their uniforms brilliant against the great swathe of green. It was an inspired piece of theatre, and we tingled with the battle cries, the victory chants and the strange and rousing music. It is said that when Mozart heard the Mehter, he gave a standing ovation, crying out, 'This is music!'.

In the Golden Horn, open boats tied to the shore pitched in the wash from the passing traffic while men cooked over pans of boiling oil on the decks. We ate lunch of salted fish fried in oil and placed between two pieces of bread with a handful of parsley and a dollop of garlic sauce. It tasted delicious, but made us sick. Farther along were stalls selling the unusual combination of mussels and intestines. The mussels are threaded onto a long skewer, dipped in a light batter and then fried, doused with a herb sauce and placed between layers of bread.

The intestines we left for others to enjoy, although the aroma was enticing. The grey tubes are wound around a stick covered in stuffing to form a sausage about half a metre long and as thick as a fist. This is then slowly cooked over hot coals, slipped off the stick, chopped into short lengths and once again served between two layers of bread.

In Istanbul we ate the best and cheapest cherries we had ever seen, apart from the black ones in the mountains of Pelion. There were barrow loads of ripe and luscious fruit throughout the city: cherries, apricots, early peaches, strawberries and raspberries.

At the end of the first week in Istanbul, Oldan informed us that the owner of the mooring was expected the next day. It was time to move on. We had heard of a small, free harbour used by fishermen, ten kilometres south of Istanbul at Yeşilköy, so we sailed once more along the Bosphorus, past the Golden Horn and the wondrous skyline of Istanbul to our new anchorage.

Yeşilköy was also a pretty waterside suburb built around the harbour and a sandy beach where the water appeared clear, although in the adjoining harbour we sat in a putrid black soup and often the stench was so strong that we breathed in short puffs. In one section of Istanbul harbour on our way to Yeşilköy, the water had been so polluted that the depth sounder stopped. At first we had thought it was broken, but once in the clearer water of the bay it worked as before.

Trains ran through Yeşilköy into Istanbul and we missed the civilised customs of the Bosphorus buses. There were no such refinements on the trains which were often packed tight with sly men who stared coldly when I pushed away their wandering hands. On one occasion an obviously liberated and wealthy woman, festooned with striking gold jewellery and dressed in a designer suit, yelled angrily at a man who persisted in rubbing his arm against me as he pretended to hang onto a support. I tried to thank her but she turned her back and stared out of the window as though nothing had happened. The man pushed hard against me when he left at the next stop. In the peak-hour trains men would push erections against me while staring innocently ahead. Others would deliberately breathe in my face. Some would just stare with loathing.

One morning on the train I felt faint. There were no seats and the only wall to lean against was taken up by men, none of whom were likely to make room for me. But one did. A tall young man in his 20s eased me into his space.

'You'll feel better with some fresh air,' he commented as he made an unsuccessful attempt to push open a window.

'You're from Australia,' I said, recognising the accent. It turned out he had come from Sydney with his two sisters and his parents who were scattered throughout the crowded carriage. His father had insisted that the children visit Turkey to become acquainted with their heritage.

'But we hate it here,' the young man said. 'My sisters and I are homesick. We want to go back. We wish we hadn't come.'

'Do your parents feel the same way?' I asked.

'Oh no, they love it,' he replied. 'They were born here. It's an emotional experience for them. They've been talking about taking us on this trip for years, so we can't tell them that we want to return to Sydney early.'

I looked across at his two attractive sisters in their late teens. 'How do your sisters cope with Turkish men?' I asked.

'They think Turkish men are shits. Always mauling and being crude. They would never marry one, thank Christ. We all speak Turkish, though, so it's easier for us. How do you manage?'

'With difficulty,' I assured him.

Between Beyazit Square and the Galata Bridge which spans the Golden Horn is an old part of Istanbul that is noisy with the clamour of shoppers and vendors, hawkers and porters, cars and trucks, horse-drawn carts and the strange music of the arabesque. In this area of bazaars and markets, the artisans and tradespeople are grouped in narrow streets, so there is the street of the coppersmiths, the street of silversmiths, of goldsmiths, of booksellers, of antique dealers.

In the midst of the timeless activity is the Kapali Çarşi or Covered Bazaar, a fascinating labyrinth of more than 4000 shops. We imagined it would be full of tourists, but we saw a mere handful. It was packed with Turkish people following shopping patterns that had been established centuries ago, of caravanasi and souks, of scented teas and long, hard bargaining.

Nearby there are streets of fabric shops interspersed with lace shops, braid shops, button and buckle shops, ribbon shops and shops of trims for every conceivable purpose. My palms grew clammy with excitement, I could not make decisions and Alan's patience was in delicate balance, so we left without buying anything. But we would return.

I felt angry that I could not go there alone to browse and shop instead of dragging poor Alan along, but the whole area is a male enclave. There are no women in the world of fabrics in Istanbul, so a foreign women alone would find it impossible to survive without some serious mauling.

Nearby is the grand old Hotel Pera. Agatha Christie had regarded it as home and she had written *Murder on the Orient Express* there. Her rooms were being repainted so we could not see them, but Atatürk's suite, now a museum, was open. As we walked through the severe and sensible set of rooms with their brown leather upholstery, I wondered why the austere and great man had chosen to spend the last days of his life in the harem of Dölmabahce Palace. Atatürk, like his subjects, was an enigma — or so it seemed to me.

Of all the palaces of Istanbul, the Beylerbeyi Sarayi was our favourite. You enter the garden through a long arched tunnel with an end wall of stained glass. Then suddenly there is sunlight sparkling on the white marble facade of an enchanting building. Sultan Abdul Aziz, a man of refined taste and sensitivity, had

found it impossible to live in the suffocating vulgarity of Dölmabahce Palace, so he had constructed the Beylerbeyi Sarayi on
the opposite side of the Bosphorus.

Our guide, a pompous man with a Hitler moustache, tried to
bully our group of three along as if we were taking part in an
athletic event.

'My name's Mr Demirsar,' he informed us, tapping the name
tag on his lapel where it was clearly printed. 'I'm your leader.
Now hurry along. There's a lot to see.'

The third member of the group was a dour dark-suited man of
middle age who never spoke. Even when addressed, he refused
to answer, and he seemed so serious that Alan and I referred to
him as Mr Jolly.

We followed Mr Demirsar as he strode from room to room.
The only way to slow him down was to stubbornly take one's
time and to ask questions. When Alan asked him something, Mr
Demirsar would respond with a detailed answer but when I
asked, he directed his answer to Alan. I found him abrasive.

'This room is where the men talked,' he told us. Then farther
on he said, 'This room is where the women gossiped.'

Referring to the many sultans who had been poisoned (usually
by scheming family members), Mr Demirsar explained that food
tasters had been used.

'Of course they were always women,' he announced smugly.

'Perhaps women's sense of taste is more refined than men's,'
I suggested, teasing him, and hoping he would overlook the
great chefs of the world. He glared, then added coldly, this time
looking me in the eye, 'Women were dispensable.'

In the lovely harem section Mr Demirsar remarked, 'Of course
the foreigners think that the sultans were licentious and lacking
in restraint. They laugh about them. But that's because the foreigners are ignorant of what really happened. In those days
Turkish men could have many wives.'

'But even with many wives they apparently felt the need to
have concubines as well,' I pointed out. 'One can hardly describe
the sex life of the sultans as restrained.'

'Madam doesn't understand,' our guide said. 'It is true there were many women in the harem but they were there to do the work, to look after the Sultan's children, to teach them, to amuse them, to play with them.'

'I'll bet they played adult games as well,' Alan whispered.

The harem bathroom had a shower of unusual design. Directly beneath the ornate shower rose, another smaller rose projected from the floor to just the right height.

'Wowee! What fun!' I exclaimed to the humourless Mr Demirsar. He sucked in his lips and rudely turned off the light, forcing us to leave. The man whom Alan and I had christened Mr Jolly suddenly spoke the only words we ever heard him utter.

'Jolly!' he exclaimed, smiling.

We stared at him in amazement.

In 1700 or thereabouts, Selim the Grim had built the enormous barracks that during the Crimean War housed the hospital run by Florence Nightingale. She had fired me with admiration as a child in primary school when I read about her exploits in what was known as The Brown Reader. Constantinople was a world away then. But here I was. Her hospital had been preserved within the barracks and I wanted to see it.

It seemed, though, that forces were working against us. The barracks, still in use today, were enclosed by a high wire fence that stretched for kilometres in an area of cantonments and vast silent spaces devoid of traffic and people. We walked and walked, but never came to anything that even vaguely resembled an entrance.

Eventually, after hailing the only taxi we had seen, we were dropped at the massive stone gates. They were bristling with serious armed guards, their rifles at the ready. The taxi drove away and we were left standing there.

'Perhaps this isn't a good idea,' I said to Alan.

But he bravely strode to the watch-house and explained why we had come.

'Wait here! You must wait here!' the guard snapped.

So we waited, the line of soldiers steady and alert before us.

Finally an officer approached and escorted us through the gates. On either side of the long gravel drive stretched lines of armed soldiers, their eyes unwavering as we passed between the rows. I felt like running away.

At the entrance to the barracks stood a guncarriage ready to receive a coffin. We skirted it and walked into the entrance hall with its glass-fronted cabinets full of army memorabilia, crossed swords above the doors and a large photograph of Atatürk in battledress in an oval frame.

'The Major will see you now,' the officer informed us. He knocked on the nearest panelled door and we were ushered into a large room with glass doors that followed the curve of a verandah which opened onto manicured gardens and lawns.

The major sat behind a leather-trimmed desk. His face was unsmiling.

'Why are you here?' he asked.

Alan explained, and then added, 'I'm sorry that we've come at an inconvenient time. With your permission, we could come back another day.'

The major relaxed and smiled.

'Please sit down,' he said. 'Yes, it's most inconvenient today. Impossible really. Security is very tight and everyone is engaged in funeral duties. One of our high-ranking officers has died suddenly. There's no-one who could escort you through the Florence Nightingale Museum.' He turned to me. 'Are you a nurse?' he asked.

'No, I'm interested in her as a woman,' I tried to explain. The major nodded thoughtfully, pursing his lips and slowly nodding.

Just across from Hagia Sofia is the Basilica Cistern, an eerie underground chamber with 366 columns supporting the enormous roof. You may ask why one would bother to visit a water-storage tank. But this one was built by Justinian, halfway through the 1st century AD. Now it is a cool, ethereal space with a continuous sound and light show as you wander along suspended walkways in the dripping gloom. It is evocative of cathedrals and things spiritual.

That was our last day in Istanbul. We strolled for a while along the banks of the Bosphorus, inevitably sad. How could it be otherwise? Istanbul is a fascinating and beautiful city. It represents the two faces of Turkey, one turning towards the east and the other towards the west. It is a mixture of old and new: 16th century masterpieces and bazaars, modern technology and designer clothes. But after weeks exploring its treasures, it was time to say *'Allahaismarlardik'*.

North or south? That was the dilemma. To the north lay Bucharest, the Danube, Odessa and other tempting places. But *Anaconda* and *Syrah* were already in the Ukraine and their experiences, relayed by radio, were not positive. Law and order had broken down in some places. *Syrah*'s dinghy had been stolen and JB had had several unpleasant encounters with officials and was returning with all speed to Istanbul. We sailed south, back down the Dardanelles.

A letter from Des on *Panache* arrived the day before we left Istanbul. The Dardanelles is a sombre place at the best of times and Des's news added to the gloom. Laurie had leukemia and was not expected to live. She had first felt tired in the Red Sea but had blamed her lack of energy on the headwinds and the tough sailing. It was not until they reached Cyprus that tests were done and the diagnosis made. Their son Tod was with them. *Panache* would stay on the hard in Larnaca while Laurie and Des flew home to New Zealand so that Laurie could undergo further treatment and be with the rest of their family. Sometimes miracles happen. Laurie was a strong and positive woman who would not easily accept defeat. Still, we were sad.

*return to the Aegean • toothache in Athens
the waterman of Galixidhi • into the Ionian*

Yiasas, fair Greece. We felt a lift to our spirits on returning. Once more we headed across the Aegean towards Athens where this time we would meet Trevor and Christine, our friends from Rhode Island in the US whom we had not seen for several years. The passage down the Dardanelles was fast, *Windigo* running 'wing and wing' with the *meltemi* behind her, and the sombre killing fields sliding silently past on either side.

The island of Lesbos is famous for many things, including the best olive oil in Greece. However, it is probably best known as the birthplace of the poetess Sappho who wrote in a poem back in 612 BC, 'I was in love with you once, Atthis, long ago.' Atthis was a woman, which caused people to think, 'Ah, ha!', and hence the word 'lesbian'. As it turned out, however, Sappho was basically heterosexual. She died in her 50s when she jumped off a cliff on the island of Levkas after being rejected by her male lover.

Theophilos, the famous Greek painter, lived and worked on Lesbos, as did Epicurus, Aristotle, Aesop and a host of lesser-known musicians, writers and artists. On the other hand, from this gentle community also came the dreaded pirate, Barbarossa.

Mytilini, the main town on Lesbos, is a mixture of old mansions, concrete blocks and winding Levantine streets lined with market stalls and craft shops. And on the wharf in the crowded harbour was a Greek rarity — a waterman with a gracious manner and a generous spirit. The waterman is king of the harbour in Greece during the summer months. The harbourmaster may not agree, but that is a minor point. These purveyors of the precious liquid to boats are almost invariably perverse and cranky men who cause havoc in the crowded harbours with a range of tactics destined to turn normally reasonable boat crews into aggressive combatants.

As the days passed, I was able to abandon the survival tactics developed in Turkey — like avoiding eye contact with a man, covering the body, wearing an impassive expression, foregoing perfume. Normal relations, without threat or innuendo, were a pleasure again, as most Greek men, despite their machismo, generally treat women with respect.

Alan and I continued west across the Aegean to the island of Aegina, 12 miles south-west of Athens, where there is a boatyard with facilities for lifting yachts out of the water. *Windigo* had had virtually no maintenance on her hull since leaving Darwin more than three years before. As well as anti-fouling and painting, we needed to check the propeller and the rudder, and to perform the various other tasks that can only be done when the boat is out of the water.

Aegina is a popular island with tourists as well as with Athenians, for it is only a 30-minute ride by hydrofoil from the capital, which we called 'cockroaches' because of the resemblance as they skimmed along the surface of the water. The island was once a rich trading port with an illustrious maritime history and, in the Battle of Salamis, the Aegina fleet was said by Herodotus to have distinguished itself above all the rest.

Today the crescent-shaped harbour is packed with *caiques*, ferries, cruisers and yachts, and tied to the harbour wall are five or six covered fishing boats from which the island's fruit and vegetables are sold. Following the curve of the crescent are tavernas and tourist shops selling a range of island crafts and produce, several specialising in pistachio nuts, known to the Athenians as 'Aegina peanuts', for which the island is famous. But perhaps its greatest claim to fame is that it was here that Nikos Kazanzakis wrote his most famous novel, *Zorba the Greek*.

Ten kilometres across the island is the Aegina Boatyard owned by the two Asprakis brothers — Gregory, an attractive blond Greek with charming manners, and Theo, his dark-haired brother who, despite his excellent English, lacked the grace to say even *kalimera*.

Gregory lived in style in a villa high above the boatyard with his wife and two young children. I asked if his wife worked, and was told that she worked very hard.

'She's a village girl so she's used to hard work,' Gregory explained. 'She helps the gardener with the flowers and vegetables, and in the season she collects the olives and the pistachios. And when she's not working, she plays with her horse.'

'Is horse riding popular in Greece?' I asked.

'Oh, she doesn't ride it,' Gregory laughed.

One day while walking through the grounds with Gregory, I noticed six motorbikes through the open door of a shed and farther on, an elegant and gleaming black and red horse-drawn carriage in the shade of the pines. When I asked Gregory about these, he replied, 'I collect motor bikes and my wife collects carriages.' He laughed and then continued. 'I was joking. I bought the carriage as a wedding present for my wife. That's why she has the horse. We like to go out driving in the cool of the evenings.'

While we suffered in the heatwave of our first week on land, we imagined the Asprakis family trotting sedately through the olive groves. The heatwave engulfed Athens and the surrounding countryside, causing several deaths in the badly polluted capital. With the temperatures in the 40s for days, we had to be disciplined to get much work done. The Aegean, tranquil and clear, lapped a few metres from where we worked so it was easy to cool off, but hard to leave the water again.

The Greeks do not even pretend to cope with the heat. They work in the early mornings, disappear until late afternoon, work until dark at around 9 p.m. and eat between 10 p.m. and 11 p.m. We could not break the habit of a lifetime and, besides, we were paying for our time on the hard.

For at least a month one of my front teeth had been bothersome. Finally, I had to agree with Alan that something would have to be done about it. Therefore we returned from Aegina to Porto Rafti to be in a safe anchorage on a bus route into Athens. We visited a chemist in Ormonia Square the next day. They usually speak English and would possibly be au fait with the medical and dental arrangements of the city.

'My sister's a dentist,' exclaimed the chemist. 'She'll help you. Her name is Yana and she's very good. She trained in America.'

Yana was young with apricot-coloured hair, a clear olive complexion and intelligent olive-green eyes. I had hoped for someone with a little more experience but she was kind and her hands inspired confidence. Nevertheless, I found it difficult to imagine her struggling with stubborn molars, blood and pain. After X-rays and some prodding about, she announced that the task was beyond her skills; the root was shattered, a surgeon was needed. My worst fears were being realised.

'I can help you with the cost of the operation,' Yana said when she learned that we were on a tight cruising budget. 'I work two days a week in the Faculty of Dentistry at the University of Athens. You can go there and be operated on by one of the best surgeons in Greece and it won't cost you more than a few dollars.' She studied my white face, and then added, 'If you like, I'll be the nurse.'

I was grateful, but then Alan almost ruined the arrangement.

'The last time Olma had something like this done, it was the surgeon and the nurse who emerged white-faced and shaking. She's a terrible patient,' he told Yana.

But it was no joking matter. For the next week my face resembled a rotten potato and I hastily sewed a burka in which to hide from Alan and the world. The Greek fishermen stopped giving me friendly waves and averted their eyes, as men are supposed to do with Muslim women.

We spent three weeks in Porto Rafti, which left us short of

time to get to Rome before the winter storms began, so we headed towards the Corinth Canal instead of around the Peloponnese as originally planned. The reason for building the canal in the first place was to cut 200 miles off the distance.

If Emperor Nero could see the Corinth Canal, he would be amazed, because he had been the first to imagine such a project, and indeed began work himself with a silver spade and 6000 slaves. But the task was beyond them. It was not until the end of the 19th century that a French company succeeded in cutting the five-kilometre-long cleft through the rocky isthmus that separates the Aegean Sea from the Ionian.

The Gulf of Corinth is a lovely waterway with a deeply indented coastline and a backdrop of majestic purple mountains, with Mount Olympus somewhere in the clouds. At the beautiful village of Galixidhi we stopped for water. Delphi, that fabled centre of the world for the ancient Greeks, is close by and, although we had visited it on a previous trip to Greece, we wanted to see it again.

We were the only yacht on the quay when we tied up halfway through the morning, but the waterman could not be found.

'We don't know where he is,' the people said. '*Argotera, argotera*. Later, later.'

By late afternoon the quay was packed with yachts, all German. Their skippers paced up and down impatiently. They were also waiting for the waterman. I grumbled to Alan but he reassured me that as we were there first, we would be served first. I had my own thoughts about the meek and their inheritance, so I kept watch for the waterman.

At least I knew what he looked like, for the villagers had given me a clear picture.

'Oh, you can't mistake him,' they said. 'He is big. He has a big belly. He has a big moustache — like this.' They spread their arms wide and laughed loudly. Something in their manner warned me that he would be a character. When I saw him in the distance, I ran to greet him and after establishing a rapport (Greeks will ignore you if you neglect to do this) I asked if we could have water.

'Of course,' he replied. 'You can be second.'

I wanted to ask him why I could not be first but thought that discretion was probably more appropriate. The waterman unlocked the hose, dragged it across the quay and handed an end to one of the Germans. I forced myself to smile, approached the German and explained that I was to have the hose after him.

'Yes, Madam, I'll bring it to you myself — when I've finished with it,' he replied coldly.

I sat on the bow of *Windigo* and waited. Fifteen minutes later, the German, ignoring me completely, walked past with the hose and handed it to a man on the boat next door. They both ignored my shouts of outrage. The waterman said patronisingly, 'Now calm down, lady. You can be next.'

'That's what you said last time,' I reminded him.

'This time for sure,' he replied.

Alan waited at the bow of the next-door yacht and when the owner emerged with the hose, Alan determinedly took it from his hands before the German had time to collect his wits. We had filled two of our five tanks when suddenly there was no water and the hose began to slide across the deck. I leapt upon it and hung on as though it were a lifeline.

'What are you doing? We haven't finished yet,' I yelled at the waterman.

'No more water for you, lady. Kaput!' he shouted back as he tugged at the hose.

I tugged too. The hose grew slimmer and the villagers who had gathered on the dock as if they expected an incident, developed a healthy interest in the tug of war between the angry woman and the big waterman. Backwards and forwards slid the hose. I tried to get it around a winch for greater purchase, but was not quick enough. Alan could not watch. He went below muttering, 'Oh, dear God!' with his arms crossed over his head.

But it was an uneven battle. The waterman was heavy and strong and he had the flat quay on which to manoeuvre, while I was entangled in the rigging, bruising my bare feet on deck fittings and teetering on the verge of falling overboard. When he gave a last mighty tug, I let go.

The big waterman went tottering backwards like a drunken gorilla, finally landing heavily on his fat bum at the feet of the crowd. The delighted spectators slapped their thighs and laughed with raucous glee.

A German, perhaps trying to be kind said, 'Everything will be all right. Now just calm down. You can have more water later.'

'Bugger off!' I told him.

Then the waterman hauled himself onto *Windigo*, glanced around, jumped back on the quay and addressed the crowd.

'Ah, ha! I thought so. They've been hosing down their boat,' he yelled.

The audience then turned to glare accusingly at me. Hosing down a boat is a venal sin in the Greek islands because water is often in short supply in the summer. My outrage was complete, my anger choking. I stood on the bow and luxuriated in it, swearing and shouting at the fat waterman and the gaping skippers on the surrounding yachts.

Some understood everything, some very little. No-one moved. I stormed below and wept, and Alan said, 'Let's get out of here.'

The Ionian, 'the wine dark sea', derives its name from the priestess Io, one of the lovers of Zeus who turned her into a white cow in an attempt to deceive Hera, his wife. It is known in Greek as *Eptanisa*, the Seven Islands: Corfu, Kefalonia, Kythero, Ithaca, Zakynthos, Paxos and probably Levkas, although the latter is not strictly an island.

To those who expect the islands to resemble those of the rest of Greece, the Ionian islands are a surprise, beautiful in an entirely different way. They are gentle shaded places with pine and elm, and pencils of cypress piercing the skyline. The aromatic *marquis* grows wild on the uncultivated areas, and there are green fields and flowers and the silver sheen of the olive groves.

Whilst some of the architecture is typically Greek, there is an Italianate influence throughout the Ionian which dates from the period of Venetian trading in the 14th century and there are some hasty modern concrete constructions which date from the serious earthquakes of the 1950s.

After passing quickly through the Gulf of Patras, we were held up in Preveza with bad weather and a broken engine part. It was the end of October and already we could smell winter. It seemed that we had left it too late to reach Rome safely. Mike and Fiona, our friends on *Syrah*, had also reached Preveza and together we decided to spend the winter in Greece and to push on to Italy in the early spring of the following year.

CHAPTER 11

winter in Tranquil Bay
Viking and the Irish wheaten terrier
Ruff, the wolf

To the north, the craggy peaks of the Albanian mountains curve with the coast before it turns sharply to the River Thiamis and eventually flattens into the salt marshes around Preveza and Levkas. On the outskirts of Preveza are the ruins of Nikopolis, built by Octavian to celebrate his victory over Antony at the battle of Actium in 31 BC.

Levkas town, our closest source of supplies in the winter of 1993–94, had been destroyed by an earthquake in 1953 and hastily rebuilt in a chaotic jumble of bricks and corrugated iron houses and shops lining narrow streets that ring with the energy of the busy market town.

At the southern point of Levkas island is a precipitous white cliff from which the island takes its name and from which the famous poetess, Sappho of Lesbos, flung herself in despair. According to the locals, criminals were later flung from the cliff and, if they reached the sea alive, they were rescued and pardoned.

Sheltered by the mountains to its west and a long peninsula to the south and east, the tiny village of Nidri nestles on the coast a few kilometres from Levkas town. It faces a small protected bay which is ringed by softly wooded slopes of pine. Wild herbs grow in profusion amongst the rocks which the sun turns into hot meteorites that radiate warmth into the bay long after sunset. This lovely place is known as Tranquil Bay and it was here that we were to spend our second winter in the Mediterranean.

There had been madness and mayhem when we sailed through the area in the summer. Thousands of charter yachts had woven suicidal courses through the wind tunnels between the islands and hordes of tourists had crowded the tavernas and blanketed the beaches with umbrellas and pink flesh. Now they had gone and calm had returned.

The people were busy at their winter occupations. Many had two jobs, one for the summer and another for the winter. Summer jobs were invariably in the tourist industry, but immediately the invaders leave, the waiters, cooks, guides and touts metamorphose into teachers, builders, farmers and fishermen. The long-suffering acceptance of tourists and their ways was replaced by sparkles of interest in us and a return to the warmth and generosity of spirit that is common amongst the Greeks.

Early in our stay we were involved in a minor mishap at Levkas that could have cost us dearly had we not been dealing with 'winter Greeks'. Taking on diesel was a task we both dreaded and not once since leaving Darwin had we managed to do it with any degree of aplomb. One of several things invariably went wrong: we were overcharged, the hose was too big for the tanks, it was impossible to regulate the flow so the job took too long and the diesel sellers grew angry, or the fuel gushed forth and escaped through the scuppers and cockpit drains causing a multicoloured stain to form an incriminating ring around the boat.

Putting diesel in the water is an offence which carries a hefty $500 fine. We were never sure what went wrong at Levkas, but a few seconds after the pump on the wharf had been turned on, we were standing in the cockpit aghast as the tell-tale pink, mauve, purple and green shimmer spread in a circle around the boat and the expression on the face of the approaching policeman changed from benevolent bonhomie to outrage.

'What's this? What's this?' he demanded through clenched teeth.

It seemed safer to remain mute. The diesel seller tentatively approached the policeman and there was a muttered conversation in Greek. It appeared that the fuel merchant was offering some explanation on our behalf. Several times we heard him use the word 'Australian', which seemed to have a soothing effect on the nattily uniformed officer who turned towards us and said one word.

'Detergent.'

Alan jumped below and returned with the entire supply which the policeman furiously sprinkled over the diesel. He then shot us a look of disbelief, made three clicking sounds with his tongue and stomped off, the sun shining on his neat behind and ramrod back.

When we stopped at Preveza, we met a young Finnish couple who live aboard a *caique* in the harbour. Ann-Marie and Viking were their names. Viking was, as you may imagine, tall and confident with a striking mane of white-blond hair. I found his personality overpowering and his real name unpronounceable.

'Just call me Viking,' he said.

Ann-Marie, a quiet woman with the face of a madonna, gazed upon Viking as if she would follow him to the ends of the earth, and indeed she may be called upon to do so for Viking expressed his wish to sail the Pacific. The Greek *caique* was certainly seaworthy, strongly constructed with the wide beam and fine bow typical of the ancient craft.

The couple had had it built when they first arrived in Greece but the construction ate up all their funds before they were able to buy and install an engine. Undaunted, they used the *caique* under sail to fish the waters around Preveza, selling their catch at local markets until they had accumulated the funds to install a motor. The crusty Greek fishermen tolerated the sharing of the sea's resources and were generous in their support.

Above the deck, Viking had constructed a single cabin, primitive and uncomfortable despite the numerous cushions and Ann-Marie's earnest attempts to transform the makeshift addition into a home. On our first visit, a golden dog lay on the cushions.

'This is Amber,' Viking said. 'She would like you to shake hands.'

We accepted her outstretched paw. Amber was charming, her

eyes round and gentle. Viking gathered her in his arms like a baby, rocking her and kissing her soft head.

'She's an Irish wheaten terrier,' Viking explained when we admitted we had not seen her breed before.

Four years previously Viking had been living in an isolated Costa Rican village. He did not explain why he was there. Two weeks before he was to leave the village, a tiny golden pup attached itself to him, and nothing he did could shake it off, it was always there behind him. Viking was puzzled because the other village dogs were of the Balinese type — scrawny, mean, and ill-treated — while his new friend was clean and sleek.

The night before his departure it was raining hard, so Viking weakened, allowing the pup to come into his room, whereas previously it had slept outside his door. The tiny creature was snuggled into Viking's neck when he woke in the morning and he realised that he could not leave her behind.

Viking's airline seat was booked but he cancelled it. He made another booking two weeks ahead hoping that would give him time to get through the formalities that would allow him to take the pup into Finland. But there was a three month quarantine period.

Viking could not wait three months so he hired a shady lawyer to falsify the documents and once again made preparations to leave. Then the airline company refused to accept the pup. Determined, Viking bought a child's ticket for it. When the crew discovered the pup, however, all hell broke loose. But Viking argued that he had paid for the extra seat and as far as he was concerned, the pup was his child. So persuasive was Viking that when he received his tray of food, the pup received a special doggie tray.

On arrival at Helsinki, Viking phoned Ann-Marie and announced that he was bringing a beautiful blonde Costa Rican girl home to live with them, and quickly hung up. Ann-Marie met him at the airport, ready to murder them both, but she was completely captivated by the tiny, golden bundle. How the relatively exotic puppy came to be wandering lost in a Costa Rican village was something that Viking could not explain. The whole affair cost him US$3000.

In the first week of November the weather suddenly turned cold and snow covered the distant peaks. We took out our winter woollies and unpacked the heater from its summer storage space beneath our bunk. The foliage glowed with autumn colours and smoke hung in the still air. Dressed in their three layers of black pleated skirts, the village women added the first of the traditional brown crocheted shawls.

Alan returned from Preveza with a two-litre gas cylinder from which to decant for the heater. He paid $64. We groaned at the price but then thought, 'Oh well, it doesn't matter because we'll get the deposit back when we return it.'

The woman from whom he bought it owned a small corner shop close to the centre of town, and she had other ideas. She was of the village, but it was clear that she did not consider herself so. No black garb or headscarf for her, but rather an ensemble of purple jersey and a fierce henna rinse through lac-quered hair that framed a sullen face.

The flicker of recognition that lit her eyes at the sight of Alan was swiftly replaced by a studied nonchalance when he asked for the refund. Perhaps she had not understood. Disregarding my past failures to communicate with pictures, I grabbed a biro and a piece of paper from the counter and began sketching cylinders and banknotes and arrows. But it was obvious that the only way to retrieve the deposit was to knock her down and take it. We left cursing our lack of Greek and feeling angry and defeated.

It was then that we remembered the pretty girl at the tourist information office. She spoke excellent English.

'Take a seat. I'll help you,' she said when she heard of our predicament. Her voice on the phone to 'henna head' was calm and reasonable, but finally she replaced the receiver quite firmly.

'I can't help you,' she said. 'She won't listen to me. You must go to the Prefecture.'

The Prefecture was a functional concrete building on the second floor of which was the office of the Prefect, a man with an air of quiet competence. He also spoke excellent English. He listened to our story without interruption, but when he spoke there was a note of apology in his voice.

'Well, I'm afraid that all I can do is take her to court,' he said, as though we had wanted her shot. Alan explained that we would be in the area for some months so taking her to court would be adequate but, really, all we wanted was our money back. The head of the Prefecture then shouted an order to someone hovering in the corridor and within seconds another man entered the office. They talked in Greek for a few seconds.

'This is Constantine,' the Prefect said. 'He'll look after you.'

Constantine was a compact man who walked with a purposeful step.

'Come with me,' he ordered and before we had time to fully explain, we were approaching the gas shop.

'*Po-po-po!* Greek Mafia,' Constantine exclaimed. (*Po-po-po!* is something like the French, *Oh la la!*)

This did not inspire confidence but it appeared that events had gathered their own momentum and it was too late to flee.

Constantine began in a persuasive tone, but 'henna head' interrupted angrily and delivered a tirade in our direction. Constantine tried again. 'Henna head' was clearly agitated. She shouted him down. The situation was fast developing into a full-blown brawl as passers-by formed a group in the doorway. Soon they would be adding their ten cents' worth and I moaned to Alan that this was not turning out the way we had hoped. Alan advised me to remain silent.

Then Constantine thrust a single sheet of paper in front of 'henna head' and softly spoke two words. The effect was dramatic. 'Henna head' lowered her eyes and her facial muscles slumped. She opened the cash register, extracted the money and placed it on the counter before us, but her eyes were venomous when they met Alan's.

Outside the shop we thanked Constantine. As he and Alan shook hands, Alan asked, 'By the way, what did you say in there?'. The answering smile on Constantine's face was enigmatic. He shrugged his shoulders, gave a friendly wave of farewell and was gone.

While exploring Levkas town, we stumbled upon a new super-market near the quay. We felt a rush of inexplicable sensations as we entered. There was something familiar about the way the goods were displayed. A young Greek man, whom we imagined to be the owner, approached with an outstretched hand and a warm smile.

'Hi there! I'm Stavro. Welcome to the Stavropoulos Supermarket.'

His accent was broad Australian and his manner relaxed and friendly. Soon we were joined by Lini, his Asian wife, a confident and feisty young woman. Both had been born and raised in Sydney where Stavro had worked as an accountant before acqui-escing to his father's wish that the family return to Levkas town, the birthplace of the parents. Stavro's father had inherited the piece of land on which we now stood. We chatted for a while before I asked the inevitable question, 'How do you enjoy living in Greece after a lifetime in Australia?'

Their reply was guarded.

'Oh, it's fine. We like it,' they said, their eyes wandering into the distance.

The cheese counter was near the back of the shop. When I moved towards it, Stavro's father, a tough-looking, gnarled man in his 60s, came to serve me. He wore a sloppy joe with the words 'Botany Bay' in bold letters across the chest. We chatted about Sydney, and the local cheeses. When I asked if he enjoyed being back in Greece, his eyes glazed in typical Greek fashion and for a few seconds I feared he would ignore my question.

Finally he answered, struggling to control strong emotions.

'Look! I lived in Australia for 30 years. I'm Australian,' he said. 'I love Botany Bay. I kept my fishing boat in Cooks River and I went fishing every day. It's different here. It's OK — but different.' His eyes filled. 'That's all I want to say.'

I felt moved by his dilemma and decided against any further intrusion into the old man's feelings. As I turned away, he fixed fierce eyes upon me.

'There's just one thing I hate about Australia,' he said.

'Oh, what is that?'

'I hate all those bloody Asians,' he replied.

Alan and Stavro continued to chat in the front of the shop while I inspected the range of goods on display. In the pasta section I noticed a neatly dressed woman about the same age as Stavro's father. She caught my attention because in that part of Greece women of her age wear black, but she was dressed in a tailored woollen skirt with a pale blue pullover and a pearly necklace. Once again I experienced feelings of familiarity. She raised sad eyes to mine.

'I'm Stavro's mother.'

I offered my hand, and she continued to hold it as she spoke.

'We don't often see Aussie people. You know, I miss Aussie people. I love Australia. Australia is my home. This is not my home. I don't want to come back here but my husband make me. I tell him I don't go but he say you my wife. You must go.'

She paused for breath and I wondered what to say. She removed her hand from mine and leaned against the shelves before continuing.

'I had a lovely home in Australia. Is beautiful home. In Sans Souci. You know Sans Souci? Every thing nice, eh. The garden too. All very nice. I make the curtains, the covers for the beds. I work hard in the factory sewing the bras for Berlei and I spend everything on my house. Make it all beautiful. And then my husband, he sell it. He sell it for peanuts. I cry and cry but he don't listen. Now I must live above this shop. Is not my home. Is not beautiful.'

I put my arm around her and she wept.

'Perhaps you will all return to Australia some day,' I suggested.

'Perhaps — but I think no,' she replied. 'My home is gone, my garden is gone. What I do with new house, new garden? I want the old one.'

'Well, at least you have your family around you. That must be a comfort,' I told her.

'The two little boys, sons of Stavro, they don't like it here. They don't speak Greek, they don't like Greek school, don't understand the games. They cry and cry.'

We stood in silence, both sad. The children would probably adapt and be enriched by the experience. They would become bilingual and at ease in another culture. And in the future, the pull of *their* birthplace may reverse the process.

I had just finished reading Clive James's autobiography *Unreliable Memoirs*. At the end of the book, after decades away, he writes, 'Sydney is so real in my recollection that I can taste it. It tastes like happiness. I have never ceased to feel orphaned.'

As Christmas approached I had already made friends with Yannis at the fish shop in Nidri village. The overseas telephone exchange in Nidri had closed for the winter and the only place to make an international phone call was the local fish shop.

It was nothing like a fish shop as we knew and loved them, but rather something of a meeting place for the fishermen and friends and customers of Yannis, the owner. Yannis spoke no English but he responded to me with warmth and a twinkle. I found him irresistible. A peppery, passionate man with a strong Belmondo face, his moods ranged from cantankerous, when he was prone to kick fish and wandering dogs, to gentle and solicitous. His wife, Ireni, was strangely similar in temperament, and the couple's daily clashes reverberated along the main street, causing the passing villagers to smile knowingly and shrug their shoulders.

Those who gathered in the shop were mostly fishermen from

the small *caiques* bobbing in the bay. They lugged their catches from the quay and dumped the boxes with reckless abandon onto the slippery concrete floor of the shop. Fish jumped from the boxes and leapt about, often spilling over the footpath onto which the entire front of the shop opened.

Fish were not actually displayed, there being no display area. Instead, the boxes were arranged in steps, sardines and mussels and small fish in front, large fish like tuna and the mighty octopuses at the back. Most of the fish were foreign to us so I usually held one up for Yannis to assess and if he clicked his tongue whilst giving the thumbs up sign, I bought it. But he always did that, come to think of it.

Before Christmas, the weather turned foul. It rained so heavily and for so long that it cleaned the skies and the water we caught in buckets was clear for the first time since reaching the Mediterranean. Everything inside the boat was damp. Alan felt depressed, the sheets felt clammy, our books swelled, the towels stank, mould appeared at an alarming pace, and Velia's photo on the saloon bulkhead kept fogging up and she periodically faded from sight.

I sewed and tried to ignore the elements. The new Turkish upholstery would take weeks to complete, but I felt a sense of purpose once I began. There were virtually no right angles on the boat so each cushion was a different shape requiring its own pattern. The ones I had completed looked attractive, but very tropical. They were hardly in keeping with the climate, but they would be fine in the Caribbean.

Although happy sewing, there were other things I dreamed of doing before the winter passed: wandering through the villages, making marmalade from the luscious citrus fruit grown in the area, improving my Italian, baking a cake, pickling some onions, reading, knitting, generally being hedonistic. My southern Italian bread soup, however, was a success. The recipe passed around the anchorage and soon everyone was eating bread soup.

We spent Christmas in a taverna at Vliko, a tiny village in the neighbouring bay. There were about 20 of us, friends and acquaintances from the anchorage. Several days before Christmas we held a meeting to plan the event and it was decided that the women would 'do the vegies' on Christmas Eve. I could not understand why the men could not peel a spud or two and was just about to say so when Fiona, quick on her feet, suggested that, with my assistance, she could be responsible for the table decorations.

We rowed ashore to gather wild holly, berries and pine from the bushland around Dorphelt's old home. Then we wired them into wreaths and added touches of tinsel and red ribbons.

On Christmas Day everyone trudged the three kilometres to Vliko in freezing weather to find the steam-filled taverna as hot as a sauna. There was plain boiled cabbage, plain boiled carrots, plain boiled dried peas, sloppy mashed potatoes and rock-hard baked ones — not exactly festive fare. But the turkey, cooked in the local Greek bakery, was excellent, as was the pudding, homemade and brought from Ireland by a guest on an Irish boat. A couple of people performed funny acts, and we sang rowdy songs and danced Irish jigs until well after dark.

As the winter progressed, we made new friends. Nearby was the luxurious yacht *Wavedance*, owned by two Yorkshire ex-policemen and their wives. They had hit on a workable solution to the high cost of owning and maintaining a yacht by pooling their resources and sharing expenses. The couples took turns at living aboard, changing over every few months. Sometimes their visits overlapped but they appeared to enjoy each other's company.

Accustomed as we were to the puzzling affluence of some Sydney police, we were suspicious of our new-found friends, but Mick and John assured us that they had never been offered a bribe, had no knowledge of drugs and had seldom seen violence.

In his younger days Mick had served for some years with the Queensland police force and his tales of life in the far north amused us. On his return to the UK he was chatting one night to a mate who had also spent some time in Queensland.

'Yes, Mick, I agree with you. It's a good life down-under,' his friend had said. 'I had a wonderful time out there too. The

Aussies are great people. Couldn't meet better. They shout you drinks at the pub, take you out fishing, invite you home to dinner. But the whites are proper bastards.'

Two of our favourite people in the anchorage were Jenny and Keith, a Welsh couple spending their fourth winter in Tranquil Bay aboard their solid old motor cruiser, *Victorina*. Keith was large, strong and tanned, with luxuriant white shoulder-length locks that were kept under control beneath a florid, hand-knitted cap which also served as an oil rag. He spent hours mucking about in *Victorina*'s massive engine room, and was, without doubt, a most unusual retired women's hairdresser.

Most things about Keith were big: his personality; his wife; his boat; and his dog, a shaggy alsatian named Ruff, or was it Rough? The dog tolerated yachties but hated Greeks. The Greeks reciprocated. They said that Ruff was a wolf. Certainly, the dog's behaviour ashore did little to change their opinion.

Ruff was noisy and aggressive, striking fear into the villagers and their dogs, both of whom scampered for cover when Ruff broke loose. Keith argued that Ruff was guilty by association because the Greeks hated all alsatians, a legacy of the war years when the Germans used alsatians to flush out partisans and to round up the villagers. Under the circumstances, the Greeks appeared amazingly tolerant in that they allowed the dog to stay for four years.

I also thought Ruff was a wolf. When I visited *Victorina*, he fixed me with little pig eyes. The hair along his back rose and stiffened, his upper lip curled away from poisonous yellow fangs and an ominous rumble rolled from deep in his throat. It was at that stage that Keith dragged him to the aft cabin and locked him in.

'I don't know what's got into Ruff today. He's usually so gentle,' he always said.

Keith and Jenny's daughter lived on *Zipcode*, a small yacht anchored near us, and their son lived on a boat near the opposite shore. It was a close-knit floating family, watched over with pride by the warm and generous Jenny.

Also on the far side of the bay were Keerin and Koonar, two

wild Irish brothers who were fine sailors and enthusiastic Irish jiggers. They were delighted at the arrival of their sister with the Christmas pudding from the Emerald Isle.

Steve and Jo owned a *felucca* which was tied up at the village quay. They used it in the summer months to show groups of back-packers around the Gulf of Amvrakia, near Preveza. Jo was bubbly and fun-loving, a perfect foil for the more serious Steve, a young man famous in his lifetime. He had sailed a 14-foot skiff from Nidri across the Mediterranean and up the Nile to Aswan, where he had been joined by Jo for the return voyage. Surviving the vicissitudes of Mediterranean winter weather and the venality of some Egyptian officials in a tiny craft without a cabin is a feat deserving of the glowing eulogies he received in the British press.

Lias and Julia, Swedish and Norwegian respectively, were spending their second winter in Tranquil Bay. Not for them the traumas of wind shifts and gales while swinging at anchor. They simply ran their boat aground in the mud at the beginning of winter and kedged it off again in the spring. The idea had strong appeal, but I believed that Alan and I would have felt trapped.

Halfway through January we heard someone calling our names and we looked through the companionway hatch to see Viking and Ann-Marie circling *Windigo* in their *caique*.

'Come to dinner,' I called.

That evening, we heard their dinghy bang against *Windigo*'s hull and the first one aboard was the dog. I was delighted to meet her again but had not expected Viking and Ann-Marie to bring the dog to dinner. Neither of us gets wildly excited about having dogs below, especially with the heater. But below she tumbled, crazy with excitement. She ripped from one end of the boat to the other while I quickly extinguished the heater.

'Far better to shiver than to have a singed dog or, worse still, a fire on board,' I reasoned.

Eventually Amber settled down and I stopped worrying about

her. She appeared to be sleeping, so I relaxed and enjoyed listening to our guests tell their latest news. Viking as usual did most of the talking, filling the boat with his flamboyance.

Then, to my horror, I noticed the dog suddenly jump up and assume the shitting position in the middle of the new Greek carpet that we had finished laying earlier that day. When I uttered a strangled cry, Ann-Marie calmly informed me that the dog had 'a bit of a problem'.

'She's taking pills for it so nothing will come out,' she said.

That was nice to know, but hardly reassuring. Each time Amber squatted and strained I held my breath, certain that something would come out. I sent frantic signals with my eyes to Alan but he assumed the pose of innocence that he practises when he knows something unpleasant is happening. Finally Amber fell asleep on the floor.

After dinner, we sat around chatting, Viking making his contribution from the cockpit where he had gone to smoke. The dog was lying in front of me and I absent-mindedly stroked her back with my bare foot. I thought I heard Viking saying, 'Would you like me to do that to you?' but I did not answer nor stop what I was doing because it seemed a strange thing to say. I did not know what he meant, nor was I certain that he had even said it.

'Would you like me to do that to you?'

He had said it again. Not in my wildest dreams did I imagine that I was doing anything wrong. I could feel myself blushing with confusion. Did the question have a sexual connotation? Was there perhaps something a bit kinky about Viking and Ann-Marie? Were they interested in swapping partners? Group sex? An orgy!

Suddenly Viking was standing before me. He was trembling with rage. His voice when he spoke, was deep with menace.

'Don't do that to my dog,' he said through clenched teeth. 'Get your filthy feet away from her. I warned you twice, but you kept on doing it. You put shit on my dog.'

I glanced at Ann-Marie but her eyes were fixed upon Viking's face, and they were luminous with love.

'You insult Amber and you insult me,' Viking continued. 'Get away from her. Amber's a member of my family — my child. She's to be treated with respect. I would kill anyone who harmed her. Never do that to my dog again. Never.'

I crumbled with shame and embarrassment. It seemed that I had committed the most egregious folly. Fighting hard to keep back tears, I listened while Alan said a stilted farewell to our dinner guests.

Early in 1994 there was a letter from *Panache* with wonderful news. Laurie was out of hospital, having won the battle against leukemia. The doctors referred to her victory as a miracle although she had a two year supply of bone marrow in storage just in case. At the end of that time, all being well, she and Des would return to Cyprus to continue their circumnavigation. They were living in a caravan and working hard to build up their depleted funds. The medical bill in Cyprus amounted to $65 000.

Halfway through February we farewelled *Syrah*. Mike and Fiona were determined to push ahead early to England, but we were content to remain until the weather became more stable. Mike was happy to be leaving as he could not adapt to the Greek way, interpreting independence as rudeness and making an inadequate effort to establish a rapport. The Greeks reacted accordingly.

It is not difficult to tell when some Greeks dislike you — they spit on your feet. On a couple of occasions in Preveza while strolling in the market place, I noticed gnarled old peasants give me the evil eye before directing a globule onto my shoe. When my anger subsided, I rationalised that they probably thought I was German.

On our last visit to Preveza we were hungry in the crisp morning air and bought two slices of pizza. The main street was noisy and busy with nowhere to sit, but in a side lane there was a low, whitewashed wall. A man from the house opposite walked through his front door to hang his canaries in the sun and after glancing at us and saying good morning, he hastily retreated. Minutes later he reappeared with two slices of steaming hot, freshly baked spinach and fetta pie.

'Throw away pizza,' he ordered. 'Pizza no good. My wife make good Greek food. You eat good Greek food instead.'

In early spring we received wonderful news from Velia and Graeme — they would fly to Europe again in the September of that year. We danced for joy in the main street of Levkas town and immediately we arrived back on board we dragged out the charts and tried to plan where we could be in September that would be thrilling for them and safe for *Windigo*.

Seville in Spain sounded perfect. It was 80 kilometres inland on the Guadalquivir River and therefore protected from the sea. The one piece of tourist literature on Spain that we had on board told us that Seville was in Andalucia and was a product of two great cultures, Arab and Christian, with a Moorish style and influence in its architecture. It was famous for ornamental ironwork, lace, pottery, tapestry, leather, gold and silver work, the third-largest cathedral in the world after St Peter's and St Paul's, and the oldest bullring in Spain. We imagined that Velia and Graeme would fly to Madrid.

In the inky darkness we awoke one night to feel the boat behaving in an arbitrary manner, the rhythmic rocking replaced by a capricious jerking and shuddering as if some hideous sea monster were gambolling beneath us. The air seemed filled with its raucous, rumbling cry. We scrambled from the bunk in terror, never having experienced anything like it before, but then we had never before been on a boat during an earthquake.

I had visions of great chasms opening in the seabed into which we would be sucked. Alan calmed me a little by insisting that we were safer on the shock-absorbing water than on land, and, indeed, when we peered out, it seemed that the boats in the bay were all swinging calmly on their anchors. All were bright with lights, though, and it was obvious that we were not the only ones awake and worried. From the shore came sounds of turmoil — shouting, crashing, the barking of dogs.

When we rowed ashore at dawn the villagers were already busy repairing the damage. On the Richter Scale the quake had registered 5.6 but there had been no loss of life. Several of the older houses had tumbled down, things had been thrown hither and thither, and many buildings had sustained minor damage, the worst being the liquor shop. A group of dejected men stood watching precious liqueurs seep across the concrete and into a drain. The earthquake's epicentre was in the sea off Levkas town. I could not help wondering what would happen to a yacht anchored directly over an epicentre.

In mid-February we made a short cruise of the neighbouring Ionian islands, calling at several villages as we sailed along the coast of Levkas before crossing to Cephalonia, the largest of the Ionian islands. In the earthquake of 1953, every town and village on the island had been destroyed except Fiskardo. No-one has ever worked out why it was spared, but as a result it remains a charming, 19th century waterside village looking like something transposed from Venice.

With a name like Euphemia, one expects a village to be feminine and pretty, but Euphemia was ugly — one of those villages that turn their backs on the sea. From the bay it seemed that we were looking up her skirts at rows of dirty underwear.

'Come in a spirit of excitement' said our guide book to Ithaca. And we did. The fabled island hid in a swirling mist. It remained invisible until we were almost upon it and could see its peaks pushing through the dense cloud and its cliffs rising from foaming waves. At anchor in the harbour at Vathi, we looked across to a natural amphitheatre ringed by a backdrop of high mountains behind green terraced hills and rich valleys.

We rode our bikes up the widest valley to the foothills where we were forced to leave them and walk until my winter legs refused to function. Alan powered on in search of nymphs while I sat and contemplated the view. The word 'bucolic' sprang to mind but I dislike the sound. 'Arcadian' is softer, and it is Greek. Homer had described the island as 'rocky and severe' and parts of it are, but Ithaca appealed to us and we felt we were communicating in spirit with Ulysses, for this was his island home.

At the end of February the weather finally became warm. Vernal breezes wafted from the land, sweet with the smell of warm rocks and new grass. In the late afternoons we walked through the cypresses and olive groves with butterflies in our hair and a carpet of daisies beneath our feet. At dusk the silver disc of Vliko Bay shimmered in the distance and lights flickered and reflected in the still waters. Donkeys picked their way along the narrow paths leading home to the village, their bells tinkling in the still air. We made preparations to leave.

After almost a year in Greece we felt sad that we had to go. The death of Melina Mercourie added to the melancholy. The passing of a Pope could not compare with the catastrophe that befell the silent and anguished Greeks with the death of the beautiful woman who had been passionate in her fight for freedom and democracy in Greece.

So farewell to that little corner of the Ionian and its quirky, generous people. Yannis and Ireni were not in their fish shop when I went to say goodbye. It appeared that the shop was running on trust with customers serving themselves. No-one knew where the owners had gone, nor when they would return. I placed the red roses I had brought on top of the till, and quickly walked away.

In Levkas town we shook hands with the sausage and salami seller, the carpet merchant, the wine seller who also sold cucumbers that he had preserved in a thick, sweet syrup, the offal seller who shouted his wares in English, French and Italian, the mono-syllabic clockmaker, the purveyor of scarves and caps. To all of them we said goodbye, leaving until last Stavro and his torn family at the Stavropoulos Supermarket.

CHAPTER 12

*the people never came
singing in Dionysius' ear
'non mangio piu' at Agropoli
a rapscallion in Salerno • the Pontine Islands*

'Italia! Oh, Italia! Thou hast the fatal gift of beauty.' So said Byron. Nevertheless, we did not expect the coast of Calabria to entrance us with its beauty but, from the sea, it did. It appeared a gentle landscape, of the kind that could have inspired Capability Brown and his colleagues when they set about reshaping the English countryside.

From our viewpoint half a mile offshore, we watched a slowly moving panorama of green valleys and rolling hills, villages clinging to the sides of mountains, tree-lined streams and startling cliffs, their limestone faces gleaming white in the sun. Toy trains snaked in slow motion along the coastline and rows of *paesani* in the grey-green fields harvested something that looked like *carciofi*, or globe artichokes, through the binoculars.

On the tip of Italy's toe is a spot with the lovely name of Saline Ioniche. But Saline Ioniche is not a lovely place, for it epitomises the gross waste that is a festering sore in the south of Italy; *un cancro* that causes the people of the north to scream, *'Disgrazia!'*, when they see their taxes flowing through Rome to the Mafia-controlled south.

In this region of perpetual poverty, we sailed into a grand artificial harbour, an enormous construction for the use of big ships — tankers and similar vessels. But all it contained was a handful of tiny fishing boats, and *Windigo*.

On arrival, we became confused by so much unutilised harbour space, and the feeling that there were no people bothered us. It was as if a mysterious disease had wiped them all out and we were the first to enter this modern ruin. We were cautious, however, so we pulled *Windigo* well out from the quay to provide a barrier against thieves and rats.

A few minutes later, we heard a voice.

'*Benvenuto Windigo.* Where's your passarelle? I can't get on board,' the voice called.

On the quay stood a tough-looking small man with a brown, leathery face. His haircut was so recent that the skin of his scalp showed white through the stubble on the sides of his head, on top of which was a thatch of black.

'We don't own a passarelle,' Alan explained.

'No passarelle!' the man exclaimed. 'But I can't get on board,' he repeated.

'No. Well, as you see, we are all tied down for the night,' Alan replied.

'I'll come back another time then,' the visitor said good naturedly. 'I used to live in Australia.'

As he walked away, Alan called after him.

'What happened to all the people?' he asked, sweeping his arm over the landscape.

'The people never came,' the man replied.

The next morning, while Alan worked on the boat, I set off on foot to find a post office and to buy fruit and vegetables, but the farther I walked, the more I wished the excursion had not been necessary. From the sea Calabria beckoned like a jewel, but at Saline Ioniche it was all an illusion.

A pitted road ran parallel to the shore, its sides littered with rubbish: plastic containers grown brittle in the sun, old tyres, a collapsed pram, an ancient fuel stove on its side, a decomposing dog, hessian bags with something soft inside. Crumbling concrete apartment blocks were separated by vacant allotments overgrown with weeds and littered with debris. In some, a donkey or a goat stood swishing away the flies in the shade of a makeshift shelter or under dust-coated grape vines on rickety terraces.

The old men I met on the way were silent, and guarded like Turks, their trousers too short and their felt hats brown or black. Few answered my cheery *'Buongiorno, signor'*. The one young man I met responded in a friendly way and told me where to find the post office. It was simply farther along the interminable road.

'Is there somewhere I can buy fruit and vegetables?' I asked.

'A kilometre or so farther on is a village. You may find some there,' the young man replied.

The village barely existed. It was simply a more densely populated part of that endless road. Its one shop had a few cardboard boxes that contained the remnants of rotting vegetables: tomatoes too soft to pick up, shrivelled celery, crinkled carrots and desiccated cabbage. It smelled of despair.

The five women in the shop were the first I had seen. When I spoke to them in my rusty Italian, they laughed with delight and all babbled together. But their dialect was strange and I understood little. They were all plump, three wore widows' black and the youngest two who did not had teeth missing in the front.

'Is this the only shop?' I asked them.

'*Si, signora.* But there's a big supermarket three kilometres farther on. They sell everything.'

'Not everything. Not any more,' said another.

It appeared that an enormous *supermercato* had been built to service the thousands of people who were to live and work in the industrial complex at Saline Ioniche. Now, according to the women, many shelves were empty and fewer and fewer people worked there.

I trudged back along the dusty road, wishing I had stayed on board. There was no traffic apart from two teenage boys on a motorbike. They passed three times, summing me up, and I worried until a man began to walk behind me, begging for money and cigarettes. I felt safer with him there. He stayed for perhaps a kilometre before disappearing into an apartment block not far from the harbour.

In the late afternoon we sat in the cockpit and gazed across to Mount Etna which was fuming on the island of Sicily. Where should we go? North or south? To Rome or to Sicily? Why not both?

Syracuse was once the most important city in the entire Mediterranean region, superior even to Athens. Founded in 734 BC by colonists from Corinth, it is resonant with history and in over two millennia its basic layout has remained virtually unchanged. Ortigia, the ancient half, is still the heart and soul of the city. Originally an island, it is joined to the mainland and Achradina, its modern half, by a causeway.

Like Rhodes, the city reveals its splendour suddenly to those who approach it from the sea. Rounding Castellucio lighthouse, one enters Grand Harbour, its shores a crescent of medieval buildings, baroque palaces and a massive Norman castle. Such was the glory of Syracusa that it attracted people like Plato, Archimedes, Aeschylus, the evil Dionysius and later, Caravaggio, though perhaps the city's most loved citizen is Santa Lucia, the patron saint of Syracuse who was murdered for her faith by Diocletian in 304 BC.

The police were helpful and gracious when we checked in. Alan mentioned our concern about crime. Would we be affected by it? What precautions should we take? The handsome head of police smiled as he spoke.

'It is not always wise to believe everything you hear, *amico mio*,' he began. 'Syracuse is no more crime-ridden than anywhere else. However, you must always be alert for bag snatchers on bikes. You, Alan, must always walk on the curbside and you should both keep your wits about you at all times.'

'Perhaps I shouldn't carry a shoulder bag in Syracuse,' I commented.

'That would be wise,' he replied, and added, 'Keep your boat locked, remove everything from the deck, and never leave the boat after dark.'

Like city dwellers throughout Italy, the people were elegantly and fashionably dressed. They chatted noisily in the bars and outdoor restaurants facing the bay. It was mid-morning but, even at that hour, groups of men stood gossiping in the sunny squares, preening, posturing, gesticulating, hugging each other in flamboyant greeting or farewell. We noticed several expensively dressed young men cruising the squares in open sports cars, mostly red in colour, and those with motor bikes congregated in groups of Elvis look-alikes. There were few tourists, not even the ubiquitous Germans.

We wandered the alleyways and palace-lined squares of the old city to the strange Duomo, once the Temple of Athena, with its baroque facade and column-crammed interior. Built in the 6th century BC, it was at various stages a Byzantine church, an Islamic mosque, a Norman church and a Spanish barracks and evidence of the four styles was everywhere.

In Achradina, we saw cryptic signs pointing to 'Dionysius' Ear' in the same direction as the Greek theatre. His ear turned out to be a large, deep cavern with delicately curving walls that had been excavated by Dionysius' slaves, who were then imprisoned there until they died. So perfect were the acoustics in the cathedral-like space that Dionysius could hear even the softest whisper of rebellion or plots to escape through a small crack in the ceiling. While we stood in the dark drum, an Italian burst into song, his tenor voice ringing in the stillness like a bell. And the song? 'Santa Lucia'.

Since ancient times, passage through the Strait of Messina in small craft has been considered hazardous and, as *Windigo* passed through, it was impossible not to think of the sufferings of Ulysses: 'Thus we sailed up the straits, groaning in terror, for on one side we had Scylla, while on the other the mysterious

Charybdis sucked down the salt sea water in her dreadful way.'

We saw Scylla's cave high on a cliff, a dark hole from which she drooped her six long necks to snatch sailors from their ships as they passed beneath. And at one stage, there were whirlpools around us but the effect was minimal, nothing like the Charybdis which had the power to suck ships down and belch them out again. The whirlpools, however, intensify at certain times of the month and, until they were subdued by an earthquake in 1783, they were a force to be reckoned with.

The town of Agropoli stands upon a promontory that juts out into the Gulf of Salerno. It is an attractive place where the medieval village rises steeply from the harbour on one side, while the more modern town rises in a series of steps from the water's edge on the other. We had planned to stay in Agropoli for two days, but ended up staying for two weeks.

It all began with Enzo and Antonio. *'Benvenuti ad Agropoli'*, they called as they passed *Windigo* on their way to their own yachts farther along the quay. Later, the four of us sat in *Windigo*'s cockpit drinking vino while they talked of boats, their dreams of sailing around the world, of Agropoli, and of food.

'The cuisine of Campania is the best in all Italy,' Antonio announced, his round face creasing with mischief.

'The people of Bologna may not agree,' I countered. 'Isn't the region of Emilia-Romagna supposed to have the best cuisine in Italy?'

'Ah, the northerners think everything they do is the best,' Antonio replied. 'But apart from bland and boring mortadella, what else is there?'

'There's Parmigiano,' Enzo reminded him. 'Where would we be without it?'

Then turning to us he said, 'Come to our house for dinner tonight. You too, Antonio,' he added, turning to his friend. 'Bring Letizia. Perhaps you should cook, Antonio. As you know, Bibiana is beautiful and talented but she doesn't cook well.'

Enzo, a teacher at the local *Scuola Media*, was endowed with film-star good looks and a passion for poetry. With his wife,

Bibiana, he lived in a smart garden apartment with separate guest accommodation across a small courtyard. Just inside the entrance was a sleek black bird in a cage. It called *'Amore, amore'*, at the top of its lungs and sometimes *'Amore Enzo'*. They explained that it was an Indian lovebird and that it was in love with Enzo but totally indifferent to Bibiana who looked after it.

The walls of the living area were lined with an eclectic array of paintings, masks and photographs.

'Bibiana has a fine arts degree,' Enzo explained when he noticed our interest.

'But I have no job,' Bibiana moaned. 'I work as a cinematographer but there's little work available in that field south of Naples.'

Antonio's fiancee, Letitzia, was also a Fine Arts graduate. She worked in Salerno as a restorer of medieval frescoes and she bubbled with a vivacious, whacky humour, the pile of red hair knotted on top of her head bouncing as she laughed. In very short time, Antonio had prepared a superb first course of pasta with squid in its own ink, followed by a platter of seafood: prawns, octopus and two types of local shellfish served with a mixed green salad. Bibiana excels at cooking cakes, so there was also a savoury Easter cake, a sweet Easter cake and small Easter eggs filled with ice-cream. The latter, accompanied by Bibiana's homemade lemon liqueur, were sensational.

Towards the end of the meal two friends arrived. Rocco, a rotund and smiling professor at the University of Naples, was accompanied by his wife Vesna, a lawyer from Montenegro who was just establishing herself in Italy. Rocco was bearded and he wore a long black cape like a priest's robe. Both he and Vesna spoke fluent English.

It seemed to us that when Italians were not talking about food, they were talking about politics and, as the evening wore on, the room reverberated with heated discussion and good-natured laughter. The Neapolitan dialect was quite incomprehensible to me, so every few minutes one of our hosts would try to include Alan and me in the discussion by speaking in Italian or English.

Bibiana tried to explain her disillusionment with the Christian Democrats, and the betrayal she felt as a result of ex-Prime Minister Andreotti's suspected involvement with the Mafia.

'I feel betrayed, disgraced and angry. We are a country without direction,' she complained.

'What success do you think the Fascists will have in the next elections?' Alan asked.

'I'm not sure. Politically we act like children,' Bibiana answered. 'And, like children, we are not ready for democracy.'

Enzo looked worried. 'Bibiana, our guests will get the wrong impression,' he said. 'They'll think you support the Fascist Party.'

'I may do that, Enzo,' she told him. 'It offers stability. Italy needs another *duce*, someone who will tell us what to do and then see that we do it.'

Rocco said, 'Bibiana, remember what happened last time. Mussolini told us what to do, but it was the wrong thing.'

'You're the one who's acting like a child, Bibiana,' Enzo admonished.

And so the argument raged. A bottle of lemon liqueur was consumed, cigarette and cigar smoke clouded the room and sometime in the early morning, Enzo drove us back to *Windigo*, weaving merrily as he sped through the silent streets.

The next day at sunset, Enzo returned. 'I'll pick you up in a couple of hours. We're all going to Rocco's house for dinner,' he informed us.

Two friendly red setters greeted us at the door of the large stone house, built on a steep hillside above the Cilento coast. The Mediterranean gleamed silver below us in the light of the half-moon and lights twinkled in a grand arc that stretched from Punto Licusa in the south to Capri in the north. The night was cold, a fire crackled near the refectory table, and the house smelled of herbs, garlic and curing prosciutto — an Italian smell.

Italians are noisy people, flamboyant and gregarious. We drank Rocco's homemade wine and once more discussed the effects of a win for the Fascists in the *Mezzogiorno*, the untidy and neglected southern region dominated by the Mafia and seemingly resistant to change.

'We've tried everything else,' Bibiana persisted.

'We've also tried Fascism,' the others replied, while Enzo turned to us and asked if we knew Alberto Moravia's book *The Conformist*. We had read *Roman Tales* and *The Woman of Rome* but were ignorant of his other works.

'It's about a man sucked into the evils of Fascism by his desperate desire to conform.' Enzo turned to his wife. 'Fascism wouldn't suit you, *cara mia*. You're too unpredictable.'

Rocco had prepared *gnocchi* with a herby green sauce, followed by baked eel and a green salad. There were plates of sausages *fatto a casa*, cheeses made from goats' milk and hearty peasant bread with a crisp crust covered with a residue of ash. There were bottles of dessert wine, and liqueurs made from a variety of fruits. And there were amazing figs that had been soaked in liqueur, stuffed with almonds, baked in the oven and then coated with dark chocolate to become plump cushions of pleasure.

As we sat drinking coffee, Rocco announced that he would pick us up in the morning for a sightseeing tour of the area.

'The mountains behind Agropoli are magnificent in the spring and many of the villages are medieval gems. You must see them,' Rocco said.

Enzo and Bibiana came too. Alan asked how Enzo and Rocco were able to take time off work, but they gaily replied that they were simply *fortunati*. From high in the mountains near the partly restored village of Castellabate, we could see across the wide shining sweep of the Gulf of Salerno to the Amalfi coast, Capri and distant Ischia. The area around Castellabate is a national park for the preservation of the medieval towns, and the scattered monasteries and farmhouses. Rocco floated along in his flowing black cape, a passionate and learned guide.

'We didn't come to be with you and Alan. We came to listen to Rocco,' Enzo joked, giving us both a friendly hug.

On the way back to Agropoli, Rocco pontificated on another subject.

'We've been eating far too well,' he announced. 'We must show some restraint. We've been overindulgent, even gross. Whatever will our guests think of us.'

We tried to reassure him.

'No, it must stop. Tonight we'll just have a simple pizza,' he declared.

Alan and I became suspicious when Rocco parked the car in front of a restaurant.

'This isn't a pizza parlour, Rocco,' I said.

'It may not look much like one,' he replied. 'But they make the best pizzas in all Italy. Now stop complaining and let's go. *Ho molta fame!'*

Antonio and Letitzia were already there with two more friends. There was Nico, an amiable lawyer with his adoring child bride, and the chivalrous Gaetano, an elegant veterinarian. They sat at a large round table in a corner of the crowded restaurant and we could hear Antonio's laughter ringing out above the clatter as we entered.

Baskets piled high with warm, slightly toasted bread arrived immediately and the table was quickly covered with plates of ten varieties of antipasto: marinated raw fish, roasted peppers in olive oil, artichoke hearts, baby broad beans in a fresh tomato sauce, stuffed anchovies and several specialities of Agropoli, mainly shellfish prepared in different ways. The white wine was light and slightly spritzig and those who drank the red declared it ambrosia.

Then the pizzas started — four different types in quick succession. Their bases resembled samousas, thin, light, crisp and airy, and their fillings were sumptuous. Later, when Antonio was discussing dessert with the waiter, Rocco interrupted, 'No, no, no, Antonio! Our guests have not yet tried the most famous of Agropoli dishes. Now is the season.'

I groaned. '*Sono piena*, Rocco. I am full. *Non mangio piu.'*

'You can forego the sweets,' he replied. 'Just have fruit and cheese.'

So we were served plates of short pasta with a sauce made

from anchovy fingerlings. They resembled a pile of white worms and tasted like buttery crab.

As we left the restaurant it began to rain.

'If it's raining in the morning, I won't take you to Paestum,' Bibiana told me and Alan. 'It will be more fun when it's warm and sunny.'

Alan and I prayed for rain. We were exhausted by the hospitality and joyful zest for life of our new circle of friends. They appeared to have perfected a lifestyle that had a happy balance between work and play. Just being alive seemed so amazing to them. They sparkled with fun and passion and generosity of spirit and made me think of something that E.M. Forster had written, 'Love and understand the Italians, for the people are more marvellous than the land.'

The morning dawned cold and wet and we thanked the powers that be, and stayed in bed for most of the day. In the late afternoon, an elderly man approached with two bottles of wine and a cake. He was a serious man, softly spoken.

'Please accept this cake and this wine,' he said. 'My wife made the cake and I made the wine. Both are very good. You are welcome in Agropoli.'

We asked him to come aboard but he politely waved away the invitation and was gone.

Eboli is a little town that was made famous by Carlo Levi in the 1940s when he wrote a sombre book called *Christ Stopped at Eboli*, about life in a southern Italian village. He actually wrote the book farther south in Basilicata, and possibly never visited Eboli but, according to our friends, the effect of the book is that tourists now come to the area.

Twenty-five kilometres south of Eboli is Paestum where three great Doric temples stand close together in a green field surrounded by rose gardens. The temples of Poseidon, Ceres and Basilicata are the most complete and splendid of all the Greek temples in Italy. No doubt one factor that contributed to their preservation was the low-lying malarial swamp that surrounds them, for it kept the area empty of people who would otherwise have used the stone to build houses and other structures.

Seen from a distance the columns appear intact, gigantic and indestructible, but when you sit on the grass at their base and gaze at the sky through the golden shafts, they appear ethereal. Nearby is a small museum and Bibiana was an informed and enthusiastic guide.

'We'll have a late lunch at my place,' she said. 'But first we must go to the buffalo farm.'

The area around Paestum is famous for the best mozzarella in Italy, and Bibiana lost no time in educating us.

'A buffalo must be happy to give sweet milk. Like a mother, eh,' she explained. 'Here we have extensive marshes, so the buffaloes can wallow around in the mud and this makes them happy. They produce mozzarella in other parts of Italy but they don't have enough mud, you see. So the taste is not so good.'

The farm produced fresh mozzarella daily but still Bibiana complained that it would not be as good as if we had come in the early morning.

'It will taste the same to us,' I assured her, but she looked slightly shocked at such nonchalance about food. She chose a range of types and sizes from the large trays where the shiny plump shapes floated in whey, and after we had been seated in her sunny courtyard at Agropoli, she arranged the cheeses on an old earthenware platter with wedges of ripe tomatoes and sprigs of glossy fresh basil. To the table she added a pepper grinder, a bottle of green olive oil, a loaf of peasant bread, a bottle of chilled wine, and we had a feast.

It was time to move on, to leave Agropoli, but we dreaded telling her.

'Oh no. Please don't go,' she cried. 'We're all having such fun. Enzo will be sad. I will cry. Rocco will grow morose and Antonio will also cry. And you haven't really got to know Nico and Gaetano yet.'

Nevertheless, the next day we set about preparing *Windigo* for sea. Gaetano called in with a bottle of wine and an invitation to dine at his house. We told him we were leaving. Antonio came to check that we had remembered his invitation to dinner at his house the following night.

'You're the skipper,' I said to Alan. 'You must make it clear to them that we have to go.'

'You speak the lingo, my love. You must make it clear,' he replied.

When we pick up a *Domus* magazine with features like 'Farm Houses of the Amalfi Coast', we expect to find Antonio's house featured there. Built on top of his parents' stone farm house and extended out from it with balconies, it is entered by a wide exterior staircase. The house sits on the slopes above the Mediterranean and is surrounded by olive trees, grape vines and a vegetable garden. The interior of the house is classic white with restored timber furniture and tiled floors, and Letitzia's light and sure touches of colour. A fire blazed in the big whitewashed fireplace and Antonio was busy at the stove when we arrived. The room quickly filled with noisy friends, and finally Rocco shouted that he was weak from hunger. *'Sono debile per la fame, Antonio!'*

We ate *orecchi e fagioli* (ears and beans), a pasta dish in which the pieces are shaped like ears and served with borlotti beans in what is really a hearty soup. I would have been content with the soup and the green salad, but this was not to be. It was accompanied by a platter of several types of *casalinga* pork sausages and an array of cheeses made by Antonio's parents. One of the cheeses resembled a large golfball and I asked Antonio what type it was.

'Unsalted butter wrapped in mozzarella. The very best.' He kissed his finger tips. There was a platter of cakes and biscuits, bottles of fiery *grappa* and the popular lemon liqueur.

Later, I sat chatting to Rocco.

'*Caro amico*, it's time for us to go, to leave Agropoli,' I told him. 'We must move with the wind and we have a long way to travel.'

'You've read *Alice in Wonderland*,' he replied. 'Do you remember the unbirthday party? A very merry unbirthday, to you?'

I assured him I remembered.

'Well, we have had the welcoming parties for you. Now we must begin the unwelcoming parties! A very merry unwelcome, to you,' he sang and they all raised their glasses and took up the chant.

'A very merry unwelcome, to you. A very merry unwelcome, to you.'

'They are incorrigible,' I thought, feeling sad at the thought of leaving them.

I tried to tell them so in my halting Italian, but they simply shrieked with laughter. Alan restored sanity by standing in front of the fire and addressing them in English.

'You are the most generous and lovable people we have met. We'll remember you always,' he told them. 'On Saturday Olma and I are holding a "farewell to Agropoli" evening on board *Windigo*. We'll feel honoured if you are there. *Grazie a tutti*.'

And so they came. Enzo and Bibiana, Rocco and Vesna, Antonio and Letitzia. There was also Nico without his child bride, and Gaetano. And there was yet another guest, one Paolo by name who appeared to be Antonio's friend. Paolo was apologetic that his work had taken him away from Agropoli just when we had come.

They arrived like a group of excited children, skipping and laughing along the quay. They piled below, filling the boat with presents of wine and cakes and fruit and cheeses. Rocco brought a plate piled high with his extraordinary chocolate-covered figs and a large panettone in the traditional Easter shape of a dove.

'We thought it best to all come together,' explained Letitzia. 'Then we won't be interrupted by each new arrival. Now we can all sit down and enjoy ourselves.'

Wine was poured and in the enforced intimacy of the saloon, they proceeded to do just that.

Alan and I had been preparing for two days. Despite the fact that I had been cooking *a la cucina Italiana* for most of my adult life, I was not prepared to pit my skills against the culinary feats of that group. I therefore chose Thai cuisine, reasoning that the tastes of Thai curries, coconut milk, Kaffir lime leaves and lemon grass would be new and exotic for Italians, who are notoriously chauvinistic about their cuisine. Fresh coriander was unavailable in the town, but fresh mint and basil made adequate substitutes. At various stages in the preceding two days I had been consumed by terror at the thought of feeding so many people in the confines of a yacht but, with everything well organised, it was possible.

The next morning Alan and I were dead and the boat was a shambles. But there is a right time to leave and this was it. We forced ourselves to clean up the mess and by late morning, we were underway. It felt like leaving home.

Salerno takes its name from *sal* (salt), the sea, and the little river Irno. Its setting in the splendid sweep of the Gulf of Salerno is beautiful, and in its siting, as well as in several other ways, it resembles Naples a few miles farther north. We knew that we would need to take care but from our research and from those who had gone before, Salerno seemed the safest place to leave the boat while we visited Pompeii. The area around Naples is *comorra* country and yachts in trouble have little redress in an area where the code of silence is a way of life.

'This is the fishing harbour. Why are you tied up here?'

A man and a small boy stood on the quay. The man's belly, inside a soiled singlet, hung over his sagging trousers and several days of black stubble covered his jowls and chin.

'Tell him that we prefer to be in the fishing harbour because the yacht harbour is too exposed,' Alan said.

I translated. The small boy, a rapscallion with matted hair framing a scowling face, eyed me with malice.

'I'm the warden of this part of the harbour,' the man told us, and then with a smarmy complicity he added, 'You have my permission to stay here for five days.'

'*Perfetto*,' I replied. 'We don't wish to stay longer.'

'You must pay me, of course.'

'As far as we know, there are no fees for the fishing harbour, only for the yacht harbour, but we'll check with the harbourmaster,' I told him.

'For you, sweet *signora*, a present will be enough. I like whisky,' he said.

'Later,' we told him, remembering the lessons of the Red Sea.

He slouched off, his sandals flapping loosely. But the boy remained, smouldering and belligerent. As we turned away, he let out a stream of abuse.

'Pigs. Filthy pigs. Madonna fuckers. Dirty bastards. Shit eaters. Go away. *Va fan culo!*'

I started to say, 'Now listen here, kid . . .', but thought it prudent to ignore the little sod. We wished that someone would say, '*Benvenuti a Salerno*'.

In the Middle Ages Salerno had been famous for its school of medicine, the *Civitas Hippocratoca*, which endured for over a thousand years, reaching the height of its glory in the 12th century. Doctors trained for eight years and all learned to perform surgery. The centre of Salerno was virtually destroyed when the Allied forces landed from the sea in 1943. The city has been rebuilt along the waterfront with wide boulevards and lines of trees, but our enjoyment of the area was marred by a persistent madman who followed us, babbling incessantly about the Madonna. At the impressive Duomo of San Matteo with its huge bronze doors brought from Constantinople in 1043, the madman disappeared.

There was one more thing we wanted to see — the view from the Castello — but I had to ask directions. I approached an expensively dressed, respectable looking *signora* with carefully coiffed hair and a lizard skin handbag. Smiling brightly, I had only uttered a few words when to my horror, she sprang a foot off the pavement and went rigid with fear, beating the air with her free hand.

'Oh No. No! No! No! No!' she screamed, as if I had tried to sell her a live snake. I was mortified. She gave me a look of loathing and ran as fast as her Cuban heels would allow, around the next corner. Perhaps she did not like foreigners, or maybe she just couldn't stand the sight of me. *Chi sa?* A bemused stallholder who had watched the strange theatrical then kindly showed us where to go.

'What exactly did you say to that woman, Olma?' Alan wanted to know. But I felt his tone was slightly accusatory so I said, 'Oh, nothing.'

From Salerno I rang my ex-husband in Venice. He knew of our plans and would be wondering where we were.

'What on earth are you doing in Salerno?' he asked. 'No-one of any refinement goes there!'

'Sailors aren't noted for their refinement,' I told him.

'Salerno is an arsehole of a place,' he continued. 'The air is foul, the water is contaminated with sewage, the people are peasants and the only thing of worth is that tatty old Duomo.'

'You're still a cultural snob, my dear Eneide,' I replied. We agreed to meet in Venice in a few weeks time.

It would be ridiculous to compare Salerno with Florence, Venice, Perugia or Assisi or any of the dozens of exquisite towns and cities of Italy, but it has its own special charm and its people love it.

'Why have you come to Salerno?' many asked.

'To see your city. To visit the Duomo.'

'*Ah, Salerno. Bella citta, eh!*' they replied.

Staccato tapping noises bounced from the deck. Someone was throwing stones at *Windigo*. Standing on the quay, his arm raised to let fly another missive, was the foul-mouthed urchin of the previous day.

'Put that down,' I yelled. 'What do you think you're doing, throwing stones at our boat.'

'I want to come on board. Please can I come on board.' He was totally unrepentant.

'No, you can't.'

'I want to come on your boat. Shorten the lines so I can get on. It's too far for me to jump,' he persisted.

'No, now go away. If you throw stones at our boat again, I'll tell the police.'

His father arrived as Alan and I sat in the cockpit enjoying the sunset. Something disingenuous in his manner should have alerted us.

'There's a fishing boat coming in. You must make room for it,' he said.

'But there's already enough room for a fishing boat to fit beside *Windigo*,' Alan pointed out.

'This is a big fishing boat. You must move.'

It took us almost an hour to pull up the two anchors at the stern, untie the lines to the shore and the fishing boats on either side, and re-position *Windigo* a few metres to starboard and then replace everything. All the time, our swarthy friend gave directions from the quay, enjoying his power.

'More to port. Too far. Now to starboard. Too far. *Madonna mia!* Watch those lines. *Porca miseria!* Forward. Back. To port. To starboard.' Alan fumed in frustration as I translated for him.

'If he'd just say where he wants us to go and then shut up, there wouldn't be a problem,' he complained.

As we were adjusting the tension on the lines and thinking about our half-consumed whiskies in the cockpit, one of the armed patrol guards with whom we had exchanged friendly greetings as we left the port area each morning sauntered across.

'Why did you move?' he asked.

'We were told to by the warden. There's a big fishing boat coming in.'

'The warden? There is no warden. I think you mean Giuseppe. He lives in that derelict boat over there with his tribe of kids and his big wife. Do not trust Giuseppe!'

'Why did he ask us to move?' I wondered aloud.

'You've somehow annoyed him,' the patrol guard answered. And as he walked away, he called out over his shoulder, '*Attenzione, miei amici!*' Be careful, my friends.'

We caught the dawn train from Salerno to Pompeii. Alan had not seen Pompeii before, so he was fascinated by everything. Part of my interest was in the changes that had taken place since my first visit in the 1950s. At that time there had been little or no restoration, just excavation, so it was a pleasure to see some of the houses now restored to the way they were when people lived there. On my first visit, women were not allowed to see the erotica, but today groups of school children on excursions giggle their way past the scenes of intercourse and Priapus weighing his enormous erection.

Early next morning we were preparing to leave Salerno when Giuseppe called out, 'Are you leaving?' We nodded.

'You owe me L 15 000 for looking after your boat.'

'We didn't ask you to look after our boat,' I told him.

'But if I hadn't looked after it, something bad would have happened to it. I kept it safe,' he replied.

'I think the patrol guards kept it safe, Giuseppe. And I don't believe that you've any right to ask for money,' I said.

Alan came on deck with a bottle of wine.

'I don't know why I'm doing this,' he said to me as he handed it to Giuseppe. 'It seems like a reward for sheer, unmitigated gall. On the other hand, he may have friends in our next anchorage.'

The days were clear and sunny as we sailed along the Amalfi coast, but crisp with a breeze that blew across new snow. From the sea the mountains are splendid, their towering crags and rocky obelisks reminding us of Phangan Bay in Thailand. So, too, did the grottoes and caves around Amalfi and Positano where the hotels and villas appeared as mere dots on grand and precipitous sites.

Passing close to the cluster of the Galli Islands, we thought again of Ulysses. This was where the sirens had lived, and where Ulysses had had to block the ears of his crew with wax and to have himself tied to the mast, so that he could listen to the sirens' sweet song without being lured to his death.

It was here, too, that the engine began to splutter and die and Alan was forever diving below to perform mysterious rites while I watched the shore draw closer and willed the engine to start before we ran aground. Would it get us to Rome, we wondered. We longed for wind as we nursed *Windigo* along the sunny southern side of wonderful Capri and across the Bay of Naples to Baia.

The island of Procida loomed out of the golden smoke haze with an air of decaying opulence. Like an Indian city reflected in the Ganges, its layered buildings, painted in faded lemon, pinks and Roman red, shimmered in the still sea. Nearby Ischia, by contrast, was organised and leafy, bustling with tourists and decorated with the weird and whimsical mansions of those who have more money than taste.

The Pontine Islands lie scattered across the sea between Naples and Rome. The islands of Ventotene and San Stefano were until recently serious penal settlements, and it was in the circular prison on the latter island that Caligula's sisters had been imprisoned. Some German yachties we had met in Greece had said, 'Don't miss Ventotene!', and it is indeed picturesque. The island is formed from volcanic rock into which the people have carved houses, tunnels and restaurants, Flintstone-style. A more conventional town has been built on top of the subterranean dwellings.

CHAPTER 13

Fiumicino • Rome • Michael, the Ukrainian
the Monster of Florence
the Arsenale in Venice

Fiumicino is Rome's main outlet to the sea. The town is built on either side of the canal that runs from the Tyrrhenian Sea to join the Tiber before the river bends to enter the sea a few kilometres farther south. Opening bridges allow access to yachts and trawlers, and cramming the northern side of the canal are scores of fishing boats that supply the Rome fish markets, and the 54 fish restaurants of Fiumicino.

The town is well organised and thriving, a pleasant base from which to explore Rome, which is only an hour away by train or bus. Ostia Antica, the port of ancient Rome and one of the finest of Roman ruins, is close by. We tied the boat to the canal wall in the centre of the town next to a supply of free fresh water.

From the moment we arrived, the people were insatiably curious about us, the boat and our lifestyle.

'I don't want to be adopted again just yet,' Alan said. 'It's too exhausting and we have too much to see and do. Perhaps later.'

Being tied up in the canal was like living in a fishbowl so we rigged up the cockpit awning to give privacy from the street beside us, and left it open to the canal and the town on the opposite bank.

'What flag is that?' someone asked as we sat hidden behind the awning.

'It's British, I think.'

'No, that's not the British flag. That one has stars on it. Five small ones and a big one. See?'

'No idea, then. Could be from anywhere.'

'Does Britain still have colonies?'

'Yes, I think so.'

'Could be from anywhere, then.'

'Why don't we ask them?'

'There doesn't appear to be anyone on board.'

Rome, City of the Soul! Where does one begin to explore that rich and often confusing city where every few steps brings to light something to wonder at and to think about? One needs a lifetime. We had visited Rome several times in the past, indeed, it was our favourite city. Although not as ordered as Florence or Venice, Rome surpasses both in its complexity, in its special brand of haphazard charm and in its raw Italian spirit.

It seemed appropriate to visit St Peter's first. There it was — grand, awe-inspiring and beautiful as always. And, as always, it was covered in grime, pigeon droppings and the pollution of Rome. The authorities are agonisingly slow about passing legislation to curb the excesses of the motor car. We spent the morning in the great cathedral's cool interior, content to sit and marvel at the unsurpassed tribute to genius.

Walking along Via della Conciliazione to Castel Sant Angelo, we marvelled at how little the city had changed since we were last there. The phrase 'the Eternal City' had a ring of truth about it. Trees were bursting with spring growth along the Tiber. Ponte Sant Angelo, that most elegant of bridges with its statues of St Peter and St Paul and Bernini's ten baroque angels crosses the river here, so we followed its lead to Piazza Navona, from where we returned to Pyramid Station by bus.

Not long after our arrival we looked up to see two people staring down into the boat through the open saloon hatch. A change in atmospheric pressure had caused the water level to drop and

Windigo was now well below the level of the footpath. The man and woman, silhouetted against the sky, hovered above us like two birds of prey, blocking out the sun.

'Hello, down there. I'm Michael. This is my mother, Eva,' called the man.

He was well over six feet, an enormous man in his 30s with closely cropped fair hair, bulging muscles and an aggressive stance.

'I see you're from Australia,' he said. 'We want to go to Australia. We hear it's a beautiful country. Free. The people can do as they please there.'

'Well, it's not quite that free,' I said. 'And yes, it's beautiful.'

'I've taught myself to speak English so that I can go to Australia. I also speak good Italian. Can we look at your boat?'

'The water's too low,' I pointed out. 'You couldn't get on board.'

'Where's your passarelle?' Michael asked.

'We don't have one,' I replied.

They wandered off, obviously disappointed.

A couple of days later they returned, all spruced up and bearing a bottle of champagne. What could we do but ask them aboard?

It was obvious that Eva was a strong and determined woman, but she acted in a tactile and mothering way towards me that made me feel ill-at-ease. Michael, who filled the saloon with his bulk and bravado, told their story, slipping easily from English to Italian and then back to English when he saw that Alan was not following.

They had fled from the Ukraine to escape the communists and were refugees without passports — stateless people. Italy is a compassionate country where officials turn a blind eye to some of the finer points of people's existence, so Michael and his family had been able to live and work there without harassment.

'You're lucky, Michael,' I said. 'Italy has been generous to you.'

'Italians are lazy,' he replied. 'I want to go to Australia where I can work hard when I want to. Here there is the siesta. I don't like the siesta. I like to work all day, but the boss tells me to go and have a sleep. *Porco miseria!* I want to be my own boss. I don't like anyone telling me what to do.'

'You won't be able to enter Australia without passports,' Alan pointed out. 'Getting that sorted out should be your priority.'

The unexpected suddenness of Michael's next question startled us.

'Can I look at your engine?'

'Are you interested in engines?' Alan asked, taken aback.

'Yes, of course,' Michael answered. 'I used to be in the merchant navy. I understand boats and engines. Now can I see it?'

Michael and Eva squatted at the engine room door, speaking earnestly in Ukrainian. 'Good, you have looked after it well,' Michael said to Alan, rather like a headmaster patting a pupil on the head for a job well done.

'Now on Sunday,' he continued, 'we're taking you on a picnic to Frascati. We're preparing a Ukrainian barbecue. With a sausage as long as your arm!'. He gave a raucous belly laugh and I felt myself withdrawing from him.

'Perhaps we shouldn't go,' I said to Alan later.

'Well, it's too late now,' he replied. 'We've no way of getting in touch with them.' Then he added, 'Relax and enjoy the day. Frascati wine is famous, and we may get to see that lovely villa. Villa Aldobrandini, I think it's called.'

At precisely 10 a.m. Michael arrived in a battered old Fiat Uno. First we had to go to Michael's place to pick up the food, his mother, and his son, an overweight lad of 14 called Dennis. Home was a tent and an old caravan surrounded by at least ten similar makeshift homes that belonged to other refugees. The dwellings were untidy heaps that had been extended with packing cases and pieces of iron, and held together with ropes and wire. The area of wasteland in the scrub a few kilometres from Fiumicino was littered with broken-down cars, old fridges, bent bicycles and similar cast-offs.

Michael's grandmother, a wizened woman without teeth, sat on an upturned drum nursing a diseased hen, and there were several more ailing birds scratching lethargically in the dust, their scaly raw skin showing through the sparse feathers on their backs and craws. A long hose running into the bush was the only source of water.

Lunch was piled into baskets and off we went, not in the direction of Frascati as promised but in the opposite direction. In the back seat with Eva on one side, her arm possessively around my shoulders, and clammy Dennis on the other, I sat cramped and miserable.

'Isn't Frascati in the opposite direction?' Alan asked Michael.

'We're not going to Frascati,' he replied, a note of finality in his voice as if he were speaking to a persistent child. There was no further explanation.

The spring countryside was pretty with blossoms and eventually Michael stopped the car beside a farm gate where a stream tumbled through a causeway under the road and continued across a green field with willows. The gate was locked.

'Climb over!' Michael ordered.

'But someone owns this land,' I protested.

'That doesn't matter. We often come here,' Michael replied.

Italians are generous people so perhaps it did not matter. On the other hand, it would be a brave farmer who would make an enemy of big Michael. We followed the family to a grassy bank beside the stream and Michael lit a fire.

'Eat,' he ordered.

From a large plastic bowl, Eva dished out piles of meatballs that floated in a thin sauce.

'I can't possibly eat that much,' I told her.

'These are special,' she replied. 'Minced turkey cooked in yoghurt. You're too thin, Olma. I'll make you big and strong.' She looked at Alan. 'You're built like a man but there's not enough meat on your bones. Eat up. You're almost Michael's height and only half his size.'

'I like Alan the way he is,' I told her.

'*Stupida!*' she replied, using one of the few words of Italian she had learned.

Michael shovelled meatballs into his mouth while he barbecued chicken pieces on green sticks he had cut from the willow trees. The long sausage was not mentioned again, but I worried about the origin of the chicken pieces.

'I suppose Australians eat plenty of meat,' Michael commented. 'Ukrainians also. Meat makes people big and strong. Not like Italians. They're small and weak because they eat cattle fodder. All that pasta and green salad stuff. Grass, I call it. That's why they can't work hard and they tire quickly. That's why they must have a siesta.'

'Perhaps it's because it's sensible to work in the cooler parts of the day and sleep in the heat,' Alan suggested.

'No, it's because they're not real men. At least 50 per cent of Italians are homosexuals.'

'Michael, that is ridiculous!' I said. 'Not that it matters one way or the other, but there are probably fewer homosexuals in Italy than anywhere else.'

He gave me a searching look. 'You like Italians then?'

'Yes, of course I do,' I replied. 'And as they appear to annoy you so much, perhaps you should go elsewhere!'

Who wants to argue with a giant and his vulpine mother when one is a long way from the boat on a lonely dirt road. In the awkward silence, I looked at Michael throwing things into the baskets. There was something unmanageable about him. I felt he could quickly become choleric, violent even. I wondered about Dennis's mother. What had become of her?

But the next minute Michael was ebullient again, wrestling with the complaining Dennis and kicking grass into the wine.

'Let's go!' he shouted. 'We'll drive around Lake Bracciano and stop at the Etruscan tombs.'

It was a tedious drive, made more so by Michael's comments, which he made, not for any nefarious purpose, but simply because he believed what he said.

'There are no homosexuals in the Ukraine.'

'Of course there are, Michael.'

'It doesn't matter,' said Alan.

'The world will end in the year 2000. Jesus and Nostradamas said so.'

'That is ridiculous, Michael.'

'It doesn't matter,' said Alan.

'Women have no intellect. God only intended them for breeding.'

'Look, Michael . . .'

'It doesn't matter,' said Alan.

Later in the safety of the saloon, we tried to be philosophical about the day.

'You have to admire their courage,' Alan reasoned. 'They escaped from behind the Iron Curtain before *perestroika* and *glasnost* eased the way. They succeeded despite near-starvation, armed guards, tracker dogs and raging rivers. And all that with Michael carrying his grandmother on his back for much of the way.'

'I never want to see them again!' I declared. 'Should we be worried about *Windigo*, I wonder. What will happen to her when we go to Venice?'

'If I were them, I would certainly be tempted,' Alan replied. 'And yes, we'll have to take some precautions I suppose.'

We felt more at home in Fiumicino as the weeks passed and people began to greet us in the streets and the marketplace. The town had an air of purpose and its own steady rhythm that flowed with the canal and the arrival and departure of the shellfish trawlers and the scores of smaller boats that fished closer to shore.

The people who regularly walked along our side of the canal often stopped to talk. Gisella, a smiling woman with a kind face walked her dog each afternoon and stopped for a chat if we were on board.

'You must come for dinner,' she would say.

'Thankyou Gisella, we would love to come soon,' I would reply.

Piero, a small spidery man, rode a pushbike. He brought red

roses that he stole from people's gardens as he rode by. *'Per la bella signora'*, he said as he ceremoniously presented them.

Moko, a young black man from the Gambia passed each morning on his way to sell sunglasses and headbands at the bus stop.

'When you gonna buy new sunglasses, eh?' he joked, and together we chanted, 'Not today. Maybe tomorrow,' and he would walk away laughing.

Donello, elegant in Armani style, often strolled by at sunset, always alone. We were surprised to find he was married.

'I walk alone because my wife is German,' he said one evening. When he saw the looks of puzzlement on our faces, he laughed and added, 'Well, the Germans don't like the *passeggiata*. They don't understand. You must meet my wife. On Sunday we'll pick you up, take you for a drive and then to the yacht club for drinks and something to eat.'

Donello was a successful engineer and he owned a small, sleek yacht, which he kept in the yacht club marina in the Tiber. Michelle, his wife, not only refused to walk but she also refused to sail. Donello looked at Alan and said, 'You're so lucky to have a woman who will sail,' to which Alan replied, 'Yes, but getting her to walk is the problem!'. They laughed, while Michelle confided in me her frustration with the Italian psyche.

'It's difficult for me in Italy, Olma. No, it isn't the war. They seem to have forgotten that. It's something else. Italy has an ancient and sophisticated civilisation, so over the centuries Italians have developed clever ways of doing things, unusual methods of solving problems, shall we say. Beneath the charm they are devious, shrewd, inventive, imaginative. They themselves invented the word for it. Machiavellian! He epitomised the way they are. Germans aren't like that. We say what we mean. We don't play games. We're decisive and direct.'

I had no words of wisdom for Michelle. The world is as it is.

The only visitor who bothered us was a spivvy-looking little man who did not speak, nor even smile. He simply stood and stared, his face blank and his fly held together with a safety pin. No doubt he was mad and I found myself thinking about the man on the stairs: 'He wasn't there again today, Oh, how I wish he'd go away.'

Disappointed that the summer crowds had already begun, we joined the queue at the Vatican Museum and headed for the Sistine Chapel. On previous visits I had been saddened by its lack of lustre, the genius of Michelangelo struggling beneath the patina of grime. On that visit we witnessed a miracle.

The entire interior of the chapel has been cleaned and restored. It glowed and sparkled, a riot of colour with every detail crisp and the colours luminous and resplendent. We felt like dancing and, indeed, the noise in the chapel as the excited crowd gasped and exclaimed became so loud that a guide shouted at the top of his voice, '*Silencio!* Be quiet! Silence please!'. This is a hallowed place, not a circus!'. For a few minutes there was calm until those people moved through and a new crowd gathered.

'*Silencio!* Be quiet! Silence please!'

Afterwards, we wandered along the Tiber, its banks now leafy and inviting, past the imposing law courts to Piazza Navona. One probably should not view another church so soon after the incomparable Sistine Chapel, but we could not walk past Sant Ignazio where the Jesuit priest, Andrea Pozzo had created his amazing trompe l'oeil ceiling. And then to the Trevi Fountain and the Spanish Steps where memories of Velia flooded back.

As a child, Velia had been terrified by a mad woman on the Via Condotti. The poor soul had wanted to be friendly but her appearance had been witch-like and Velia had run shaking to hide behind Alan. We remembered, too, the steaming hot mandarincino liqueurs that the three of us sipped every evening in the bar on the corner before setting off in the winter cold to find a restaurant that would meet with Velia's approval.

We had not seen the Ukrainians since the picnic and had not thought about them either, so it was with some dismay that we heard them calling from the shore late one afternoon.

'You must come with us now for a bath,' Michael ordered.

We were slightly taken aback because we knew we needed one.

'We're taking you up into the mountains to the hot springs. It's only 80 kilometres away. It's good for your skins. Gets all the filth out of the . . . how do you say it? Pores, that's it.'

'No thank you, Michael.'

'We've made a special trip to pick you up. Now let's go!' he persisted.

'No Michael. We're not going,' I repeated.

He stiffened and for a second he seemed to fight for control. Then, just as suddenly, he relaxed.

'Next time then,' he said cheerily enough and they were gone.

The spring weather was glorious and on a clear singing day we packed a picnic lunch and set off for Ostia Antica where the ancient port city of Rome, preserved since antiquity in the dried mud of the Tiber, is still being excavated. It is an evocative site, conjuring up visions of the city as it was in the time of Claudius.

Once through the massive Roman Gate, a road paved in large slabs of stone leads through an avenue of trees to the city centre where the streets are lined with warehouses, shops and dwellings. There are temples and baths, brothels and fountains, and a fine theatre. And in the marketplace, not far from the Thermopolium, the hot drinks stall, is a sign in Latin, which translated says, 'Read, and know that there is a lot of gossiping in the market.'

At the entrance to the city proper was a new notice board with a sign in Italian. *'Sono disponibili gli obiettori di conscienza in qualita di accompagnatori per gli scavi'*. The English translation was underneath. 'English speaking conscientious objectors are available to accompany you through the excavations.'

We were intrigued. Should we have one, we wondered. I asked the woman in the ticket booth what it meant.

'In Italy there are many conscientious objectors who refuse to do national service,' she explained. 'It would be unfair on the others if the conscientious objectors didn't serve at all, so instead they must work for the benefit of the community. They help the poor and the needy, the elderly and the sick. Those who speak a foreign language help the tourists.'

'That seems an admirable arrangement,' I said.

'Would you like a conscientious objector to accompany you?' the woman asked.

We declined, not through any ideological belief but simply because the day was ours and we preferred to wander alone. It was lovely there. Ivy crept over some of the ruins, wild flowers adorned others, swallows dipped and weaved against the curve of the sky and the air tinkled with the songs of hundreds of small birds. On the outskirts, where the ruins disappeared under the surrounding crops of grain, which were now shoulder high, we ate lunch on a grassy mound and pondered on what lay hidden in the earth beneath us.

La lingua Toscana, the Tuscan tongue, was the basis of my Italian learned in Florence many years ago. I usually find the language of other regions incomprehensible and in Rome, where the language is strongly idiomatic, I was often at a loss. Seldom, however, did I make clangers as big as the one I made in a Fiumicino chandlery to which I accompanied Alan so that I could translate his requests for engine equipment.

'Tell them I need some penetrating oil,' he requested.

I tried to wriggle out of it. I felt it would not be straightforward but apparently life aboard *Windigo* would be untenable without penetrating oil. I consulted the dictionary and blundered forth.

My request riveted the three young men behind the counter to the spot and I knew immediately that everything was not as it should be. They showed admirable restraint, however, despite their desperate eyes and sharp intake of breath before they disappeared into the stock section. But worse was to come.

When they returned, one of them triumphantly brandishing a can, Alan looked at it and in glorious innocence said, 'This won't do. Tell them it's too light. We need something much heavier.'

The three young men collapsed in agony behind the counter before once more retreating to the stock area from where we could hear strangled moans. I am still not certain exactly what went wrong, but Alan grew self-righteous and refused to admit that the request was fraught with peril from the beginning.

At the top of the Via Veneto is a fine renaissance palace that houses the high-security American Embassy. We successfully negotiated the various checks, and entered.

'You want a United States visa!' shouted the belligerent young woman behind the security screen, as though we had asked for the crown jewels. 'Are you residents of Italy?'

'At the moment we are.'

'But not permanent residents. That's no good. You must be permanent residents.'

'It's difficult for us to become permanent residents of anywhere because of our lifestyle,' I told her.

Alan explained. The young woman's face turned to granite.

'Then you should have obtained the visas while you were residents of your own country,' she pointed out.

We explained that we had left our country more than three years before and at that stage we had had little idea about which countries we would wish to visit.

'What are your jobs?'

'Right now we have no work.'

'No work. No work! How do you eat?' she exclaimed.

'We own our house. We try to live off the rent.'

'But no work!' she repeated in disbelief. 'They will not give you a visa, you know. You can fill out these forms, but it's a waste of time. Yours and mine.'

Our circumstances and our plight were now known to many in the waiting crowd who studied us with interest. Feeling slightly ridiculous, we buried our heads in a corner and filled out the forms. Then we sat and waited for three hours. When an American woman who had been staring at Alan for some time approached, we felt almost grateful.

'I just have to tell you, you're the spittin' image of my nephew back in the good ol' US of A!'

She and Alan talked of ancestors and forefathers and inherited characteristics for some time while the waiting crowd once again followed the ups and downs with interest. But in the end Alan and his American acquaintance could not decide whether they were related or not, and interest flagged.

Eventually we were summoned to a bulletproof booth by a young American, one of those 'Let's get this show on the road' types. He looked us up and down, decided we were acceptable and said, 'I'm sorry you were kept waiting. Please come back at four o'clock and you can have your visas.'

The siesta was well under way, so we ate our picnic lunch in the Borghese Gardens, that idyllic part of Rome with lakes, ponds, fountains and follies, passionate lovers and black Africans selling long-stemmed red roses. Then we window-shopped along the Via Veneto back to the embassy.

Obtaining a Spanish visa was even more involved, with three separate visits to the Spanish Consulate in Via di Campo Marzio, where the officials were helpful to everyone else, but cold and obstructive to us when they realised we were Australian. Some years ago, so the story goes, a Spanish soccer team arrived in Melbourne without visas and the players were told that they could not enter the country. Australian travellers have been treated differently from other nationalities ever since.

The Monster of Florence, Pietro Pasciani, had been accused of eight double murders in lonely bush parking places on the outskirts of Florence. The four murdered couples were all young lovers whom Pasciani is said to have killed in acts of violent sexual sadism. The trial of the semi-literate farmer was transmitted daily on national television to millions of Italians and every day the country quivered with the shocking revelations, while the behaviour of the grey-haired old man alternated between angry outbursts and protracted sobbing.

In the early stages we believed Pasciani innocent, but after watching the prosecutor's interrogation of the man's 14-year-old younger daughter, we felt sickened and believed him capable of anything. There she sat, her body from the neck down filling the screen. She sat with her knees apart, her short bare legs dangling like a child's, her stubby fingers clutching at the arms of the chair or twisting the material of her skirt into tight knots. Obviously retarded, she was scared and squirming.

'Did your father wear a rubber cover on his penis when he made love to you?' the prosecutor asked.

'Yes, he always wore one of those things,' she replied.

It got worse. We turned it off. Some time later, Pietro Pasciani appealed and was found innocent and released. The case is still unsolved.

Before the Pasciani trial there was another which lacked the titillation of the Monster mystery and was simply gruesome. On trial was a mother who had murdered her daughter. Her bloated porcine face was expressionless as she blubbered her answers and it must have been obvious to all that she was incapable of rational thought. With their backs to the camera, her other two daughters gave evidence, one for, one against.

Abysmal as they were, we sometimes laughed at the sex shows. Compered by a sleazy pimp and a brassy blonde with mounds of silicon, the shows outrageously pander to the male ego. Suggestive song and dance routines are punctuated by advertisements for scantily attired prostitutes who writhe and purr on the screen whilst their phone numbers flash in a corner.

Italian 'Candid Camera' is a cruel and shocking program in which the celebrity guests are 'set up' in a way that reminded us of the victims of the sickening thrills at the Colosseum. We watched as a handsome film star was inveigled into taking part in a magician's act in which the star was locked into a pillory board which, he was assured, would be opened by the magician. The camera focused on his smiling face.

'This is all such fun. Great PR!' he thought.

Suddenly, a simulated fire broke out — smoke, sirens, the works. Everyone rushed out, except, of course, the handsome film star. He was terrified. He screamed for help, his eyes bulged in their sockets, his hands clawed at the timber of the pillory board, his legs thrashed. He was no longer handsome.

Gisella brought her husband, Aldo, to meet us. She spoke of him often so we knew that he worked in administration for Alitalia. Gisella had been a hostess on international flights and that was how they had met. Aldo was as we had imagined him, patrician in appearance with the amusing and entertaining manner of a raconteur.

'Gisella tells me that you won't come to dinner. I must insist that you do!' he said. 'Tomorrow night we will prepare a typical Italian meal for you.'

Their house was a few minutes' walk from the boat and we felt slightly embarrassed that we had not accepted an invitation earlier, having walked past their house in Via Tempio della Fortuna many times without realising that they lived there. The house was tastefully furnished and set in a large garden with fruit trees and grape vines.

Antipasto was a dish of fresh ripe tomatoes chopped finely with fresh basil and served with warmed, crisp bread, a bowl of cut garlic to rub on the bread and green olive oil to pour over it. *Spaghetti alle vongole* was followed by thin slices of baby veal cooked lightly in olive oil with herbs and lemon and served with a green salad. Gisella had made a luscious *tiramisu* to end the meal. Aldo and Gisella also owned a yacht, so we talked of sailing, of cruising, of travel, and of experiences in far-flung places.

It is so easy to fall in love with Italians. Gisella and Aldo, like others before them, knew that we would sail away and possibly never be seen again. Their friendship and hospitality was mag-nanimous and without ulterior motive.

In the dinghy, Alan and I explored the canal for a couple of kilometres inland and finally found, tucked into the willow-lined shore, a small boatyard with sufficient space to leave *Windigo* while we were in Venice. The owner was a roguish ex-sailor from the merchant navy and next to us was a New Zealand cruising couple who offered to keep an eye on *Windigo*. We were grateful to them, particularly as the security guard was a tiny Sri Lankan who, with his gentle demeanour, seemed most unlikely to dis-suade intruders, and the watchdog, a big friendly black animal covered in plump ticks, trusted and licked everyone. Still, it was the best we could do.

We had not seen the Ukrainians for several days and we anticipated that if they noticed that *Windigo* was not in her usual spot they would presume that we had already left for Sardinia. But the day before our departure for Venice, there they were, peering intently at our overnight bags airing in the sun on the foredeck.

'Where are you going? Ah, Venice. Then I'll sleep on your boat and look after it,' Michael declared. 'My mother can stay here too so there'll be someone to cook for me and to be on board during the day when I'm at work. Dennis can come too. He'd like that.'

Why did Michael always make me feel threatened? It was a kind offer that under different circumstances we may have accepted. Perhaps our fears were groundless. Were we becoming paranoid? Being a refugee does not make one a boat thief. But . . .

'Thank you Michael,' Alan was saying. 'It's kind of you to offer but we've already made other arrangements.'

'Other arrangements will cost you money. We'd do it for nothing,' Michael replied, obviously disappointed. 'Where will you go?'

We were noncommittal. 'There are several boatyards around here. Maybe we'll leave it with one of them, maybe in the Tiber.'

'I'll come with you. The currents are strong so you'll need help,' Michael said.

Alan explained that we could manage without help and we preferred to do things our way. The four of us stood in awkward silence until Michael finally spoke.

'Our car was stolen last night,' he said. 'We had to take a taxi to come here. We may not be able to come and see you again. It's too expensive by taxi.'

We shook hands across the water and watched them slowly walk away.

The Arsenale in Venice, commenced in the early years of the 12th century, takes its name from the Arabic *dar accina'ah*, and in its derivation points to the strength of Venice's early links with the eastern Mediterranean. At the height of the city's power, the Arsenale was the base for no fewer than 300 shipping companies, extensive wharves and warehouses, and thousands of *arsenalotti*, boatbuilders whose skill and efficiency were legendary.

Napoleon burned the wharves in 1797 and confiscated the remains of the Venetian navy. Parts of the Arsenale are still used by the Italian navy for storage and the naval museum is housed there in an old granary.

It is in this now quiet and picturesque part of Venice that my ex-husband, Eneide, and his wife, Rosie, live, and it was nearby that Rosie found us an apartment that would be vacant for the first three days of our stay, such space, such luxury, after the confines of the boat. We felt tempted to simply sit in the sun and watch the life of the Arsenale unfold in the *piazza* below us. But Venice awaited, her buildings decked out in cascades of flowers.

There it was as it has always been, floating in the warm Canaletto light on that milky turquoise sea, the insidious slow sinking invisible, the dank rot hidden. One day Venice may no longer exist and the world will be without that rarest of treasures. You feel the pathos as the floor of San Marco undulates beneath your feet.

We spent the days wandering the twisting *calle*, visiting churches, museums and galleries, and one day we caught the *vaporetto* to Murano, the glass-making island that, for one reason or another, we had never before visited.

At the end of the week, within a few hours of leaving Venice, we were back aboard *Windigo*. She seemed to have shrunk in our absence but she was otherwise as we had left her.

'I suppose you'll soon be leaving,' Aldo said on our return to the old spot in the centre of town. We explained that we had only to collect our engine parts and make a last trip into Rome.

'We'll take you for a farewell pizza tomorrow evening,' Aldo said. 'Nothing grand, just a pizza!' Alan and I ate only fruit for lunch, remembering Agropoli.

And of course it was grand and, yes, pizzas were served, but the diners appeared to be there for other purposes. Antipasto was presented on two large circular tables from which you helped yourself in a clockwise direction.

'This is marvellous!' exclaimed Alan, his eyes glinting as if the antipasto were gold bars.

'Gluttony's a sin,' I reminded him.

Aldo then became assertive and insisted that we all have fettuccine with a sauce made from special mushrooms that appeared under pines for only a few days each year.

'This is the season. You must try them,' insisted Aldo. 'It could be a once in a lifetime experience!'

The sauce was almost black. It tasted earthy and strong and it clung to the pasta like rich cream. We enjoyed it, but the helpings were too generous to finish. The pasta was followed by tender barbecued lamb and salads, a rich ice-cream, and a fiery liqueur that Aldo described as a digestive, 'to settle the stomach and prevent the staggers.'

I should have noticed the zeal of the zealot in Alan as we caught the early morning bus into Rome for the last time. Baroque churches were one of his passions.

'How shall we spend the last day?' I asked.

'I want to look at churches again if we have time,' he replied.

That was fine by me so we started with Sant Agostino with its Caravaggio, and then Sant Agnese with its Borromini facade, followed by San Bernardo, San Carlo alle Quitter Fontanel, Sant Andrea al Quirinale, Santa Maria della Vittoria, San Giovanni in Laterano, San Clemente, San Stefano Rotondo.

'Stop! Please stop,' I panted. The details had begun to blur and I begged for mercy. How apt were the words of Saint Theresa of Avila: 'The pain was so sharp that I cried aloud but at the same time, I experienced such delight that I wished it would last forever.'

There were two more visits to make — a final pilgrimage if you like. We strolled through the Forum to the exquisite little temple, the Velia, then to the Trevi Fountain to throw in our coins. One can say *ciao* to Rome but not *arrivederci. Ciao Roma, bella citta!*

CHAPTER 14

*Corsica and Sardinia • a marine procession
in the Balearic Islands
Moors and Christians • the Alhambra
Gibraltar • the Guadalquivir River
reunion in Seville*

Our intention when we left Rome in June 1994 was to sail to Sardinia, but southerly winds forced us north to the island of Elba with its pretty Tuscan landscape, wooded mountains, and a 'Dracula' castle high on a pinnacle. Elba, Italy's third largest island after Sicily and Sardinia, is the place of Napoleon's exile. From there on a clear day he could probably have seen Corsica, his birthplace.

But for us the day was not clear, the pollution so thick that we could not see big ships until they were almost on top of us. Ashore, Elba was polluted by tourism with Ye Oldes and Merry Englands so much in evidence in the capital, Portoferraio, that we wondered why the English do not stay at home for their holidays. It was not yet high summer and already the streets were congested.

The pall of unclean air had spread to Corsica, and for hours we motored along that island's eastern shore without seeing the land, apart from the jagged high peaks of Corte, the island's wild inner region. Corsica smelt inviting, though, as the perfume of its sweet *maquis* and wild lavender wafted out to sea on the warm air.

The few French cruising yachts that we saw flew the Corsican flag, a black Moor's head on a white background beneath the tricolour. It seemed a prudent thing to do because the Corsicans have an active separatist movement and are easily upset if they feel you have no respect for their cultural identity and their demands for independence from France. And I suppose they are thoroughly tired of being the bad guys in French films.

Our days in Corsica were spent on white sand beaches where we swam in water of stunning clarity. Not a scrap of rubbish was to be seen, and when the wind blew the smog away, the air sparkled and we were in Paradise. The coast of Corsica is a place of great beauty.

One of the cruising guides we had on board described Sardinia as the best part of Italy, and perhaps it is for the yachting fraternity. It is certainly a mysterious, undeveloped and wild place with wonderful cruising grounds. Separated from Corsica by the treacherous Straits of Bonifacio, the north coast of Sardinia is a series of deeply indented bays and small islands with a background of the raw, wind-sculptured granite mountains of its lonely interior. High in the Barbagia region lives the closed society of shepherds who have a reputation for kidnapping the rich and famous, of which there are many along the 16-kilometre stretch of the extraordinary Costa Smeralda.

For the pleasure of the glitterati, as well as to fund his own extravagant lifestyle, the Aga Khan developed this piece of coast with lavish and often tasteful accommodation and an exclusive marina. The local regional authority laid down strict guidelines before construction began, so there are no high-rise buildings, garish hoardings or fast-food restaurants, or indeed any of the crassness of most holiday resorts.

While having lunch at Olbia, south of the Costa Smeralda, I discovered an unattached tooth in my mouth. *Dio mio!* We began the search for a dentist as we had in Athens. The pharmacist, a strong young man who looked as if he worked out with weights, took a quick look and smiled.

'You can go to my dentist,' he said. 'He's my brother and his surgery is directly opposite, across the *piazza*.'

The dentist, built like a heavyweight boxer, was a much larger man than his brother and he approached my broken tooth with the gaiety and vigour of a happy athlete. This was not the kind of dentist I had come to know and fear.

'Not a problem. Easy. Easy,' he proclaimed after inspecting the damage. 'Relax. Just relax. Enjoy yourself *signora*.' And then he added, 'I am.'

Within a short time, he had rebuilt the tooth.

'How long will it last?' I asked.

'Up to you,' he replied, then, laughing, he added, 'I know you won't be back.'

Garibaldi spent the last years of his life on the uninhabited wooded island of Caprera, after leading the fight for the unification of Italy. His home on the island is now a museum and a place of pilgrimage for Italians, who approach it from the island of Maddalena to which it is joined by a causeway.

We approached the house from our anchorage on the opposite side, after a long hike through the heat along dusty tracks that all seemed to converge there. The house in its park-like setting appeared comfortable rather than grand.

People were walking straight past the ticketseller at the front gate so we did the same. I remember wondering why he was there.

'*Scusi, scusi!* You haven't paid,' he called after us.

'Everyone else walked past. Sorry.'

'I don't think you're Italian,' he said. 'Italians don't have to pay to visit Garibaldi's house. Everyone else must pay.'

'That's fair,' we assured him.

Garibaldi's red shirt and his cloak still hang there, along with his saddles in the stables across the courtyard, and Marsala, his famous white horse, is buried nearby. Garibaldi's bed stands in the centre of the living room where he had it moved so that he could watch the turquoise waters of the bay as he died.

Like the *meltemi* of the Aegean, the *mistral* can blow for days at a time. When we were ready to leave Sardinia for the Balearics, it blew for five consecutive days and was then followed by blissful calm. We entered Mahon (or Mayon), the capital of Menorca, at night after a smooth two-day crossing and for the first time in our lives we were in Spain.

We approached the harbour from the blackness of a moonless night and, as we rounded the headland which hid the town from the sea, it was like entering a fairyland, the water so still that we appeared to be gliding over coloured glass that reflected lights from around the bay and the hills beyond.

In the morning it was still a magic world, the brilliant white of the waterfront buildings sparkling behind the palms that lined the long bay, the architecture a mixture of Spanish and English colonial. Above us, nestled in the trees, was a delicate pink and white mansion where Admiral Nelson had once lived with Lady Hamilton.

We knew that the Spanish loved processions, but we were not expecting to see one so soon after our arrival. But no sooner had we entered the cockpit to survey our new world than we heard a great honking like the braying of a thousand donkeys, a blowing of trumpets, a clashing of cymbals, and a banging of drums. Bells pealed, and all around the harbour and on the tops of the surrounding hills and mountains, enfilades of bonfires sprang into life as if lit by an unseen hand.

Down the harbour in slow procession came an armada of boats, scores of them, all decorated and festive with streamers and flags and coloured balloons. An effigy of a richly gowned saint stood at the head of the procession in the bow of a grey navy vessel whose sailors lined the decks in drill formation. We were thrilled as the procession slowly passed by *Windigo* and out of sight.

Then, from the direction in which the boats had disappeared, we heard another great hullabaloo, and suddenly there was the procession again, heading towards us at a perilous pace. The boats were racing. The saint, no longer on the navy vessel, now leaned alarmingly in the bow of one of the leading small boats, her gown and white lace headdress blowing behind her like those of the Arab brides in Akko harbour.

The participants were racing the effigy to the finish line. The boats wove and rocked and plunged as they ploughed through the wake of those in front, and the faces of the contestants were wild with excitement and the threat of collision.

Like mainland Spain, the Balearic Islands have been settled by numerous invaders: the Phoenicians, the Greeks and the Romans. The Arabs, who took over in AD 711, saw the islands as stepping stones to the domination of the known world and the ultimate defeat of the Christian enemy. But they, too, were eventually overtaken and the islands are now part of Spain.

There are five islands in the group: Mallorca, Ibiza, Menorca and tiny Formentera and Cabrera. They lie off Spain's Costa del Azahar. Except perhaps for Menorca where the wealthier tourists go, the coastlines of Mallorca and Ibiza are tarnished with the concrete towns of the package holiday crowds, ersatz Spanish villages and noisy discos. The crowds that roam the streets of Ibiza are young and I often found their language brutal and their attitude threatening.

When we approached Ibiza, however, it rose from the sea in the late afternoon and we were entranced. Pine-covered and green, its spectacular cliffs hung above us in shades of salmon, grey, and white, seared by the still fierce heat of the setting sun, and it appeared that we were the only visitors to this splendid island. Eventually, though, we reached Puerto di Sant Antonio Abad to find the Balearic equivalent of Surfers Paradise; no surf, of course, but lines of towering apartment blocks, hotels, flashing neons, noise, glitter, and the smell of stale cooking oil.

In the town of Sant Antonio Abad we ordered cold drinks at a bar in which several people were lolling at tables littered with dirty coffee cups and overflowing ashtrays. Our drinks were placed in front of us on the bar, when suddenly the place emptied, except for one man who moved close to Alan. He casually fondled a ball of something soft and brown.

'Get out,' Alan said to me.

'But we haven't had our drinks,' I remonstrated as he propelled me towards the door. Why was he behaving in this way? The two men in the car parked just outside the door were waiting for us, but the signal from their colleague inside had not been the one they expected. The drug entrapment had been unsuccessful and we vowed to choose our refreshment stops more wisely in the future.

Landfall on the Spanish mainland was at Calpe on the Costa Blanca which seemed an odd name, as the only things *blanca* about it were the ubiquitous holiday apartments. Five miles farther west, we crossed the Greenwich meridian, and most of Europe lay behind us. Still we were not halfway around the world. At the resort town of Benidorm, the water close to shore was a mass of dark heads and the bodies on the beach formed a solid mat, with many people forced to stand.

At last at Alicante we left the tourists behind and the real Spain began, although the tourists would return at Malaga on the Costa del Sol farther south. Alicante is an attractive town with streets paved in patterns of coloured tiles. A large covered market sold unfamiliar Spanish foods: intriguing fish; a confusion of sausages; some preserved in vats of lard; cheeses that we had not seen before; meat we could not recognise; trays of testicles; soft unlaid eggs; stalls selling the strong-smelling *bacalao* or salt cod and others selling *churros*, a type of doughnut formed as the dough is squeezed through a pipe into boiling oil.

Throughout the regions of Alicante and Valencia there are more than 60 towns and villages that hold annual 'Moors and Christians' festivals, the most famous being at Alcoi. The historical beginnings of the mock battles between the followers of the Cross and the Crescent Moon go back to the battle of Lepanto.

The event was later celebrated in the streets and squares of these two southern provinces.

Over the centuries the battle has taken on a more local character, with each town seeing its patron saint as having wrought the miracle of the defeat of the infidel. During the celebrations, the people wear elaborate costumes which they begin planning and preparing months before each festival.

We heard that one such festival was to be held at La Villa Joiosa, a village on the coast 64 kilometres from Alicante. The village had apparently held a special attraction for Berbers and Turks who had raided it on a fairly regular basis. In 1538, however, Turkish corsairs sailed into port in four galleys and 30 galliots, only to be defeated by the brave townspeople, with some help from above in the form of a sudden downpour which swelled the River Sella so that the enemy vessels anchored at its mouth were swamped, and many sank.

From the local television channel we learned, entirely wrongly (or maybe it was my poor understanding of Spanish), that the battle would take place at 2 p.m. We actually commented that this was siesta and therefore a strange time to be holding a battle in medieval costume in the fierce heat of summer. Nevertheless, we caught a bus to the village and arrived around lunchtime.

La Villa Joiosa was certainly decorated for a festival, particularly in the old quarter of the town near the small beach. Here the narrow streets and alleyways were covered in canopies of streamers and coloured lights and outside each door stood a small round table covered in a white lace cloth, on which sat a vase of flowers. There were scores of tables, charming in their repetition as one looked along the street. A man lay as if dead in one of the doorways but when we stopped, concerned, the two other people in the street laughed.

'Don't worry about him,' they said. 'He's just a drunken sailor. He comes to watch the battle every year, and he gets drunk every year.'

Most of the streets, though, were deserted, and as we walked across the bridge over the River Sella, a magnificent Moor in gold robes gave a tired wave and passed in the opposite direction, while ahead another Moor and a couple of Christians wandered listlessly. An air of languor hung over the village.

'I've a feeling we've missed the battle,' Alan said. 'Let's have lunch and see what happens.'

The town had indeed closed down but near the river we found a small, modern restaurant with people inside. It was airconditioned. Bliss! The first course of salad was an unusual combination of pickled and fresh vegetables served with olive oil. They were followed by *tapas* which in that instance was a platter of delicacies, each served on half of a small toasted bread roll.

Some were hot like the spicy grilled sausages, the slices of pork with rosemary, and the thinly sliced beef with garlic and black pepper. Some were warm like the blood sausage, the brains and the omelette. Some were cold like the roe, the salmon, the wind-cured ham, and a couple of things we did not recognise even after we had eaten them. With a large bottle of icy San Miguel beer, it was a fine lunch and the *tapas* were the best we would find while we were in Spain.

'Did you see the battle?' one of the diners asked. We explained that we had apparently come too late.

'*Que lastima!* But it will all take place again later,' he explained. 'You can see it then. It's often better at night.'

'What time will it begin?' Alan asked.

'After dinner. No set time. Just when everyone is ready.'

Dinner in Spain is late. The sun does not set until around 9.30 p.m., and dinner is not until 10.30 p.m. or later. It was possible that the battle would not even start until around midnight. There would be no trains or buses back to Alicante at that hour. *Que lastima!* What a pity!

We sailed past Torreviaja and the moonscape region of Murcia to Almeria and continued to Motril where the harbour was safe enough to leave *Windigo* while we visited the Alhambra at Granada.

On the other side of the Sierra Nevada mountain range from Motril, Granada is built on and around three cone-shaped crests in the foothills, one of which is called the Alhambra. Upon it floats the beautiful airy palace of the same name, which in Arabic means 'the red palace' after the soil on which the palace is built.

The Alhambra is the world's only remaining medieval Arab palace. It is constructed from the materials of the site: rocks, bricks and stucco instead of the stone and marble of more substantial buildings. The interior has a fragile quality, sensuous and romantic.

Built as a pleasure palace in the 14th century for the ruler Abdul Yusuf, it would no doubt have fallen into ruin like all the rest had it not been for Ferdinand and Isabella who had loved it. Its halls and pavilions, floating like the decorated tents of the Ottoman armies that we had loved in Istanbul, are covered in splendidly elaborate stucco designs like gorgeous mantillas, and all around is the sound of water from the high Sierra Nevadas, in streams, lakes, fountains, pools. The water gurgles and splashes through the Court of the Myrtles and the wonderful Court of the Lions, and through the cloisters and courtyards of the Generalife, the stylised garden and orangery that hugs the sides of the hill. The only building I can think of to compare with the Alhambra is the Taj Mahal — they are both great fantasy creations, one a tribute to love, the other to pleasure.

If it had not been for a strong outgoing current in the Strait of Gibraltar pulling us westward, we would not have been able to progress against the winds that funnelled through the strait from the Atlantic Ocean. At last, though, the lion's head towered above us, while the mysterious purple mountains of Morocco across the water formed a jagged outline against the sky.

The Rock of Gibraltar has always been associated in our minds with 'true British grit' and Empire, and Britannia ruling the waves, so we expected something splendid, grand, even. But we have seen much better rocks in other places. This one is quite ugly, a second-rate rock as rocks go, surrounded by industrial complexes that belch smoke and bile.

Gibraltar, a British crown colony, is obviously part of Spain but the British have always shown a reluctance to give it back. The 'rock scorpions', as the people of Gibraltar are known (though I'm not sure why), enjoy being a crown colony, a duty-free port and an active smuggling centre where the *contrabandistas* rip around the harbour after dark in sleek, black, high-powered speedboats and we, along with everyone else except perhaps the *Guardia Civil*, look the other way. The inhabitants of the narrow strait, a convergent zone for shipping, have an ancient culture of smuggling, still evident in the illicit trade in such items as whisky and cigarettes and (before Spain's acceptance of birth control) contraceptives.

In mythological times Gibraltar was one of the Pillars of Hercules, its twin pillar being eight miles across the strait at Jebl Musa. Perhaps we were officially in the Atlantic Ocean but, because the strait is 36 miles long, it was difficult to tell just where the Atlantic began and the Mediterranean ended. The water was no longer blue, but sea-green.

Main Street is a mixture of 18th and 19th century architecture with Andalusian and Genoese inspiration in the facades above the duty-free shops and English pubs and clubs. We bought Marmite, English marmalade, New Zealand lamb and a Spanish spray-can of cockroach poison in the hope of eradicating the latest plague, picked up in the canal at Fiumicino.

For the first few days we lived in relative luxury at Gibraltar's newest marina at the base of the mist-tipped rock where the Barbary apes live, and then we moved across the bay to Algeciras to await the servicing of *Windigo*'s liferaft. The small fishing harbour was a molasses-black sewer, and when the wind blew from the land, luckily not often, we gagged with the stench. Algeciras is a noisy, dirty industrial city where oil refineries, steel plants, factories, mills and sewerage plants belch their poisons into the air and sea, while a couple of kilometres to the south, the guests at the expensive resorts swim from the beaches.

We hated Algeciras in the beginning, but as the days passed we grew to accept it, even to like it. There was an energy and a purpose about the place, especially around the waterfront. Algeciras is the bustling ferry port to Morocco and the rest of Africa and the wharf area is an explosion of colour and a pageant of people. Moroccans in their bright *djellabahs* mingle with hooded Muslim women, and Africans in caftans and *jubbahs* rub shoulders with sari-clad Indian women and white-robed Arabs.

A market in a circular covered pavilion was located adjacent to the ferry wharves, and the narrow streets surrounding it were lined with the stalls of the smaller merchants, the farmers from the surrounding villages, the second-hand traders and itinerant hawkers. Shopping for food in Algeciras was an event that could, and sometimes did, take up most of the morning.

Cabo Trafalgar, a few kilometres west of Gibraltar, was the scene of Nelson's great victory. It was here that he sighted the French and Spanish fleets, and the ensuing battle, which began at noon, was over by mid-afternoon. Napoleon's plan to invade England was foiled, but Nelson was dead, killed by a sniper's bullet from high in the rigging of an enemy ship.

We stopped briefly at nearby Cadiz. The town juts into the sea on a spit of rock and guards one of the world's oldest harbours, built as early as 1100 BC. It is a clean and organised old place with a massive cathedral that towers over all.

The Guadalquivir River rises in the sierras at Cazorla and flows across Andalucia to enter the Atlantic Ocean at Bonanza. The Romans had called the river the Betis, but the Moors renamed it *Guad-al-Quivir* (the Great River). The river certainly has an illustrious history, for it was from there that ships left for the New World, and from nearby Palos de la Frontera Columbus set sail in 1492 for what he believed to be India.

Through the aptly named Bonanza and up the river to Seville, 80 kilometres inland, poured the gold and treasures of the Americas that had established Seville's position as a city of fabulous riches and Spain's place as the paramount power of Europe. Magellan also sailed from Seville when he set out on the world's first circumnavigation.

We had only ever navigated short stretches of rivers before, so we left Bonanza in August 1994 with some trepidation. It would take three days to reach Seville, because it was possible to travel only on the incoming tides. In the beginning navigation was easy because the river was wide and deep as it flowed through the salt marshes near its mouth, but farther inland the river narrowed as it squeezed through rolling hills and farmlands. This was an entirely different experience for those who had grown accustomed to being at sea with sea smells, sea sounds, constant movement, and the infinite blankness of the ocean.

Here was a gentle world with the strong fragrance of fecundity, of mud and trees and growing things. All around were cattle in the shallows, goats along the banks, farmers waving from their fields, irrigation systems, haystacks and white haciendas. The solitary screech of a seabird was replaced by the twittering of myriads of small land birds, thrushes and warblers, larks and finches. Eagles and black kites circled overhead and ducks, herons and the occasional flamingo fished near the banks.

Often we saw trees entirely covered with white egrets that seemed oblivious to us gliding by, as did the brilliant kingfishers darting through the foliage and the small, long-beaked birds that flitted in and out of tunnels in the banks. At night we heard the croaking of frogs, the plops of invisible mud creatures and the sibilant sounds of insects. The land world is largely taken for granted by those who never leave it, but to us it was new again and we gathered it around us like a comforting cloak.

On the morning of the third day the spires and towers of Seville rose slowly from the simmering plain. Ahead was the city of Carmen, Don Juan, the Barber, Figaro, Fidelio, and Murillo and Velazquez, flamenco and the *corrida de toros*.

We had read that there was a small affordable marina near the centre of the city but after negotiating the lock that regulates the water at the outskirts, it was obvious that the marina had been demolished, probably in preparation for Expo which was held in Seville in 1992. Nearby, however, was a small and elegant timber wharf with Venetian-type poles tipped in gold paint. An overgrown garden covered the steeply sloping site, on top of which was an old mansion, to all appearances uninhabited. We pulled *Windigo* under the willows and tied up, barely able to contain our excitement at finding so perfect a mooring.

A narrow path led up through the garden to a high stone wall which we climbed without great difficulty and from our vantage point we looked across to the wondrous Plaza de Espana and the enormous Maria Luisa Park with its fountains and follies, gleaming tiled surfaces and flocks of gentle white doves. We felt like Alice discovering Wonderland and we quickly returned to the boat to collect our bikes so that we could explore further.

To our surprise we were no longer alone. Tied alongside *Windigo* was an American yacht named *Arion* with Doug and Ann aboard. We had become friendly with them on the passage Gibraltar, liking the way in which the two opposites lived happily together on a small boat. Doug was a lanky, relaxed man who viewed the world with a humorous and tolerant affection. Ann, on the other hand, was intense, energetic and so supremely organised that we laughed with glee if she made the slightest gaffe.

'What a wonderful spot you've found,' Doug called in greeting as we scrambled through the bushes and lowered ourselves onto the wharf. 'Didn't think you'd mind if we joined you.'

'We're delighted,' we assured them.

'How long can we get away with being in this great place?' Ann wondered.

There was no way of knowing how long our luck would hold and we thought it unwise to ask anyone, so Doug and Ann bolted their bikes together and the four of us set out to explore. We enjoyed their company and admired their experience and nautical skills. They had left America several years before, crossing the Pacific to Australia, where they had worked and toured extensively, growing to love the outback and its people.

'I remember once we were backpacking through western Queensland and we camped one night near the road in someone's property,' Doug reminisced. 'In the morning, the owner rode up on horseback and when we told him what we were doing he said, "That's a silly idea, mate. Too bloody risky. Take one of my cars, keep it for as long as you like. I'll see you when you get back." So that's what we did and we were away for two months. There are some mighty fine people in your country.'

The first time Doug and Ann came on board at Seville they noticed the cockroaches scurrying across the ceiling. 'My God,' exclaimed Doug, 'It's an invasion. Why don't you get rid of them?'

'We've tried everything,' we explained. 'Like rats, they'll only leave when the ship is sinking. They're indestructible.'

'Rubbish!' said Ann. 'Mix boracic powder with sweetened condensed milk to a smooth paste, then form it into small balls about the size of a pea. Place these everywhere, in the back of lockers, under the sink, in the head. In a few days, voila!, no more brown bugs. They can't resist the condensed milk, and the boracic is deadly to a cockroach.'

Doug's face shone with malice. 'They die a painful death,' he explained. 'The boracic binds them up inside until they burst. Pow! Then their mates eat them and they explode too. Pow! In a few days there won't be a cockroach on the boat.'

We took their advice and by the time Velia and Graeme arrived a week later, there was not a live cockroach to be seen.

'Oy! Captain, Captain. *Hola! Hola!*'

Standing above us were two men in the uniforms of the *Guardia Civil*, their faces set and serious.

'You are not permitted to be here. You must go — now,' the angrier of the two announced.

'We're very sorry if we've done something wrong,' Alan replied. 'We've been here for four days now so we presumed it was all right to stay.'

'Four days? Four days! *Por Dios!*' the officer exclaimed. 'We've only just noticed you from the other side of the river. It's not permitted. It's strictly forbidden.'

We all mumbled apologies and told the officer we would go immediately, and for the first time, he smiled.

'Well, probably tomorrow will do,' he said. 'You can go around to Guelves on the other arm of the river. There you can anchor, and the bus into town takes only 20 minutes.'

The arm of the Guadalquivir River at Guelves was quiet and peaceful, the banks lined with shadowy gums in which the white egrets nested in the evenings. Cicadas sang and fish jumped and we could almost have been on the Murray River back home. Away from the river, though, we were most definitely in Spain. Guelves was really a suburb of Seville, its white and pink houses stretching along the river in a ribbon. There was a marketplace and bus stop opposite the anchorage and, farther along the road, the biggest and best supermarket we had ever seen. It had 55 checkouts and many of the staff wore roller skates.

We had not seen Velia and Graeme since their last holiday with us in the Aegean a year and a half before. Arriving far too early at Seville's modern airport, we paced about, drank several cups of strong Spanish coffee, and ended up feeling jittery and weak. But then they were there, and we hugged and kissed them and felt strong again.

'I remembered! I remembered!' Velia sang as she waved a package in front of us. Alan and I could not have left the relative safety of the Mediterranean region without a fully functional radio, so it was with relief that we accepted the part she had forgotten to bring the year before.

Those were marvellous days in Seville. Alan and I thought of it as 'our city' and we showed it to Velia and Graeme with a proprietary interest, gratified when they responded with delight as we had done. It is an easy city to explore on foot because most of Seville's famous monuments and parks are clustered within a few hundred metres. They are linked by the flow of the city and contained by the Guadalquivir River.

Seville's most imposing landmark is the massive Gothic Cathedral. One enters and is instantly lost in its cavernous and dim interior, where priceless treasures are dwarfed almost into insignificance. Easier to comprehend is one of Seville's best known landmarks, the Giralda, a soaring tower beside the cathedral. It rises from a paved Moorish courtyard of orange trees, and was originally a 12th century minaret, on top of which was added a fanciful top storey with a weathervane at the apex.

Close to the Giralda is the Alcazar, fashioned on the Alhambra and combining renaissance and Moorish architecture in a style known as Mudejar It is a sumptuous and splendid building, its cool interior glowing with the colours of the tiled surfaces, the gilt, and the painted stucco.

Seville's history goes back more than 3000 years and this is reflected in the city. From the Torre del Oro, the golden tower beside the river, to the wonderful pink bullring, the Maestranza, and the old tobacco factory, now part of the university, where the mythical Carmen rolled cigars, it is constantly rewarding. Often we packed lunch so that we could eat in one of Seville's lovely parks, sometimes we ate at one of the outdoor restaurants in the Burrio de Santa Cruz, the picturesque old Jewish quarter with its iron balconies, flowers and wandering minstrels, or in Triana, the gypsy part of town on the other side of the river.

It was the time of Seville's annual Flamenco Festival and one evening in the packed modern theatre near the bullring we shared the suppressed fervour of the audience which sat in wrapt concentration, aware of every nuance. The complicated elements of flamenco, like those of the *corrida*, are part of the Spanish heritage, ingrained from childhood, incomprehensible to all others except the *aficionados*. We responded to the gypsy music, the clapping, the tapping, the plucked strings and the plaintive songs on another level but, nevertheless, for us it was a galvanising experience. We will always remember the *zapoteo* (tapping), the *tapoteo* (clapping), and the sad *cante jondo*, the melancholy sweet songs of Andalucia.

In the churches, we wondered at the strange icons and the fanciful madonnas that no longer possessed the attributes of sculpture but rather resembled dead bodies or wax dummies in clothing. They were dressed in rich fabrics, their cheeks rouged and their hair real. La Macarena, the most loved madonna of Seville, is gloriously enthroned. She sits serenely with white lace ruffles around her face, a crown of precious stones in her hair, and glass tears on her cheeks.

The bullfight season was in full swing with daily television coverage. In Seville, posters plastered every centimetre of spare space. They advertised an appearance in the Maestranza by Spain's greatest bullfighter, the charismatic and talented Marillo Jesulin de Ubrique. Tickets went on sale at dawn in the dank, cave-like basement of the Maestranza, but when we arrived in the pre-dawn, the queues had already formed and there was an air of solid determination and palpable intensity in the waiting crowds.

We soon realised that the purchasing of tickets for a bullfight was an experience in itself. There were so many options, so many queues for so many different categories of seating depending on whether one wanted to sit in the *sol* (full sun), or *sombre* (shade), or in half sun and half shade, or in covered seats or private boxes, facing the chute, or behind it, or on either side. We stood feeling conspicuous and slightly silly, four confused and naive foreigners in a sea of *aficionados*, one of whom took Graeme by the arm.

'You'll get the best seats if you sit with us. Join this queue,' he said.

'We don't think we can stand full sun,' Graeme told him.

'The sun moves, *amigo*,' the young man said. 'These seats will be perfect. We know this bullring.'

He included his two friends in a sweep of his arm. They smiled at us and we all shook hands. Fernandez, the one who spoke English, was a tough-looking man with shrewd black eyes. He chewed on a toothpick. He and his friends, Atanacio and Alvaro, were dressed in dusty work clothes.

'Have you been to a bullfight before?' Fernandez asked. 'No? Well, you have chosen to see the best matador in Spain. Jesulin is an artist, a magician.'

'We seem to be the only foreigners buying tickets,' Graeme commented after we had been there for some time.

'That's because you're on a boat and not at one of the hotels which have tickets for their guests. But you won't see many foreigners at the *corrida de toros*. They don't like the bullfight.'

'We may not like it either,' Velia told him. 'We may find it a cruel sport.'

'It's not a sport!' Fernandez exclaimed. 'When we want to watch sport we go to the soccer. This is a fiesta, a ritual where man dances with the animal. Then the man kills the animal. Man is superior to the animal and the bullfight reminds us of that. Cruel! What is cruel? Do you eat meat?'

The queue began to move slowly towards the window.

'I'll buy your tickets for you,' said Fernandez, taking the roll of notes from Graeme's hand and dealing with the ticket seller.

'See you at the bullfight,' he called as the three of them hurried away to work, and we climbed the stone stairs to explore the most beautiful and ancient of Spanish bullrings in the calm of the morning. It is an elegant baroque creation in white and deep pink, trimmed with wrought iron balconies and accoutrements. Inside, below the seating, there are the stables, the pens for the bulls, the wardrobe and dressing rooms, the taurine museum, a small modern hospital, and the chapel.

On the day of the bullfight we arrived early but already the arena was crowded. Fernandez and his two friends had obviously been watching for us and we soon saw them standing and waving to attract our attention. The seats were in an excellent position, close to the ring but still high enough to look down upon the entire arena. They were directly behind the chute from which the bulls would enter. Soon the sun would move and be behind us and eventually the high back of the ring would cast its shadow over us.

As the seats filled with the capacity crowd and trumpets were heard in the distance, it seemed that a band of electricity encircled the bullring, a barely controlled turbulence, something volcanic. A disturbance broke out on the opposite side of the ring where the spectators would soon have the sun in their eyes, and a few minutes later there was another volatile brawl a few seats behind us. People thumped and yelled and pushed, and a wave of around 20 people swayed across the seats.

'We'll be squashed,' screamed Velia. 'I want to go.'

'You'll never get out. They'll calm down,' Graeme tried to reassure her.

For the second time in Seville we felt engulfed by the passions of the crowd. We knew less about bullfighting than we knew of flamenco, but we could not help but be caught up in the emotion and suppressed elation.

Behind us sat two elderly peasants with wrinkled brown faces and eyes grown small from squinting into the sun. Like many of the people around us, they drank in long draughts from the *porron*, the skin wine bag at their feet, and every little while they would tap us on the shoulder and offer the wine bag and hunks of a flattish yellow loaf of bread. Obviously they enjoyed the spectacle of the mess we made of ourselves for they laughed uproariously and clapped fit to burst when Graeme displayed some talent in getting the thin stream of red liquid into his mouth. We felt dazed by the sun, the wine and the waiting, the dust and the sweat. The words of Garcia Lorca's poem with its reeling repetitious 'at five o'clock in the afternoon' kept swimming in my head: Oh white bull of Spain! Oh black bull of grief!

A buzz passed through the crowd as the President of the bullfight entered his balcony. He would direct the *corrida*. Then the parade began — a glittering line of horses, matadors, picadors and banderilleros led by the *alguacilillos* (mounted police). The costumes flashed and sparkled in the sun as the parade moved around the ring to the rousing music of the *pasodoble*. Velia gripped my hand. The fight was about to begin, and we both felt apprehensive — perhaps we should not have come. Then there was the clear pure sound of the clarion call to signal the beginning of the *corrida*. The picadors sat waiting on their padded horses, lances at the ready, and the crowd was hushed.

Suddenly, the gate burst open and a massive black bull charged into the ring, his muscles rippling beneath the glistening hide and his eyes wild. He baulked and pawed the dust, unsure of what to do. People in the crowd began to shout, taunting him, urging him to move. The two old peasants directly behind me and Velia stood on their seats and shouted and shook their fists.

Perhaps it was that sudden movement that caught the bull's attention because with a tremendous surge of power and speed it charged directly at us. We were too amazed to move as it hurled itself across the ring. So great was its power and so intense its fury that it broke through the top rails of the arena wall, sending pieces of timber flying into the air, and it was propelled across the *callejon*, the safety gutter between the ring and the spectators, There, its momentum broken, it fell back.

'I'm definitely leaving,' cried Velia, trying in vain to scramble along a row of knees. But the owners pushed her away so they could stand and cheer like everyone else. There was no escape for Velia. A great wall of sound rose from the crowd, a resonant, boiling roar at the bull's sudden show of bravado. Picadors and their assistants quickly forced the beast back into the ring and the crowd settled down again.

When Jesulin entered the ring there was silence, intense and absolute. He stood before his bull, handsome and arrogant, his lithe body moulded into exaggerated maleness by the tight pants and the squared and tasselled shoulders of the glittering coat and as he worked his cape around the bull we watched enthralled at his grace and courage. Finally, with his whole body poised on the balls of his feet, and his shoulders hunched forward, he delivered the final thrust, and the bull crumpled at his feet. I am not sure why we were moved, but we were.

The two ears and the tail were sliced off the bull and the President awarded them to Jesulin. The crowd went wild, women threw parts of their apparel into the ring, men threw their wine bags. Jesulin kissed each piece of clothing and drank from the wine bags before throwing them back into the stands. The ring was littered with flowers as the bull was dragged away behind two stocky horses and Jesulin was carried shoulder-high in triumph around the ring.

'You are lucky!' Fernandez enthused. 'You'll remember that for ever.'

Yes, we would. But we would also remember the less skilled matadors on the program that day, because they reminded us that this strange ritual is indeed barbaric. There are those in Spain and elsewhere who want it banned. I find it impossible to make a judgement on the topic. Suffice it to say that none of us wishes to see another bullfight.

The Jesulin phenomenon continued to intrigue. Some days later, we watched him kill six bulls on national television at a special *corrida* for women. Jesulin was the only man allowed into the huge Plaza de Toros, apart from the priest, I suppose. Women of all ages packed the arena. The President was a woman, as were the picadors and the other matadors, the police, the attendants. At the end of the *corrida*, thousands of women scrambled across the *callejon* and into the ring where woman fought woman in a desperate attempt to touch the magic matador. Then he who fought the bulls raced in terror from the women and disappeared from sight into the relative safety of the bull chute.

Adeu, Jesulin! Adeu, España!

CHAPTER 15

*the Canary Islands • Teneriffe lace
Madonna of the Candles
across the Atlantic*

In the Atlantic Ocean a few hundred kilometres off the coast of Africa lie the seven small specks of the Canary Islands. They have been part of Spain since the 15th century when the Spanish finally subdued their tough Stone Age inhabitants, the Guanches.

The islands are volcanic, Lanzarote having more than 300 volcanic cones. Teneriffe, the largest island in the group, but only 80 kilometres long, is a mixture of prolific growth and barren volcanic zones of stratified lava. High in the centre of the island, Mount Teide rises to some 3500 metres.

By yacht, a passage from Bonanza to Las Palmas on Gran Canaria should take five days but strong headwinds, rough seas, and gear and engine failure kept us at sea for eight days. Instead of reaching Las Palmas as planned, we were blown off course towards Teneriffe and it seemed easier to make our landfall there.

That passage was sobering. The sea is unforgiving of those who venture forth unprepared and after so long making short hops in the Mediterranean, we had grown complacent. We had forgotten the fearsome power of the oceans.

An engine part sheared off and it was too rough to make repairs. Without the engine to power them for some days, the fridge and freezer stopped functioning and most of the fresh and frozen food had to be thrown overboard. Protective patches on the sails were in tatters and stitching had ripped on some of the seams.

On our first evening at sea we had seen a sunset unlike any we had ever seen before: too brilliant, too spectacular. We should have heeded the sign and turned back to Bonanza, but we pressed on. The winds blew from the south instead of the north and depressions formed around the Azores and added to our stress.

Our original intention had been to spend a month cruising in the Canaries before crossing 'the pond' to the Caribbean, but instead, we booked into the new marina at Santa Cruz de Teneriffe, the capital city of the island, and set to work to repair the damage and to strengthen as much of the gear as possible.

Years before, I had met a gentle woman of 85, whose hobby was making Teneriffe lace. Such was my ignorance that I had had no knowledge of the significance of the intricate and delicate craft, nor any understanding of the whereabouts of Teneriffe. Certainly, I had no idea that one day I would be there.

The lace was all around: a living craft. Patterns based on ancient motifs fluttered from the windows and decorated the altars and chapels. Women wore the lace in their blouses and it hung as the decoration on the fine linen napery that spilled from the shops in the narrow streets of Santa Cruz de Teneriffe, the small bustling capital by the sea.

It seemed strange to us that way out there, surrounded by the rolling green mountains of the great Atlantic, there was a cluster of tiny islands where life was just as sophisticated and organised as it was in mainland Spain. There were concerts and opera, galleries and good restaurants, as well as hotels and resorts, for most of the islands' wealth comes from tourism.

Carlos, the marina manager, was a young man with an outsized walrus moustache. He was a worrier and he made us nervous.

'Check your lines <i>Windigo</i>. The swells are mounting. Bad weather is on the way.'

'Seabirds are coming in. There'll be storms.'

'When the air is so clear that you can see the summit of Teide, it can mean that a hurricane is on the way.'

One day he surprised us. 'I love your country,' he said.

'Have you been to Australia?' I asked.

'Oh yes,' he replied. 'I'm really a journalist but there are no jobs on Teneriffe and I'm now married, so I must do something else. A couple of years ago, I covered a four-wheel-drive rally across Australia for a Spanish automobile magazine.' Then he smiled and added, 'That's why I agreed to you paying such a low rate at this marina. I like Australians.'

A few days after our arrival the marina was full and yachts were beginning to raft up two and three deep along the harbour wall. All were preparing for the Atlantic crossing while they waited for the hurricane season to end. Had it been an Australian marina, there would have been camaraderie, cockpit parties and a sharing of expertise, but the Europeans who filled the berths kept to themselves and there was little interaction.

Our neighbours on the port side were a family from Manchester. Sylvia, the mother, was a blonde chain-smoking bulging woman who often needed to borrow things. 'A cup of milk, please, luv. The boys drank it all on me again. I'll pay you back.'

The father and his three teenage sons were friendly, too, but they were tough, tattooed and boisterous, forever chiacking and lashing out at each other. The males of the family were virtually monosyllabic in that their most-used word was 'fuckin'' with a handful of nouns thrown in for good measure like 'dog', 'sea', 'boat', 'women', and 'politicians'.

'Would you like to borrow a book on the Caribbean?' Alan asked the father one day.

'No thanks, pal. Don't read fuckin' books. We're going for the climate, not the fuckin' culture,' he replied.

When a large American yacht called *Gone With the Wind* pulled alongside one day, the skipper yelled across.

'I see you're from Australia,' he said. 'Perhaps you know my friend.'

It was some time since anyone had said that to us.

'I doubt it,' Alan replied. 'Australia's a very big country.'

Undeterred, the American persisted.

'My friend's from Adelaide and he sails a boat called *New Address*. Col Harrison's his name. Just thought you may have bumped into him.'

'Yes, we know him!' we shouted back.

When he told us that he was actually a friend of Col's fiancée, we were surprised. Our romantic friend had at last been lassoed.

'Jeannie's a sailor too,' the American explained. 'She's already circumnavigated on her own yacht and now she's joined Col to sail back to Australia with him. You'll probably meet up with them in Panama.'

While in Santa Cruz, we received mail and news from several sources. A sad letter from Ellen on *Maisie Dotes* told of Woody's death soon after completing the circumnavigation. JB and Rosa on *Anaconda* were already home in New Orleans, having passed through the Mediterranean in one season, and Andre and Barbara, their dreams of circumnavigating unfulfilled, had flown home from Malta, leaving *Northern Lights* to be sailed across the Atlantic by a paid skipper and crew.

Burramys was heading towards England to meet up with Bret and Debbie from *Interlude* who were working there, and *Anhinga* was already in the Pacific heading for Brisbane.

There was a letter from Mike and Fiona in the south of France where they had attended a bullfight with all the colour and pageantry of a Spanish *corrida* but without the cruelty, the blood and the death. They did not mention how the matador tired the bull, but his aim had been to pluck a red rose from between the bull's horns. As I read the letter I thought, 'That's the way it should be.' And yet ... and yet ... *muy complicado*, as they say in Spanish whenever there's a difficult decision.

The people of the island of Teneriffe believe that the Virgin's mother came from the village of Candelaria, about 24 kilometres along the coast from Santa Cruz. In the village church there is a lovely madonna, the Madonna of the Candles. She is dark-skinned, and richly ornamented with lace and glistening silver, candles and glass — a fairy princess on a silver carriage.

Despite the weight of so much finery, she appears ethereal, floating like a crystal vision in the sunlight, sometimes silhouetted against the inky blue of the sea and sometimes against the black lava flows as the people carry her along the coast road from Candelaria to the Cathedral in Santa Cruz for the blessing. As the slow procession passed, I was reminded of Oscar and Lucinda and the shimmering glass church as it floated on the river.

Sometimes while Alan worked on the boat, I assembled one of the bikes and rode to the tiny seaside *pueblo* of San Juan. It was a charming medieval village with its shops hidden in houses in the narrow alleyways. The bakery made an ash-encrusted loaf of robust peasant bread that lasted for days and we liked its sourdough flavour.

At each visit I puzzled over the golden sand beach that ran along the length of the village.

'It should be black,' I said to the baker one day.

'We prefer yellow,' he replied. 'So we brought the sand from Africa. It's not that far away.'

As a respite from the work on *Windigo*, we sometimes took bus trips into the mountains. The ear-popping rides to tiny towns with winter climates brought on a ravenous hunger and soon caused us to crave the heat of the seaside below. One day we caught the bus that wound along the Atlantic shores to Los Christianos, 75 kilometres to the east, but the old town had all but disappeared under the bingo barns, pubs, tatty resorts and razz-matazz of yet another tourist enclave.

Towards the end of November, weather conditions across the Atlantic had stabilised. The harbour was less crowded, there were empty berths on the marina and Carlos was now worried about making money. It was time to go.

We set sail on 4 December 1994 precisely at noon. With so far to go, it mattered little when we left but 'noon precisely' had a ring to it and we were searching for symbols. It would be our longest passage so far, 21 days we anticipated, and after the dif-ficult trip from Spain to the Canaries we were feeling apprehen-sive. The Atlantic is a mighty ocean and even though we would be in its tropical waters, we wondered about its personality, its wave trains, its contrariness.

When darkness came, the lights of Teneriffe were twinkling invitingly on the horizon, but they soon sank irrevocably into the sea and we were on our own with 3000 nautical miles of ocean ahead of us before we reached the Caribbean. By heading south to pass close by the Cape Verde Islands, we hoped to pick up the trade winds sooner than if we stuck to the rhumb line.

For the first week the conditions were miserable, the seas short and choppy and the wind strong. We took it in turns to sleep on the saloon floor where we could wedge ourselves in with cushions. Alan found two radio skeds operating, one run by a woman named Trudy in Barbados, and when we listened to other sailors being brave and gung-ho about the conditions, we felt wimpy and dis-consolate. One day on the radio we picked up our Japanese friends, Kuni and Nobby, whom we had not seen since South-East Asia. It was great to talk to them but they were hundreds of miles away. Perhaps we would see them in the Caribbean.

During the second and third weeks *Windigo* moved smoothly up and down the deep blue mountains that rolled from the north, sometimes becoming huge walls of water that towered above us as if they would bury us. But each time, *Windigo* rode the waves like a brave little cork and we lived our lives in reasonable comfort. On a couple of occasions there were calms and we motored until the fuel supply had to be conserved for powering the batteries. Halfway across I cooked a fine baked dinner with a leg of New Zealand lamb, potatoes, pumpkin, sweet potatoes, onion, eggplant and frozen green peas. There was mint sauce and gravy as well. And champagne.

We caught our first dorado in the second week: a beautiful golden creature sprinkled with silver, with a round head and soulful eyes. As it broke the surface of the water it shimmered in the sun, the greenish-blue of its back iridescent and glistening. But as we struggled with it in the cockpit, its El Dorado colours slowly drained away with its lifeforce until the once beautiful pelagic fish became the colour of mullet.

Dorado, also called *mahi-mahi* or dolphin fish, mate for life. 'We will choke on this fish!' I told Alan, so he cut off its head with the soulful eyes, and we felt better.

As we neared the Caribbean, graceful tropical birds circled above the boat, their forked tails flying behind them like silken ribbons. The sea turned translucent and pale green with the warm currents, and brilliant crimson sunsets lit the evening skies.

On Christmas Day we were 40 nautical miles from Barbados and we debated whether or not to make our landfall in its capital, Bridgetown, or to continue to the small island of Bequia in the Grenadines, where we could expect to find a more protected anchorage. After 25 days at sea, we opted for a calm place to rest, and so dropped anchor at Port Elizabeth on the island of Bequia the next night.

It had been a trouble-free passage, due to meticulous preparation and good luck with the weather. The only gear failure was a ripped genoa but we managed to rig up the spare headsail instead. We were now safely halfway around the world, the big bad Atlantic behind us and the tropical paradise of the Caribbean awaiting. We opened another bottle of champagne and drank to the half of the world ahead of us.

CHAPTER 16

Caribs and cannibals • the Rastafarians
Island in the Sun • Mr Boozo, optician
'phallus duratus'

The Caribbean Sea is one of the world's most seductive bodies of water. It is defined by the island chain of the Greater Antilles in the north, the Lesser Antilles in the east, and by the landmasses of South America and Central America. It is the thousands of tropical islands, however, that give the Caribbean Sea its allure.

The name Caribbean derives from the early inhabitants of the islands, the Caribs, who invaded from the south in the pre-Columbian period. These warring tribes were ferocious warriors who gave us the word 'cannibal' (from 'caribal' or Carib). As well as eating their victims, they had other diabolical customs like emasculating boys and fattening them up for future feasts. There are historians, though, who maintain that the cruelty of the Caribs was a fiction invented by the early European explorers and buccaneers to excuse their own cruel and bloody extermination of the entire Carib race.

Columbus arrived in 1492, and so began the domination of this tropical paradise by European nations that were fascinated by its wealth, its charm and its strategic position. Spain, England and France were the main contenders, but Holland, Denmark and Sweden also became embroiled in the affairs of the Caribbean.

Despite the invasion of white people, it is noteworthy and, indeed, just that the black slaves brought from Africa by the early settlers now outnumber all the other groups so that most parts of the Caribbean are black republics with blacks in all positions of power. When the slaves were freed in the 19th century, thousands of Hindus and Muslims from India were brought in as indentured labour, and their descendants remain.

The Caribbean has never been an entirely tranquil place, because most of it is in the path of the terrible and destructive hurricanes that roar across the southern Atlantic from their spawning grounds in Africa, flattening towns and villages, destroying plantations and killing thousands of people. Nor has the area been calm historically, for, like the hurricanes, the early explorers and the fortune seekers rampaged through the area with scant regard for those who lived there. Sir John Hawkins, Sir Francis Drake, Sir Walter Raleigh were in many respects no better than plundering pirates, egotistical and irrational; Captain Henry Morgan and 'Bluebeard' Teach were also unscrupulous buccaneers who pillaged and raped their way through the islands.

Our landfall at Bequia was in the minuscule nation of Saint Vincent and the Grenadines in the Lesser Antilles, a nation well known to yachties but off the beaten track for tourists. Its 30 small islands and cays, most of them too small to show on a map, form a splendid crescent of emeralds in a turquoise sea. Bequia is a simple seaside village with a history of whaling and boat building and its people have always been seafarers.

In the beginning, the most startling aspect of being in the Caribbean was the quality of the light. After being so long in the Mediterranean, this was a shock and, like the early painters in Australia, we found that it took time to adjust to the surprising clarity, the hard outline and the clear delineation of detail.

Here was the kind of island paradise that people fantasise about: powder-soft beaches encircling tranquil bays, swaying palms, balmy climate, fish and coral, and the pulsating rhythm of calypso. From the water at Admiralty Bay, the main harbour of Bequia, little is visible through the thick trees but a stroll inland reveals a range of small boutiques, bars, restaurants and shops, and a bakery that makes sweet bread flavoured with nutmeg. All are there to cater for the couple of hundred yachts at anchor at any one time, as well as the cruise ships that anchor on the outskirts where the water is deeper.

On our first visit ashore a black lad of about 16 spat at me and said something in his lilting language that sounded like 'Go home honky'. Admittedly, I had told him, politely, I assure you, that we did not require his assistance to drag our dinghy onto the beach ('Only one dollar, man'), but I still felt annoyed. 'You must be very careful in the Caribbean,' people had warned us. But then they had said that about Italy, Spain, Indonesia and most of the other countries through which we had safely sailed.

'Forget it!' Alan said.

Near the landing stage was an airy fruit and vegetable market where most of the stalls appeared to be run by Rastafarians. Of all the colourful groups in the Caribbean, the Rastafarians are the most exotic, insisting that the smoking of *ganga* (marijuana) is part of the sacrament, and idolising the Jamaican reggae singer, Bob Marley.

Often very tall and thin with matted dreadlocks stuffed into their floppy knitted caps, they sport Bob Marley T-shirts or those proclaiming the late Emperor of Ethiopia, Haile Selassie, as the Saviour, the Black Messiah. Their sensational clothes emphasise red for blood, gold for wealth and green for fertility, and they team these colours with purple, turquoise and lime so that the effect is theatrical and startling.

On our first visit to the market, an open pavilion beside the sea, we were approached by two wild and lanky stallholders. They were young men with large, even, white teeth, elaborate dreadlocks and matted beards and moustaches, for the Rastafarians believe that they must follow the teachings of the Bible when it says, 'He shall be holy, and shall let the locks of the hair of his head grow.'

'What you like buy?' one asked.

'It all seems very expensive,' I replied. 'I don't think we can afford to buy anything.'

'Yuh, is expensive. The people on the yachts are wealthy. That's why!'

'Not all people on yachts are wealthy. We're not wealthy.'

'Then you gotta go to Saint Vincent island to buy, man! It's cheaper there. You know what I mean.'

We warmed towards the two strange men with their wide white smiles and friendly eyes.

'What are your names?' Alan asked.

'Just call me Roots, man,' the wilder of the two replied. 'And this here is my friend, Malcolm X.'

Despite the fact that Rastafarians are not supposed to have physical contact with whites, we all shook hands.

'See, I am a man of God and me come to do God's work,' said Malcolm X. 'In Australia, you whites make black man get raw deal. One day I go there to help the black people. So *Jah* (God) say!'

'Malcolm X right, man,' Roots said. 'You treat black people bad in that country. If something wrong in a country, then every ear hears it. Ears hear "White Australia!"'

'That was a long time ago. We no longer have a "White Australia Policy",' Alan replied. 'Australia is a multicultural society now.'

'Black people there still get raw deal, man. Nothing change for them. Ears hear!'

We tried to explain that things were changing, that things were improving, but beneath their level and unflinching gaze we felt censured and accused.

As the days passed, it became apparent that our Caribbean paradise was also flawed, and that many Bequians lived a mean existence in dilapidated clapboard shacks that nestled behind croton hedges under the picturesque deception of hibiscus and flame trees. The yachtie dollars are filtered into European hands, and prices are so high that even the wealthy Europeans in their mega yachts complain bitterly.

The Bequians certainly cannot afford to buy and, to add to their misery, the jobs on the island generally go to people from other islands, rather than to them. Perhaps we, therefore, should not blame the people for stealing from the yachts while they are left unattended in the bay at night, their occupants spending freely at the restaurants and boutiques. We decided that we would never leave *Windigo* after dark in the Caribbean and, despite the heat, we locked ourselves in each night and slept with the fan whirring and only a small slit open in the hatch above our heads, for there were many stories of machete-wielding youths climbing aboard yachts while the occupants were asleep.

On Sundays the hills rang with fervent gospel singing that floated from the open-sided churches and mingled in the hot, still air. Everyone wore Sunday best. For girls and young women, this was an above-the-knee garment that resembled a chopped off bouffant ballroom-dancing gown, all nylon petticoats and puffs in bright greens, oranges and reds. They covered their hair with bows of different colours and they fluttered along the forest paths like so many wonderful butterflies.

The young men affected an exaggerated American Negro style — hip, flashy and loud with outsize sneakers in iridescent pink, lime green and puce. Older people dressed conservatively, the women in old-fashioned dresses and head scarves and the men in hats.

One morning, mounds of bright red fleshy flowers were piled on rickety tables near the beach and on stalls in the market. The flowers appeared suddenly and all the stallholders had them. Malcolm X waved us over, obviously prepared to overlook our failings.

'Sorrel time!' he called, picking up handfuls of the flowers and letting them fall back onto the pile. 'This is sorrel. Season only short. You buy now, man.'

'What does one do with it?' I asked.

'Drink! You make sorrel drink. Very good at New Year after you drink too much rum. Just boil it up with this here.'

He piled sticks of cinnamon, knobs of ginger, nutmeg nuts and some of their lacy orange coating of mace into my hands, saying as he did so, 'Spices free for you. You buy sorrel.' So we did, a great gleaming pile of the shiny crimson fruit.

In the large pot we used for cooking crabs, I boiled the flowers and the spices with sugar, strained the liquid and bottled it, and took one bottle back to Roots and Malcolm X as a present. In a tall glass with ice and a curl of lime, it was a refreshing and visually sensuous drink with a spicy piquant favour and, despite the splashes of red all over the galley, we decided it was worth making again if the opportunity arose.

We had left Sydney in 1990 and now it was 1995. We were beginning to feel homesick. Perhaps if we had decided to fly home in the European winters we would not have felt such pangs, but then we would not have had the experiences of wintering in Turkey and Greece. We had considered bypassing America and continuing into the Pacific, and the more we thought about it, the more attractive the idea had become.

Rested and optimistic after a couple of weeks in Bequia, we finally made the decision to return home a year earlier than planned. Perhaps we needed a change from the lifestyle for a while. We missed the earth, the garden, the birds, lovely Pittwater, the vitality of Sydney, our house and the comforts of home like long hot showers, a washing machine and a phone, a library, our family and friends.

The island of Saint Vincent, 10 nautical miles to the north of Bequia, is thickly forested, mountainous and beautiful. Its domestic architecture is typical of most of the Caribbean islands, with timber houses being painted in the 1960s colours of lime, pink, turquoise and lemon under corrugated iron roofs. In the capital, Kingstown, there were also faded double-storey buildings with gingerbread trims, latticework and painted wooden shutters.

The sensual throbbing of Kingstown was almost overpowering. Loud with drum beats and calypso music, the town exuded energy — a pulsing, rhythmic exuberance — and the people danced rather than walked along the streets, yelling to each other, laughing, pushing and slapping like unruly children. Men and women wore brightly patterned, offbeat clothes, and either plaited their hair into long strands which they then fashioned into complicated structures on top of their heads or they had it straightened and dyed blonde or red, or a combination of the two colours.

On Saturdays the town moved to a different piper as the large Seventh Day Adventist population attended their services and the churches overflowed with men in dark suits and women in white satin dresses and white straw hats with flowers in the brims. Little girls flounced about in frills and lace with coloured plastic clothes pegs scattered through their hair.

In the shops were bottles of Caribbean sauces, piles of plantain and sweet potato, loaves of bread spiced with cinnamon and nutmeg, huge green papaya and plastic bags of frozen pigs' ears and pigs' tails and trotters.

The island of Mustique was a surprise, first in its relatively open woodland environment, and then in its welcoming attitude to yachties. The island even provides free moorings! Mustique is the Caribbean holiday island of the British royals and other rich and famous people like Mick Jagger and David Bowie. Most of the mansions are hidden in huge grounds with thick plantings and, in fact, the entire island resembles a park with rolling lawns, flowering shrubs and trees, palms, ponds of waterlilies, a lagoon and a bird sanctuary. We especially loved the humming birds — tiny, iridescent, blue-green gems against the pink and yellow blossoms, their wings whirring tirelessly like small fans.

The famous Tobago Cays, a short distance from Mustique, is an uninhabited system of reefs, lagoons and dots of islands but there were literally hundreds of yachts, cruise liners and pleasure craft scattered across the surface of the cays: a floating town no less. We could hear snorkellers and divers gasping in amazement at the sights beneath the surface, but when we dived in the same places, we saw nothing to compare with Australia's Great Barrier Reef.

'Wonderful, isn't it?' an English snorkeller shouted to us as he paddled by.

'Yes, wonderful,' we replied.

The country of Grenada, comprises the eponymous main island, 'the Island of Spice', the islands of Carriacou and Petit Martinique and three or four islets. Saint George, the capital of Grenada, is built around a large blue lagoon and the setting is magical. Here the people appeared much less flamboyant, more European in their dress and demeanour. The shops were a little more sophisticated, the spice sellers and hasslers more insistent, no doubt imagining that we were from one of the cruise ships that unloaded streams of tourists each day.

Grenada is the fabled island of the film, *Island in the Sun*, in which Harry Belafonte played Eric Gairy, a local revolutionary hero who began with the true interests of his people at heart, but later, after becoming Prime Minister, resorted to brutality and murder in order to retain power. His orders were carried out by a group of thugs known as the Mongoose Gang, who later met their match in the opposition's New Jewels. Even political parties have colourful names in the Caribbean.

Gran Etang National Park is situated high in the jungle-covered mountains of Grenada's rainy interior and our minibus groaned its way through thickly forested countryside swathed with misty green valleys, streams and waterfalls. At the national park headquarters beside a crater lake, a beautiful macaw was systematically demolishing a door with its bulletproof beak, screeching defiantly as it did so. Birds, monkeys and armadillos live in the park, but the latter two are now endangered species as the locals insist upon eating them for their supposed aphrodisiac qualities.

The lake was overgrown with reeds, the tracks slippery and muddy, the air freezing and the only monkey we saw quickly turned its bum towards us and hurried away into the treetops.

Alan's glasses disappeared overboard in the Careenage at Saint George. We remembered having seen an optometrist near the market, so we found the prescription and hurried there.

'You must sit and wait,' the humourless young assistant said.

'Are there any magazines?' I asked.

'No.'

We sat on the wooden bench in the old-fashioned shop and read the signs tacked to the walls.

'No admission.'

'Keep out.'

'Immediate payment required.'

'No eating or drinking.'

'No spitting.'

'Nothing to do? Do it somewhere else.'

'Keep quiet!'

It was some time before we realised that we were pressing our bodies against the back of the seat, and that our arms were folded tightly across our chests.

'I wish there had been somewhere else,' I whispered to Alan who sat staring straight ahead in silence. The young black woman and her small son who had entered just after us, also sat staring straight ahead in silence. They both wore dark glasses.

I was just about to repeat my whispered wish to Alan when the optician entered from beneath the 'No admission' sign. He was a small-boned, plump white man with skin the colour of suet and strands of lank brown hair sticking to his wet forehead. His tight shirt was sweat-stained and it gaped where a button was missing on his belly, and his trousers had ridden up into his crutch.

Mr Boozo, for that was the obnoxious man's name, sat beside the small boy and proceeded to carry out a consultation, the details of which we, by our proximity on the bench, could not fail to be acutely aware. Apparently the child was recovering from an operation to remove a tumour which had resulted in the loss of one eye. In two weeks he would fly to the US for surgery that would determine whether or not the other eye had been affected. The young mother sobbed and held her child to her. She could not afford to accompany him to the US and she knew no-one there who could visit him in hospital.

'I would give my life to save his one good eye,' she wept while we fought back our own tears.

'That's a stupid thing to say!' the optician curtly admonished. 'Now be a sensible woman and do as you are told.'

'I can't bear him to be blind. I can't bear it,' the mother moaned. 'I don't know what to do. He's my only child.'

'Pray, woman. That's all you can do,' the optician said.

With that, the man jumped up, disappeared behind the counter and returned with a dusty black case with a hinged lid, something like a small display case for butterflies. He sat once more between us and the small boy and his mother and, snapping back the lid of the black box, said, 'This is what he needs right now!'.

We gasped in horror, for in the box were rows of glass eyes on wire stilts. They stared in all directions and changed their focus whenever Mr Boozo moved his knees, sometimes peering accusingly at us, at others staring in all directions at once. They were grouped in different colours. It was horrible. The child let out a piercing scream, his mother moaned as if in a faint and Alan said, 'Let's wait outside until this is over,' and we staggered through the door and walked quickly away. It was not for a couple of hours that we felt recovered enough to return for Alan's glasses.

The food shops of Georgetown are often called supermarkets, but they remained simple establishments with basic supplies of the usual tropical things like bananas and papaya, breadfruit and sweet potato, and in the freezers there were bags of hairy goat ears, chopped hunks of cows' hooves, and twisted intestines.

The bottle sections were often intriguing with a range of curious beverages, one of which caught our eye. It featured a lurid drawing of a naked woman. Behind her stood a man with one hand over the woman's genitals and the other over one of her breasts. 'Island Pride' was printed in large letters above the drawing and below it, the following:

DOUBLE TROUBLE SEA MOSS
Aphrodesia Marina
PHALLUS DURATUS
(Delicious with evaporated milk)

Crime and violence in the Caribbean were worse than we had anticipated and we found the constant fear of something painful or terminal happening to us very wearing. Stealing from boats was common, and all yachties were warned to avoid particular bays because of drugs and violence towards foreigners.

Even in the Careenage, three yachts were boarded by thugs while we were there. Above us sat the prison, known as the

Yellow House, a pleasant building with views of the lagoon, and we could imagine the prisoners planning their attacks as they studied the ways of the yachties from the vantage point above.

I no longer believed that poverty was the major cause of crime. We had been in poorer countries where we had not felt threatened, so it seemed that it had something to do with pride, attitude and possibly vengeance. Should we be armed like many other yachties, I wondered. Alan and I often debated the issue, especially after our arrival in the Caribbean, but Alan would not consider carrying firearms. He was probably right, for it was in port that one needed protection and a gun must be handed in on arrival. The alternative was to hide it, but the consequences of it being discovered in a customs search were serious. There was no easy solution, but I did feel vulnerable.

CHAPTER 17

liming in Port-of-Spain • Carnival warnings
Dirty Mas and Pretty Mas • Joseph and Hannah
Australia versus West Indies in Trinidad

The whimsical coat of arms of Trinidad and Tobago combines a white-capped sea lapping on rocky shores with the three peaks of Trinidad rising above the waves. It shows three birds: the hummingbird, the scarlet ibis of Trinidad and the *cocrico*, the Tobago pheasant. Above the birds sprout the symmetrical sprays of the *chaconia*, the flaming red forest flower, a coconut palm and a capstan. The three galleons of Columbus, representing the Holy Trinity, together with the three peaks that prompted Columbus to call the larger of the two islands Trinidad, also figure on the emblem.

The coat of arms tells us something of the people and their history, but it does not prepare us for the vitality, the infectious joie de vivre and the unabashed sexuality of the inhabitants.

'Here every creed and race find an equal place,' they sing in their national anthem, and this appears to be more the case in Trinidad than anywhere else we had visited. These distinctive people are a mixture coming from many sources: the remnants of the Caribs; slaves from Africa and the descendants of their English, French and Spanish masters; some Portuguese and Italians; Indians who had been brought in to work the plantations when slavery was abolished; and Chinese and Middle Eastern traders.

Each of the different ethnic groups, together with the mixed race members of the population, has distinct cultural traits and it would be unrealistic to believe that there is no friction. But the differences appear to be openly discussed, solutions sought and anger diffused with humour and satire rather than violence. The concept of nationhood, of being a Trinidadian, is strong in this volatile grouping and we were interested in the reasons for it.

Perhaps it is in the language, for all Trinidadians speak a lilting shared lingua franca, a type of Creole that is derived from English but which contains words and expressions from French, African and Hindi. In the beginning we found its melodious lilt and strange syntax incomprehensible, but then the flexible Trinidadians would slip into English if they were educated, and if they spoke only Creole we managed with laughter and mime, at which the Trinidadians display a Marcel Marceau facility.

Maybe their cohesion lies in their shared culture, for all Trinidadians, regardless of ethnic origin, love their heroes: the writer V.S. Naipaul, the designer and artist Peter Minchell, the beloved Brian Lara, and the kings and queens of Carnival. Carnival belongs to all Trinidadians and is of national concern.

The answer could very well be in their music — calypso originated in Trinidad and has its roots in the songs of the slaves. The lyrics of the leading vocal exponents, the calypsonians, are a mixture of social commentary, bawdy sexual innuendo, scandal and satire all linked with wit and wisdom and nonsense rhymes. The famous calypsonian, David Rudder, sang in his classic 'Calypso Music' that there will be 'lyrics to make a politician cringe or turn a woman's body into jelly.'

In Trinidad, young and old share the same music and the same dance and the same fun, and one is not conscious of a generation gap. The 86-year-old Roaring Lion who wrote the famous song 'Mary Ann' is still recording in Trinidad and the world's leading calypso singer, the Mighty Sparrow, is a living legend loved and respected by people of all ages.

Size is also a factor, I suppose. The population of the two islands is only 1.3 million and this in itself is a reason to learn to live together in harmony.

We chose to anchor in Chaguaramas Bay, 16 kilometres from the capital, Port-of-Spain. A jungle ridge of mountains protected us from the northerly winds and Gaspar Grande island from the southerlies. Venezuela was a mere seven miles away across the Gulf of Paria, its waters muddied by the mighty Orinoco River.

There was already a large contingent of cruising yachts in the bay when we arrived and the first people we bumped into were Harry and Olive from *Sunbird* whom we had not seen since Suez. They were also on their way home. Trinidad is a gathering place for yachts at Carnival time and there were several Australian and New Zealand yachts in port, some we had met before and some we had only heard of. It was to be a busy social time.

Port-of-Spain is a sprawling and unruly city of modern sky-scrapers, old colonial buildings, gingerbread houses, untidy clapboard structures, boutiques and bazaars, raucous vendors, vagrants, and street stalls from which calypso music blares forth. There are Creole, Indian and Chinese restaurants; and churches, mosques and temples. And dotted all over the city are pan yards, the home bases of the numerous steel bands, and mas camps, which are masquerade headquarters where the Carnival preparations for the various theme groups take place.

Unlike many other Caribbean towns, Port-of-Spain makes no concessions for tourists who must either join in or go away. There are no five-star hotels or swish resorts and little infrastructure. Nevertheless, you are warmly received on the assumption that because you are there you are prepared to be involved.

As we walked through the streets on our first visit, we grew increasingly apprehensive because it seemed as though the city had a serious crime problem. The evil razor-wire was much in evidence, most of the buildings had substantial iron bars and heavy security screens, and armed guards stood at the doors to many establishments. Small items like ice-creams and soft drinks were sold through holes in security screens, and outside several shops the customers were required to wait on the footpath until they were ushered through the door in groups of three or four at a time. Firms advertising 'Stolen Car Retrievals' seemed to imply a crime economy like that of Colombia.

'I'm beginning to think we shouldn't have come here,' Alan commented.

'We came for Carnival,' I reminded him. 'Let's just see how things work out. Have you noticed that no-one smokes, there's no vandalism, and there's no graffiti, not even a heart?'

Two young men, who were obviously not beggars, brazenly asked us for money and a little farther on, a third tried to involve us in a scam with bus tickets. These are normally sold from security booths so that the bus drivers do not need to carry money which could tempt someone to rob them. A fourth man offered us drugs. Oh well, in a strange town the new-comers are conspicuous and it usually takes a few days for things to settle down.

In Port-of-Spain, liming is almost an art form. This concept is exclusive to this part of the world and it means to enjoy oneself by doing nothing, apart from sitting around with your friends, gossiping, drinking or playing about. One hangs loose, man. It appears to be mainly an activity of the men, although sometimes there are women in the groups. Those who disapprove of liming call it loitering.

Port-of-Spain is famous for several things, one of which is its marvellous fabric shops. There are dozens of these shops, each with a Carnival section displaying brocades, satins and sequined materials and a range of costume paraphernalia. Alan, knowing my weakness for fabrics, advised restraint for the first few visits.

'Try not to buy until you get to know the market,' he warned. 'Remember the confusion in Istanbul. Just look today.'

At the first emporium, the tall security guard glared coldly as I crossed the threshold. I thought that perhaps I was supposed to say something.

'Good morning. May I go in?'

The guard would not answer so I repeated the question. Still he refused to answer. I teetered foolishly in the doorway before finally deciding to risk entering, but as I stopped to look at the first display, another guard strode angrily towards me and stood exceedingly close, his breath in my hair. What is wrong with these people, I wondered. This is obviously a shop, so presumably these fabrics are for sale and therefore I have a perfect right to look at them. But why won't they speak?

One must also touch fabrics, feel them, explore their texture, their composition, their quality. Each time I tried, the guard rolled his eyes in disgust, snatched the loose end from my grasp, swished it through the air like a mad matador and then with exaggerated fastidiousness, rearranged the end over the bolt and stared at me defiantly. After several attempts at ignoring his odd behaviour, I spoke.

'I appear to be doing the wrong thing but I presumed that it was all right to inspect before I bought.'

His body tightened into a spring of suppressed fury and he stared at me in silent outrage. I looked around the shop. There were three or four customers happily inspecting materials without a hovering and surly guard at their side. It seemed that we two were caught up in something surreal and bizarre. I retreated from the shop, confused and angry, and found Alan.

'I've just heard that there were riots outside that shop last night,' he said. 'The people are still jumpy. We'll come back when things settle down.'

There were plenty of other shops. I was never to return to that one.

We tried to hire a television set before we returned to Chagauramas. Ours would not function in Trinidad because it was not compatible with the American system, but all the sets had been rented for Carnival. We missed not having that window into the culture, so we began tuning in to the local radio. 'Carnival Warning to Trinidadians' was one of the first announcements we heard and it was repeated every few hours day and night:

- Securely lock all doors and windows of your houses.
- Do not drive alone. Drive in convoy.

- Check the back seat of your cars. Someone could be lurking there.
- Do not walk alone. Stay in a group.
- Have your car and house keys ready. Do not waste time fumbling.
- Do not wear jewellery. Do not carry valuables.

There were several more items, all sensible and all frightening.

We also bought the *Trinidad Guardian* each day in the hope of being able to understand what to do at Carnival. It seemed that there were many ways to celebrate but, after studying the timetable of events, it appeared that sleep would be out of the question for the duration of the Carnival. Nor did the *Trinidad Guardian* enlighten us a great deal on the finer points, for we could not understand the patois. Under a heading 'Carnival is . . .' on the front page, we read what someone called Eric Williams had to say.

'Jump up and get on bad. Play yourself. Especially the women. Ash Wednesday morning they don't know you, when you see them in the street, they watchin' you cut eye. They don't know you, and you done touch up they body!'

And we read things like 'A good fete is jumping, wining, grinding. Feel that bass line slam your chest. Jump up and get on bad!' So we asked Jamie, a Trinidadian friend to explain.

'It's easy, man. A fete is a jump-up, a dance. Wining has nothing to do with wine. It's to do with the hips which you gotta swing in a figure of eight. Like this man. Grinding is to grind your body hard against someone else's body. It's not necessary to know them 'cause any body will do. Dingolaying is the best. That's grinding while wining down to the ground.'

'Is there a word for what you do when you get down there?' Alan asked mischievously.

'Yuh, we have word for that!' our friend laughed. 'Same as yours.'

From the newspaper we also learned that there had been 17 murders in Trinidad in the six weeks since Christmas, and one morning we saw on the front page a large photo of two French yachties with whom we had shared a maxi-taxi to Port-of-Spain on the previous day. They had been mugged in the main shopping street soon after their arrival in the capital. We read that three men had just been hanged in Grenada for drug offences, but in Port-of-Spain a man convicted of drug dealing had been sent to prison for the duration of Carnival. The same punishment had been given to a man who had failed to remain still during the singing of the national anthem at one of the Carnival events.

Soon after that we saw an advertisement for a Carnival seminar to be held at a nearby yacht club and this made us feel better. If it was necessary to run a seminar, it must mean that others were confused as well. A large group of yachties had gathered and the seminar was conducted by two Americans in their 40s or early 50s, both escapees from the world of advertising.

The two Americans loved Carnival and each year they returned (this was their sixth year) to join a mas group and to organise those yachties who were experiencing it for the first time. Not only did they explain the historical and social significance of various aspects, and what would happen at each event, but they had organised a large fleet of maxi-taxis to transport the yachties to the various venues, since wandering around Trinidad at Carnival time was dangerous. The maxi-taxis would pick up and let down at each of the four anchorages along the coast between Chagauramas and Port-of-Spain. Everyone was relieved and grateful.

Carnival really began with the French and takes place each year before the austerity of Lent begins. The word derives from *carne vale* (flesh, farewell). When the old Spanish and Amerindian society was taken over by the French, Trinidad became a colony whose language was French or French patois, but after the abolition of slavery in the 1830s, the whole character of Carnival changed. Instead of being an elegant amusement for the white elite, it became a euphoric Afro-Trinidadian festival that grew out of defiance and the yearning for freedom.

As well as mocking and satirising the colonial masters, Carnival confronted and provoked them by drumming, noise, mayhem and bad taste. The harder the authorities tried to control Carnival, the more entrenched it became, until now there is virtually no segment of society that does not participate.

The three main elements of Carnival are procession, music and dance, or 'mas', 'pan' and 'calypso'. With its roots in the praise and satire songs of Africa, calypso was also a source of information and humour for the black people, but it scandalised the whites. When the British foolishly banned the African drum in 1883, the people rioted and thumped on bamboo and sticks, then on a variety of metallic substitutes for drums, such as tins and machinery parts and finally during the Second World War they discovered the possibilities of 44-gallon drums. These were cut, shaped, polished and tuned into a new musical instrument — the steel drums of Trinidad — and so pan was born.

Above all, though, Carnival is about people. Each year the Trinidadians come into the streets in their thousands to claim for themselves an alternative reality, to pretend they are something or someone that they can never be: a king or a queen, an Indian chief, a drunken sailor or a sex symbol.

Dressing up — the masquerade — allows people to behave without inhibition. Only the person of the masquerade is real, the person of the mask. So those who wish to participate join bands or masquerade groups and they parade in the costumes of those groups during the two principal days of Carnival. This is called Pretty Mas.

Visitors are encouraged to join mas groups too. They pay for their costume and go along to the mas camps in the weeks before Carnival to help in the preparations. We were tempted, but we felt that we had arrived too late. Also we doubted that we would have the stamina to dance through the streets for two days and nights in the steamy heat when the temperature was usually in the mid-30s to 40s.

How can poor people afford to take part in Carnival when new costumes are required each year, we wondered. I am not sure of the logistics but outside the banks in Port-of-Spain there were posters advertising 'Loans for Carnival costumes. Low interest rates.'

Each mas band has a theme and a designer, many of whom are famous in their field, like Peter Minshall who designed the Barcelona Olympics opening ceremony and the 'Dance of the nations' at the World Cup Soccer finals, and Wayne Berkeley who has worked at the Barbican and Albert Hall in London and La Scala in Milan. So Carnival brings together artists, designers, dancers, musicians, satirists, comedians, mime artists, costume makers, choreographers, singers, poets, songwriters, organisers and planners in an inspired explosion of talent and energy.

Carnival is also a highly organised and government-sponsored competition which has the backing of most local and some international business firms, and intense partisan support flares around the leading protagonists. Which group will win the pan competition? Who is the best designer? Who will be the Calypsonian of the Year? Who will be Queen? or King? Which will be the winning Carnival song this year, 'Ode to Brian Lara' or 'Jump up and Dance' or one of about 20 others? Everyone has an opinion based upon a deep understanding, for all rehearsal venues, mas camps, pan yards, calypso tents and jump-ups are open to everyone, day and night.

The Pentecostals were outraged by Peter Minshall's use of the title 'Hallelujah' for his masquerade group with a theme of peace and joy. They claimed that 'hallelujah' was their word, and they argued that only a heretic would use it as a Carnival title. The *Trinidad Guardian* published the answer from The Carnival Kingdom (the organising committee) to be sung to the tune of 'Glory, Glory Hallelujah':

Does any pastor have a monopoly on God?
Praise God, Hallelujah!
Can a prime minister tell me how I should praise my Lord?

If, in the face of the Devil, I capitulate
The Holy Spirit would tell me, ye of little faith!
People! All I want to do is praise my Lord.
Only demons stop a man from praising God

Then followed the rousing chorus: 'Hallelujah! Hallelujah! Sing it through Trinidad and Tobago!'. Other groups with names like 'Hot, Hot, Hot', 'Tribal Passions', 'Poison' and 'Barbarossa' were left in peace to pursue their particular brand of fantasy.

Letters to the papers concentrated on Carnival and they ranged from impassioned support for the new crop of road songs to complaints about the influences that American pop was having on the music and lyrics of soca and calypso. The great singer and teacher, Chalkdust, wrote, 'We cannot have our children singing words like "bumsy",' whereupon the children turned the word into a catch-cry of delight.

As well as Pretty Mas there is Dirty Mas or *J'Ouvert*, which begins soon after 2 a.m. and, as its name implies, opens Carnival. It is a hedonistic, bacchanalian riot of fun to which people wear lewd and bizarre costumes, tattered clothes or very little clothing at all. The celebration is characterised by brain-shattering soca music, wild dancing, the drinking of copious amounts of rum, and gangs of masked demons who smear axle grease and mud over as many participants as possible.

Alan and I did not have the courage to take part in Dirty Mas. Nor did we have the stamina, for at 2 a.m. that morning we were returning to *Windigo* from the Savannah, after attending Dimanche Gras, the flamboyant presentation of the winners of the various Carnival competitions to a 'standing room only' audience of ebullient Trinidadians.

Queen's Park Savannah is an open space in the centre of Port-of-Spain. It surrounds an enormous pavilion capable of seating thousands. Down its centre runs a catwalk large enough to accommodate the hundreds of people in each masquerade group as well as the bands of more than 100 pannists, each with a 44-gallon drum.

Slowly the big catwalk fills with the shining silver pans mounted on moveable trolleys and decorated with glitter and tinsel. The players, dressed in the costume of their pan yard, assemble behind their instruments. At some invisible signal they all begin to play.

Imagine the din of 100 pannists striking their pans, the rush of sound belting you against the back of your seat, flattening you out, exploding your brain, assaulting you. The pannists do not just beat their pans. They leap and jump and gyrate in a frenzy, their energy pulsating through the vast audience until the people are lifted from their seats and they, too, jump and twist and dance with an energy that is almost frightening.

Most of the players do not read music. Like the Balinese gamelan players, they must memorise the entire repertoire which ranges from calypso to classical. Often the music is loud and persistent, but it can also be soft and sweet and as abstract as a haiku.

On the night of Panorama, however, the bands played the songs of this year's Carnival. New songs are written each year and the entire population learns the lyrics and sings the songs in the streets, the home and in the workplace, 'All day, all night, Mary Ann'.

From Sunday until Ash Wednesday, everything closes in Port-of-Spain and excitement reaches fever pitch with all night jump-ups, parties, calypso tents, rum and noise as the people make their final preparations for Carnival. Alan and I had purchased reserve tickets for the Savannah so that we could watch the parade in some comfort, or at least in the shade, but when we reached Port-of-Spain we got caught up in the crowd and we never reached the Savannah.

Sitting in the gutter with crowds of effervescent people in searing heat for eight hours at a stretch is not normally our idea of fun, but that is what we did, and we were entranced for the entire time as thousands upon thousands of Trinidadians danced their way through the streets like an irresistible river of colour, sound and explosive and sensual joy. It is a dazzling parade, a universal festival, a potent hypnotic force.

It takes eight hours for each group to pass in a rough circle through each of the four judging points, only one of which is the Savannah. Each mas group is led by its soca or pan band assembled on semitrailers with batteries of loudspeakers. The music is so *fortissimo* that it changes the rhythm of one's heartbeat and for a few minutes we feared we would die. Behind each mas band is the group's booze bus, to ensure that the rum and beer never cease flowing. I was not sure how people sustained such energy, but it was probably a combination of training, adrenalin, rum, dope, euphoria, trance and, above all, the beat of the drums.

The air was heavy with the dust of thousands of dancing feet, the smell of sweat, rum, beer, eau-de-cologne, boiled corn, coconuts and *callaloo* (rice and peas), as people of all ages and shapes took on their Carnival persona and threw their inhibitions aside. Dancing along somewhere in the melee was the Prime Minister and several members of his Cabinet. Mick Jagger and David Bowie and their famous friends had come across from Mustique but they, too, were invisible as they acted out their fantasy egos somewhere in the moving mass. Carnival was for everyone.

When I saw the first grinders I thought, 'Surely they're not doing what I think they're doing,' but as no-one else paid the slightest attention to their antics, I decided that it was normal Carnival behaviour, totally acceptable in this God-fearing island. Sometimes they grind in groups, often in threes, but usually in twos. Sometimes they snatch a stranger of the opposite sex from the crowd, grind and then 'chip off' as though nothing had happened. Being a spectator is no guarantee against a grinding if someone likes the look of you, but neither Alan nor I was ground.

The leading characters with the most elaborate costumes paraded at the head of each mas band. Peter Minshall's group, 'Hallelujah', was led by an apparition in white called 'Joy to the World'. She floated beneath many great wings of fine silk six metres high, that moved as if they had life of their own, and her elaborate gown and headdress sparkled with imitation crystals and diamonds. The people were silent with awe as she floated by as Queen of the Carnival.

Finally it was all over. Alan and I felt the limp exhaustion that follows a sustained obsession. Like a luminous cloud that blots out the rest of the world, Carnival had taken over our lives and an ancient and tribal rhythm had captured our souls. For two days we slept and limed about, but reality returned on the third day, clear and bright, and we set about organising ourselves for the next phase.

On our first trip into town after Carnival we wondered if things would be different. Perhaps the people would no longer bounce along the streets in Carnival mood. They could even be dull and ordinary. We need not have worried, for they were as they always had been — cheeky, funny, outrageous, endearing.

Not long into the trip, this time by bus instead of maxi-taxi, a black woman of about 80 years jumped aboard with the alacrity of a girl. She was slim, supple and still good-looking, and her eyes sparkled with humour. The dozen or so passengers smiled at her for she was irresistible. A few miles farther on, an equally elderly man entered. He, too, was smartly dressed and attractive, but not so agile, and he balanced on his walking stick while he surveyed the available seats. Then his eyes caught those of the woman and he walked towards the front of the bus and sat opposite her in the section where the seats faced each other. They smiled and nodded at each other, the woman coquettish, the man relaxed.

'They call me Joseph,' he said to her. 'What about you?'

'They call me Hannah, man,' she replied. 'What's it to you?'

'Just wondrin'. Hannah, ey. Nice name for a nice woman.' He bowed graciously from the waist.

'I'm not too nice,' Hannah laughed flirtatiously with emphasis on the 'too'.

'That's good,' Joseph replied. 'I wouldn't want you to be too nice!'

The passengers, who had taken an unabashed interest in the little drama, now laughed and two or three offered encouragement, much to the amusement of everyone, including the two on centre stage.

'How about you and me get together some time soon?' Joseph asked her and the passengers silently pursed their lips and nodded approval.

'Is you askin' for a date, man?' Hannah asked with a charming smile.

Joseph grinned and leaned back in his seat, his arm along the back of the one next to him. 'Guess I am. How about it, Hannah?' he drawled.

'Problem is, I gotta get off this bus right now, man,' Hannah protested as we neared the outskirts of Port-of-Spain and she jumped to her feet. Her voice was tinged with disappointment and the passengers waited in silence as if they were holding their breath.

'Then I will join you,' said Joseph decisively.

They stood together, Joseph with one hand on his walking stick and the other around Hannah's waist as he guided her off the bus, and as they stood smiling at each other on the footpath, the passengers shouted and waved encouragement through the open windows. Alan and I held hands on the bus, and felt that the world was as it should be.

Immediately Carnival was over, most of the American and European yachts left Trinidad, and the Australians and New Zealanders entertained on each others' boats, seeking to become better acquainted, because everyone would need assistance to negotiate the Panama Canal, as well as comradeship and support across the Pacific. So we made new friends, laughed a lot and sometimes grew maudlin in our shared homesickness, since all were longing for the blue ridges and sun-kissed soils of home.

Two people we admired were Mike and Lois, whom we had met briefly in Gibraltar. Fifteen years previously they had travelled from their home in Queensland, through the Red Sea to Europe in a small fishing boat, returning by the same route as they were not dependent on the winds and they wished to avoid the large oceans. The next time the wanderlust grabbed them, they learned to sail and were now, like the rest of us, completing a circumnavigation.

Mike was a snowy-haired, intense and hard drinking man with a fiery disposition. Lois, on the other hand, said little, laughed with genuine amusement at Mike's stories and was gentle and calm. She was also one of Australia's few female Master Mariners. Their children were scattered around the world, their eldest son working on a square-rigger in England.

Travelling north through the Red Sea on their first trip, they had anchored one afternoon near Marsa Terifa, where they met a Saudi prince while they were ashore stretching their legs. With a retinue of servants and a couple of his royal friends, the prince was on a hunting expedition and he and the two friends had walked from a base camp several kilometres from the anchorage in search of game.

'There we were, just me and Lois, in the middle of this bloody great desert,' Mike told us. 'Who should walk out of the dunes in front of us but these three guys in long white gowns carrying guns. "It's only a mirage," I said to Lois. "Relax love, they are not real".'

Lois replied that they appeared real enough to her and turned to run full-pelt back towards the marsa where the boat was anchored. Eventually, though, it was all sorted out and the Saudi prince had insisted that Mike and Lois join his party for dinner that night. Just on sunset, they were picked up at the anchorage and driven in a four-wheel-drive vehicle to the hunting camp in the desert, where decorated tents were pitched in a semicircle, each one guarded by huge black men with bulging muscles and shiny scimitars.

'It was like something out of the Arabian Nights,' Mike said. 'We thought we were on a magic carpet. And you should have seen the meal. And the furnishings. The urns and pitchers, the goblets and salvers. Wonderfully lavish!'

Mike, as usual, had drunk a considerable amount by the end of the meal and needed to take a walk in the desert. He excused himself and wandered across the dunes until he was out of sight of the guards with their flashing scimitars because as he said, 'I did not like the looks in their eyes.'

Much relieved, he was admiring the stars as he strolled back towards the main tent. Suddenly, a robed figure emerged from the darkness and stood in front of him. The apparition carried a large and ornately decorated silver chalice that twinkled in the starlight and without warning, he reached for Mike's fly and unzipped it.

'Leave me alone!' Mike screamed as he sprang back, clutching himself. 'Don't you dare touch me, you foul bastard. Bugger off!'

'But I must, sir,' the man replied. 'You are unclean. I must wash you. You cannot be unclean!'

'Well, if you say so,' Mike replied, not too sure of his ground.

The servant expertly pulled out Mike's willy, washed it, dried it, powdered it, replaced it, and zipped him up again. As Mike admitted, it wasn't an entirely unpleasant experience but it was still some minutes before he had regained his composure and was able to join the others in the tent. As Lois tells it, before Mike resumed his place beside their host, he walked past her, his face white and troubled, and he bent over and whispered frantically in her ear.

'Lois, do not . . . I repeat, do not go for a pee!'

Cricket fever swept through Trinidad a few days after Carnival. Australia was to play a one-day match against the West Indies in

Port-of-Spain, and local boy wonder, Brian Lara, would be in the West Indian team. It seemed churlish to leave when 'our boys' would be severely outnumbered; far better to stay on for a few extra days to cheer them on. To be honest, though, we had caught cricket fever from the Trinidadians who seemed determined to engulf us in their enthusiasms.

'Leave before the one-day match! You must be crazy, man.'

'But you are Australian, aren't you? How can you leave?'

'Have you ever seen Lara play? He's a miracle, man.'

Like most other things in Trinidad, a cricket match is unlike a cricket match anywhere else. It is a grand affair with steel bands and Trini flair. In Trinidad cricket is loved by all, even though it can cause friction, as it did some years ago when the Indian community barracked for a visiting Indian team.

Not knowing exactly what to expect, we queued for tickets in the early morning when they went on sale some days before the match. We hoped for seats in one of the stands.

'Those seats go long ago,' we were told by others in the queue. 'Them only for rich people and their friends.'

'And the politicians and their friends!' someone else said.

Our seats were for the bicycle track in full sun.

'Bring big hats and lots an' lots of beer,' we were advised.

Neither of us knew a great deal about the game of cricket but I had heard of *aficionados* inspecting the pitch before the match so I suggested to Alan that perhaps we should do that. Also inspecting the pitch was a small group of four Indian *cognoscenti*. One was a Buddha-shaped gentleman with a noisy, bossy personality and long white hair and beard like a guru, which was in fact what he said he was.

'In what field are you a guru?' I asked him.

'Cricket,' he replied. 'Here, have some *ganga*,' and he offered a handful of rolled joints around the group. We declined, but the others lit up and we chatted for a while.

'You must be sitting with us at the cricket!' the guru exclaimed eventually. 'I will direct my wife to cook extra samousas and pokhoras and roti for you, and there will be plenty of rum and *ganga*. I'll explain the rules of cricket to you during the match so you'll understand everything that is happening.'

With Alan's weakness for Indian food, I had to think fast.

'You're kind, my friend,' I said. 'But we've already made arrangements to share lunch with a group of yachties from the anchorage at Chagauramas.'

This was not altogether true, but it was probably what would ultimately happen.

At 4.30 a.m. on the day of the match we were up and away, but when we reached Queen's Park Oval there was little room left. We squeezed our way to the sloping concrete track and people good-naturedly made space for the small group waving green and gold kangaroo flags.

We sat in a sea of Trinidadians who were in great high spirits, for they were convinced of victory. The temperature quickly soared to 40 degrees and we huddled under hats and drank copious amounts of Carib beer poured over large containers of crushed ice sold by enterprising Indians. And we sweated so profusely that no-one needed to use the toilets for the entire day.

The noise was profound as people cheered, whistled, stamped, banged on drums and bottles and cans and blew conch shells. Sometimes, as if to a hidden signal, only the conch shells would sound and it was as though thousands of testosterone-tormented bulls were joined in lament. Wild-eyed Rastafarians led Mexican waves and when two of them saw the Australian flags, they loudly attacked the group on our treatment of the Aborigines, but we sat in embarrassed silence and they soon moved away.

We were delighted when Australia won, but at the same time sad for the crestfallen Trinidadians. Brian Lara had been impressive but the Australian team had played a brilliant game. Then, despite their loss and disappointment, the Trinidadians came in dozens to shake hands with the Australians scattered through the crowd and we were moved by their generous spirit.

CHAPTER 18

vampires off Venezuela
Curaçao in the ABC islands
shopping in a mansion in Colombia
the beautiful San Blas Islands • Panama

So intimidating were the grapevine stories of muggings and boardings along the Venezuelan coast that we sailed well out to sea without making a landfall. But there was another reason for avoiding the coast — the humid basin of the Orinoco River was the home of vampire bats, and we could not free our minds of the experience of one yachtie couple who had anchored in a bay on the Venezuelan coast to catch up on some sleep.

The wife had woken around midnight, sensing a presence in the cabin. Turning on the light, she found the mattress and pillows soaked with blood and both she and her husband bleeding profusely, because the bats inject an anticoagulant before they start drinking. In a state of shock the couple up-anchored and sailed to the nearest town for assistance, which included anti-rabies injections as the bats are carriers.

One black night while on watch, I smelt something putrid in the air and, suspecting that a fishing boat was upwind, I switched off the cabin lights and hurried into the cockpit to investigate. Instead of landing on cool steel, my bare foot pressed down on something warm and soft and alive.

'Vampires!' I screamed. 'Wake up, Alan. Help! There's a vampire in the cockpit!'

I sprang below and banged shut the hatch as Alan stumbled from the aft cabin.

'Calm down, Olma. You're imagining things,' he said when he saw the state I was in.

'No, I am not. I felt it. And I feel sick,' I told him.

While I cowered in the galley, he opened the companionway hatch and was immediately attacked by an enormous seabird, its snapping beak and flailing wings filling the cockpit. Alan slammed down the hatch just as I had done.

'I'm not going out there with that thing,' he announced. 'That's the biggest bird I've ever seen.'

'But you must. I can't keep watch,' I persisted.

So he climbed out through the aft cabin hatch and approached the cockpit from the rear, but the enormous bird was strong, aggressive and determined. It would not budge from the cockpit. Alan tried various methods, but each time the bird outmanoeuvred him, its long thrust and dangerous beak making it impossible to get near. He tried enveloping it in an old painting sheet, but it fought and pecked and shat in fury. Finally, with a boathook, he was able to trip it, push it onto the side deck and force it overboard. With its two-metre wingspan, it was probably an albatross, and we immediately thought of the Ancient Mariner and prayed that the bird would live.

Two days later we made landfall on Curaçao, in the ABC islands. Aruba, Bonaire and Curaçao are part of the Netherlands Antilles that lie slightly to the east of the Gulf of Venezuela. They were discovered at the end of the 15th century by Spanish mariners, but the Dutch ousted the Spanish in the 17th century and developed a successful economy based on smuggling, slave-trading and farming.

Today, the islands are probably the most prosperous in the Caribbean. One reason is that oil refineries had been set up by foreign interests in Aruba and Curaçao to refine Venezuelan oil brought in by tankers. The refineries have provided jobs and given the people a high standard of living. Another reason for their greater prosperity is that they have remained dependent territories of Holland, which takes care of expensive national items like defence and membership of various international bodies, and the upkeep of embassies and consulates. Internal affairs are managed by the islanders who appear happy with their way of life.

The official language of the islands is Dutch, but the lingua franca is Papiamento, a mixture of Dutch, English, French, African and local Indian dominated by Spanish, because of strong trade links with Venezuela. In Papiamento, the word itself means 'babble' which seems an apt description. On Curaçao the signs are all in Papiamento so we had little chance of understanding and there were few clues to help us. *Un macacu ta subi palu di sumpinja un biahe so*, means, 'A monkey climbs a cactus but once.'

One does not expect to stumble upon a miniature Amsterdam in the Caribbean Sea, but Willemstad, the capital of Curaçao, is like that. Cut in half by the waters of Santa Anna Bay, Punda, the downtown area, is on one side and Otrabanda (literally 'the other side') on the other. The buildings that line the shores are similar to those along the banks of the canals in old Amsterdam. They are painted and gabled with rows of attic windows and roofs of red tiles brought from Holland as ballast in the holds of trading ships.

As in Amsterdam, the boats and bridges are central to the life of Willemstad. The high and graceful Juliana Bridge allows ships to pass underneath, but the old favourite, Queen Emma, is a pontoon bridge which swings open at least 30 times each day to allow seagoing vessels to pass through. Built in 1888, a toll once had to be paid by all who crossed it wearing shoes. Barefoot people were able to pass free, but today it is free to all.

The streets, with names like Heerenstraat, Gomezplein and Madurostraat, are lined with shops that sell products we had not seen since Europe — French perfumes, English knitwear, Italian fashions, Swiss watches and Japanese cameras. The people are of mixed race, smartly dressed and conservative but welcoming. We formed the impression that there would be little, if any, crime on the island of Curaçao.

As is often the case, we found the area around the market to be the most colourful part of town. In Curaçao the market floated like the one on the Greek island of Aegina, being formed from rafted-up Venezuelan trading vessels laden with tropical fruits, vegetables and fish.

Perhaps the island of Curaçao is most famous for its singular liqueur of the same name, for it is only here that the oranges from which it is made will grow. At the time of the Spanish, Seville oranges had been planted all over the island but for some reason they had not grown as expected, turning instead into small hard green fruit with an unusual flavour. They were useless for everything — except for making the rare and expensive Curaçao liqueur which forms the basis of several family distilleries that are scattered across the island.

There is an old Chinese curse which says, 'May you live in interesting times.' Anything we had ever read about Colombia indicated that it had been through more than its share of interesting times, and we had no wish to be part of them. Yet, circumstances caused us to re-examine our position and head for the old Spanish city of Cartagena on Colombia's Caribbean coast.

Cartagena is one of the artistic and cultural treasures of South America and it has won World Heritage listing for its fine Spanish colonial architecture. Its harbour provides a convenient stopover for yachts sailing west towards Panama.

None of these temptations was enough in itself to lure us there, but when we heard from yachties ahead that the harbour was relatively safe from boardings, we were interested. *Sunbird* was already there.

'Yes, it's perfectly safe,' Harry reassured us on the radio.

'But how can that be when Colombia is in such a mess?' Alan asked.

'This part of the town's like an armed camp,' Harry replied. 'But the biggest safety factor is that the President of Colombia, as well as the local drug barons, keep their mega-yachts here.'

Colombia has a history of violence which is probably unequalled in South America. It has guerilla armies, murder squads, muggers, robbers, killers and thugs. There is crime, corruption, censorship, inequality, exploitation, poverty on a grand scale, juntas, tyranny, political unrest and powerful drug cartels that control 80 per cent of the world's cocaine production.

In the obsessive search for the mythical El Dorado, the cruelty of the Spanish conquistadors knew no bounds, and their excesses set in motion a cycle of violence that has remained as part of the psyche of the people, mostly below the surface but sometimes erupting like a volcano spewing blood. In 1948, a period of violence, '*La Violencia*', began in Bogota and lasted for a decade. It swept the country in a bloodbath of murder, torture and horror that left 300 000 people dead. The vendettas flared across the land, brother killed brother, family fought family and entire towns and villages fought their neighbours.

The cities swelled with the thousands of refugees fleeing from the terror in the countryside. Children who had seen their families raped and slain quickly came to believe that life was cheap so they formed their own gangs, the *gamines*. Later these grew into groups of thugs that in their turn ruled by terror, kidnapping the children of the rich and demanding huge ransoms and turning the cities into dangerous hellholes. The violence led to crime, the army formed death squads, the drug bosses and mafia bosses grew rich, while the people grew poorer and more desperate.

At the end of the 1980s, Colombia reached the brink of another bloody internal feud, but a new constitution was introduced which affirmed a more pluralist approach to government and a wider recognition of human rights. However, little change actually took place because of the power of the drug cartels and their guerrilla armies.

When Pablo Escobar and three other drug barons were forced into exile in Panama, they made an unusual proposal to the Colombian government. In return for immunity from prosecution, they would pay Colombia's entire national foreign debt of $13 billion.

After some consideration, the Government refused the offer.

Cartagena has withstood several sieges in its history, the most famous involving Francis Drake who held the city to ransom for ten million pesos, billions in today's terms. The most courageous siege commander was Blas de Lezo who, when called upon to defend the city against the British under Captain Vernon in 1741, was already minus some of his body parts. He had lost a leg in the battle of Gibraltar, an eye in Toulon and his right arm in the battle of Barcelona. Although victorious at Cartagena, he lost his remaining leg in the battle and died soon afterwards.

Simon Bolivar, South America's great liberator, gave Cartagena its well-earned name of *La Heroica* (the Heroic City) for it was one of the first towns to proclaim independence from Spain, inspiring the capital, Bogota, to follow suit.

Today the city is a fascinating blend of old and new. There is the brooding fort, the skilfully engineered and immensely strong city walls, the narrow streets and pastel-tinted colonial buildings with their archways, courtyards and fountains. The facades of the buildings are covered in balconies which not only protect the interiors from the sun and rain, but once facilitated the time-honoured Spanish tradition of people-watching and serenading. The popular name for the balconies is *panza* (belly) and they served an important social function in a society where young women were seldom allowed out of the house and never unaccompanied. In the swelling of the *panzas*, whisperings and love affairs could develop while the young women were safely inside and partly hidden by geraniums.

Cartagena's petrochemical industry has brought development and wealth, but it has also polluted the beaches where the expensive resorts and hotels are to be found. There are designer shops, up-market restaurants, and suburbs where the wealthy Spaniards live in what are virtually armed enclaves. We appeared to have anchored in one such suburb for the shore was lined with mansions and parks. At the water's edge was a small marina and bar with a pleasant outdoor dining area that projected over the water.

'You'll have to check in with Norman first,' we were told by those already there. 'He's a cranky bugger and he overcharges on drinks if he gets the chance. Just watch him.'

Norman was one of those Australians whom we wished were a Lapp or a Hottentot, for his rudeness and sloth were embarrassing. He had arrived in Colombia in the 1970s and had fallen in love with Rosita, a sharp-tongued Colombian woman who had developed a dislike for gringos, perhaps because of being married to Norman. As foreigners are not permitted to own land in Colombia, everything the couple possessed was in Rosita's name: the land, the bar and the marina. Now it appeared that Rosita's affections had strayed and Norman stood to lose everything.

He sat dejectedly at one of the tables over the water, an empty beer bottle before him and his stubbled potato face buried in folds of flesh as his head lolled on his chest.

'Norman?'

'Yeah.'

'Alan and Olma from *Windigo*. We've come to check in.'

'Sit down,' Norman growled as he shuffled off, returning five minutes later with a map of the city which he spread on the table before us.

'Life is easier all round if you yachties stay out of trouble,' he said, and he began making crosses on the map as he spoke. 'Never go into the Getsemani area. You are bound to be mugged there. Stay away from here and here and don't go anywhere near here, either. That area's dodgy too.'

'There's not much left,' Alan commented.

'No, not much,' Norman replied. 'You shouldn't go to the contraband area either but of course you will, so go in the daytime and keep your wits about you. Now I'll get you a drink. Two beers?'

'No thanks, Norman. It's a bit too early for us.'

He scowled, and we left to explore our immediate neighbourhood, the suburb of A'Manga. Perhaps the best way to give an idea of the area's opulence is to describe the local supermarket, the likes of which we shall probably never see again. Imagine a grand white *Gone With the Wind* mansion. An ornate marble facade with elegant columns and sweeping marble terraces formed the entrance to the graceful building which was set in manicured lawns and formal gardens.

The interior with its wide, curving marble staircase and stained-glass windows had been painstakingly restored and in it was housed the supermarket. For tired trolley pushers there was a reception area with antique furniture, an elegant restaurant, and upstairs was an enormous tiled bathroom and toilet in period style with fresh flowers and handtowels with floral borders. Enchanting! And through it wandered the affluent Spanish clientele wheeling their smart silver trolleys with built-in calculators.

The secluded and leafy streets of A'Manga were of a similar style to the grounds of the supermarket, and each gateway was guarded. Near the beach, more mansions and expensive apartment blocks were being constructed by dozens of dusty workmen with donkeys and carts.

It appears that contraband goods are 'legal' in Colombia, the attitude of the authorities being that, like prostitution, dealing in contraband is a fact of life so there is not much point in making a fuss. In Cartagena the dealers in contraband are grouped in one part of the city, most of them running their businesses from small outlets in a large two-storey colonial edifice built around a central courtyard. We expected the area to be sleazy and the people dangerous, but it appeared to be well organised, although those with whom we dealt were curt. Our largest purchase was three cases of whisky for $5.30 a bottle. We thought of it as cheap ballast and hoped it would last us across the Pacific.

Needing cash for our contraband goods as well as for other purchases placed us in a position where we had to go to a bank, so we chose the most imposing establishment in the Plaza de Bolivar in the old city. In its cool interior we found a seat on a raised balustraded section from where we could survey the main floor. Very few people entered the bank alone. Almost everyone came in pairs and it was soon obvious that the second man in each pair was an armed bodyguard who stood close behind the person making the transaction.

'What will we do?' I asked Alan.

'There seems no alternative but for you to keep watch while I get the money,' he replied. 'Then we'll stand close to the guard outside until a taxi comes along.'

'But taxis may not be safe, either,' I argued.

'Should we forget about Scotch for $5.30 a bottle then?'

The business of withdrawing money was painfully slow and I suspected everyone who came near Alan, barely restraining myself from yelling out a warning on a couple of occasions. Finally it was done. Then we felt even more vulnerable, as though we were carrying a million dollars in cash that the entire population of Cartagena knew about. No sooner had we reached the footpath than a vehicle resembling a taxi pulled up in front of the main door, and the smiling driver beckoned us over.

'I don't think that's a taxi,' I said to Alan. 'It looks different in some way.'

'It is a taxi,' he insisted. 'Get in before someone mugs us.'

We were barely halfway across the Plaza de Bolivar when the car was suddenly surrounded by armed soldiers, zealots in their teens with stubborn faces and guns at the ready. There were about ten of them crowding around the car, pushing their unsmiling faces against the windows.

'Shit!' I said.

'Don't say anything,' Alan whispered.

The soldiers shouted at the driver, first just a couple of them, then all together. The driver shouted back, his face black and angry. Tempers began to fray and the shouting grew wilder, a couple of soldiers raised their guns, and people began disappearing from the square.

'Alan, let's get out of here,' I begged.

He opened the back door, pushing it against a soldier.

'No!' shouted the soldiers and banged the door shut again.

'I think we're in trouble,' Alan said, his voice sounding strange.

Then suddenly the shouting stopped, the driver threw the car into gear and drove off, babbling away as he drove. Alan tried to get some sense out of him but he simply kept on babbling as if we understood. Finally he took both hands off the wheel, clapped them above his head, threw back his head and began to laugh, a throaty, joyous release of tension that filled the car with merriment. We joined him. It seemed the best thing to do.

Norman glared at us over the top of our bill when we went to pay the anchoring fee prior to leaving Cartagena.

'You have not bought one drink from my bar,' he exclaimed accusingly.

'We prefer to drink on the boat,' Alan told him.

'Bloody Australians. Tight-fisted buggers, the lot of them,' Norman replied as he grabbed the money and stormed off.

The islands of the San Blas archipelago are strung along the coast of Panama from a point near the Colombian border to the Gulf of San Blas. There are supposed to be 365 of them, one for each day of the year, but only about 50 are inhabited. Some are tiny cays with a single palm tree on a circle of sand, some are large enough for sizeable villages of palm-thatched huts. With its clear turquoise waters and palm-fringed beaches, the remote province of San Blas is one of the truly beautiful places of the world.

The people who live there are the Cuna Indians, the last of the full-blood Caribs. They are small, determined people, striking in appearance with their straight black hair cut in a short bob, and the women with brightly rouged cheeks and a black line tattooed down the bridge of the nose. They wear brightly coloured panels on the front and back of their blouses, which are tucked into short skirts and finished off with a bright sash around the waist. On their arms and legs they wear dozens of gold and silver bracelets and anklets and the women on the first couple of islands we stopped at appeared to have one nostril blocked with a silver plug. One does not like to peer too hard up other people's nostrils so we were never sure whether or not the passage was completely blocked off.

'Mola madness' afflicts everyone who passes through the San Blas and we caught the complaint at the first island we approached. A *mola* is an intricately designed and stitched piece of appliqué. Many layers of coloured fabric sections are used, cut away to reveal the layers underneath so that a complicated repeat pattern of shapes and colours and stitches and yarns is created. The *molas* are designed and made by the women to wear as panels on the front and back of their blouses, but they are treasured for their decorative qualities by yachties and collectors because the anthropomorphic designs are both naive and sophisticated.

The Cuna Indians are Panama's most highly organised people with a remarkable tenacity in guarding their traditional way of life. Marriage outside the race is forbidden and those who transgress are expelled. Dancing is a form of religious expression, and music is vital to the success of ceremonies like the puberty rites for girls when their hair is cut for the first time.

Groups of excited people rushed to the water's edge waving *molas* each time we visited an island. I soon grew tired of these reception parties, for the little boys were tedious in their perverse habit of feeling between my legs and trying to pull down my shorts while their mothers roared with laughter at my discomfort and Alan disappeared behind a hut because he could not keep a straight face. What had the boys been told about gringo women, I wondered.

At one tiny island there was an old man who spoke reasonable English, although he was rather vague about where he had learned it. His two sons and their wives and several children lived on the island but they owned little apart from a canoe, two plastic buckets in which they kept the *molas* and a few plastic dishes.

'Can we give you anything?' we asked. 'What do you need?'

'Very little,' replied the old man. 'But we're sometimes short of drinking water and we like sugar and sweet things, and I need a large strong needle to mend the sails of my fishing canoe.'

We bundled as many things as we could spare into the dinghy and took them ashore, but the old man was away fishing and the families seemed shy. For a while we wondered if we had done something to offend them, but just on dark the old man paddled out to *Windigo* in his canoe.

'Thank you for your gifts. This is all we have to give you in return,' he said placing a heavy green coconut in the scuppers.

Our time in the San Blas was like a vacation. We swam with coloured fish and a couple of gummy sharks in water like gin, explored islands, dozed in the shade on white beaches, fished and read. Sometimes big warm thunderstorms swept across the archipelago and we collected fresh water in abundance. Apart from occasional sightings of *Sunbird*, we saw no other yachts. We felt that, apart from the few San Blas islanders we met, we were alone in the world and the world was beautiful.

Portobelo is a day's sail from the northern entrance to the Panama Canal. Columbus named it 'the Beautiful Port' when he stopped there in 1502 on his fourth voyage to the New World. With the conquest of Peru, gold and treasure was shipped to Panama and then brought by mules across the isthmus to Portobelo. Its history, therefore, has some similarities with that of Cartagena, but there the likeness ends, for Portobelo now lies in dripping moss-covered ruins.

One of the world's wettest places, it is remote and isolated on the edge of a steaming jungle that encroaches inexorably on the small village that has been built in the ruins. All around there are cannons, forts and walls which are now little more than soft mounds of green moss. It feels as though primeval forces are at work in a relentless return to nature. There is a well-tended church, however, with a life-sized black Christ who vies with the spirits of *obeah* that hover in the grey mist above the village.

In the main square, a group of strange black men had gathered. Because they are superstitious, they wore their clothing inside out, and on their heads sat high peaked hats covered in feathers, tinsel, buttons and rings. On lengths of rope around their waists there was a macabre collection of amulets, talismans and fetishes like daggers, saws, jawbones, whistles, skulls, tins, toy revolvers, bugles, and the dismembered pieces of white baby dolls, the heads covered with matted blonde hair, their blue glass eyes rolling. These men were the descendants of African slaves who had turned upon their white masters in the area around Portobelo and slaughtered them. The articles around their waists were the grizzly reminders of that event.

Some of the men began to beat out a rhythm on their drums, softly at first and then loudly and insistently. Other men began to dance, spinning and leaping with wild abandon in a display of aggressive machismo. From somewhere came the women, falling upon the men like demons, and all writhed and panted in a brutal simulation of intercourse. Perhaps in the darkness, lit by a shaft of silvery moonlight, I may have found the dance/mime erotic, but in the grey mist of the afternoon, the sun struggled onto a wild and tawdry orgy.

Harry and Olive on *Sunbird* often amused us with their positive reactions to every country they visited. They are the kinds of travellers who are determined to see only the good things — a laudable objective to be sure, but one that I could never hope to achieve. My impressions of Portobelo and the dance we had seen together stimulated Harry to spring to its defence:

'Now, Olma, I don't believe that you should describe Portobelo as squalid because it's not. It's quite a nice little place really. Pleasant actually. I've seen much worse. You do realise they are poor people, don't you? Well, they are. So you really shouldn't criticise them, because they can't help it. And the dance was merely a bit of uninhibited good fun. You can't expect to find the Bolshoi here you know.'

The isthmus of Panama was originally settled by the Spanish after the explorer Rodrigo de Bastidas had sailed along its Caribbean coast in 1501, a year before Columbus on his fourth and final voyage. Panama was a province of Colombia in the 19th century, but when it slowly dawned upon the world powers that there could be a way of linking the Pacific and Atlantic oceans across its narrow isthmus, Panama assumed a new importance. Actually, though, Charles V of Spain had ordered a feasibility study for the building of a canal in the 16th century.

Four centuries later, Ferdinand de Lesseps was awarded a contract to build the Panama Canal after his successful completion of the Suez Canal, but the task was beyond him. Malaria and yellow fever killed the workers in their thousands and there were insurmountable construction problems. Then, in 1903, a revolutionary junta with the backing of the US, declared Panama to be independent, and a treaty was signed giving the US 'sovereign rights in perpetuity' over the canal zone, which extended 14 kilometres on either side of the canal.

Construction of the wonderful waterway began in 1904 and the first ship sailed through a decade later. Relations between the US and Panama, however, have always been strained because the Panamanians resented the US control of the canal and the presence of foreign troops on their soil. Finally, a new treaty promising Panama control in the year 2000 was signed, and the relationship has improved as a result.

Certainly, the Panamanians to whom we spoke did not disguise their impatience to be rid of the American presence in their country and to have complete control of the canal. It is, after all, Panama's most lucrative asset. Large ships using the canal pay a minimum of $30 000 for the right to transit.

Panama City is at the Pacific end of the Panama Canal and the twin towns of Cristobal–Colon are at the Caribbean end. We entered the latter through impressive approaches and mighty harbours where the supertankers and other large vessels waited for their clearance to proceed through the canal. In the harbour at Cristobal there were also many yachts waiting for permission to transit. The comfortable Cristobal Yacht Club was a gathering place for those who were heading into the Pacific.

We were secure within the grounds of the yacht club as it was surrounded by a high security fence and patrolled by armed guards. The Cristobal part of town was barely safe in the daytime and out of bounds at night, and Colon was quite simply dangerous, a definite no-go area at any time. Built mainly of timber, it was designed to resemble New Orleans but now the French-style buildings are leaning and falling to pieces and Colon has become a violent and dangerous slum from whence all semblance of law and order has disappeared.

In Cristobal, though, law and order is at least in evidence. The small gaol is built in the centre of town and the only thing that separates it from the population is a high wire fence through which the prisoners are clearly visible behind the bars of their cells. When we walked past they were singing, their voices turning the square into a rather festive place. When they caught sight of two gringos walking past, they waved and shouted excitedly, seemingly in the best of spirits.

Despite the violence and crime in this part of the world, we would remember the people for their warmth and vitality. One of our last contacts with the Caribbean was a Cuna Indian porter who pushed a wooden cart laden with our provisions through a crowded market area. He was a tiny man with soft brown eyes and jet-black hair cut in a silky bob. At one stage he and the trolley disappeared. We searched everywhere. I mimed, 'Have you seen a small man with a trolley piled with provisions?' but all shook their heads. Feeling crestfallen and cheated, we returned to the taxi stand.

Suddenly he was there, and when he saw us he left the trolley and ran towards us, his arms outstretched, his brown eyes joyous and his face beaming with relief. We never knew his name but the three of us liked each other.

Unlike the Suez Canal which is cut through flat desert, the Panama Canal climbs over a hump in the isthmus. In the middle is the glorious Gatun Lake, a freshwater paradise in a national park with prolific birdlife, monkeys, schools of fish, freshwater alligators, cheeky otters, and a Smithsonian Institute for the study of the jungle environment.

Boats must negotiate three locks in order to ascend to the level of the lake, cross it and then descend through three more locks to reach the level of the Pacific Ocean on the other side. The construction is a brilliant feat of engineering, and a viewing platform and museum have been set up at Miraflores Locks near Panama City.

I viewed the whole procedure with some trepidation because I had read that yachts and supertankers were often in the locks together like David and Goliath, and the wash from the latter could spin a yacht out of control and even sink it. In order to avoid accidents, the Canal Authority insists that all vessels, regardless of size, take a pilot on board.

'Oh no, not another pilot,' I moaned to Alan, remembering those in the Suez Canal.

'These are different,' he replied. 'They're well paid and all are experienced Master Mariners.' Then he added, 'And someone in the club told me they are all young and handsome.'

A further problem for yachts is the ruling that each boat must have on board the skipper plus four line handlers. This calls for some skilful negotiation and planning on the part of the skippers for most yachts are sailed by husband and wife teams, so it usually means that three yachts must band together to provide assistance to each other.

The transit takes two days to complete, so at least six days must be set aside to get three yachts through. Yachts anchor for the first night in Gatun Lake. It is pleasant to swim with the otters and to fall asleep to the sounds of the jungle. Those assisting catch the bus from Panama City back to Colon on the night of arrival to be ready at dawn on the Caribbean side for the next transit. It was stressful being out after dark in those two cities, but we hoped that being in a group would give us some protection and we were always on guard.

Line handlers in the Canal Zone are experienced professionals and the yachtie women in particular feared that their skills in line handling would not be equal to the task. I for one was terrified of being hit by a 'monkey's paw', the string-covered lead weight at the end of each line. I also worried that I would not have the strength to hold the boats true in the turbulence.

Of the three pilots, all young, professional and attractive, we liked Cesar best, perhaps because he was obviously pleased to be with a group of Australians. He arrived with a large bag of ice and as he tipped it into a bucket in the galley he said, 'I did part of my training in Australia, so I know how you Aussies like to drink.'

Despite all my fears, the transits were uneventful and finally the three yachts were safely anchored in Balboa harbour, the port for Panama City. For the first time in several years, *Windigo* was once more floating in the Pacific Ocean.

CHAPTER 19

five weeks at sea • an amorous whale
new friends • landfall in the Marquesas

O n the day we left Panama in May 1995, the Pacific seemed to welcome us and we thought how aptly it was named. How could we have been so wrong. A gentle breeze barely rippled the surface and thousands of seabirds wheeled and circled above the islands in the Gulf of Panama. The morning was hot and the sun shone from a clear sky. It seemed an auspicious beginning to what could be the longest passage of them all for, if we failed to make landfall in the Galápagos Islands, it would be at least five weeks before we again saw land in the Marquesas.

As a way of gauging time, we found ourselves thinking of the six weeks' summer holidays we had enjoyed as teachers. We thought of the times when, in South-East Asia or Europe, we had been able to fit in visits to several countries in the six weeks. We remembered the range and variety of the experiences. Now we were faced with a similar timespan in which we would not see another living soul, no land, just vast expanses of ocean — 4000 nautical miles of it.

One of our ground rules was that our adventure should never be at the expense of others. Unless the boat was literally sinking beneath us, we were determined to help ourselves, but we wondered about our capacity to be entirely self-reliant should problems arise in this isolated corner of the South Seas.

The notorious Humboldt current that runs along the coast of South America brings cold water from the south and forces a complicated series of lesser currents to form around the Galápagos Islands. The aim, of course, is to use the favourable currents and to avoid the contrary ones, but, because they are invisible and unpredictable, luck plays a part. One yacht that left a week before us ended up within sight of the coast of Ecuador before it was able to make ground westwards to the Galápagos Islands.

Yet another variable is the El Niño phenomenon, which considerably increases the warm water flow in some years. Because this happens around Christmas, it has been named El Niño, the little child, after the infant Jesus. The effects can be dismal for sailors, with increased convection activity, rain and strong winds. While still in the Caribbean, we had heard that the El Niño effect was already noticeable in the Pacific.

After a couple of days at sea we picked up *Sunbird* on the radio. Harry and Olive were also heading for the Galápagos, but they were finding, like us, that the currents were setting them off course.

'We're so happy to be at sea, though,' Harry said. 'Just so pleased to be out of Panama. It was a dreadful place, squalid and violent. We didn't like it at all. How can people live like that? Awful! Squalid and depressing. Not nice at all.'

'Is that you, Harry?' Alan asked in mock surprise.

'Yes, of course it is! Don't you know who you are talking to? It's Harry, on *Sunbird*.'

On that same day I became so ill that I wanted to curl up and die, but dying is not an option when there are only two on board. Should we turn back? No, let's try antibiotics. After five days I felt better but I had lost the taste for whisky. One of the joys of my life had suddenly become anathema, and there we were wallowing under the weight of three cases of it.

'Perhaps we should tip it overboard,' Alan commented.

'No! Maybe I will recover my taste. Let's wait and see.' But it was three weeks before I was again tempted to touch a drop.

When safe on terra firma, I love whales. Their great warm bodies, their intelligence, and their biblical and literary mystique create an aura of wonder and romance. At sea, though, I hope never to see them.

We were more than 1000 nautical miles from Panama when we encountered the first whale. Not quite as long as *Windigo*, it dived and breached and blew and cavorted around the boat in the early morning, its gleaming black bulk rising slowly from the waves like a monstrous snub-nosed serpent.

'I think it's showing off for us,' Alan commented.

'I think it's flirting with *Windigo*,' I replied, 'and I don't like it.'

As if it heard us, it then dived beneath the boat, came up on the other side and turned lazily on its back so that its huge white turquoise-tinted belly floated parallel to the hull and only a foot from it. We could have reached out and tickled its belly, but we were frightened. We had both heard stories of whales mistaking yachts for lovers.

The whale turned its massive head slightly to one side and peered at us with one eye. Alan was excited, but I was verging on hysteria.

'Let's turn on the engine,' I begged, because somewhere I had read that whales disliked the sound of a motor. But the whale continued to float on its back beside the boat, winking at us in the wash. The melancholy epitaph on Keat's tomb in Rome's Protestant Cemetery kept gnawing at my brain. 'Here lies one whose name was writ in water.' At times during the four hours that the whale was with us, it repeated its previous antics, leaping and diving and blowing before provocatively rolling over beside us again.

'Come on, you stuffy old thing,' its eye seemed to say, 'let's have some fun.'

Perhaps the whale would have eventually grown tired of *Windigo*'s disdain and would have swum off in search of a more responsive mate. Conversely, it may have reacted like a woman spurned, since we presumed from her submissive missionary position that she was a female. But eventually a large school of dolphins came leaping joyfully towards us. They also played around the boat, sometimes surfing in its bow wave, sometimes leaping along the hull, regarding us with glee as they danced beside us. Maybe the whale sensed our preference for these frolicking jokers, perhaps its ardour had dissipated, but it slid silently into the depths, its mighty bulk changing from deep turquoise to black, and then to a grey-green smudge.

It was in that area of the Pacific, just north of the Galápagos Islands, that the Robertson family of husband, wife, three children and a crew member had been attacked by a whale some years previously. Their timber yacht sank so fast that they barely had time to launch the liferaft. For 38 days they drifted with the currents, cramped and suffering, living on raw fish and collecting rainwater and dew, before being rescued by a passing ship. It is an epic survival story which is recorded in their book, *Survive the Savage Sea*, a copy of which we kept in our panic canister so that we would have something inspiring to read should we ever have the misfortune to end up in our liferaft.

Most sailors have a whale story. One morning Alan had befriended a French sailor in a bay near Gibraltar. Over coffee the Frenchman had asked if we had had any trouble with whales.

'We've seen many but so far they've stayed a safe distance from the boat,' we told him.

'I lost my last boat, a catamaran, off the coast of Africa because of a whale,' he replied.

He had been below preparing breakfast when he became conscious of an overwhelmingly revolting stench. Rushing on deck, he had found the boat surrounded by whales, one of which was vomiting the contents of its stomach into the water. Whilst the rest of the pod remained still, the tormented one had begun to thrash about, tossing the catamaran on its side as though it were a toy. The whale's huge head had become wedged between the twin hulls of the boat and, within seconds, the catamaran was broken to pieces and the Frenchman was left clinging to a scrap of debris until he was picked up the next day by a Japanese fishing vessel.

'I don't think I could have gone to sea again after that,' I commented.

'Well certainly not in a catamaran,' he agreed. 'That's why I now have a steel boat. At least you have a sporting chance.'

How wrong I had been all my life in imagining the doldrums as an area of no wind. I blamed Coleridge: 'We stuck, no breath nor motion. As idle as a painted ship upon a painted ocean.'

More accurately known as the Inter-Tropical Conversion Zone, the doldrums was for us an unpleasant stretch of ocean characterised by strong winds, squalls, heavy rain and thunder storms — a troubled area with alarming cloud formations. It was not until we had passed through the region that we found the consistent trade winds, and by that time we were past the Galápagos Islands. Some of the boats we had socialised with in Panama succeeded in reaching them; others, like us, were not so lucky.

Each morning and evening we spoke to the group on the radio and the cheerful camaraderie was great for morale. There was *Hini Moana*, with Tony and Joy on board. Tony was a tough little Irishman with the wit and sprightliness of a leprechaun. He and Joy came from Sydney where both had been in business.

'Before we went cruising, I used to be fanatical about fashion,' Joy confided. 'I would cover myself in jewellery. Everything had to match. Now, who bloody cares?'

'I do!' Tony replied. 'You looked wonderful.'

On *Dream Weaver* there was Bob, a serious New Zealander with a fleabitten old dog called Sam, whom we had met in Balboa. Sam was an alsatian with a rusty matted coat and a mean eye.

'He looks very old,' I said to Bob.

'He is old,' he replied. 'I've had him since he was a pup. As an engineer, I had to work in many countries and Sam has always come with me. He's in the contract. Now I'm taking him home.'

One morning we heard Bob talking to Tony on the radio.

'Sam's sick. He's gone in the back legs. He can't move out of the cockpit.'

'That's bad. I'm so sorry,' Tony commiserated. 'What will you do?'

'Last night I tried to kill him,' Bob replied. 'But it didn't work.'

'What happened?' Tony asked in a tight voice.

'Well, I crushed up 30 sleeping pills and mixed them in his food. Then I said farewell to Sam and went to bed and cried myself to sleep. In the morning, there he was smiling up at me as usual.'

'That's terrible, mate. What will you do now?'

'I'll just have to try for the Galápagos and have him put down. Surely someone at the Darwin Institute would do that for me.'

There were two other single-handers in the group. Brit, a bubbly blonde girl from Brisbane was sailing her yacht *Melanie* home from London, where she had worked as a photographer for five years. She, too, had a dog on board.

On the coast of Portugal, Brit had anchored in the same bay as Steve, a young British ex-commando who had just begun a circumnavigation on his yacht, *Gizelle*. They fell in love. 'At first sight, possums,' Brit explained in her Edna Everage style.

Single-handers invariably sleep little, but Brit and Steve had worked out a system of sailing in sight of each other's boat, taking it in turns to sleep and using the radio to alert each other if there was a wind shift or a change of course to make. We smiled at their longing for each other as they searched through the radio channels for one which would give them some privacy from the rest of us.

'Now stop clicking through the channels to find us, you nosy buggers,' Brit admonished. 'We must have some privacy for our sweet nothings.'

A week out of the Marquesas, a joyful Brit was the first to speak on the morning sked.

'Cooee possums. Great news! I'm pregnant. You're all invited to the wedding in Fiji. It's to be a cockpit wedding, so we'll have a big raft-up in Suva harbour.'

There was *Taina*, a large black yacht sailed by Hamish, a New Zealand dairy farmer with a sharp intelligence and the soul of a poet, and his practical wife, Lyn. We had first met them and their two teenage sons, Dougal and Jamie, in Seville. A daughter, studying medicine in Auckland, had joined them on two occasions, but the family was longing to be together again.

'Jamie's very bad lately,' Lyn would confide. 'He won't study, I think he drinks on the sly and he steals my cigarettes.'

Dougal, dark and handsome and just turned 18, had fallen in love with a beautiful fair-haired girl from a Swedish yacht bound for Nicaragua, whilst the family was in the Canary Islands. When *Taina* reached the Caribbean, Hamish and Lyn, despite the dangers, allowed Dougal to travel overland to Nicaragua to see his Juliet, for the situation was becoming tragic.

'He seems more settled now,' Hamish told us in Panama. 'But one never knows just how first loves will affect people. I'll never forget the trauma of my first affair,' he ended thoughtfully.

Also sailing with us was a rather grand yacht called *Mia Carina*, lovingly built by Wally, a fiercely proud Australian of German descent whose dream of sailing around the world with his family had not worked out entirely as he had planned. We had first met Wally at Lizard Island off the Queensland coast as both boats were making their way north, but we did not meet again until Trinidad.

In the intervening years, Wally's wife had decided that the cruising lifestyle had put too great a strain on the relationship, his daughter had fallen in love with a sailor going in the opposite direction, and Butch, his son, had returned home to be with his girlfriend, although he was now on board again to help his father sail across the Pacific.

'Why did you call your son Butch?' I asked Wally one day.

'It was the most masculine name I could think of,' he replied.

'You took a risk,' I remarked, but the significance was lost on the lusty Wally.

Then one day across the waves came the voice of our old friend Col Harrison on *New Address*.

'We're at Easter Island,' Col told us. 'Let's try to meet up in Fiji. Jeannie is looking forward to meeting you both. Hope you can come to our wedding in Adelaide.'

On the 19th day we crossed the Equator and were once again in the Southern Hemisphere. That night the exquisite constellation of the Southern Cross hung sharp and brilliant from a black orb shimmering with stars like cold white jewels, and the Milky Way arced from horizon to horizon. Phosphorescence sparkled and glowed along the hull and we sailed on luminescent lace. We were alone with the sea and the sky and we felt a sense of the numinous that inspires and uplifts and makes us human. Perhaps ocean passages were enjoyable, after all.

One morning we saw a ship cross our path several miles to our stern, the only vessel we were to see in 4000 nautical miles, but in one sense this reminder of a human presence only emphasised our isolation and closeness to each other. We often laughed about the lack of mental privacy, for we could read each other's thoughts, and words were becoming unnecessary.

As we neared the Marquesas we picked up snippets of information from those already there. We knew that the mosquitoes would be fierce and the sandflies diabolical, but we did not realise that dengue fever, elephantiasis and malaria were also present. Then, a few days from land we heard of a New Zealand single-hander who had been lying in his bunk with a fever when he noticed maggots crawling out of his eye. He struggled into the dinghy, rowed ashore and found someone who gave him the eyedrops which killed the maggots, the larvae of a small fly that crawls into orifices to lay its eggs.

We heard too of having to pay a bond of $1000 if we wished to stay longer than a month in French Polynesia, but the catch was that the French Government eventually refunded the money in local currency.

'It will cost me $4000,' moaned Hamish.

We voiced our concerns to *Sunbird.*

'I don't think you should take much notice of all the things you hear,' Harry advised. 'You should not jump to any conclusions. Look on the bright side. It probably won't be all that bad.

Not too bad at all, really. Probably be quite pleasant, actually.'

At the end of the passage we felt tired, but healthy and happy. I had lost weight but Alan had gained as a result of being naughty on night watches, scavenging through the lockers for the goodies that we carry for when it is too rough to cook: chocolates, dried fruits, nuts and biscuits. Finally, though, one brilliant moonlit night, alien shapes began to rise from a silver sea. Fatu Huku sat on the horizon 20 nautical miles away with the only cloud in the sky suspended in a puff over its peak. Directly above it a single bright star cast a thread of silver light towards us. Nuku Hiva, the island where we would make our landfall, was farther on and we first saw it through the mist of early morning, a grey pointed shape rising steeply from the sea.

CHAPTER 20

*evading French Customs • a Garden of Eden
Moorea and Tahiti • Suvarov Atoll in the Cooks
an 'umu' with Lelei and Punipuao in Samoa*

Rising like giant spires from the ocean floor, the emerald-green islands of the Marquesas are the most spectacular and remote islands we have ever seen. Volcanic in origin, they lack the surrounding reefs that give protection from the ocean swells, so the sea foams at the feet of black rocky cliffs and it was not until the anchorage on Nuka Hiva opened up before us that we felt confident to approach the land.

Deeply furrowed, and buttressed with ridges of rock, a series of steeples rises from mysterious and misty valleys, and everywhere there are waterfalls that tumble into the dark recesses. Closer in, we could see noddies and terns wheeling above the cliffs and frigate birds circling overhead in the updraughts.

There are 12 small fertile islands in the isolated archipelago and they exert a powerful pull on those with a yen for seclusion. It was on Fatu Hiva that Thor Heyerdahl and his wife set out to live for a year, with their only concessions to civilisation being an iron pot and a machete. The experiment, however, was a dismal failure and Heyerdahl painstakingly describes their misery in his book *Fatu Hiva: Back to Nature*.

Jacques Brell is Alive and Well and Living in Paris may well be true in one sense, but the singer's remains are in the cemetery on the island of Hiva Oa, along with those of Paul Gauguin who spent the last years of his life on the island.

The six major islands of the Marquesas were originally settled by Polynesian mariners who travelled vast distances by canoe. The first white man to visit them was a Spanish explorer, Alvaro de Mendana, who named them after the wife of the Viceroy of Peru. Captain Cook called in 1774 and subsequent visits by whalers and slave traders reduced the population of around 50 000 to little more than a thousand, for the people had no resistance to the diseases brought by the visitors. Today there are around 8000 Marquesans.

The islands became a French Protectorate in 1842 and have remained so ever since. The people live a subsidised existence in a dream-like setting. Perhaps they want to shake off the yoke of colonialism, but I doubt it, for life is easy for them and they appear to lack any incentive to change. However, when the French have finished allowing their seas to be fished out and have polluted their environment with radioactivity, the Marquesans might very well be dumped in their island paradise with no resources.

As we dropped anchor in the caldera-shaped bay at Nuka Hiva, we noticed an ominous grey Customs launch anchored near the wharf. Never before had we encountered a Customs vessel in an isolated anchorage and we wondered why it was there.

'Haven't you heard, mate?' a passing yachtie replied when we called out. 'Last week the French introduced an import duty of A$12 per bottle on all grog found on yachts. You'd better hide yours fast. Better still, invite everyone over for drinks tonight.'

'I doubt that would solve our problem', Alan ruefully replied.

It is not easy to hide 36 bottles of whisky on a yacht, certainly not well enough to outfox a determined Customs officer, but we tried. Like everyone else in the bay, we felt that the recently introduced system was one of entrapment, because there had been no warning of a change of policy. We were yachts 'in transit' and therefore should have been governed by the same laws that applied in all other places. Not even in Muslim countries had we been asked to pay duty. Alcohol was simply placed in bond until the vessel left port.

Could it be that because the majority of yachts in the Marquesas were Australians and New Zealanders, the French were simply getting even because of those two countries' vociferous criticism of French nuclear testing in the Pacific? Furthermore, ships calling in were not required to pay duty and, according to maritime law, yachts are subject to the same rules as ships.

As the boat could not be broken into with impunity, it seemed wise to go ashore early in the morning and to remain there until the Customs officials knocked off for lunch and siesta, after which there appeared to be little action. A couple of wealthy skippers paid the duty after spectacular arguments with the authorities, some refused and were fined, but stubborn Irish Tony on *Hini Moana* refused to do either when he was boarded one afternoon.

'Take it, my dears, and I hope it chokes you,' he told the officials. 'And when I get to Papeete I will lodge an official complaint.'

After so long at sea we craved fresh fruit and vegetables, but there was virtually nothing for sale apart from a few withered offerings like wizened beans sold in bundles of ten, fossilised carrots, and imported cabbage hearts for A$8 each. We bought a cabbage heart because we were desperate.

The locals appeared to live on breadfruit and canned fish. They are big people. Even the young girls bulge and wobble beneath their *pareau*, and the tattoos of the men are stretched tightly across their rotund bodies. The size and weight of the inhabitants caused us to pity the island ponies for many people ride horses, lovely creatures, dainty and fine-boned like the creamy-brown ponies in Gauguin's *Riders on the Shore*.

Behind the village with its bakery, bureau de poste, hospital, two shops and the gendarmerie is a lush and beautiful landscape brilliant with hibiscus, frangipani, bougainvillea and a riot of other tropical flowering plants. Everywhere there are fruit trees dripping with abundance; Tahitian limes, mango, papaya, bananas, huge pink-fleshed grapefruit, and the ubiquitous bread-fruit trees. Fruit lies rotting on the grass beneath the trees. No-one appears to have the energy nor the inclination to do anything with it. My hunter–gatherer instincts were aroused but Alan steadfastly maintained that they were criminal instincts.

'The fruit belongs to someone, Olma. Everything is owned. If you pick it up, you'll be stealing', he argued. I had already managed to eat a mango behind his back by pretending that I could not keep up on the hills. After five weeks at sea it was ambrosia and I wanted more.

'Look, Mr Holier Than Thou, you have hidden 36 bottles of whisky on your boat. That's criminal.'

'I did it for you, and you know it,' Alan replied. 'It's our boat, remember.'

Bartering is against the law in the Marquesas, but the people are generous so I decided to ask the next Polynesian I saw to give me some fruit. We came to a particularly large garden with a profusion of fruit trees, the grass beneath them littered with mangoes, limes and papaya. At an open window of a timber bungalow set back from the road, a Polynesian girl was sewing.

Alan sat on the grass beside the road while I pushed through the fruit trees, stepping carefully between the precious pieces on the grass. I approached the open window. The girl looked up in surprise so I stopped and smiled and asked in what I thought was reasonable French, if I could gather some fruit. Her body went rigid, her pretty mouth opened wide, and, like the respectable signora in Salerno, she began to yell. *Mon Dieu*, what had I said.

From somewhere behind the girl an attractive woman appeared, tying her pareau above her breasts as she approached.

'Qu'est ce que vous voulez?'

I explained, and I think she said, 'Go to the shop', so I replied that the only fruit in the shop were withered New Zealand pears and apples for A$1.30 each. I was beginning to wish I had not come.

Suddenly she was at the front door, her manner completely changed. She grabbed hold of me in a very friendly fashion and, with her arm firmly around my waist, guided me through the house and into the back garden, calling, 'Alain! Alain!' as we went. A slim, fair-haired man appeared from a small shed. He, too, was tying a *pareau* as he emerged. Alain, I presumed.

For a split second he seemed to be sizing me up, then he advanced towards me with outstretched arms, pulled me to him and kissed me slowly and tenderly on both cheeks.

'Ah, how happy we are that you've come,' he sighed, his lips in my hair. 'We've been expecting you.'

'But you don't know me. You couldn't have known I would come.'

'I hoped that you would.'

'I came for some fruit,' I mumbled apologetically.

'Of course you did, and fruit you shall have. All kinds of sweet and juicy fruit. Everything you have ever fantasised about. I have wonderful bananas, almost ripe.'

I nodded, not sure of what to say. Then both proceeded to fill bags with luscious fruit from the trees, reaching high into the branches, seemingly unaware of their unabashed display of pale flesh and dark, shadowy patches as their *pareaus* were swept open in the breeze. When they saw me looking at them, they simply smiled.

'I'll help you,' I said.

'No, you just watch,' Alain replied. But the bags were quickly filled and when Alain placed them at my feet, I bent to pick them up.

'Now, let's get to know each other better,' he said, his hand on my shoulder. 'Eva will pour us some wine and later I'll drive you back to the harbour.'

'I'm not alone,' I said. 'My partner is waiting outside. I must go.'

'Magnifique! Then we will be a foursome. Eva will be happy too.'

'No! No! You've been kind and generous, but I won't stay.

Thank you for the fruit.' The bags were like a leaden weight as I struggled with them into the road. Alan laughed when he saw me staggering.

'You look as though you've found the Garden of Eden,' he said.

'It's funny you should say that,' I replied.

Beside the anchorage on the shores of Taiohae Bay, there are remains of the islanders' past from a time when the people were cannibals and carvers of stone. While waiting for the Customs vessel to disappear, we often read and gossiped under the trees there. The ancient ceremonial area, the *tohua*, is defined by stone platforms and altar-like structures for the worship of the spirits of the dead, while grim *tikis* carved from the black volcanic rock are dotted through it.

The *tohua* was an excellent vantage point with a clear view of the entire bay. On the third day, the grey launch left and we began the task of cleaning and repacking the boat, after the long passage from Panama, before exploring the next protected anchorage and visiting the nearby wilderness island of Oa Pau.

Our intention on leaving the Marquesas was to stop for a few days in the lagoon of Roa Hinga in the Tuamotus Archipelago, but during the five days it took to reach there the weather turned foul and by the time we arrived, waves were breaking across the narrow opening to the lagoon making it impossible to enter. Perhaps the grey skies clouded our appreciation of those coral atolls because they appeared lonely and impermanent, floating there in an immense and empty ocean, so low and insignificant. These characteristics have made them a graveyard for ships and yachts, as many have come to grief in that forbidding place of treacherous currents and cruel reefs.

The name *Tuamotus* means 'low and dangerous archipelago' and when one considers that Mururoa Atoll is part of the Tuamotus, the word 'dangerous' is indeed apt, as is 'low' to describe the actions of the French regarding nuclear testing in that once pristine Pacific environment.

So breathtakingly lovely is the island of Moorea, 12 miles across the strait from Tahiti, that we soon forgot our disappointment at not being able to stop in the Tuamotus. It quickly joined Skorpios and Mustique on our list of favourite islands. Similar in character to Nuka Hiva with its spires and peaks, it floats in the centre of a circular translucent green lagoon, a clear and tranquil ring outlined by foamy white, where the waves of the darker ocean break on the coral.

We were in the Society Islands, so named by the indefatigable Captain Cook because to him the islands were so close together as to resemble a society of islands. This is not altogether true, for there are really two parts of the Society Islands, the *Iles du Vent* (the Windwards) and the *Iles sous le Vent* (the Leewards).

Unlike Tahiti, Moorea has managed to blend most of its hotels and resorts into the landscape in a way that does not offend. It is an island where everything is a reminder of a Gauguin painting. His *Tahitian Women* gossip beneath the trees in tropical lushness, their ample brown bodies wrapped in bright *pareaus*, hibiscus in their hair as if they have just stepped through the frame.

Apart from the painted wooden bus that meets the ferry from Papeete, there is little public transport on the island of Moorea. Taxis, like everything else in French Polynesia, are prohibitively expensive. We assembled our bikes, realising that we would have to push them half of the way, but at least we could coast our way down when we went up.

The interior of Moorea is an area of sweet-smelling verdant valleys with grazing cattle and cool mountain streams and waterfalls. There are coffee and vanilla plantations, and flowering trees and exotic ferns and plants. The people obviously respect their gorgeous environment, adding flowers to the plantings and keeping the island clean and rubbish free.

The Belvedere, high in the hills, was the setting for the most recent *Mutiny on the Bounty* film with Mel Gibson and Anthony

Hopkins, but below it at a fork in the road, my yachtie legs could go no farther.

'Is it far?' I asked four hikers who, with wobbly knees and damp hair, stumbled down the track towards us.

'Oui, quatre kilomètres'.

Alan continued while I minded his bike and read a book on the bank of a stream.

Tahiti, the largest of the Society Islands, is shaped like a figure eight, the two sections joined by the isthmus of Taravao. Like its neighbour Moorea, it is a lush and sensual island and, over the last couple of centuries, its aura of romance has enthralled people like Gauguin and Matisse, Cook and Thor Heyerdahl, Robert Louis Stevenson and Somerset Maugham.

But that is the past. Today, the island and its capital Papeete are overrun by tourism and prices for most commodities are ridiculously high. The artists, writers and adventurers of the past were regrettably far too successful in bringing an awareness of Tahiti's allure to the world.

For us, an exciting part of being in Papeete was meeting *New Address* again. In Jeannie, Col had obviously found a soulmate since she was an experienced sailor in her own right. She was also extremely confident and forthright, but when she looked at Colin, her eyes melted so that we were relieved and happy for him.

In Papeete we received sad news of cruising friends Lois and Mike, he of the pampered willy. Their son, in his early 20s, was missing, believed drowned, after being washed overboard when the vessel on which he was working was wrecked off the coast of Cornwall. Eleven people were rescued but two were never found. It is difficult to grieve without a body, so Mike and Lois were simply sailing home as fast as they could.

Tied up near *New Address* were Tony and Joy. Tony had stormed into the Customs office on arrival demanding that he be recompensed for the alcohol removed from *Hini Moana*.

'We've been expecting you,' the officer calmly said. 'You may have your drink back.' He pushed the cartons under the counter-top.

'This is ridiculous!' said Tony. 'Why did you take it in the first place?'

'We expected you to pay the duty, of course,' the officer replied.

Early in July, Alan and I set sail from Cooks Bay, Moorea, for the tiny Suvarov Atoll 800 miles to the north-west. Remote and unspoiled, the Atoll lies in the northern part of the Cook Islands. The isolated group of *motus*, dotted across a wide lagoon, had for years had but one inhabitant, Tom Neale. A man of solitary habits with a love of nature and the sea, he described his experiences in a book entitled, not unnaturally, *An Island to Oneself*.

There are 15 Cook islands scattered across a wide stretch of ocean. The people are Polynesian Maoris and most of them live on the main island of Rarotonga, the administrative centre. In 1901 the administration of the islands was taken over by New Zealand and the Cook islanders now enjoy New Zealand citizenship. Hundreds leave each year for the brighter lights of Auckland.

The Reverend John Williams of the London Missionary Society arrived in Rarotonga early in the 19th century and quickly converted the islanders. As a result, the church still plays a dominant role in Cook Islands affairs and the people are deeply religious and conservative.

After eight gruesome days of squalls, screeching winds and big seas, the brown smudges of the coconut palms that cover the *motus* of Suvarov appeared on the horizon. As we passed inside the outer reef, the waves abated and the angry dark blue of the sea changed to a soft aquamarine world speckled with sunlight. Alan stood in the spreaders from where he could easily see the channel of dark blue that marked the deep water between the lighter blues and the turquoise nearer the reefs. I steered the boat by following the direction of his arm above me. It seemed that we were all alone in a wilderness of sea and sand and breakers, but as we approached the largest *motu* we noticed three yachts anchored in a curve of white beach, one German, one Swiss and one Australian.

The Australian skipper was beside us in his dinghy before we even had time to set the anchor.

'Howya goin'. Good trip? No? Well, the weather's strange this year.'

Ross, a laconic tanned young man, his mother and his girl-friend had been there for a week, diving, fishing and catching lobsters.

'We catch more than we can use,' Ross told us. 'I've brought you some coral trout, but tonight there'll be a fish barbecue ashore, so you can put this in the fridge until tomorrow.' He placed a plate of gleaming white and pink-streaked fillets on the deck. We had just finished reading John Hersey's classic, *Blues*, a treatise on fishing and the cooking of the catch and already my mind was whirling with ideas for the several meals that Ross had given us.

'You'll love it here,' Ross said as he paddled away.

We thought we would but, despite the dancing light, the crystal water and the perfect palm-shaded *motu*, we felt vulnerable sitting in infinite space with only the reef and the thick thatch of palms to protect us from the ocean forces. Gradually, though, we grew accustomed to the booming of the waves on the outer reef and settled down to enjoy the wild and beautiful place, where thousands of seabirds wheeled and cried overhead.

There were kilometres of reefs, their yellows, creams and tans marbling the sapphire surface. Brilliant fish swam lazily by, seemingly unperturbed by our presence. And there were sharks. When we asked Ross if there had been any attacks in the lagoon, his answer caused us to cease exploring forthwith.

'Yes, people have died. Suvarov is so far from anywhere that medical assistance is of little use. You're on your own out here, mate.'

Alan and I were never entirely at ease in the water after that and as Ross provided more fish than we could eat, we tended to swim in the shallows where alien shapes and their shadows were clearly visible against the white sand bottom.

Barbecues ashore had a formality that is usually missing from the typical yachtie gathering, for we were guests of the owner of that remote atoll. Smiling Jimmy was a charming old man with shrewd brown eyes and a gentlemanly demeanour. He managed to convey, without actually saying so, that the small island was his home and that those who visited it had better do the right thing.

'You are most welcome on this island,' he said, taking our hands in both of his dry brown ones and graciously leading us along the beach, 'Come and meet my family.' Walking towards us was an exceedingly buxom and attractive woman of around 40. She wore a *pareau* and led a small brown boy by the hand.

'This is my daughter Frances and her son, Tojay.'

'Can you sing?' Frances asked as soon as the introductions were over. We were uneasy. I feared that we may be called upon to sing a solo around the campfire after the barbecue. Or perhaps there would be a karaoke. Neither thought was pleasant.

'No, we can't sing,' I answered with firmness.

'That's a shame,' Frances replied, looking genuinely disappointed. 'When people sing, our Sunday service is so much more enjoyable. By the way, we start at 11 a.m. sharp and after the service, we all have lunch together.' That we may not have wished to attend Sunday service seemed of little consequence.

As Smiling Jimmy and Frances piled logs on the fire, Alan and I chatted to the others and we were soon joined by a young man with a body of bulging muscles and a face with flashy good looks.

'Welcome,' he said. 'They call me Tomorrow. I'm the boyfriend of Frances and Tojay is our son.'

Well, that cleared up that little mystery. Mounds of grouper steaks were cooked over a bed of coals. There were coconuts to drink, and copious quantities of palm heart and breadfruit. Each of the yachts had brought something to share but no-one liked my spicy contribution, so Alan and I ate it the next day. Before the meal, Smiling Jimmy said grace, a long and heartfelt thanks to God for all the blessings bestowed upon that tiny speck of coral, while the grouper steaks grew cold and wept juice beside the fire.

By Sunday another two yachts had arrived and there were 20 people in the congregation in the large airy room of the family home in the centre of the island — Tom Neale's old house with additions. Frances led the singing in a clear, confident voice and Smiling Jimmy and Tomorrow provided the harmony with the rest of us helping out in the choruses. Then Smiling Jimmy gave communion but there were only two candidates from amongst the yachties.

During lunch, another fish barbecue, Smiling Jimmy sidled up to Alan.

'God has asked me to go to Penrhyn Island,' he said. 'But I've no way of getting there.'

'How far is it?' asked Alan while I held my breath.

'Oh, only two or three day's sail,' Smiling Jimmy replied. 'Will you take me there?'

But Alan declined, suggesting that our host ask someone with more time to spare as we were leaving the next morning for Samoa and a two day jaunt to Penrhyn Island could easily set us back a week, or more if the weather turned nasty. Hamish and his family on *Taina* took him a couple of weeks later, so the Lord's will prevailed, despite the lack of support from *Windigo*.

Western Samoa is believed to be the legendary heartland of Polynesia. The Samoan people are closely related to the Hawaiians, Tahitians, Tongans, and Maoris, and the Samoans themselves believe that they are the last remaining true Polynesians. Although the Samoas are populated by the same people with family members in both parts, the islands are politically divided between American Samoa, a US territory, and Western Samoa. The latter was a German colony from 1899 until the First World

War, after which it was administered by the League of Nations. Since the Second World War it had been a protectorate of New Zealand, finally gaining independence in 1962.

The social structure of the islands is built around the *aiga*, an extended family with sometimes thousands of relatives. At the head of the *aiga* are the *matais*, the chiefs who control land and property, care for the well-being of the *aiga*, and represent it on government councils. In Western Samoa, the traditions and customs of the *aiga* are so strong that visitors who disregard them will cause offence, and some knowledge of '*Fa'a Samoa*' (the Samoan Way) can save visiting yachties from the wrath of the *matais* that will surely be incurred should anyone anchor in a bay without obtaining permission. There are strange rules such as closing one's umbrella while walking past a meeting of the chiefs, and the strong missionary zeal of the churches makes work on the Sabbath a strictly observed taboo.

After a week's sail from Suvarov, Apia harbour looked sublime. Glassy calm, it was protected from the sea by reefs and a rock wall. There were nine yachts at anchor, all German, although an Australian catamaran arrived the next day. One lone ship was unloading at the dock. For the capital of a country, it was the quietest harbour we had ever seen. When the smiling Customs officer came on board, we were relieved at his relaxed style because we still had a considerable amount of whisky on board. He eyed the bottle in the teak holder near the galley.

'Is that bottle of whisky just for show or can I have a drop?' he asked.

I handed him the bottle and he poured enough whisky into his orange juice to make a rhinoceros stumble. After swigging it down he announced, 'I won't need to search your boat. Everything seems OK. I'll go now.'

Like its harbour, Apia is sleepy and relaxed. Along its foreshore runs the main street, Beach Street, with traffic lights so recently installed that the locals are still not sure of what to do, and accidents are common where before they had been few. The street, like the rest of the city, is in transition. There is a handful of modern structures, but mostly the streets are lined with crumbling colonial buildings interspersed with patched 1950s architecture. There is an air of acceptance, a ramshackle quality. Nevertheless, the town nestles in a splendid setting beside the coral-fringed bay.

At the southern end of the bay stands the famous Aggie Gray Hotel. We anchored in front of it because it is the most attractive building on the entire island of Upolu. Pseudo-colonial, painted in white, pale olive green and grey, it sits in tropical gardens and was built to replace the hotel built by Aggie years before. During the Second World War, Samoa was home to the US military, and Aggie grasped the opportunity by setting up a small bar and restaurant on the beach. The food was good, Aggie was generous and she prospered. It was there that James Michener met her and later credited her with playing a part in getting him started on his *Tales of the South Pacific*.

Michener was not the only writer who gathered inspiration in the Samoas. It was there that Somerset Maugham wrote *Rain*. In the hills above Apia, Robert Louis Stevenson lived and wrote during the last years of his life, and on the island of Ta'u in the Manua Group, Margaret Mead wrote her controversial *Coming of Age in Samoa*.

Apart from the cabbage we had bought in the Marquesas and a few beans in Moorea, we had not eaten fresh vegetables since the Panama supply had run out. The sight of the Apia market thrilled us. It was a large open pavilion filled with piles of tomatoes, cucumber, lettuce, beans, zucchini, and capsicum. There were even larger mounds of cassava, taro, sweet potato and other hairy root vegetables, but we ignored them in favour of the less starchy and more familiar. Here we could afford to eat well again and for a few *tala* we could buy more than we could carry back to the boat.

The people were friendly, but the women behind the mounds of root vegetables looked puzzled when we ignored their produce.

'These are for the *umu*. You'll need some of these,' one of the women told me.

'We live on a boat. We can't do the *umu* on a boat,' I explained.

The women thought about this for a moment or two.

'If you stay on Upolu for a few days, someone will surely ask you to one,' another women replied. 'It's better to be part of a family.'

She was right, at least on the first observation. A couple of days later, Alan returned from a dinghy trip across the bay to the supermarket.

'I've just met a young man called Lelei, the accountant at the supermarket. He's asked us to the family *umu* on Sunday and it seemed churlish to refuse. Tomorrow he'll come for lunch so you can meet him.'

There was something about Lelei that made me feel ill at ease. Built like a thugby player, which indeed he was in his spare time, he was tall with muscled shoulders and a thick thatch of black hair that completely covered his forehead. His eyes were dark and troubled. Perhaps that was why I felt uneasy. The fact that he asked my age as soon as he sat in the cockpit had nothing to do with my misgivings because I had already read that age is important in Samoa. Youth defers to age and age elicits respect, so Lelei would find it strange to be waited upon by an older person. But as Alan and I were both older than our guest, there seemed little alternative.

'How old are you, missus Alan?'

'Lelei, in Australia some people don't like to tell their age. It's a secret,' I replied.

Water off a duck's back. Lelei stared at me as if I had taken leave of my senses.

'Lelei has been to Australia,' Alan said in the awkward silence. 'Haven't you, Lelei?'

'Yes, I went to Sydney last year to stay with my uncle and aunt at Bankstown,' he replied. 'My uncle is a preacher with the Church of Christ. He went to Australia to tell the people how to banish Satan from their lives.'

'Is he having much success?' I asked.

'Satan is still very strong down there,' Lelei replied earnestly.

On Sunday Lelei picked us up in a friend's car and we drove through the garden suburbs of Apia to a small weatherboard and corrugated iron house on the outskirts. The modern *fale* seems to lack the natural sense of belonging which characterises the older and more traditional thatched bungalows. A large breadfruit tree and a pink hibiscus grew in the front yard and a black pig snuffled in the grass. For many Samoan men, a good wife, many children, a *fale*, a breadfruit tree, a pig and a canoe are the basis for a happy life. Lelei had acquired most of these things, but still he appeared unfulfilled.

Punipuao, Lelei's wife, was not as I had expected. She appeared too young to have given birth to the four children who played on the floor of the large main room where we were to eat, but her pride in them was obvious and her pretty face beamed when she spoke of them.

'Lelei says we must have many children but I believe four is enough. How can we educate more than four?'

'God will take care of that,' Lelei said firmly. Then turning to me, he said, 'Punipuao's faith is shallow. I worry that God will punish her so I must be firm about what happens in the family. I understand God's ways.'

The children were told to play outside and a cloth was spread in the centre of the floor. We sat cross-legged around it while Punipuao brought bowls of food and placed them before us. Everything had been prepared the previous day and cooked in the coals while the family was at church because no work can be done on the Sabbath. Then Punipuao left the room.

'Punipuao can't eat until we've finished,' Lelei explained.

Alan and I struggled with the breadfruit, the taro and the plantains because to our tastes they are dry, starchy and bland. There was a curry of some kind of meat, probably goat. And there was our favourite Samoan dish, *palusami*, made from young taro leaves, onion and coconut cream.

When the meal was finished, Punipuao entered the room with an antique *tapa* cloth at least six metres long. The fine mats are made from the bark of the mulberry tree and they are a display of wealth in Samoa. They are handed down as an inheritance and are irreplaceable, so I presumed that Punipuao had brought it to show us in the same way as those in our society will sometimes drag out a treasured family heirloom to impress the guests. But when we had admired the lovely old mat, Punipuao folded it carefully and with both hands held it towards me.

'This is for you, Olma.'

Alan and I looked at each other in dismay. We could not accept this gift. I began to panic. Then I noticed the little girl fanning herself in a corner of the room, her clear brown eyes watching us.

'You're kind and generous but I don't need a tapa cloth, Punipuao,' I said. 'But there is something that I'd rather have as a gift. I'd love a fan.'

'A fan? But fans are worth nothing,' she replied.

'I'd find more use for a fan. It's very hot here and I don't own one,' I cajoled.

'Then you must accept our best fan,' Punipuao said and removed the most elaborate from a group of four that were stuck behind a crossbeam on the wall.

We said goodbye then, so that Punipuao could eat.

Before we left Apia we asked Lelei and Punipuao to lunch aboard *Windigo* and I explained that we would all eat together.

'That is your way,' Punipuao replied.

Alan and Lelei spoke of thugby league while Punipuao told me of her children and her husband's plans for more lucrative employment when he finished his accountancy course. But, as on previous occasions, Lelei soon managed to steer the conversation to his consuming interest in religion.

'My friend David went to Sydney to study for the church but he fell in love. That was the work of Satan.'

'But, Lelei, falling in love is hardly the work of the Devil,' I told him. 'Most people regard it as a heavenly experience.'

'It was the Devil's way of preventing my friend from doing the Lord's work.'

'Surely he could still do the Lord's work while he was in love. One passion does not necessarily cancel out all others,' I persisted.

'Satan's influence was so strong that my friend had no more energy for spreading the word of the Lord,' Lelei replied.

A few minutes later we were discussing the damage caused by the last cyclone to the neighbouring island of Savai'i. That too was the work of Satan, Lelei maintained.

'The people of that island are lazy. God allowed Satan to punish the people because they wouldn't work. Now they have to work to repair the damage.'

This time Punipuao spoke first. She came from Savai'i.

'Not all the people on that island were lazy, yet God punished them all in the same way. How can that be right? It was not Satan nor God. It was simply the weather.'

Lelei's body stiffened and his face turned black as he stared at his wife. Would she be so courageous in expressing her ideas if she were alone with him, I wondered, for he suddenly appeared to be possessed by something dark and violent and I felt uneasy for her. Then he noticed me looking at him and he forced a smile and said, 'We must be going now.'

In the last decade of the 19th century, Samoans were caught up in a power play between contesting foreign interests who treated the people badly and imprisoned some of the *matai* when they tried to protect the traditional ways. It was into this turmoil that Robert Louis Stevenson arrived to live the last few years of his life. Objecting to the way in which the Samoans were treated, he took the side of the Samoans, unlike the other *palagi*, thereby winning the Samoans' hearts. And so the writer of *Treasure Island, Kidnapped, Dr Jekyll and Mr Hyde*, and *Ebb Tide* became affectionately known as Tusitala, the teller of tales.

We set out to visit 'Vailima', the place where he had lived with his wife and family.

'Is it far to "Vailima"?' we asked a woman dressed in a bright Mother Hubbard.

'No, not far at all. Just on the outskirts.'

Samoans often tell you what they think you want to hear, so I was suspicious. And rightly so, as it turned out, for when we reached the outskirts, there was no sign that we were anywhere near. Alan asked a man how far it was to the house of Robert Louis Stevenson.

'Is he the man who is buried on top of the mountain?' the fat man asked.

'He wrote books,' Alan explained, 'He was a famous man.'

'The man on the top of the mountain is famous but he is famous because he is buried on top of the mountain.'

'It's probably the same man,' Alan remarked. We trudged ever upwards, through the foothills and into the mountains.

'Vailima' and its grounds adjoining the Botanical Gardens are attractive. Great pains have been taken to restore the mansion to the way it was when the Stevenson family lived there, and it was tantalising to imagine the elegant writer, slim and ailing, living his last years in that green and gorgeous world, surrounded by Samoan servants dressed in *pareaus* and *lava lavas* made from the Stevenson family tartan, an idea that seemed out of character in a man who had decided to live in this informal tropical paradise.

'Would you like me to sing 'Stevenson's Requiem' for you?' the young Samoan woman who had shown us through 'Vailima' suddenly asked.

'Yes, we'd feel honoured,' we replied. And in a clear, true voice she sang, 'Under the wide and starry sky, Dig the grave and let me lie . . .'

The sound of her singing echoed through the high-ceilinged rooms like the ghost of 'Vailima.'

Stevenson's old home sits at the foot of Mount Vaea. Past a waterfall that cascades into a dark rock pool, we followed a narrow path that winds through dripping ferns and buttressed banyan trees to the summit. It was along this track that the bereaved Samoans had carried the body of Tusitala to his resting place high above Apia. On the sublime point, the people built Tusitala's stark tomb and along its sides they carved his requiem.

After so long without television (last seen in the Canary Islands) we were happy to find that the system in use in Samoa permitted a clear reception. Our happiness was short-lived, however, for Samoan TV was the most irksomely parochial that we had seen.

Church affairs, preaching, hymn singing and praying take up a large slab of viewing time. Then there are the interminable birthday greetings. A photograph of the birthday person fills the screen whilst someone with the sombre tones of a preacher intones a saccharine message which invariably ends with 'Now you be a good little girl and attend church regularly,' or 'Enjoy your day, my lad.'

Sometimes a newsreader would stop suddenly in the middle of reporting an earth-shattering event (I exaggerate, for there were no such events while we were there) to say, 'These ten people who have applied for the job of teller at the Apia branch of Westpac are to be outside the bank at 9 a.m. tomorrow morning.' Then followed the names of the ten applicants. World news was invariably New Zealand news, with the emphasis on thugby union. The Northern Hemisphere seemed far, far away.

Somewhere, though, in the bowels of the studio, was a person with a healthy sense of the ridiculous. With the concentration of German yachts in the harbour, it seemed more than a coincidence that we were able to watch a series of riotously anti-German movies, thoroughly enjoying for the second time around *The Guns of Navarone* and Richard Burton in *Where Angels Fly*.

We had stayed long enough in Upolu. Its tattooed inhabitants had treated us well. We had heard that the Samoans were thieves, but we lost only a pair of sneakers from the dinghy. We had heard that they were big people and they are. They are also fat, and growing fatter on starchy *umus*, fast foods, and fatty off-cuts of New Zealand mutton. They say of their cousins in American Samoa, 'Now they are fat. Compared to them, we are thin. It's all that American fast food, you know.'

Perhaps the Samoan diet contributes to the somnolence, the lazy pace, the lack of animus from which we wished to escape. But more than anything we wished to be free of that quality that is all pervasive, the unctuousness of the church. Despite the natural beauty of Upolu, we had no wish to return to Samoa and the realisation shocked us because we had not felt a similar lack of enthusiasm for any country apart from Sri Lanka. In Samoa there was a tedium that was soporific, even irksome.

Outside the post office on Beach Street was a freshly painted white wall guarded by a sour-faced young man in a gaberdine *lava lava*. The wall was shaded by a giant banyan tree and one day I leaned against the wall for a few minutes' respite from the heat.

'Don't lean on that wall,' the young man snarled, his hand gripping his baton as he advanced and before I could ask, 'Why not?', Alan had yanked me away, saying, 'Olma, I know you want to ask him why not, but please don't. He's just doing his job.' Yes, it was time to leave.

On the other hand, we would remember Upolu as the place with only one beggar, and he may simply have been the island's resident nonconformist, for he sang to himself as he scrabbled in the bins along the waterfront, his long beard blowing in the wind. We would remember, too, that there was little crime despite the fact that 90 per cent of the population was unemployed. Perhaps the answer was in the power of the *matai* because Samoans fear the shame of a rebuke from the respected chiefs. Then, too, the lack of privacy in living in the open *fale* keeps a rein on behaviour as everyone is aware of the slightest indiscretion — possibly even the ancestors buried in the painted sarcophagi that decorate the front lawns of the *fale*.

Samoan children yell 'goodbye' as a greeting instead of 'hello Mister', and as we rounded the breakwater on our way to the neighbouring island of Savai'i, a group of brown children diving from the rocks, yelled 'Goodbye, Goodbye,' beckoning us to come back.

CHAPTER 21

a treacherous sunset • stooged in Suva
gossip • the Yassawas • journey's end

In August, Alan and I left Samoa for Fiji on a passage we expected would take about 12 days. The toilet broke on the eighth day and then Alan became ill with diarrhoea and an ear infection. *Windigo* was approaching the Lau group of reefs and islands to the north-east of Fiji when we heard the radio warning:

> People living on the eastern side of islands in eastern Fijian waters are warned of destructive winds and high seas. You are advised to secure your houses and to take adequate precautions.

'Bloody hell!' we said.

The brilliant 'shepherds' delight' sunset of the previous evening had made us slightly uneasy, but we reasoned that it was supposed to be a good omen in the Southern Hemisphere. We marvelled at its magnificence and had hoped that it augured fair weather, because we had come too far to turn back.

When a yacht is hit by storm-force winds in the open ocean, there is at least the reassurance that there will be adequate sea-room, that the vessel will not be blown onto rocks or reefs. But there we were close to land and reefs with the skipper feeling poorly. Slowly the wind increased to a howling pandemonium, and the seas built up until they became aggressive green walls of water with smoking peaks. We plunged and vibrated in a maelstrom of savage fury. Like those who cannot accept the death of a loved one, we could not believe that this was happening to us.

The first piece of equipment to succumb to the strain was the autopilot so we hand-steered with our safety harness clipped to the cockpit floor so that we would not be swept overboard. Breathing became difficult because the wind seemed to blow the air away before we could inhale sufficiently. Before long *Windigo* had become unmanageable in the strange convulsions of the seas. She was picked up by a mighty wave on top of which she teetered for a second before falling through the air and landing with a shuddering crash on the other side.

'We can't continue like this,' Alan shouted above the tumult.

The recommended procedures for surviving a storm at sea are 'heaving to', 'running before' or 'running under bare poles'. We understood the theories but we were unpractised in the procedures. 'Running before' the waves and wind was dangerous because the waves were too powerful by then and we would have been pooped. 'Bare poles' meant removing all sail and letting the boat fend for itself. That we were not prepared to do, except as a final resort, so Alan chose 'heaving to'. In our case that meant using a small piece of mainsail to leeward and tying down the steering wheel so that the rudder was held in the opposite direction, thus creating opposing forces. If the vessel were correctly balanced, it would bob along very slowly in the direction for which it had been set.

We removed everything from the decks, threw it below, and scrambled after it. Then we battened down the hatches, secured all locker lids, stowed everything that could move, sealed the dorade vents and turned *Windigo* into a submarine. When we sat to catch our breath we realised to our immense relief that the boat was remarkably comfortable most of the time. Sometimes a wave would break upon her and she would shudder and flounder under the weight of the water, and screws would fall from the deck lining. Once, we opened the hatch to look out but the sight was so terrifying that we vowed not to do it again.

The storm raged for 42 hours. Alan was deaf in one ear, so the sound was slightly muted for him, a small consolation. When the radio broke down, we discussed death and dying because we had no means of sending a 'mayday' if we were blown onto the reefs. We had no fear of death; it was the dying that bothered us. We hoped it would be swift, painless, and if possible, dignified. In my salt-encrusted and stressed state I felt like dying. Then we said how much we loved each other, and I cried and wanted to live.

On the third day the conditions were still dramatic, but Alan felt that with a little more sail we could control the boat and even make some progress. For the next two days and nights we hand-steered through the islands, taking it in turns for an hour and a half at a time because that was all we had the strength for in those heavy seas.

Our arrival in Suva harbour brought relief to the other yachties as they had been on the verge of notifying the authorities of our failure to respond to radio calls. We slept for two days before tackling the task of putting *Windigo* back together again. Then we felt remorse that such a lovely lady was looking so neglected, and we vowed to remain in Suva until she was gleaming again.

The island groups of Melanesia comprise Fiji, Wallis and Futuna, New Caledonia, Vanuatu, Solomons and Papua New Guinea, over a thousand islands strung across a wide swathe of the Pacific Ocean. *Melanesia* is a Greek word for 'Black Islands' and it refers to the dark skin of the inhabitants, believed to be the descendants of Malaysians and Australoids who arrived around 8000 years ago.

Fiji is a group of 332 islands and atolls. There are two large islands on which most of the people live, Viti Levu (Great Fiji) with the main cities of Suva, Nadi and Lautoka; and Vanua Levu close by to the north-east. On the eastern edge lies the Lau group of islands and to the west, the lovely Yassawas with larger islands like Taveuni, Kandavi, Mbau and Ovalau scattered between.

Abel Tasman, bound for Java in 1643, sighted the island of Taveuni but it was not until 100 years later that Captain Cook landed on the small island of Vatoa. The inhabitants fled into the jungle in fright, so Cook wrote in his journal that 'some circumstances shew'd the Natives to be Docile people'.

Captain Bligh did not find the people so docile when he was forced to sail through the islands after being set adrift by the mutineers who had seized the *Bounty*. Crossing what is now Bligh Water near the Yassawas, he and his men were pursued by two canoes of cannibals who only gave up the chase when a fierce storm capsized one of the canoes, thus allowing Bligh to continue to Dutch Timor.

Later, as captain of the warship HMS *Providence*, Bligh returned to Fiji and collected the breadfruit trees which provided the seeds for the one we had seen in the botanical gardens in Georgetown, St Vincent, in the Caribbean.

The establishment of plantations by the early settlers led to a seemingly insoluble problem which still plagues Fiji. Workers had to be found for the sugar plantations, so thousands of indentured labourers were shipped in from India just as they had been in Trinidad. In Fiji, though, the Indians were never allowed to own land and therein lies the problem, the source of bitter discontent on the part of the Indians and the basis for racist laws and regulations on the part of the Fijians, since the Indians now number more than half the population.

Because the Indians cannot own land, they have concentrated on commerce and now run most enterprises, being particularly skilled in money matters and organisation. Naturally, they also want political power. But most of all, they want to own land in the place they call home. When the Fijian yells, 'Go home Indian', the Indian replies, 'This is my home. I know no other.' The Indian boasts of his ancient culture and his business brain, the Fijian of his cannibal past and his ownership of the land.

Suva, the capital, slopes towards the sea from the rich green foothills of the dripping mountains. The city appears relatively modern and functional from the sweeping harbour. We spent our first day ashore just wandering.

Parallel to the shore is Victoria Parade, almost a boulevarde at its southern end where it runs beside a dignified lawned space in which sits the Parliament House and government buildings. Adjoining these buildings are Albert Park, the botanical gardens, and the museum. It was in Albert Park that Charles Kingsford Smith almost came to grief when he landed the 'Southern Cross' in order to refuel. He had no previous knowledge of the dimensions of the park and imagined it would be more like a paddock. As it was, until a couple of hours before his arrival, a row of coconut palms ran down the centre of the park. Luckily someone had had the foresight to insist that they be cut down in time.

At its northern end, Victoria Parade ends in the busy downtown area with its so-called duty-free shops, curry houses, restaurants, silk and sari emporia, handicraft and artefact sellers. In narrow side alleys, tiny businesses sell all manner of goods from second-hand wares to mousetraps and wicks for kerosene lanterns. In Suva, there is even a Prouds, where stepping across the threshold is like stepping back into the 1960s, because many of the goods are reminiscent of that era. I felt that much of the stock for sale in Suva was left over from Australian stores as it was old-fashioned and passé.

Our favourite place in Suva, however, was the large double-storey, pavilion-style market where Fijian, Indian and Chinese vendors sell fruit, vegetables and fish, and goods made from *masi* cloth (Fijian *tapa*) and shells. Upstairs, Indians sell potatoes and onions. I do not know why these are not sold with the vegetables downstairs but they are hawked by the Indian herb and spice sellers who strangely also sell the *kava* or *yanggona*, although only the Fijians drink this muddy brew.

In Fiji, the drinking of kava is both a ceremonial and a social custom. *Kava* is made from the root of a pepper tree, *Piper methysticum*, and is sold either as an untidy, spidery dried root or as a powder. We bought two kilos of the latter as we were not sure that we could cope with the roots. Custom dictates the presentation of *kava* to the chief of any island that one wishes to visit;

a *sevusevu* or traditional gift offered by the guests to the host as a token of respect.

Once upon a time, the *kava* was prepared by virgin girls who chewed the roots into a soft, pulpy mass before spitting it into the large wooden bowl, the *tanoa*, where the water was added. The missionaries found the practice of using virgins in this way not to their liking, unhygienic even, and eventually they persuaded the Fijians to use another method. Today, the roots are pounded with a mortar and pestle or ground by a machine and, after the water has been added, the gritty liquid is strained through cheesecloth.

Kava has varying effects upon the drinker, ranging from mild euphoria to fuzzy-headedness, numb lips and tongue. Over-indulgence causes the limbs to turn to jelly and the imbiber melts into a lethargy. Although *kava* drinking forms the basis of Fijian culture, one wonders how healthy it is for economic growth, because, while the Indians become competent traders, many Fijians waft around in a *kava* haze wondering why the ownership of land has failed to make them rich. On the other hand, the drinking of *kava* alleviates the need for alcohol and probably a *kava* induced haze is preferable to an alcoholic stupor.

Close by the market is the enormous handicraft centre where scores of Indian traders and a couple of enterprising Fijian stall-holders sell *masi* cloth bags and table mats, shell jewellery and a range of items carved from wood, most of them of little functional or aesthetic value. Possibly they make nice Christmas presents for distant relatives. There are bowls, servers with contorted handles, carvings of Christ on the Cross, serviette rings, platters, trays, grotesque cannibal forks and clubs, and grisly implements for stirring the cauldron.

'These are all the rage in Australia at the moment, Madam,' declared an obsequious Indian as he pushed a set of tiny cannibal forks towards me.

'Things have certainly changed in the last few years, then,' I told him.

'Oh yes, Madam. Now Fiji is — how do you call it? Flavour of the month.'

There were no cruise ships in the harbour so we were the only tourists in the entire complex, an annoying situation because the stallholders were desperate and snatched at us.

'Let's not do this,' Alan begged.

'But I've just seen a perfectly plain wooden bowl that I like and it was only $12.'

'I'll wait outside,' my loyal partner replied. 'But I suggest that you explore further before buying. And remember you're hopeless at bargaining.'

The grass was indeed greener a few stalls farther on where I found a slightly better bowl for $20. I offered the bowing Indian $12 and when he refused, I walked on.

'OK, OK, $12,' he called, panting after me.

As we walked back to the shop, I was already relishing telling Alan of my success but, on picking up the bowl to inspect it again, I discovered that it was not the same bowl. The $20 price tag had been transferred to a smaller bowl.

'This isn't the bowl we decided upon. This one's smaller. You've changed the price tags,' I complained.

'Oh, no, no, no. Madam is surely mistaken.'

It seemed that I should have bought the first bowl for $12, so I retraced my steps, only to find that the $12 price tag on it had just been replaced by one saying $20.

I found Alan outside in the shade of a weeping fig tree.

'Where's the bowl?' he asked.

'I changed my mind. We really don't need one at the moment.'

'You were stooged, weren't you,' he laughed.

In a small open space beside the markets, a group of Chinese dancers was performing in a manner that was distinctly amateurish, but the small crowd of smiling Fijians did not seem to care.

'They're practising for the Hibiscus Festival,' a tall Fijian youth, dressed in the traditional *sula* (skirt), informed us.

The festival began with a parade along Victoria Avenue the

next morning. The people, particularly the Indian women and girls were dressed in their finery and they chattered excitedly as though the Festival were their very own. The sun lit their bright saris and flashed on their gold jewellery as they pressed together with their more prosaic Fijian compatriots. The Fijian men in their skirts, however, certainly outshone the Indian males, most of whom wore ordinary pants and shirts. There was fellowship and good cheer and Indians and Fijians appeared at ease with each other. Perhaps it was not always so, but during our several weeks' sojourn in Fiji, we saw no evidence of racial conflict.

There was a string of perplexing floats, hundreds of scouts, a police band in white *sulus* with serrated hems, an army band in khaki *sulus* with straight hems and assorted groups that represented organisations like the Red Cross and various local enterprises. The crowd watched in silent wonder. Alan and I were happy to see them so engrossed in their parade but we left before the end.

When we walked into the Royal Suva Yacht Club, we felt that we had almost come full circle because in many ways it was similar to Darwin Yacht Club, our point of departure from Australian shores. Well-tended lawns dotted with tropical trees and shrubs sloped from the open verandahs to the water's edge, and we found it a pleasant place to join the other yachties for sundowners after working on *Windigo*.

Some boats were returning home from a circumnavigation, some were exploring the Pacific. Many we already knew and others we were meeting for the first time. The cruising community is small and close-knit so invariably there were friends or acquaintances in common. We were all waiting for the winter southerlies to subside and the northerly flow of summer to begin. Everyone was concerned with getting the timing right, because if we left too late we would risk being caught in an early cyclone.

Alan and I listened to the others discuss alternatives and we tried to make a decision about what we should do. Some yachts were going to take part in the annual Musket Cove race from Fiji to Vanuatu, and we were tempted to join them. Others intended spending time in New Caledonia. Most of the circumnavigators, however, would probably sail direct from Fiji to Australia because they were all longing for their homeland and loved ones, and most were tired of sailing after the long slog across the Pacific.

The last week of our stay in Suva was marred by grey skies and torrential rain, but stranger than the weather was the behaviour of our fellow cruisers. For three days we were ignored by friends and acquaintances. Not a soul came near *Windigo*, eyes were averted when we went ashore, our waves and smiles were ignored. We felt abandoned and offended and we searched our souls for the reason. An unkind act? A thoughtless remark? Apart from being mystified, and too proud to ask anyone for the reason, we were worried because, in the cruising fraternity, survival could depend upon the goodwill of others — and it appeared that there was little of that left towards us.

Then on the fourth day we were suddenly inundated with visitors coming to *Windigo* in droves, and on the smallest of pretences. It was as if they had held a meeting and decided that we should be forgiven for whatever crime we had committed. We were released from coventry.

'Can I borrow your voltmeter, mate?'

'Come to dinner tonight.'

'Join us for sundowners.'

'Thought we'd drop in for coffee.'

At Musket Cove a week later, I believe I identified the instigator of our fall from grace, a woman whom we had once met briefly in Santa Cruz de Teneriffe in the Canary Islands. Nancy was an intense, red-haired woman with a thick Scottish accent and a face that reminded me of an angry frog. We had both liked her husband Stan, the skipper of *Scorpio*. He was an endearing New Zealander with an easy manner and a laconic charm.

Scorpio had passed through Panama a few weeks before us, so when we saw a letter for them still sitting forlornly in the pigeonholes at Cristobal Yacht Club we collected it and dropped it in their cockpit in Moorea as they were not on board when we arrived. We did not expect thanks and none was received. Finally they anchored near us in Suva harbour, Stan friendly and spontaneous and Nancy refusing to acknowledge my presence.

'Odd,' said Alan.

'Bloody rude,' said I.

Chatting to a group of yachties beside the lagoon at Musket Cove, I noticed Stan and Nancy approaching beneath the palms, so taking the initiative, I greeted her in a clear voice so that all could hear.

'Good morning, Nancy. We've not spoken since we first met in the Canaries. How are you?'

The group held its breath and some people found a sudden interest in the clouds and the treetops, others pushed pebbles through the sand with their toes whilst they folded their arms across their chests and grew grave. Nancy looked at me with round eyes that had turned reptilian, cold and venomous, and her mouth clamped into a grim line.

'Nancy! Olma spoke to you and you didn't answer,' her husband admonished angrily.

'I did answer,' she snapped.

Everyone looked at the ground for they thought she was lying. But Nancy and I knew that she was not. Her animosity was blinding but I could not fathom the reason. After that, Stan called us daily on the radio for a chat and when we shared an anchorage, he would paddle across to have a beer or a cup of coffee. We remained in friendly radio contact until *Scorpio* had safely reached her home port in New Zealand. Stan never referred to Nancy and neither did we, but we often pondered on the mystery of life aboard *Scorpio*.

On our way to the Yassawas we motored through the narrow exit in the reef that encloses Suva harbour just as Brit and Steve were sailing in. Brit stood in the bow of *Melanie* to proudly display her large abdomen. She looked radiant and happy. We would miss the wedding, but we had waited long enough and it seemed to us that if Brit dallied too long her baby would be born in Fiji instead of Australia.

There are several 'Blue Lagoons' around the world and no doubt those who live beside them would claim that the eponymous film was shot in their blue lagoon. The Fijians are no exception. It matters little, for the anchorage at Blue Lagoon in the Yassawas is probably one of the loveliest.

Sitting cross-legged in the sand with members of his clan, the chief of the island that borders the Blue Lagoon waited beneath the palms. He was a Buddha-like brown man with calculating eyes that did not accord with his wide grin. Alan presented our gift of *kava* with both hands, placed it on the sand beside the chief, clapped once and stepped back. The chief then chanted over the gift, the others joining in the chorus. There was some rhythmic clapping and we were then told we had permission to walk on the island.

The Yassawas is a group of 60 small volcanic islands stretching in a line for 50 miles. We spent a week relaxing there before sailing to Lautoka to provision for the last ocean passage of the circumnavigation.

It proved to be the most difficult passage of them all to begin, and I was reminded of the Chinese sage who said that the hardest part of any journey is taking the first step. Even when we were fully prepared and provisioned, we lingered, daunted by the significance of that final leg. How different were our feelings from those we had experienced at the beginning of the very first passage when we had left Darwin tingling with excitement for whatever lay ahead. Then the words of the Chinese sage meant nothing; now we were filled with dread, for having come so far we feared catastrophe and we spoke to each other in proverbs.

'There's many a slip 'twixt the cup and the lip,' Alan was wont to say.

'Faint heart ne'er won fair lady,' I reminded him.

But still we lingered. It was an affliction that some cruising sailors experience from time to time.

'It's an anchor obsession,' Harry on *Sunbird* informed us. 'It's happened to me, too. But it doesn't mean anything, nothing at all really. It's just an obsession, a passing phase that you'll snap out of in a couple of days. There's nothing to worry about, nothing at all really. You'll simply snap out of it.'

One clear bright morning, moved by a shared optimism, we pulled up the anchor and pointed *Windigo*'s nose towards Bundaberg.

That final passage reminded me of a teacher speaking to students before a final examination. 'It's time to revise,' the teacher would say. 'You must practise again everything I have taught you.'

The sea was our teacher and our examiner. Sometimes there were big swells, sometimes the waves stood up short and steep, once we had calms. We used our entire wardrobe of working sails to keep *Windigo* moving in the variable conditions. Once, the winds blew at gale force, at other times we motor-sailed. We never knew what to expect.

Ten days after leaving Fiji, the heady perfume of grass, gumtips, and pandanus fruit beneath a hot sun floated out of Hervey Bay, and Fraser Island slowly rose off the port bow. We were almost home.

CHAPTER 22

boiled potatoes • reunions
a chance meeting and a blown gasket
we abandon all hope • an anticlimax

$\mathcal{B}$undaberg harbour is at Burnett Heads in Queensland where the Burnett River enters the sea. The city of Bundaberg is 10 kilometres upstream, so overseas vessels making landfall there are required to observe the check-in formalities in the harbour before proceeding to the city.

Aware of the strict quarantine regulations, we had provisioned with care in Lautoka. We knew that all meat, pulses, fruit and vegetables would be confiscated on arrival in Australia so we carefully planned our meals for two weeks. It was the first time that we had set out on a passage with so few provisions and we felt a little insecure because on all previous passages we had been prepared for remaining at sea for a couple of months should that have been necessary.

The Customs officer was welcoming, with a relaxed sense of humour.

'It's great to be home again,' I told him.

'No place like it,' he replied.

He checked our papers and was quickly on his way. The serious quarantine officer remained and the search began. Dried fruits, nuts, beans, peas, barley, milk, eggs, salami, cheese, and leftover fresh fruit and vegetables were all tossed into a large garbage bag. We watched in silence while the officer methodically checked through all the lockers. Finally he stood and stretched and we thought the search was over.

'What's in there?' he suddenly asked, pointing to a saucepan on the stove.

Alan had boiled the last of the potatoes as we approached the harbour.

'We can make a potato salad,' he said. 'It's better than wasting them.'

But the quarantine officer was relentless and the potatoes too went into the garbage bag.

'Isn't that just a bit unreasonable,' I protested.

'If you were a papaya farmer you wouldn't think so', he replied. 'This year an infestation from overseas has ruined the papaya crop. We can't be too careful.'

The next morning as *Windigo* glided through the estuarine stillness towards Bundaberg, Alan and I sat in the cockpit in an elysian state. We felt an ineffable relief, a peace, a renewal of the nexus with this land. In the years of absence we had grown unaccustomed to its spaces, its vastness, the sounds and the smells, the feel of it.

The sweeping mudflats of the estuary and the curving cyclorama of sea slowly gave way to river banks lined with casuarinas, paper barks and reeds. Pelicans fished in the shallows or sat placidly sunning themselves on strips of exposed sandbank. There were elegant ibis, waterfowl and waders, and farther inland we saw the first of the plovers, the magpies and the willy wagtails.

'I'd love to hear a kookaburra,' I said to Alan, but none was there to welcome us. In the sheltered reaches, however, we could hear the whistling and rustling of invisible small birds.

We followed the well-beaconed course past the chain ferry and the rum distillery to the pile marina in the centre of Bundaberg, a city bisected by the river. Nothing seemed to have changed in our absence and we selfishly hoped that the entire region would still be unspoiled.

Alan and I had camped many times in the Bundaberg area before we bought *Windigo*. We particularly loved historic Seventeen-Seventy and secluded Agnes Waters, the bright green of the cane fields against the tangerine-coloured soils at Childers, the turtle beach at Mon Repos and the campsites on the lazy Burrum River.

But progress is inevitable and not always detrimental, as we discovered when we explored the town. The old Bundy we remembered had undergone a facelift. It now exuded a certain refinement and a bustling prosperity. After so long in the Pacific we delighted in the cornucopia in the shops and supermarkets.

'Australia seems to have improved in our absence if this is any indication,' Alan remarked as we inspected the wide range of fruit and vegetables and the sophisticated selection of gourmet foodstuffs that would have been difficult to find in suburban Sydney before we left.

We were joined by Brit and Steve in Bundaberg. They had married in Fiji as planned and were hoping to reach Brisbane before the birth of Brit's baby. Alan and I held our breath as we watched the fiercely independent Brit manoeuvre her yacht into position between the piles. Her bulk had made her ungainly and we worried that she might fall as she hurried along the decks, squeezing past the stays and trying to avoid stepping on her beloved Sally, the small black dog that had sailed with her from London. We wondered what would happen to Sally.

'Quarantine insists on throwing out cooked potatoes so I don't like her chances,' Alan said.

While Sally dozed in sweet oblivion on *Melanie*'s deck, Brit and Steve wrangled, cajoled and pleaded with the quarantine officer for two days. They could not afford to pay to have Sally quarantined. On the third day we saw Steve rowing from the shore, his face wet with tears and we knew that Sally was dead.

'The quarantine officer was upset too,' Steve told us later. 'We bear no grudges. He had a job to do.'

At the end of October we left Bundaberg. We felt rested and we looked forward to revisiting many of the places we had loved in the past. Most of all, though, we felt buoyant at the thought of being back in Sydney in time for Christmas. Velia and Graeme were already making plans for our arrival, and our families and friends were excited.

Through the Great Sandy Strait we sailed in unsettled and unpleasant weather. In the past we had enjoyed the anchorages in this beautiful stretch of water, but they welcomed us back with cloudy skies, squalls and strong winds. The fish would not bite, the blue swimmer crabs that had been abundant in the past seemed to have disappeared, and the dugongs at the Wide Bay Bar remained hidden.

Mooloolaba welcomed us with towering black cumulus and threatening flashes of lightning. No work had been done on *Windigo*'s bottom since the Canary Islands, so her movement through the water was sluggish because of the marine growth that had established itself on her hull during the long Pacific crossing. At the popular Lawrie's marina we hauled her out of the water and cleaned and anti-fouled her bottom.

In Brisbane we anchored in the river beside the botanic gardens. The city had grown glitzy in our absence and several new glass-fronted buildings lined the banks. Tied to the pile berths was *Anhinga* with our old friends Max and Gloria on board. We had taken the detour up the Brisbane River to see them.

Max and Gloria had been back in Australia for over a year and we were interested in how the two long-term cruisers were adjusting to their new life after a decade at sea. Soon we would have to make a similar adjustment.

'It was Max's dream to go cruising, so I went along too,' Gloria explained. 'I don't regret it. But now it's my turn to do what I want.'

Gloria, looking stylish and successful, had completed an aromatherapy course and had opened a beauty salon in Brisbane. Max had worked on the boat and *Anhinga* was almost ready for sale. The couple planned to build a house in a rainforest near Brisbane.

'There's a faraway look in Max's eyes,' I said to Alan. He agreed.

Then it was on through Moreton Bay, sailing to places with evocative names like Tipplers Passage, Jumpinpin Bar, and Walley's Gutter and on through the Broadwater. At Ballina on the New South Wales coast, the bar was flat. With a feeling of relief at such an easy crossing, we entered the Richmond River and motored to one of our favourite anchorages. Sometimes in foreign ports we would remember pretty Mobbs Bay and one of us would say, 'Hope it hasn't changed.'

It was as we had remembered it. Completely enclosed except for the narrow opening in the channel training wall, it provides a natural haven for one or two yachts. There is a sandy beach at low tide. Fish jump all around and dozens of pelicans line the training wall like well-spaced sentinels.

Engrossed in boat chores below decks, Alan and I were unaware that another yacht was circling us. We were surprised, therefore, when we heard someone calling *'Windigo! Windigo!'* On reaching the cockpit we saw *Windigo*'s previous owners, Gerard and Harmke Nymeyer, waving from the deck of the circling yacht.

'What a coincidence! What luck! Welcome home, *Windigo*,' Gerard called while Harmke beamed and looked pleased with herself for she had been the one who had spotted us first. We agreed to meet in a few days time at the small marina farther up the river where we would leave *Windigo* while we visited friends at Eureka.

Despite the unsettled conditions we had experienced since leaving Bundaberg, we were making good progress. The break in the passage was pleasant and we enjoyed seeing old friends. We had no way of knowing then that the break would be much longer than expected.

Windigo's diesel engine had served us well. Apart from the usual idiosyncrasies like air in the fuel lines and worn impellers, it had given little trouble. Parts that had sheered off in Turkey and in Greece had easily been welded into place again.

'How did *Windigo*'s engine behave?' Gerard asked one day when we returned from Eureka. He sounded like an anxious father.

'No major problems,' Alan reassured him.

'I'd like to have a look at it if I may,' Gerard said.

As the two men squatted at the engine-room door deep in conversation, water started to trickle out of the engine's aircleaner and into the bilge.

'That's serious,' both men exclaimed.

The cooling system was blocked, the head gasket had blown and the injectors were damaged. Alan pulled the grey monster apart but the repairs demanded the skills of an experienced diesel mechanic with access to a workshop.

It wasn't until 14 December that we finally rounded Evans Head and continued south. The relative nonchalance we had enjoyed since Bundaberg was replaced by a disturbing sense of urgency. We thought we had left ourselves plenty of time, but the persistent southerlies and the engine failure had changed that. I rang Velia every few days.

'Please hurry,' she begged. 'Please be home for Christmas.'

The Haven at Laurieton is aptly named. Conditions were once again deteriorating as we approached the entrance to the Laurieton River. Heavy rain had reduced visibility, strong winds made the seas stand up, hail pounded the decks and lightning flashed over the land.

'It's becoming silly out here,' Alan said, 'We'll try the Haven.'

It was one of the few places on the coast that we had never entered and it seemed that forces were aligning to push us out again as we battled against the ebbing tide. Finally, though, we reached a little hamlet with the unlikely name of Dunbogan and there we dropped anchor at dusk on 16 December.

'Nine more days till Christmas,' I said to Alan.

'Plenty of time,' he replied.

Laurieton is a pleasant place to sit out a blow. The town nestles beside the river at the foot of a mountain called North Brother. The Camden Haven River rises in the creeks of the nearby mountains and flows in and out of lakes on its way to the sea. The little town feels sleepy, relaxed and friendly; like a warm enclave that time has passed by. We knew that the wind raged outside, but in Laurieton's lovely waters it was calm and protected. Even the shags and pelicans moved slowly in the velvet air.

Our intention was to arrive in Sydney a couple of days before Christmas. There were still some presents to buy and I wanted to have my hair done. Yachties tend to be casual about appearances but I would soon be dealing with landlubbers again and they might not understand. I could hear them gossiping.

'Oh, my dear. Have you seen Olma yet? All those years on a boat have certainly played havoc with her hair.'

As the days passed and the wind continued to blow from the south I gave up all hope of visiting Terrence, the hairdresser I had used for years in Sydney. I would have to visit a Laurieton salon instead.

'My hair is very fine,' I warned the young woman. 'Please be careful when you do the streaks as it quickly becomes porous.'

Perhaps she did not listen; perhaps she was incompetent. The end result was a disaster of major proportions. By the time I reached *Windigo* I was sobbing with grief. Alan helped me aboard and tried to comfort me, but I became hysterical when he said, 'Yes, I agree with you. You can't go back to Sydney looking like a yellow mop.'

Despair turned quickly to anger. I leapt into the dinghy, revved the outboard into action, sprinted up the hill to the salon and confronted the young woman who had caused my angst.

'I look like a tart,' I told her. 'You simply must fix it.'

So instead of blonde streaks I had brown streaks. The end result was more or less what it had been before I first entered the salon. But my hair was now stressed and it had lost its sheen. I consoled myself by thinking of positive things. My hair would eventually recover. I would soon be with Velia again. We would soon be home. Life was wonderful, most of the time.

On the sixth day in Laurieton I pleaded with Alan.

'Let's stick our heads out. It may not be too bad after all.'

Against his better judgement he hauled up the anchor and we motored the four miles to the sea. We even hoisted the main and tried to sail but the wild and unpredictable Tasman was belting at the coast and even tacking was out of the question. Once again we battled back in against the ebbing tide and re-anchored in our old spot.

The thrust and momentum of the attempt to sail had made me feel buoyant for a while but despondency returned as the weather bureau continued to forecast strong winds from the south. I fished from the boat without success and fantasised about homecomings.

Thousands of people crowded every nook and cranny of the rocky outcrops and headlands of Pittwater. They waved flags and bright banners. Millions of coloured balloons floated into the air as *Windigo* rounded West Head, and as she turned through the entrance beside Barrenjoey, squadrons of planes dipped their wings in salute and the crowd sent forth a mighty cheer.

'The waiting has affected your brain,' Alan said when I described the scene.

There comes a time when one must abandon all hope. We moved *Windigo* onto a mooring near the boatshed at Dunbogan and on Christmas Eve we caught a bus to Sydney.

Velia and Graeme had prepared a champagne and seafood luncheon. There were nuts and cherries and sweets, and panettone sprinkled with cognac. We relaxed in their sunny inner-city courtyard and drank toasts to the future.

Early in January 1996 Alan and I returned to Laurieton and prepared *Windigo* for the passage to Pittwater. When we rounded West Head two days later, there were no crowds to

an anticlimax

welcome us, no banners, no flags or balloons, no squadrons of
lanes. But as we sailed past Barrenjoey we knew that our home-
oming was just as we had wished it to be — private, personal,
ncandescent with the joy of being alive.

'O Captain! My Captain!
our fearful trip is done,
The ship has weather'd every wrack,
the prize we sought is won,
The port is near, the bells I hear,
the people all exulting,
While follow eyes the steady keel,
the vessel grim and daring.'

Walt Whitman

EPILOGUE

At the end of his wanderings, Ulysses was given advice by Teiresias. The blind soothsayer told him to balance his oar on his shoulder and to walk until he came to a place where the oar meant nothing; where people assumed that the oar was a shovel carved for winnowing the corn. There Ulysses must settle far from the sea.

A year and a half has passed since Alan and I completed the circumnavigation and we have not felt the urge to escape from the sea. When the tenants moved out, we returned to our house overlooking Pittwater. *Windigo* floats below in the bay, beckoning and tantalising. Financially, it would have been wise to sell her but we cannot. She is the stuff of dreams and we are still dreamers.

One voyage has ended for we have sailed full circle. Nevertheless, we still find ourselves unpacking the journey piece by precious piece. Most of it will remain in our memories, and every little while we will take it out, shake it, laugh at it, and treasure it. It is a well of memories that nourishes us: a Bernini sculpture, a dish of fine food, a Greek fisherman's brusque greeting, a ruined temple in Turkey, the patina of a painted door in Aden.

Other journeys have already begun, because the circumnavigation changed our lives. Alan returned to teaching for a couple of months immediately after our return but he found the classroom stifling after the wide blue sea. So, with his oar across his shoulder, he found work with a company that operates cruisers on Sydney harbour. He re-enrolled at Brookvale TAFE and quickly passed his coxswain's and engineer's examinations and he is now studying for his master mariner's ticket. For the present, he is happy working with boats in Sydney Harbour.

I am happy, too, for I am having an adventure of the mind. I discovered in writing *The Watcher on the Quay* that I enjoy expressing myself with words, and already I have another work in progress. And I feel relief and joy at being close to Velia once more.

Neither Alan nor I will 'rust unburnished' but when and where we will wander next, I know not. What I do know is that we have been changed and enriched by our experiences. We are as much a part of all those we met as they are of us. We cherish the elation of being able to remain in control during a crisis, and we feel a deeper, more sensual involvement with the world than the watchers on the quay will ever know.